THE NATION'S REGION

Series Editors
Jon Smith, The University of Montevallo
Riché Richardson, University of California, Davis

Advisory Board
Houston A. Baker Jr., Vanderbilt University
Jennifer Greeson, Princeton University
Trudier Harris, The University of North Carolina, Chapel Hill
John T. Matthews, Boston University
Tara McPherson, The University of Southern California
Scott Romine, The University of North Carolina, Greensboro

LEIGH ANNE DUCK

The Nation's Region

Southern Modernism, Segregation, and U.S. Nationalism

The University of Georgia Press | *Athens and London*

Paperback edition, 2009
© 2006 by the University of Georgia Press
Athens, Georgia 30602
www.ugapress.org
All rights reserved
Set in Sabon by Bookcomp, Inc.

Printed digitally in the United States of America

The Library of Congress has cataloged the
hardcover edition of this book as follows:

Duck, Leigh Anne, 1967–
The nation's region : southern modernism, segregation,
and U.S. nationalism / Leigh Anne Duck.
x, 340 p. ; 24 cm. — (The new southern studies)
Includes bibliographical references (p. 291–329) and index.
ISBN-13: 978-0-8203-2810-2 (alk. paper)
ISBN-10: 0-8203-2810-3 (alk. paper)
1. Caldwell, Erskine, 1903–1987—Criticism and
interpretation. 2. Hurston, Zora Neale—Criticism and
interpretation. 3. Faulkner, William, 1897–1962—
Criticism and interpretation. 4. American literature—
Southern States—History and criticism. 5. American
literature—20th century—History and criticism.
6. Regionalism in literature. 7. Segregation in literature.
8. Nationalism in literature. 9. Modernism (Literature)—
United States. 10. Southern States—In literature.
I. Title. II. Series.
PS261.D825 2006
810.9'9750904—dc22   2005035686

Paperback ISBN-13: 978-0-8203-3418-9
          ISBN-10: 0-8203-3418-9

British Library Cataloging-in-Publication Data available

Parts of chapter 4 appeared in a slightly different version in
"'Go There tuh *Know* There': Zora Neale Hurston and the
Chronotope of the Folk," *American Literary History* 13,
no. 2 (Spring 2001): 266–94, published by Oxford
University Press.

Parts of chapters 5 and 7 appeared in a different version in
"Haunting Yoknapatawpha: Faulkner and Traumatic
Memory," *Faulkner in the Twenty-First Century: Faulkner
and Yoknapatawpha* 2000, edited by Robert W. Hamblin
and Ann J. Abadie (2003), 89–106, published by the
University Press of Mississippi.

To my parents and to Mike

Contents

Acknowledgments ix

INTRODUCTION
American and Southern Exceptionalisms 1

PART ONE. IMAGINING AFFILIATION

ONE
Region, Race, and Nation 17

TWO
Economy Crisis 50

PART TWO. MODERNIST MAPPINGS

THREE
    Erskine Caldwell and the Abject South 85

FOUR
    Zora Neale Hurston and the Chronotope of the Folk 115

FIVE
    William Faulkner and the Haunted Plantation 146

PART THREE. THE SHIFTING "SOUTH"

SIX
    Provincial Cosmopolitanism 177

SEVEN
    The Nation's Region Redux 212

    Notes 249

    Works Cited 291

    Index 331

Acknowledgments

This book has been many years in the making, a process sustained by both personal and institutional support. I begin with thanks to my dissertation advisers at the University of Chicago—Bill Brown, Ken Warren, and Lisa Ruddick—each of whom provided inspiration vital in directing this book toward its final form. My early research on this topic was sponsored by a University of Chicago Century Fellowship, a Mellon Foundation Summer Research Fellowship, and a Walter and Carol Blair Dissertation Fellowship. The American Studies/U.S. Culture and History Workshop and the Avant-Garde Workshop provided rigorous, helpful audiences for early versions of these arguments. These early stages of the project depended on the support of fellow dissertation writers Lisa McNair, Emily Bloch, Elizabeth Ceppi, and Mary Jane Nigro.

Since then, a University of Memphis Faculty Research Grant enabled me to hire a phenomenally skilled and endlessly enthusiastic research assistant—Nathan Tipton—and I learned more during my year as a Fellow of the American Psychoanalytic Association than I could have hoped. Both undergraduate and graduate students at the University of Memphis have helped me to refine and strengthen the ideas in this book, as have my colleagues Shara McCallum, Loel Kim, Kim Magowan, and Jean-Pierre Reed. Barbara Ching and Jennifer Wagner-Lawlor offered valuable publication advice, as did Bill and Ken at Chicago. I am particularly thankful to Brad Evans and Sabine Haenni, who have provided a rich intellectual exchange since the earliest inklings of this project, contributing greatly to its improvement.

It has been a privilege to participate in a scholarly network with people who are transforming the field of southern studies and who are also remarkably generous and supportive. Deborah Cohn, George Handley, Katie McKee, Annette Trefzer, and Riché Richardson have offered important questions and great advice. Scott Romine and Jack Matthews provided helpful and generous responses to this book. Special thanks go to Jon Smith, who has been an unfailing source of encouragement and who recruited this book for the series. And it has been a pleasure to work with the University of Georgia Press: Nancy Grayson and Jennifer Reichlin have been models of professionalism, in its very best sense, and all participants in this project have been quick and generous in their responses to every query. As copy editor, Polly Kummel was deft, thorough, and very helpful.

Finally, this book is dedicated to my best supporters. My parents have, at every stage, been embodiments of faith, and it is a testimony to my husband's perseverance that, having lived with this book every day for many years, he is still excited about it. Their confidence has bolstered my own, and for that—as for much else—I am ever grateful.

THE NATION'S REGION

INTRODUCTION

American and Southern Exceptionalisms

THE THEORY OF American exceptionalism has proved remarkably resilient. In recent decades, the nation's history of violence and discrimination has been broadly acknowledged, as has, to a lesser extent, continuation of these problems. Nonetheless, the United States continues to be touted as the attempted instantiation of a civic ideal—a political entity in which membership is constituted not through ancestry or common traditions but through shared commitment to individual rights and capitalist progress. Liberal thinkers who commend U.S. nationalism, such as David Hollinger and Richard Rorty, also recognize its inequity; critical of the nation-state, they seek to promote the democratic structures of belief they consider particularly significant in U.S. culture.[1] They note that, throughout the nation's history, prominent formulations of national membership have presented it as broad in accessibility and narrow in significance—open to people of diverse backgrounds and mandating no homogenizing panoply of traits or beliefs.[2] But this model of national affiliation has consistently coexisted with exclusive and constitutive ones that specify, for example, the race, religion, or sexual desires of the normative U.S. citizen. Accordingly, scholars such as Rogers Smith and Gary Gerstle seek to understand relationships among the "multiple traditions" of U.S. nationalism—the ways in which classical liberalism and republicanism have coexisted with more restrictive models of the national collective.[3]

Despite the periodic release of books proclaiming the "Americanization of Dixie" or the "southernization of America," formulations of U.S. southern exceptionalism have been only slightly less tenacious and have regularly served as foils to that of the nation. But while various oppositions between region and nation have elicited ample commentary—describing, for example, the intellectual habits of "Cavalier" and "Yankee," the cultural consequences of agrarian and industrial economies, and the political philosophies of premodern paternalists and late bourgeois individualists—the ideological functioning of these antipodal images has, until quite recently, received little sustained scholarly attention.[4] In one early contribution to this field of inquiry, the sociologist Larry Griffin argued that scholars have been reluctant to consider "the problem South as a social construction" because the "objective" differences between region and nation are so flagrant, particularly the disproportionate predominance of slavery and segregation in southern history.[5] In contrast, analysis of "imagined geography," as influentially exemplified in Edward Said's *Orientalism*, holds that fantasies of "other" spaces depend largely on "projection"—not merely "a very unrigorous idea of what is 'out there'" but also a dynamic shaped chiefly by the psychological needs and material desires of contemplative agents.[6] Historically, complaints concerning antisouthern stereotypes have coincided with denial of the region's worst problems, a pattern that accentuates the need to acknowledge the distinctness, even where not absolute, of southern practices. Still, it is useful to examine how the substantial cultural and institutional connections between the South and the larger nation produce and are shaped by projective fantasies.

Such analysis discloses what Ralph Ellison described as a form of repression in U.S. history—the way in which discussions of an anomalous South regularly displace fundamental questions about political affiliation from discourse concerning the nation-state.[7] While associating the nation with democracy and change and the region with racism and tradition, twentieth-century U.S. nationalism repeatedly celebrated the latter paradigm, failing either to address its incongruity with liberalism or to analyze the desires that rendered this restrictive model of collectivity attractive to so many national audiences. Concomitantly, when national discourse has acknowledged the conflict between southern conservatism and national democracy, it has typically done so in ways that localize this conflict—a "backward South" and a modern or "enlightened nation"; such models fail to incorporate a conceptual structure for assessing an ongoing conflict between prominent cultural and political models of national affiliation. Nowhere has this pattern been more apparent and destructive than in political and legal representations of southern racial segregation, which argued that apartheid was a necessary concession to a backward culture. These formulations disavowed both the contemporaneity of the South with the larger nation and the presence of apartheid in other areas of the country.

This book focuses on efforts of southern modernists to think their way through the purported temporal divide between the South and the larger nation during a period when understandings of each were unstable—when the nation, in intellectual and popular discourse, attested to its need for a sustaining culture, and the region, in economic and political struggle, confirmed a need for change. These writers' efforts to create a dialogue between tradition and modernization staged vital and largely unresolved questions regarding the meaning of collective life in a capitalist and purportedly liberal nation. Investigating the central frameworks through which southern exceptionalism was routinely asserted—devolution, folkloric authenticity, romanticism, and gothicism—these writers tested and challenged a model of binding and determinate group identification that was simultaneously courted and disavowed in U.S. nationalism. Such analysis was largely foreclosed in the 1950s, which paradoxically witnessed both increased federal challenges to southern apartheid and renewed celebration, in nationalist discourse, of the trope of the backward—and reliably anticommunist—South. But the previous interlude in the opposition of national and regional exceptionalisms had nonetheless briefly disrupted an ideological structure serving to contain the contradictions of racial segregation amid a purportedly liberal democracy.

By approaching this issue through the paradigm of southern apartheid, I do not mean to suggest that racial inequity has been limited to the South or has been practiced only against African Americans but rather to note that southern antiblack oppression has provided a potent and prominent model for understanding U.S. racial discrimination more generally. As George Lipsitz points out in portraying "California [as] the Mississippi of the 1990s," U.S. nationalism practices a "simultaneous disavowal and embrace of racism," insisting on the nation-state's commitment to liberalism while casting substantial disputes about the meanings of national citizenship as questions of how to negotiate the particularities of local cultures.[8] In order to forestall this dynamic, I often use the word *apartheid*—an Afrikaans word meaning "separateness"—when I refer to de jure segregation; the term *apartheid* is typically, though not exclusively, associated with South African segregation, which is well known to have been supported by the state.[9] Rhetoric concerning U.S. racial segregation has tended to understate that it, too, was codified and enforced by law and constituted a systematic (albeit more assertive than analytic) understanding of how collective life should be structured. Instead, U.S. nationalism has generally represented southern apartheid as a cultural practice tolerated by the liberal state.[10]

This ideological distinction between a nation of liberal laws and a region of racist practice depends on yet another distinction, which often serves to idealize regional cultures—the idea that the nation-state and its regions mobilize fundamentally different and temporally coded forms of affiliation. Contrary to a popular self-representation of nations—that each constitutes "a solid community moving steadily down (or up) history"—the United States was perceived, in the late nineteenth and early twentieth centuries, as a collection of communities moving at different rates in trajectories characterized by different customs, goals, and belief systems.[11] Increasingly, after the Civil War, the dominant national time was understood to be that of capitalist modernity—a linear, progressive temporality allowing new mobility and opportunity; thus the United States was represented chiefly as an administrative or economic unit rather than as a collective based on shared customs.[12] This modern national "chronotype," or collection of temporally coded traits, was positioned against those of regional cultures, which were understood to be shaped by tradition.[13] This seemingly benign way of thinking about the relationship between cohesive local cultures and a national administration had profound political consequences, as the regions' ostensible customs included racial discrimination. As the historian Thomas Holt argues, understanding racial oppression strictly through the framework of cultural patterns inherited from the past configures it as a problem against which liberal politics—historically wedded to the time of capitalist modernity—cannot easily intervene.[14] This is precisely how the U.S. Supreme Court, in *Plessy v. Ferguson* (1896), treated apartheid—as the result of "racial instincts" in Louisiana against which "legislation is powerless."[15]

Such temporal delineations have often, and in different ways, provided the ideological underpinnings for U.S. racial oppression. For while the teleology of liberalism is famously universal, its temporality is not. As Peter Osborne argues, classical liberalism represented itself as the product of a particular stage of social and economic development and, accordingly, embraced ideas concerning the "*non-contemporaneousness* of *geographically diverse* but *chronologically simultaneous* times," such that "certain people's presents [are seen as] other people's futures"—a transition in which imperialism, for example, is said to aid.[16] Thus, in the U.S. nation-state, even civic or liberal understandings of citizenship, which depict the nation as a protector of rights without regard to race, have been delimited by boundaries constructed as both racial and temporal. Labeling nonwhite peoples as savage or backward, for example, U.S. nationalism excluded Native Americans and residents of U.S. colonies from the temporality in which one exercises the right of political self-determination.[17]

In seeking to institutionalize apartheid, late nineteenth-century white southern elites mobilized a two-pronged temporal strategy, portraying southern African Americans as unprepared for full participation in U.S. political and economic life and also depicting southern society more generally as one shaped by traditional affiliative principles unassimilable to liberal paradigms. The "New South" spokesman Henry Grady, for example, proclaimed his commitment to economic modernization but argued that southern race relations should be negotiated within the norms of a tightly bound regional society: "The Negro . . . should be left to those among whom his lot is cast, with whom he is indissolubly connected."[18] Such arguments, as the historian Charles Payne explains, successfully established a "southern paradigm" for understanding U.S. race relations, describing racial injustice as an issue embedded in interpersonal rather than structural relations.[19] Through the early twentieth century, the trope of the backward South comprised not only alarm at differences in economic and cultural development but also celebration of communal forms of affiliation: the region was said to maintain social values that modernization was purportedly eroding in the broader nation. As one *Scribner's* essayist wrote in 1925, the South comprised "a genuine aristocracy of simplicity, kindness, wit, and culture" to set against "the vulgarity which besets our commercial civilization."[20] In this way, discourse concerning the South both demonstrated and contained a broader ambivalence toward the more limited ties and egalitarian structures of classical liberalism. On the one hand, images of the region provided a venue through which national audiences could imagine restrictive but stable and sustaining bonds, and, on the other, they represented the conflict between U.S. democratic rhetoric and discriminatory practice as a difference between national and regional cultures.

But during the Depression, southern traditionalism was increasingly seen as a threatening chronotype; no longer an effective container for the nation's disavowed antiliberalism, the trope of the backward South began to comprise an image of what the United States could become. As the economic crisis and the New Deal challenged previously dominant beliefs about the indefatigability of the national economy, the centrality of enterprise to national culture, and the ideal function of the federal government, they also drew attention to the already dire status of southern poverty, the influence of antiliberal traditions, and the necessity of including the region in federal attempts to reenergize the U.S. economy. Concerns about southern poverty and racism were intensified by the growth of European fascism, which, particularly in view of African American and leftist protest, highlighted the contradiction between southern apartheid and democratic governance.[21] By the end of the 1930s, that dichotomy itself was questioned as writers and activists exposed the degree to which southern racial practices corresponded, rather than conflicted, with those of the larger nation.[22] This reconsideration of the relationship between region and nation entailed not only demand for the full extension of liberal principles but, more substantially, investigation of how cultural forms considered anachronistic could coexist in often vital relationships with those recognized as central to modernization.

This book traces these changes by examining how popular and experimental narratives of the period configured the relationship between the South and the United States, focusing on representations of time and of cultural cohesiveness. Aesthetic narratives provide particular insight into imagined geographies because they offer a formally mediated and often emotively charged venue in which individual conceptions of space (both writers' and readers') and societal models interact.[23] Though other forms of writing, such as policy debates and journalism, also specify spatial and temporal characteristics, literature and film are notable for the fullness with which they combine conceptual depictions of imagined worlds—delineating, for example, the geography and social structure of a locale—with representation of the ways in which such spaces and times are experienced, as demonstrated through plot, imagery, and characters' thoughts and behaviors. Modernism, in particular, mobilized formal innovations designed to explore the potentially unsettling experience of modernity's multiple temporal forms: the progressive linear time of the capitalist market and the workplace; the cyclical or contemplative time of tradition and ritual; the temporal disjunctures of uneven development; the fixated, spasmodic time of post-traumatic experience; and the idiosyncratic time of individual consciousness.[24]

In southern experimental fictions, this complexity also included representations of the imagined temporal divide between the region and the larger nation. Modernist writing was not, of course, unique for its interest in temporal multiplicity; the famous montage of national monuments in Frank Capra's *Mr. Smith Goes to Washington* (1939), for example, stages an individual's subjective experience of a coalescence of mundane linear time, sudden biographical disruption, and epic history in a temporal logic reminiscent of William Faulkner's work.[25] Nor was investigation of a distinctly southern temporality unique to aesthetic narrative; such interests appeared also in journalistic and social scientific writing. But southern literary modernism is noteworthy for its temporal collisions, moments in which the region's and the nation's multiple temporal forms convulsively intersect. These figurative explorations of regional time suggested the difficulties facing people who sought to understand relationships between modernization and tradition in a larger society ambivalent about both.

These elaborate and seemingly hyperbolic representations of southern time are vital to understanding the history of how apartheid was perceived, because, by the 1930s, the ideology of southern backwardness was exhibiting considerable strain. Defenders of the status quo continued to insist that the South constituted a static but organic society in which all residents were accustomed to and enjoyed their cultural roles; this account remained broadly influential, though it was now, in national discourse, more often gothicized than wistfully romanticized. But despite an extensive system of laws and enforced behaviors designed to prevent the appearance of cultural change, the region was experiencing profound transformations, including urbanization, industrialization, the increased presence of mass media and federal government programs, and also residents' changing experience and demands of race relations. Writing retrospectively, Ralph Ellison used the metaphor of the Jim Crow bus to argue that southern apartheid, though it might appear to be a phenomenon of developmental stagnation, required extraordinary energy to maintain: "As the phantomized bus went lurching and fuming along its treadmill of a trajectory, the struggle within scuffled and raged in fitful retrograde. Thus, as it moved without moving, those trapped inside played out their roles like figures in dreams—with one group ever forcing the other to the backmost part, and the other ever watching and waiting as they bowed to force and clung to sanity."[26] Depicting both apparent stasis and intersubjective recognition of incessant force and resistance, this representation suggests that southern segregation was notable less for the ways in which it lingered than for the ways in which it was continually reproduced. In exploring the temporal relationships between region and nation, then, southern writers of this era recorded and responded to the paradoxically frenetic production of southern backwardness, which they placed in dialogue with equally assertive accounts of national progressiveness.

This literature's investment in changing understandings of the relationship between region and nation has not been widely noted, as the strangeness of southern modernism has often been understood directly to reflect a strangely backward regional culture. As I demonstrate in this book, Depression-era reviews of experimental southern fiction—particularly those from the publishing center of New York—reflect an "interpretive community" convinced that the South constituted a site of profound cultural alterity.[27] For much of its history, the field of southern studies has tended to facilitate such understandings by focusing on issues of enduring regional distinctiveness.[28] Even studies focused on regional transformation have often positioned it in a different framework from national or global change, elucidating a specifically southern version of the tension between modernity and traditionalism.[29] In a vital and largely quite recent move, southern literary scholarship has sought to comprehend and challenge the ways in which understandings of "the South" have been constructed; these works, however, examine chiefly the effects of such models on the region's history and contemporary culture.[30] Scholars seeking to position the region in broader geopolitical frameworks note that the idea of a recalcitrant South in a modernizing and liberal United States has been remarkably difficult to dislodge; seeking in part to overcome such nationalist paradigms, they focus on the region's relationships with Caribbean and Latin American cultures.[31] But while these latter approaches have productively expanded our understandings of how ideas of region and nation function, they have left open the problem of situating southern modernists in relation to a shifting U.S. nationalism. Many of these writers also struggled to think their way through a conception of the region that facilitated both the nation-state's liberal triumphalism and its racism.

In observing these shifting understandings of region and nation, this book examines a dynamic period in U.S. nationalism, one that led to reconsiderations of regional and national time, space, and modes of affiliation. To consider how individuals may have imagined their own affiliations with these chronotypes and collectives, my method is not only formal and historicist but also psychoanalytic. Often criticized for its ahistoricist and universalist assumptions—leading to accounts that fail, in Claudia Tate's words, to "examin[e] the relationship of social oppression to family dysfunction and the blighted inner worlds of individuals"— psychoanalysis nonetheless offers resources for understanding the profound interactions between psychology and social life.[32] In particular, it provides rubrics for considering how beliefs concerning group identity may reverberate with individual desires and fears, how anxieties concerning individual selfhood may seek satisfaction in fantasies concerning collective affiliation, and how political groups may mobilize psychological dynamics to shape public belief about the forms of social cohesion necessary in social life.[33] These mutual influences encompass the potential for extraordinary multiplicity, as single individuals identify with diverse collectives and dynamics of identification vary. Freud's work alone

provides at least two prominent models for theorizing group affiliation—
the melancholic identification with loved authority figures, whose shared
cultural beliefs produce "social feelings" in subsequent generations that
"hav[e] the same ego ideal," and the possessive and phantasmic bond to
a collective with, often, a charismatic leader.[34] But this proliferation of
possibilities—in both targets for and forms of identification—does not
suggest unlimited flexibility in any given social context. Rather, psychoanalysis provides tools for examining how powerful institutions, particularly nation-states, elicit among their citizenry fantasies that facilitate
support for their authority.[35]

The first section of this book, "Imagining Affiliation," provides a theoretical and historical model for thinking about the role of regions in
U.S. nationalism, arguing that the nation's avowed embrace of regional
cultures has provided a vehicle for it to endorse both cultural nationalism
and cultural diversity; this dual function has shifted through history and
in accord with the goals of cultural activists. The first chapter briefly traces
how southern apartheid, from its legal instantiation in the 1890s to the
beginnings of the civil rights movement in the late 1930s, was understood
in relation to the larger nation. Observing how regional representations
have played an ambivalent role in U.S. history—providing both alterna-
tives and supplements to national models of affiliation—I illustrate how
plantation romances, particularly Thomas Dixon's *The Clansman* (1905)
and D. W. Griffith's *The Birth of a Nation* (1915), constitute virulent ex-
emplars of this dichotomy by insisting on the value of white supremacy
as a source for not only regional but national passions. The next chapter demonstrates how Depression-era regionalists sought to display diverse local traditions as ballast for the widely criticized effects of consumer culture; the hope that regional values could resuscitate a cynical
nation was prominently narrativized, for example, in Capra's *Mr. Smith
Goes to Washington* (1939). Depression-era representations of the South,
however, were more ambivalent. Embraced by cultural conservatives and
in narratives chronologically separated from the contemporary United
States, such as Margaret Mitchell's and David O. Selznick's *Gone with*

the Wind (1936 and 1939), these images also suggested a form of affiliation that would, unlike those mobilized in other regionalist narratives, inherently oppose the goals of the liberal nation-state.

The three chapters in my second section, "Modernist Mappings," demonstrate how the formal strategies of three Depression-era experimental writers enabled them to scrutinize the seeming dichotomy between southern and national times, each in relation to a fundamental trope in understandings of the backward South. In Erskine Caldwell's representations of southern poverty, Zora Neale Hurston's depictions of southern African American culture, and William Faulkner's portrayals of white southern fixations on the past, ideas of temporal difference are explored for both formal and psychological implications. Representing conflicts among spatial, temporal, and cultural norms, these narratives depict individuals in the process of delineating their own temporal boundaries—situating themselves in idiosyncratic relationships to modernization, folklore, or antebellum history. This literature models diverse ways of positioning selves in space and society and often insists on the multiplicity of temporal descriptors applicable within the region.

Such narrative focuses have often been said to limit the relevance of these works to questions of local psychology or culture; accordingly, the southern grotesque, southern folklore, and southern gothic are often considered apolitical or even inherently conservative literary modes, which necessarily construct monolithic and unbridgeable boundaries around the region. I argue, however, that modernist authors used these literary forms to explore and often to challenge the ways in which ideas of an anachronistic region limited broader understandings of both local and national collectivities. Hence, these literary modes demonstrate alternate possibilities for interpretation, even though initial critics of these works accepted them as further confirmation of the trope of the backward South. The political implications of representing southern time and culture as uneven, fragmented, and alienating appear chiefly in comparison with other Depression-era discourses that described, for example, the rigid temporal norms of the nation, an undifferentiated and backward African American folk, or a hierarchical but static and cohesive regional society. But these authors' investigations may have facilitated the temporal mapping that developed in southern literature at the end of the 1930s, which, in concert with the emerging antiapartheid movement, explicitly staged intersections among southern, national, and global temporalities.

This chronology may appear to rehearse the triumphalism that it initially critiqued, describing how U.S. culture, with its focus on change and mobility, has historically overcome the more tradition-bound cultures that impede democratic practice.[36] But the final section of my book, "The Shifting 'South,'" argues that this post-Depression writing, which traced the mutual influences and dependencies between U.S. liberalism and southern apartheid, offered possibilities for examining the relationship between liberal state ideology and local forms of oppression that have largely gone unfulfilled. As I demonstrate in chapter 6, progressive southern writers from the late 1930s and early 1940s sought new ways to experience and conceptualize group affiliation. In contrast with the writing of James Agee, widely praised for its confrontational and tormented attention to the alterity of southern poverty, other authors explored ways of traversing apparent temporal and psychological impediments to productive alliance. But such investigations confronted a changed ideological terrain by the 1950s, at which point U.S. and southern cultures again began to be understood chiefly through a dichotomy. My concluding chapter examines novels written during the early years of this transition, William Faulkner's *Requiem for a Nun* (1951) and Ralph Ellison's *Invisible Man* (1952), which explicitly juxtapose rural southern locales with metropolitan and national institutions. Though each writer was embraced by intellectuals seeking evidence of a vigorous national culture, these novels describe individual characters' inability to discern, amid the clash of southern and U.S. cultures, vocabularies and social networks that would enable them effectively to comprehend and confront injustice. In each case, this difficulty is linked to a truncated understanding of national time that inhibits comprehension of damages exceeding the linear narrative of progressive nation-state development.

In tracing this historical trajectory, I do not attempt a comprehensive account of southern literary works but seek rather to demonstrate that southern writers have used the region as a productive entryway for discussions of multiplicity in U.S. practice and experience. I am studying a period in U.S. history in which both activists and liberal government officials saw regionalism and nationalism as ideologies that could facilitate democratic social change; accordingly, I do not dismiss the possibility that either might provide one threshold of affiliation at which to develop or encourage more beneficial forms of political and social life.[37] Though critiques of nationalism and liberalism have hardly been exhausted, it remains important that democratic nationalist ideals constituted one prominent tool in the struggle against apartheid. Even regionalism, which many critics have come to understand as an inevitably conservative form of mystification, need not result from nostalgic or essentialist ideas of cultural identity; it could instead provide opportunities for organizing around goals vital to geographies and cultures not bound by national borders, shared economic or environmental concerns, or challenges to aspects of the nation-state that suppress democratic possibility.[38] But such developments can only be supported by a clearer understanding of the ways in which U.S. nationalism has tended to code its investments in racial hierarchies as regional traits.

PART ONE

Imagining Affiliation

CHAPTER ONE

Region, Race, and Nation

DURING WORLD WAR II, when southern racial segregation had begun to provoke intense national controversy, the prolific and influential southern sociologist Howard Odum claimed that white southerners were genuinely shocked, protesting, "Who ever thought the South would abandon segregation anyhow?"[1] This complaint reflected profound indifference to the history of African American activism but also registered awareness of national policy: before the late 1930s southern segregation laws had met with few prominent challenges and had instead extended their reach into other regions of the nation and into more aspects of southern life.[2] The early years of the Great Depression were characterized by increased liberalism in national rhetoric but relatively little challenge to white southerners' racial practices.[3] During this period, African American writers and activists tended to focus on issues other than desegregation, which seemed unattainable and perhaps undesirable. As James

Weldon Johnson wrote, "There come times when the most persistent integrationist becomes an isolationist, when he curses the White world and consigns it to hell."[4] Between the beginning and the end of the 1930s, then, the predominant understanding of southern apartheid shifted such that what had been widely seen as an inherent component of regional culture was recognized as an urgent national problem.[5]

During this transformation, images of the South proliferated in national discourse—an eruption of representations in fiction, journalism, and the social sciences especially notable because, between 1916 and 1928, not one book on a southern subject had appeared on the annual best-seller lists.[6] Long configured in U.S. discourse as a region removed from contemporary national culture, the South was increasingly seen, during the 1930s, as a threat to national economic and political structures. Notably, however, such concerns evoked not only calls for reform and socioeconomic analysis but also a proliferation of gothic tropes, as editors, artists, and even social scientists described the "tremendous and ghastly visions" of the South's white supremacists, the Dantean "inferno" of its agricultural districts, the "lunatic, disintegrating wildness" of its evangelical Protestantism, and its culture "linger[ing] in the dark backward abysm of time."[7] Such uncanny imagery, in Sigmund Freud's assessment, would indicate that material evoking such shudders must threaten, in its not-quite strangeness, to unravel a repression.[8] Following that interpretive model, this chapter suggests that national cultures, like individuals, generate fantasies that depend on disavowal in the process of cultivating an identity. In particular, I argue that images of the South facilitated such disavowal in U.S. nationalism before the 1930s—a history that may have lent later representations some of their uncanny charge.

My argument treats fantasies concerning national identity—as seen, for example, in nationalist celebrations and rhetoric, debates concerning state policy and practice, and popular narratives—as vectors of implicit political philosophies. In modeling what the nation is (its defining traits, its epic past, or its desired future), such representations—whether imagined or encoded in aesthetic work or public ceremony—also stage the ways in which citizens are bound to the nation (what they share, how they feel about their country and each other, the affects that comprise their allegiance).[9] To the extent that the nation is defined as the collective body of an ethnic group, for example, its citizens may believe themselves to share not only language but also beliefs, traditions, and certain social behaviors, as well as memories of common familial patterns.[10] In contrast, if the nation is imagined chiefly as the people associated with a particular governmental structure, its citizens may understand themselves to share little beyond their commitment to that form of governance—an attachment that, however passionate, lacks the "thick" commonality of the former model. Often described as cultural (or particularist) nationalism and civic (or liberal) nationalism, these two ways of imagining national identity and affiliation never exist in a pure form but rather combine, in different ways, to shape citizens' understanding of their relationship to the nation-state.[11]

This chapter, then, argues that, from the institutionalization of southern racial segregation to the beginning of the civil rights movement (i.e., from the 1890s to the late 1930s), monolithic understandings of "the South" served to contain contradictions between divergent models of U.S. citizenship. Often configured as an exemplar of civic nationalism unified chiefly in its citizens' commitment to individual rights and to democracy as a governmental form, the United States has nonetheless, throughout its history, restricted inclusion according to ascribed aspects of identity—association with such preset social categories as race, gender, sexuality, religion, or class.[12] This latter strand of U.S. nationalism has also emphasized forms of commonality that exceed shared beliefs concerning governmental structure—commitments to religious dogma, custom, or white supremacy. These two models of affiliation—civic and particularist—explicitly competed in the Supreme Court ruling in *Plessy v. Ferguson*, which legitimated racial segregation in 1896. Weighing African Americans' rights to mobility and participation within public spaces and institutions against "the established usages, customs and traditions of the people," the Court chose in favor of the latter.[13] Thus, as I explain in the first section of this chapter, the edifice of widespread local laws constituting U.S. apartheid rested on federal support for a model of affiliation rhetorically associated with the South. Represented as a concession to white southerners and even to southerners more generally—"public peace and good order"—the denial of African Americans' citizenship rights was separated from the state ideology of liberalism, which continued to be promoted as a defining feature of U.S. identity.

This divergence was naturalized through popular aesthetic narratives that staged a distinct and organically hierarchical southern social order. Depictions of the region's slaveholding past—epitomized by the filmic and literary genres of "plantation romance"—presented it less as an anomaly in a liberal nation than as a privileged site of a coherent and binding white culture. While southern cultural difference was posited through the idealization of the region's past, it was also asserted in an opposite way—through rigorous attention to the "problem South," a site in need of economic and social reform.[14] But this combination of celebration and concern did not impede what David Brion Davis has called the "Confederacy's ideological victory" in shaping national memory and federal policy.[15] Rather, this tension between nostalgia and critique maintained a prominent role in national discourse well into the twentieth century. H. L. Mencken's famous 1920 critique of twentieth-century southern cultural "steril[ity]," for example, nonetheless proclaimed the antebellum South "a civilization of manifold excellences—perhaps the best that the Western Hemisphere has ever seen—undoubtedly the best that These States have ever seen."[16] While the insistence on regional difference served to disavow southern racism as the archaic remainder of a backward culture—preserving the nation-state's emphasis on its liberalism and modernization—the romanticization of the southern past served to retain white supremacist conceptions of a national people as a prominent trope in U.S. nationalism.

This mutual support between the U.S. nation-state and the idea of thick and binding regional cultures is not, as I note in the second section of this chapter, confined to this period or to relationships between the South and the nation. Rather, this arrangement reflects a more general pattern in U.S. nationalism, in which abstract models of national citizenship coexist with images of regional cultures bound by shared custom and belief. In this way, particularist aspects of U.S. nationalism have been both cultivated as vital to the national character—in celebrations, for example, of the nation's many regional traditions—and disavowed as irrelevant to the nation-state. The vision of white cultural collectivity associated with the South, however, has been remarkable for its prominence and virulence. My final section shows how popular Reconstruction narratives, in particular, staged a fantasy of collective affiliation that, while antithetical to liberal conceptions of statehood, played an influential role in U.S. nationalism. This chapter, then, provides important background to this book's examination of the 1930s and 1940s; it helps to explain why, in considering the relationship between the South and the larger nation, later writers and readers so often plunged into speculation concerning the very structures and meanings of U.S. affiliation.

Mapping "Jim Crow"

It is readily apparent that the federal government chose not to challenge U.S. apartheid until the 1940s and instead practiced racial segregation in such national institutions as the armed forces. But it still seems paradoxical for white southerners to have believed, as Howard Odum insisted they did, that the World War II–era challenge to segregation came suddenly and in a "flood"—"as if . . . the South was initiating backward policies in which it boldly challenged the rest of the world in new reaches of injustice and discrimination."[17] On the one hand, southern apartheid had developed over decades and was, by the 1930s, thoroughly established.[18] On the other, southern backwardness was a prominent topic in Depression-era discourse, which often depicted the region as a threat to U.S. progress. Such understandings were promoted during the 1930s by, for example, sociological studies of white southern cultural homogeneity and isolation; sociological accounts of the oppression, illiteracy, and poverty experienced by southern African Americans; popular exposés of chain-gang labor in the southern prison system; economic reports of southern lags in production and consumption of items considered necessary elsewhere; popular historical accounts arguing that the South's purpose in the Civil War had been to defend an agrarian way of life against industrialization; regionalist manifestoes claiming that the South still maintained that agrarian role in national life; and sociopsychological accounts of white southern vigilance regarding class and racial hierarchies.[19]

Southern apartheid, however, was not threatened by such critiques; rather, it had relied since its inception on ideas of the region's isolation from national time. Indeed, an appeal to fixed cultural patterns had been the defense of segregation laws since before the Civil War.[20] This precedent, established in *Sarah C. Roberts v. The City of Boston* (1847) by the Supreme Judicial Court of Massachusetts, was affirmed by the U.S. Supreme Court in *Plessy v. Ferguson*, in which the justices ruled that state law could neither be held responsible for nor intervene in the "racial instincts" that shaped local social structures.[21] By 1906, this legal reasoning corresponded with a popular and influential volume in sociology—William Graham Sumner's *Folkways*—that emphasized the temporal distinctness of southern culture.[22] Sumner argued that social mores—beliefs embedded in cultural practices—could not be changed by rational discussion, for they "are elevated into 'principles' of truth and right" and "present themselves as final and unchangeable."[23] He considered the United States generally immune to such fixation, as it had conformed to "the modern scientific world philosophy," a system of mores unique for its self-representation as "incomplete, and liable to be set aside to-morrow by more knowledge."[24] In contrast, he presented the South as a region arrested in the social patterns of the slaveholding era; its stasis could be altered only through "a great natural convulsion." By the convergence of these legal and sociological discourses, southern apartheid—the most explicit and extensively codified system of racial segregation in the nation—was deemed impervious to governmental intervention. The precedent of *Plessy* also sheltered segregationist practices in other regions from the possibility of federal interference.[25]

Much as perceptions of southern cultural fixation protected racial segregation from legal challenge, the representation of African American oppression as a specifically southern problem cast the conflict between egalitarian democracy and white supremacy as a dichotomy between national and regional practice. This contrast was especially important during the 1930s, as official U.S. discourse became increasingly liberal: where policy in the 1920s was prominently characterized by white supremacist views, the Franklin D. Roosevelt administration conspicuously shifted to a more civic nationalism.[26] Accordingly, as the Swedish social scientist Gunnar Myrdal began conducting interviews for his Carnegie-supported study of U.S. race relations, *An American Dilemma*, he suspected that the divergence between U.S. democratic ideals and the actualities of racial segregation and discrimination must create an "ever-raging conflict" in the thoughts and affects of the citizenry. He discovered, however, that such concerns were muted in all regions by the belief that racial oppression was chiefly restricted to the South, a region ordered by unassailable folkways and noted for its cultural difference from the nation.[27]

That this understanding persisted for so many decades suggests disavowal of the increasing ties between southern and national cultures. For while it is true that the southern states had not experienced the degree of urbanization, industrialization, and secularization seen in the larger United States, they were, by the 1930s, engaged in increasing exchange with national culture. The notorious 1925 Scopes "monkey trial," for example, so often cited as evidence of a specifically southern prejudice against a more modern and scientific secularism, situated that prejudice at the center of a notably modern and national media event.[28] Rather than simply revealing the alterity of a spatially and temporally isolated population, the trial served as a forum through which both regional and national audiences could examine the cultural dislocations caused by modernization, a process that continued to affect the entire United States.[29] Regional and national institutions and culture also overlapped in many ways: racial segregation appeared in many locales outside the South, and, on the other hand, media and consumer culture—of which blues and country recordings were a vital part—increasingly provided shared references throughout the nation.[30] Nonetheless, even as film distribution began to alter national culture, studios claimed to be restrained by southern audiences, whose cultural sensitivities were said to render many scripts too controversial to play in the region.[31]

Continued assessments that the South could not change both supported regional and national apartheid and denied evidence to the contrary. Societal shifts in the region were not necessarily consistent nor, in many cases, liberalizing, but they nonetheless suggest, unsurprisingly, that the region could not remain unaltered while part of a nation overtly devoted to change. The extent of the southern vote for Herbert Hoover in 1928, for example, excited great attention at the time; this substantial defection from the Democratic Party elicited numerous explanatory theories—including hostility toward the Democratic candidate's Catholicism, commitment to Prohibition, a waning of white supremacy because of the Great Migration, increased immigration into the South from other regions, increased economic prosperity, or even the "softness" of what had been a supposedly "Solid South"—and briefly disrupted the national consensus on southern political immutability.[32] Subsequent votes for Franklin Roosevelt, of course, demonstrated southern support for a political program that would substantially alter both the federal government and its role in southern society. In emphasizing regional political shifts, I do not mean to dismiss the role of race-baiting in southern politics, as evidenced by the 1928 presidential campaign and later by the "Dixiecrat Revolt," but rather to argue that such movements indicated not mere tradition and stasis. Instead, they constituted a continuing process of change and reassessment in political strategies that involved, in many cases, reprioritizing white supremacy. Indeed, reports from the 1930s suggest that southern race relations exhibited escalating strain throughout the decade.[33]

In sum, apartheid was enfolded into national law through an understanding of the South's cultural, political, and temporal discontinuity from the nation, although apartheid emerged in the United States long before the nation's most severe sectional conflict and irrespective of regional boundaries, and continued amid the increasing commonalities between the South and the larger nation.[34] In the early decades of the twentieth century, white southern propagandists vigorously defended segregationist policies through appeals to the region's distinct cultural status, an argument also mobilized against the 1922 federal antilynching bill.[35] Whereas, through the sweeping institution of segregation laws in the 1890s, southern legislatures manifested what Etienne Balibar calls "(official) state racism," such that racist policy was a defining characteristic of the region, the United States was represented as a government harboring "racism *within the state*," making it a chiefly egalitarian nation that was unable to restrain its antidemocratic elements.[36] But because, before the 1940s, the United States readily conceded this inability, antiracist appeals to the liberal principles that ostensibly defined the nation were effectively blocked.[37] Meanwhile, southern state governments, explicitly white supremacist in belief and practice, offered little opportunity for African American advancement outside economic and cultural separatism, the position embraced by W. E. B. Du Bois during the 1930s.[38]

Coming from a writer and leader who had previously challenged not only segregation but also accommodationist African American leaders, this shift suggests how successfully citations of a static southern culture served to restrict progress in U.S. racial policy. In both sociological description and theoretical formulas, Du Bois's earlier writing had challenged the logic by which southern culture and politics were bracketed from U.S. policy. In *Darkwater* (1920), he argued that, despite regional specificities, "Jim-Crow" segregation was used to manage labor competition in industrial centers throughout the nation.[39] His influential *The Souls of Black Folk* (1903) included extensive sociological commentary on the particularities of southern apartheid but depicted the temporal difference through which that apartheid was often explained—southern backwardness—as a contradiction in the U.S. ideology of progress. In this account, African Americans in all regions experience multiple temporal forms, "swept on by the currents of the nineteenth while yet struggling in the eddies of the fifteenth century."[40] By the mid-1930s, however, Du Bois considered southern backwardness an overwhelming actuality: "They are going to continue [lynching and judicial injustice] until the South becomes civilized, and no one living is going to see that day."[41]

Du Bois's reversal corresponded with his efforts to support African American gains amid a rigid system of regional and national apartheid, but ideas of southern "otherness," as suggested by numerous scholars, also played a role in enabling white nonsoutherners to disavow the centrality of white supremacy in U.S. nationalism.[42] This formulation relies on the understanding that, in large groups as in individuals, the development and maintenance of an imagined identity requires the assertion of internal coherence and the defensive projection onto another body, object, or space of any quality that threatens this idealized image.[43] More than an analogy, this theory reflects both the mutually constitutive relationships among group and individual identities and the ways in which each is supported by societal systems of representation and practice.[44] Individual Americans, for example, identify themselves as such through their affective attachment to national symbols and stories, such that nationality becomes a vital component of their concept and experience of selfhood.[45] When this aspect of their identities causes discomfort because of internal or external contradiction (between national and individual value systems, for example, or between national rhetoric and practice), individuals may analyze and address this apparent conflict—a response that one scholar of nationalism describes as unrealistic and frustrating—or may instead disavow the contradiction, attributing it to others inside or outside the nation.[46]

But while it is clear that understandings of southern cultural difference served to suppress public concern about the presence of racial segregation in an ostensibly liberal democracy, it is important to note that, for much of the apartheid era, this containment transpired less through repudiation than embrace of white supremacy as a specifically southern cultural trait. A deluge of romanticized images of the slaveholding South—many of which were produced by northern writers—accompanied the institutionalization of apartheid, allowing Lost Cause mythology to achieve, in the historian David Blight's words, "nearly a stranglehold on the cultural memory of the [Civil War] era."[47] These narratives corresponded to Timothy Brennan's account of nationalistic form, by insisting on the South's cultural coherence while depicting its "*composite* nature: a hotch potch of the ostensibly separate 'levels of style' corresponding to class; a jumble of poetry, drama, newspaper report, memoir and speech; a mixture of the jargons of race and ethnicity."[48] Literary partisans of southern elites also promulgated explicit arguments for African American disenfranchisement and white southern sovereignty in managing regional race relations. Through the voice of Uncle Remus, for example, Joel Chandler Harris argued against education for African Americans, explaining that "a nigger is done gradyated de minnit you puts de plough handles in his han's," and Thomas Nelson Page's white southern characters opined that Yankee reformers exacerbated southern racial conflict, complaining that they "don't seem to like niggers and git along with 'em easylike and nat'ral as we all do."[49] Despite its implied demands for regional autonomy, this literature was both popular and influential, leading the African American writer and educator Anna Julia Cooper to question how "Southern influence, Southern ideas, and Southern ideals . . . dictated to and domineered over the brain and sinew of this nation."[50]

Late nineteenth-century white U.S. narrative, then, depicted the South not only as debased but also as illustrious, a site for valued cultural patterns.[51] Southern representations functioned in U.S. discourse of this period as both other and exemplar, providing, in their insistent cultural difference, a logic through which U.S. apartheid could be considered separately from the state ideology of liberalism, and also providing, in their romanticization, images of white supremacy that white U.S. audiences embraced. But while it appears, as Grace Elizabeth Hale argues, that "the metaphoric South" provides a "reservoir of many cherished [white] American self-perceptions," the structure of beliefs through which ideas of a region could serve this function in national culture merits further examination.[52] The role of the South in U.S. nationalism is not simply unique but rather exemplifies how conceptions of regional cultures can serve as vehicles for the particularist models of collective affiliation that liberal nationalism disavows. Though this pattern has shifted through time, it constitutes a vital dynamic in how U.S. nationhood has been theorized.

The Nation and Its Supplements

Writing in the early 1920s, decades after formulating his influential thesis concerning the role of the West in the development of U.S. national character, Frederick Jackson Turner argued that U.S. regions seem more conventionally nationalistic than the nation itself: "We are like a United States of Europe would be . . . a federation of sections rather than of states."[53] Presenting the nation chiefly as a set of institutions and traits through which federation takes place—"the unifying influence of parties and a common legislative body . . . a common set of institutions, a common law, and a common language"—he vaguely asserts, "There is an American spirit. There are American ideals."[54] He starkly contrasts the nation's meager role in citizens' experience and character, however, with the significance of the region. Turner holds sectionalism to generate, in politics, both grievances and agitation for participatory democracy; in economics, the "material interests . . . of business, manufacturing, mining, agriculture, transportation"; and in culture, "a special flavor, social, psychological, literary, even religious."[55] Though the space of the United States is defined by the boundaries of federal sovereignty, the nation's cultures are distributed into regions: "We think sectionally and do not fully understand one another."[56] This dichotomy has been repeatedly proposed in U.S. history: where affiliation with the nation is represented as abstract and pragmatic, affiliation with the region suggests commonality and rootedness—a connection with the land and its past.[57] This is why Turner likens U.S. regions to nations and the United States to the then-hypothetical European Union. But though he implies that the United States lacks the cultural coherence that should serve as a vital connecting force in nationalism, he suggests that as long the nation can avert sectional division, the cultural bonds of regionalism could be mobilized on behalf of the nation-state.

Though regionalists in diverse national contexts avow that regions comprise more authentic cultural identities than nations, each of these forms of spatial identification has been produced through history, and their affiliative and imaginative styles result from a mix of circumstance and strategy.[58] This developmental similarity may be obscured in the United States by the notable difference between nation and regions: only the nation, with the brief but significant exception of the Confederacy, is identified with a central government, whereas such broadly recognized regions as New England and the Midwest have not constituted bureaucratic political entities. Such geopolitical units have asserted their common interests since the institution of the United States, however, vitally affecting its form; the process of creating and maintaining a united nation-state entailed negotiation not only among existing colonial governments but also among regional groups of states.[59] For the United States as for nations more generally, the nationalist project has comprised a determined effort to produce a coherent spatial identity; this effort has entailed such media as broadly distributed images and maps, national census data, representational spaces (including museums and civic monuments), and aestheticized representations of a national landscape imbued with intimately felt group meaning.[60] But these nationalizing efforts have served, in many instances, not to displace but to accentuate regional specificities through the argument that distinct regions contribute in important ways to U.S. national character.

That regional conflict has so threatened U.S. unity makes the nation-state's continuing interest in regional identities all the more noteworthy.[61] Scholars of European nationalism note that capitalist states tend to promote cultural commonality within a nation's boundaries in order to support both the government's political legitimacy and the development of markets.[62] But in shifting and various ways, ideas of regional difference have played an important role in contesting and defining U.S. national identity. In the early Republic, for example, the relatively homogeneous

New England was positioned against the Mid-Atlantic states as a cultural model for the new nation; northern states more generally depicted the South as undeveloped, brutal, and antidemocratic, and southerners represented the North as a site of unbridled and inherently radical change.[63] Each of these sectional agendas, in the years before the Civil War, constituted an effort to define U.S. political culture and coexisted with a more unifying ideology that also relied on sectional tropes—the frontier as symbol and guarantor of U.S. democracy.[64]

During and after Reconstruction, as the United States consolidated its identity as a nation devoted to capitalist expansion, the role of regionalism in national culture shifted, serving less as a mode of contestation and more as a way of demonstrating the presence of binding traditions within the nation. This is not to deny that some regionalists sought to challenge emerging trends in U.S. nationhood but rather to argue that they did so by insisting on the importance of regional distinctness. For example, when the populist writer Hamlin Garland asserted, "Local color means national character," he was confronting what he viewed as centralizing forces in national culture.[65] But while much local color fiction of the late nineteenth century produced, in Carrie Tirado Bramen's terms, "a modern critique of social and spatial marginalization," reception of this work was "inscribed within the very eastern metropolitan values" that such artists were challenging.[66] In effect, the literature that Garland championed did not disrupt consolidation of the nation's identity so much as suggest that regional customs and beliefs might lend a broader temporal dimension to a nation so focused on progress. Following Richard Brodhead's account of such representations, one could argue that they staged both a national present and regional pasts, providing the "cultural service of imaging Americans different in habits, speech, and appearance from a norm this form helps render normative" and suggesting "a history of [quaint regional locales'] supersession by a modern order now risen to national dominance."[67]

Rather than merely supplanting regions, such a logic would assign them a vital role in nationalist discourse, which, as Homi Bhabha argues, routinely struggles to balance its commitments to the binding "authority that is based on the pre-given ... historical origin *in the past*" and to the "prodigious, living principles of the people as contemporaneity."⁶⁸ In a period centrally concerned, in Bill Brown's words, with the nationalist project of "Americanizing memory," local color offered scenes that could demonstrate the nation's communal histories; images of provincial life served this purpose even when presented to readers who conceived of their own spatial and social relationships in quite different ways—less local than cosmopolitan, less collective and traditional than individualist and modern.⁶⁹ But while configuring regional cultures as vital elements in forming U.S. identity, this fiction also often displaced or denigrated U.S. racial and ethnic diversity by omitting representation of racial minorities, portraying them in demeaning and influential stereotypes, or naturalizing local racial hierarchies; its typical focus on stable local populations further obscured the coexistence of this fiction with concentrated immigration to the United States.⁷⁰

To be clear, I am not attempting to assess the politics of local color fiction, a project that has elicited numerous conflicting, substantial, and, to me, simultaneously persuasive arguments—even concerning the single example of Sarah Orne Jewett.⁷¹ Rather, I am suggesting that the difficulty of such analyses is compounded by the way in which regionalism mobilizes forms of affiliation that are simultaneously active and disavowed within U.S. nationalism. As proponents argue, the specificity of regionalism provides "a form of critique grounded in the local," one that challenges nationalist depictions of "regions ... in effect as internal colonies."⁷² Insisting on the importance of cultural differences, regionalist writing models "empathy, the capacity to imagine how someone else might feel," and challenges the "presumed universality" of national culture.⁷³ The concentration of racial or ethnic groups in certain regions—such as Mexican Americans in the Southwest or Asian Americans along the West Coast—suggests that regionalism, in its prioritization of local experience, could serve as a vehicle to promote broader recognition of the nation's diversity.⁷⁴ But while progressive writers may use regionalist representations to expand and enrich democratic and critical discourse, regionalism may also be used to support or to mask particularist currents within U.S. nationalism. At their most expansionist, for example, regionalists may propose local cultural norms to displace the nation's more abstract models of membership, creating a new threshold for national exclusivity. Conservative nationalists, in contrast, may associate *only* regions with ethnic or racial diversity, displacing recognition of an identity group's spatial dispersal in order to discount U.S. diversity.[75]

The most troubling aspect of regionalist representations, as historically mobilized in the United States, may be their tendency to promote understandings of a binding form of affiliation typically discounted in models of liberal nationalism; political theorists, however, consider such forms of attachment psychologically attractive. The United States is often described as a distinctly liberal nation; focused on future accomplishment rather than a commonality grounded in the past, national membership seems to allow for both diversity and change.[76] But by combining egalitarian rhetoric with marginalizing beliefs, practices, and laws, U.S. nationalism suggests that normative affiliation can be manifested only by people invulnerable to such discrimination and exemplary of upward economic mobility—conditions few citizens can confidently claim.[77] In contrast, culturally particularist collectives, such as those seen in late nineteenth-century aesthetic regionalism, are said to provide their members with a sense of secure and organic affiliation, a form of attachment perhaps more readily able to inspire, as Rogers M. Smith argues, "the senses of belonging and commitment that the imperatives of collective political life have always demanded."[78] Through their ostensible provision of thick cultural belonging beneath the threshold of the nation, then, regional identities have offered amelioration for precisely the damage that U.S. nationality threatens to inflict: though citizens may justly fear being "left out of" or "left behind in" U.S. capitalist progress, identification with regions is held to be sustained—determined by roots—and, concomitantly, sustaining. Facts concerning the diversity and discrimination that exist within U.S. regions are, in this ideological configuration, either elided or celebrated as signs of stable cultural hierarchy.

Thus regionalism, as a cultural discourse, has often functioned as a supplement to U.S. nationalism; it serves to suggest that, at the local level, the United States maintains precisely the kind of the cultural particularities that the state ideology of liberalism disavows. Identified with modernization and abstract structures of government, the nation-state is nonetheless shown to enfold regional cultures marked by communal life and shared traditions. Upheld as a distinction of regions, this purported embeddedness is displayed as a national lack, but in the development of U.S. nationalism, this lack may be seen as productive.[79] Refusing secure or organic affiliation while presenting itself as a signifier of viability and success, U.S. liberal nationalism denies its attachments to stable or traditional cultural content while initiating the desire for what Slavoj Žižek calls "fundamentalisms"—powerful attachments to traditions not labeled as national—among its adherents; the nation-state condones or even encourages such "ways of life" within its regions.[80]

A more prominently cited supplement to contractual nationalism is racism, which functions in a quite different way from regionalism.[81] Where regionalism gestures inward, proffering organic models of affiliation beneath the boundaries of the nation, racism gestures throughout and beyond national space; where regionalism presents claims for inclusion of local habits within a dominant national culture, racism presents claims for exclusion. Neither manages to fill the gaps in a nation's construction of itself without difficulty: the multiple groundings of regionalism root the nation in disunity, and as racism seeks to guarantee the commonality of the national polity by exclusions, it finds the contrasts among races impossible to assure.[82] Both, however, have played important roles in the history of U.S. nationhood, despite a liberal ideology that would seem antithetical to either.

To a great extent, racism and regionalism have eluded this ostensible opposition in concert: regionalism masks national participation in racism, and racism celebrates and maintains certain regionalist tropes. For example, many nineteenth-century representations of regional cultures—such as minstrel depictions of southern African Americans, "Wild West" shows, and local color fiction—prominently featured racialized models of affiliation and cultural difference—such as specifically "Negro" leisure practices, patterns of conflict between "cowboys and Indians," or the family gathering that demonstrates Norman ethnic traits in Jewett's *The Country of the Pointed Firs*. These entertainments suggested that the U.S. nation-state, however abstract and liberal its norms of membership might be, enveloped racially homogeneous or hierarchical cultures. To the extent that these cultural forms provided stereotypical representation of nonwhite subjects—as minstrelsy, in Eric Lott's words, injected "'blackness' into the public sphere"—they also placed such subjects in regions famous for racial hierarchy and violence.[83] By insistently locating racialized groups in regionalized spaces, which were suggested to maintain cultural traditions outside the control of the liberal state, these representations dissociated such groups from potential claims to national citizenship. Except in recognizably activist writing, this logic has been prominent in U.S. discourse, as representations of interracial abuse and interracial exchange—relationships that served as the sources, in Michael Rogin's words, for a "distinctive [U.S.] national culture"—are situated in distinctive regional locales.[84]

Whether through racial hierarchy and expropriation or through insistent racial or ethnic homogeneity, regional representations have provided a venue in which to stage the sorts of particularistic and possessive fantasies that psychoanalytic studies associate with nationalism.[85] Further, regional representations demonstrate the nation-state's ability to allot space to such fantasies and to facilitate their sharing and emergence. Though U.S. rhetoric does not focus on the nation-state's ability to provide a sense of racial connection and completion, it often presents local spaces as the sites of precisely such satisfaction for national subjects. (Though this logic is typically associated with white supremacy, it also appears in representations of minoritized ethnic and racial communities, which are suggested, however, to cohesively resist oppression—and, in some cases, incorporation in the nation.[86]) Thus, in order to understand how U.S. nationalism has managed to combine liberal democracy with the exclusionary fantasies often presented as its opposite, we might consider how such fantasies have been distributed to the regions in narratives of U.S. nationhood. It is in this way that, as Houston Baker argues, "the manifest content of what might be termed [U.S.] 'deep-structural principles' often derives more from the local than the federal."[87]

While understandings of the South are not unique in serving this role in U.S. nationalism, they have done so to extraordinary effect. This history resulted, in part, from the chronological convergence of the desire for sectional reconciliation with the increase of immigration and U.S. imperialism.[88] In this context, plantation romances served much as the Latin American nationalist novels described by Doris Sommer, depicting couples from North and South as previously divided white "lovers who are 'naturally' attracted and right for one another" and valuing these unions as sites of national unity and racial reproduction.[89] Such representations modeled a form of cultural and political affiliation that maintained strict class and racial hierarchies during a period when the United States was experiencing expanded racial and ethnic diversity as well as labor unrest.[90] As Amy Kaplan argues, plantation fiction, with its insistence on a natural southern Anglo-Saxon aristocracy, also provided tropes mobilized in later representations of chivalric national figures engaged in imperialistic adventures.[91] Most basically, while presenting racial difference as an element of regional culture, southern representations suggested that this mode of organizing social hierarchies and affiliations could be portable; as Walter Benn Michaels usefully notes, they did so in an era when both European and U.S. nationalisms appear to have experienced "the political appeal of the racialized state."[92]

Thus the South's role as the institutional center of U.S. apartheid facilitated its emergence as an icon in discourse seeking to limit the parameters of U.S. liberal nationalism. This function can still be observed in presidential politics, as questions of national identity and policy are framed in terms of whether the nation should tolerate signs of southern intolerance, and, conversely, whether the South will permit liberalization of the nation. In the 2000 campaign, for example, Republicans and Democrats vied over whether South Carolina's display of the Confederate flag constituted an issue for state residents to decide and perhaps a matter of heritage, or whether such arguments constituted an endorsement of regional bigotry by national political figures.[93] Such discussions affect not only the symbols with which the nation is identified but also the goals; for example, the question of whether a candidate who supports gay rights could win in the South was prominent in early media coverage of the 2004 campaign, as pundits and, reportedly, strategists argued the merits of allowing understandings of regional conservatism to set the national Democratic Party agenda.[94]

But while this logic, through which understandings of a white supremacist or otherwise culturally conservative South link particularist content to U.S. nationalism, has played a prominent role in U.S. political life, it has not been uncontested. As Kenneth Warren argues, it was directly challenged during its post-Reconstruction emergence by George Washington Cable; before that, Albion Tourgée posited southern regionalism as a source of Reconstruction's failure.[95] As regional apartheid became more firmly instituted and more violently enforced, the African American writers Anna Julia Cooper and Charles Chesnutt criticized and explored its expanding influence on national policy. Nor has the relationship between conservative regionalism and nationalism been static. During the 1930s, as I discuss in later chapters, openly white supremacist celebrations of the South coexisted uneasily with more pluralist approaches to regionalism, and exploration of this dichotomy, for many writers, yielded insight into the multiple and contradictory understandings of affiliation that were shaping U.S. society.

Even in their most hegemonic forms, however, narratives of a southern cultural collective reveal some of the contradictions in U.S. nationalism, which seeks to facilitate passionate attachment to a political entity in which, as Ralph Ellison argued, the most widely shared experience may be excruciating awareness of the potential for "upward—yes, and *downward*—mobility."[96] Ensconced in a nation-state said to generate a particularly scarifying form of political identity, southern white supremacists have explicitly exploited the tension between the goals of economic competition and national unity.[97] Implying that liberal principles cannot procure sufficient social cohesion to counter the conflicts that emerge in a capitalist society, segregationist Reconstruction narratives posited in their place the securing bonds of white supremacy.

The Erotics of Region

In U.S. history, racism and regionalism have converged perhaps most prominently in the white supremacist account of Reconstruction, a plotline popularized not only through literature and drama but also in textbooks. As Michelle Wallace explains, these narratives typically emphasized white southern suffering and argued that African Americans were unsuited to participatory democracy; diverging as to whether this inability was essential to the race or the result of life in slavery, such narratives routinely blamed the failure of Reconstruction on black southerners, rather than on white southern terrorism and political activism or on northern ambivalence in enacting Reconstruction policies.[98] Examining five decades of U.S. historiography, W. E. B. Du Bois argued in 1935 that "in order to paint the South as a martyr to inescapable fate, to make the North the magnanimous emancipator, and to ridicule the Negro as the impossible joke in the whole development," historians had produced a dangerous "romance"; in both aesthetic and scholarly presentations, this narrative conflicted with liberal nationalism, advocating "embrace and worship [of] the color bar as social salvation" and "loss of democratic ideals."[99] This problem is most vividly demonstrated in D. W. Griffith's influential epic *The Birth of a Nation* (1915), widely cited for its achievements in cinematic narration and visual aesthetics as well as for the virulence of its racism.

Though many scholars have sought to articulate the role of this film in U.S. cultural history, these arguments are sometimes deflected by its limited spatial scope. Despite its claims to national significance, it focuses on a specific regional setting and uses as source material the writing of Thomas Dixon, an avowed white southern apologist and promoter of the Ku Klux Klan. The film demonstrates its regional bias not only by its predominantly southern settings but also through its rhetoric, in which the antebellum "Southland," for example, is presented as a site "where life runs in a quaintly way that is to be no more" and in which the federal government is threatening and intrusive. Such phrasing would have been familiar to contemporary audiences not only from earlier plantation romances but also from white southern political propaganda, which sought to defend regional racial segregation and lynching from national critique; these defenses were also characterized by the racial and sexual hysteria so prominent in *Birth of a Nation*. In a nation-state that continued to claim adherence to liberalism, despite its increasing racial segregation, the film's racial panic and sectional bias render doubly incoherent its claims to promote "America[n] 'Liberty and union, one and inseparable.'" Thus critics disagree about whether the film offered "a screen memory, in both meanings of that term, through which Americans were to understand their collective past and enact their future," or whether it merely promoted a southern *"nation that never was."*[100]

But the film evades alternate versions of U.S. nationalism precisely by positing the South as a scene of national and racial affiliation. In depicting white southerners as a group that must be saved, this narrative both staged a fantasy of thick and binding racial collectivity and elided the incongruity of that fantasy with other ideas concerning the basis of national affiliation, such as pluralism or cosmopolitanism. As discourses and practices of Americanization sought to guarantee a distinct national identity amid substantial immigration, Griffith's white supremacy, like Dixon's writing before it, was, in Walter Benn Michaels's terms, "hierarchical and assimilationist . . . ma[king] possible the Americanization of the [European] immigrant."[101] In the African American press the implications of depicting collective affiliation in this way were nicely illustrated by a 1915 *Chicago Defender* cartoon titled "The Melting Pot?" in which Thomas Dixon, drawn as the devil, uses a stick tagged *The Birth of a Nation* to stir a cauldron labeled Chicago.[102] Though African Americans and liberal activists sought to debunk the film's narrative of Reconstruction and prevent its dissemination, arguing both that it was false and that it promoted racism as nationalism, only in such protests was the conflict between white supremacist and liberal nationalisms engaged.[103]

Griffith's film describes the crisis and triumphant unification of U.S. white supremacy, staging a post–Civil War reunion between white southerners and northerners who join forces to discipline a southern black population. Intertitles explain that "the bringing of the African to America planted the first seed of disunion" and that, ultimately, "the former enemies of North and South are united again in common defense of their Aryan birthright." Vividly insisting on its national import through Civil War scenes, the film stresses its commitment to peace and domesticity through its romance plot and its depiction of antebellum white family life, in both North and South, as a scene of ceaseless affection, in which "Hostilities!" consist only of conflict between puppies and kittens. Against these depictions of white affiliation and comfort, *Birth of a Nation* poses the threat of African American political influence—indirectly, through political and literal miscegenation, or directly, through enfranchisement of African Americans, an act the film presents as producing a "Black Empire." This histrionic rhetoric is supported by scenes dismissing African Americans' efforts after emancipation and enfranchisement, arguing that they ceased to labor, caroused in the state legislature, sold votes, and chiefly pursued the demand for mixed-race marriages[104]; the film insists upon its veracity by describing its representation of the state legislature as a "historical facsimile." Relying heavily on the tropes of the minstrel tradition, Griffith also denigrates African Americans through stereotypical representations,[105] exceeding even Dixon's *The Clansman* (1905) in this respect.

A popular novel later transformed into a play and Griffith's chief source, Dixon's work argues far more vehemently than *Birth of a Nation* for black "barbarism," but in comparison with the film, the novel's male ex-slaves, when loyal to their former owners, are granted a greater degree of sympathy and agency; this inconsistency underwrites Dixon's more prominent argument concerning the racial basis of democratic nationhood.[106] Dixon repeatedly deems democracy itself the special achievement of white southerners, associating both the region and the nation with this *Staatsvolk*, a "breed" that "has conquered every foot of soil . . . their feet have pressed" and that has been central "in the growth of American nationality."[107] Though white southerners are represented as people with a remarkable "power of assimilation" to whom some slaves become attached, this loyalty is not valued by the novel's organic political elite whose "way" differs from those of the freedmen (276, 234). The novel insists, somewhat paradoxically, that the problem with multiple races' living within one nation is not only the inexorable "challenge of race against race to mortal combat" but also the inevitable interracial alliance and intraracial division.[108] The white Reconstructionist Austin Stoneman, for example, is influenced by the "yellow vampire" who works as his housekeeper, and the black servant Jake is abandoned by his family and church for his friendship with his "ole marster" (275, 371, 250).

By prioritizing racial loyalty, *The Clansman* repeatedly mocks nonracialized civic nationalism as an ideology of "hate and madness" (41). Stoneman's explanation that he is "but fulfilling the largest vision of universal democracy that ever stirred the soul of man—a democracy that shall know neither rich nor poor, bond nor free, white nor black" is countered by the proposition that "there is a moral force at the bottom of every living race of men" (182, 290). The novel asserts black inferiority in the most degrading of terms, but it further suggests that even if "assimilation" of African Americans were "possible," it would not be "desirable" (46). For Lincoln, described as the man destined "to build the foundations of the New Nation . . . in love and wisdom to endure forever," civic nationalism is inherently racial nationalism; in order for every American to be a "citizen king," there cannot be "distinct races" in the nation, paradoxically suggesting that the goal of political equality mandates a "duty to exclude" (45, 46).

Thus the racist hatreds of this novel are overtly orchestrated with the goal of eliciting passionate national attachments. Critical discussions of this narrative often focus on the subplot in which an ex-slave, Gus, rapes a white woman, Marion Lenoir, and is subsequently killed by the Klan. This spotlight emerges from multiple factors, including the centrality of victim and villain in the genre of melodrama to which Dixon plainly aspires; the strangeness of Dixon's narration, which recounts the rape through Gus's repetition of the scene while under hypnosis in front of Klan members; and the historical context in which the lynching of black men was almost consistently explained as punishment for the rape of white women.[109] But Dixon and later Griffith are surprisingly straightforward in showing that rape is peripheral to the formation and action of the Klan, whose mission, as Dixon expresses it, is neither revenge nor punishment but "revolution" (335, 374). The reenactment of the rape, however, produces "a frenzy of uncontrollable emotion" in its witnesses, allotting narrative space in which they spontaneously enact their passion for their "people," an eruption that, in its spread, "revealed the unity of the racial life" and portends "the resistless movement of a race" (324, 341). The response to this rape demonstrates the zeal that Dixon deems necessary to racial affiliation, which is held to complement the regional and national affection to which Lincoln attests[110]: "I love the South! It is a part of this Union. I love every foot of its soil, every hill and valley, mountain, lake, and sea, and every man, woman, and child that breathes beneath its skies. I am an American. . . . We fought the South because we loved her and would not let her go" (54).

This language of possessive heterosexual longing does not merely constitute Dixon's model for national affiliation but further reflects his mechanism for describing how people experience regional and racial affiliation. When the southern Dr. Cameron is imprisoned in Washington, D.C., his wife, who has always regarded him as "the lover and the undimmed hero of her girlish dreams," is newly "inspir[ed]" by her "heritage of centuries of heroic blood from the martyrs of old Scotland," which leads her to almost incessant political activity (102). The northern Phil Stoneman, upon arriving in the South, is persuaded to racial and regional unity both by his love for the southern Margaret Cameron and by his "amaze[ment]" at how the regional "climate" "favour[ed] marriage"—the "tremendous earnestness" with which young southern white men "pursued the work of courting," the "divinity... claimed and received" by "the young Southern woman," and the "impossib[ility]" of divorce (210–11). Walter Benn Michaels argues that, for Dixon, "the family represents a threat to... racial 'purity' " because a family can be multiracial; nonetheless, the family is vital to Dixon's understanding of collective affiliation.[111] Thus the plot of *The Clansman* arranges for white southerners to see that the threat of interracial relationships targets their families directly: as an object of male desire and female admiration, Marion Lenoir becomes "the one human being everybody had agreed to love," such that her rape by a black man can provoke a "moral, mental, and physical earthquake" (254, 341).

Dixon is, of course, hardly unique in exploiting romantic and erotic rhetoric to model and explain collectivist passions, which often exhibit an energy for which social norms and political interests do not suffice to account. In early psychoanalytic attempts to explain such phenomena, Freud argued that "civilization... aims at binding the members of the community together in a libidinal way" and derives the "psychical energy" necessary for this purpose from individuals' sexuality.[112] Noting precisely the aspects of group feeling that Dixon sought to mobilize—"the lack of emotional restraint, the incapacity for moderation and delay, the inclination to exceed every limit in the expression of emotion and to work it off completely in action"—Freud, in contrast, characterized these traits as regressed.[113] Nonetheless, he represented collectivist passion as inevitable and even necessary.

Arguing that cultural values work almost inherently to suppress erotic pleasure and to encourage individuals to release aggression against themselves, Freud repeatedly suggested that the most complete collectivities provide some compensatory pleasure—a libidinal attachment to a sustaining and powerful leader as well as to other members of the community.[114] Noting the power of the "narcissism of minor differences," in which a community coheres by directing its hostilities toward a near or neighboring group, he claimed that group psychology is "most threatening where the bonds of a society are chiefly constituted by the identification of its members with one another, while individuals of the leader type do not acquire the importance that should fall to them," a problem demonstrated by "the present cultural state of America."[115] That Freud penned these words while Adolf Hitler was vigorously promoting a version of nationalism that valorized both a strong leader and genocide of minority groups may be less an irony than a reflection of the circumstances of late Weimar Germany, which was characterized by a failure of diverse groups to cohere into an effective democracy as well as by its increasing anti-Semitism.[116] In this context, Freud singled out for psychological concern the nation that had insisted most vigorously on Germany's democratization and was notorious for its own failure to provide minority rights—the United States.[117]

Such psychoanalytic qualms about liberal nationalism are most prominently associated today with Slavoj Žižek, who maintains that formal democracy is "always tied to the 'pathological' fact of a nation-state."[118] In affiliating with a democratic collective, subjects defy the very idea of democracy, which designates participants as "pure singularit[ies], emptied of all content, freed of all substantial ties"; this rejection of abstraction in favor of group loyalty demonstrates not the inability to separate oneself from "concrete human content" and "genuine . . . community links" but rather the actual evanescence of such content and links, perceptions that fantasy seeks to deny (164–65, 163). Accordingly, the collective, in the form of the nation-state, offers itself as a site of plenitude and connection, containing "all the details by which is made visible the unique way a community *organizes its enjoyment*"; this "way of life," or "Thing," proffers precisely the sort of substantial particularity from which democracy, in its abstraction and potential universality, seeks to separate.[119] In arguing that the nation-state binds its subjects to a Lacanian Thing, Žižek, like Freud, describes collectivist passion as a response to the subject's earliest desire, fear, and loss—the quest for the "unforgettable Other," "the mother," "a forbidden good."[120] Accordingly, his theory ascribes profound psychological power to the tendency, in any form of nationalism, toward the impassioned and potentially tyrannical protection of an imagined national bond.[121]

This conviction that liberalism not only coincides with but even activates forms of fundamentalism with which it purports to be incompatible concerns thinkers for whom democracy still holds progressive promise; Geoffrey Galt Harpham, for example, points out that Žižek's account of ideology is "psychoanalytic rather than social or historical."[122] This theory provides, however, one framework for understanding the historical and continued prominence of particularist desire—racial, religious, and so on—in U.S. nationalism, despite its continuing valorization of democratic nationhood. In Žižek's assessment, the desire for the nation's "Thing" is overdetermined, shaped both by the subject's early experience of alienation and by the aggressive and exclusionary practices of capitalism. This economic structure creates anxiety and belies liberalism's suggestions of egalitarianism, leading subjects to seek redress of each problem through the nation: "What one demands is the establishment of a stable and clearly defined social body which will restrain capitalism's destructive potential by cutting off the 'excessive' element; and since this social body is experienced as that of a nation, the cause of any imbalance 'spontaneously' assumes the form of a 'national enemy.'"[123] In an economy that inherently produces "social antagonism," fantasy—"mediated by a symbolic-ideological structure"—aims at coherence and connection, a sense of mutually facilitated and fulfilling enjoyment, and attributes any perceived instability in the collective to an "Other."[124]

For Griffith, as for Dixon, the South and the white supremacist account of Reconstruction provide a setting and a plot through which to stage precisely such a defense of thick and binding collectivity. Though criticism of *Birth of a Nation* has often articulated a " 'good' first half," juxtaposing domestic life and an epically filmed Civil War, and a " 'bad' second half," demonizing African Americans and glorifying the Ku Klux Klan,[125] it is actually the first half that launches a nationalist affiliative appeal. Insisting unremittingly on white enjoyment, it renders every domestic relationship a scene of play and desire. As the northern Stoneman brothers send their southern friend Ben a letter, proposing a visit, their sister Elsie spies on them, playing with her kitten and flouncing her skirts. Ben's own youngest sister is explicitly labeled a pet, and, when the Stonemans arrive, the two younger brothers immediately begin to wrestle, alternately punching and hugging. The film reminds us that this is not merely an idiosyncratic friendship but a model of national affiliation by labeling them "Chums . . . North and South"; the pathos of the Civil War is later staged when "true to their promise, the chums meet again," dying together on the battlefield. Critics have noted the inconsistency through which the Camerons and their guests wander so regularly through a plantation that appears to be theirs when the film repeatedly shows their house on the town's main street, but this spatial linkage supports *Birth of a Nation*'s thematic extension of intimately held property and affection to a larger white collective.[126] Accordingly, settings of economic production—slaves working in a cotton field—are presented as backdrops for white transregional desire: Phil Stoneman and Margaret Cameron travel "Over the plantation . . . By way of Love Valley." In a film widely noted for its lavish chase and battle scenes, much of the narrative centers on gazes of longing, as characters look not on loved ones but on emblems of those loved ones—photographs and letters.

Through its repeated inclusion of letters and avidly, anxiously read newspapers, *Birth of a Nation* presents passionate affiliations that encompass the span of the United States and are explicitly aligned with national concerns; accordingly, it presents, in Homi Bhabha's useful phrase, "nationness as a form of social and textual affiliation"—one limited, however, by race.[127] For while the white characters of the film's first half enjoy their slaves, slaves' enjoyment—except through falsification of the circumstances of slave labor—is not considered.[128] An early shot, for example, depicts slave children falling off a wagon as it drives through town, amusing surrounding whites but angering older slaves, who whip the children; later, Ben Cameron's inspiration for Klan costumes emerges from the play of white children who are frightening black children. As Michael

Rogin points out, Griffith's strict reliance on white actors in blackface for principal black roles guarantees also that only whites will enjoy the production of his fantasy.[129]

Notoriously, the film stages crises as black or mulatto men announce plans to marry white women, leading Elsie to faint and Ben's "pet sister" to leap to her death. Where Dixon's villain, Gus, rapes his victim, Miriam, Griffith's Gus is, in the film's current form, presented more ambivalently: though the score and shot arrangements suggest that Flora is greatly menaced, and though the original film is said to have included a rape, Gus's dialogue in intertitles proclaims that he wants only to talk, and the actor's gestures and expressions are largely hesitant.[130] But the current film holds that for Flora—who spends much of this extended sequence playing in the landscape, interacting with a squirrel—even Gus's desire for interaction threatens her enjoyment so greatly that she finds "sweeter the *opal gates of death*." Thus the scenes of sexual hysteria that follow—Ben's tentative yet desperate dabbing at the blood that trickles from Flora's mouth, the killing and originally filmed castration of Gus, the soaking of the Confederate flag in Flora's blood—result not in response to any sexual act but to the suggestion of sexual interest. This interest, like the film's Reconstruction scenes of black publicity, is presented as an inherent violation, regardless of whether it leads to specific acts or relationships, as it symbolizes the potential penetration of African Americans into the previously closed circle of white political and communal affiliation.

This is not to displace the significance of the film's sexual hysteria, so effectively studied in critical analyses, but rather to underscore the ways in which it is mobilized to represent and assure affiliative passions. Psychological readings of white supremacy sometimes present individualized sexual traumas or anxieties as the secret, or hidden kernel, of racist fantasy.[131] Psychoanalytic theory, however, argues that perceived alienation from the desired other—a loss for which the fantasy of racial cohesion either compensates or attributes blame—is at least as formative as castration anxiety and sexual identification, and provides much of the affective energy engaged in these later developmental dynamics. The sexual hysteria of white supremacist discourse presents itself, in Lacanian terms, as an "embarrassing plethora" relentlessly located in plain sight; accordingly, it is less likely to encode the "censored chapter" of the racist's history than "the lie" blocking access to that history.[132]

The excess or "loon[iness]" of this hysteria is motivated not solely by intrapsychic pressures but also by intersubjective need; it draws audience attention to a deception that, at some level, deludes the racist as well.[133] White supremacist fixations on the threat of miscegenation were patently absurd; there was no African American movement to pursue interracial sex. But as this quite obvious lie succeeded, for sympathetic listeners, in promoting ideas of black licentiousness and justifying the practice of lynching, it also distracted attention from a fact that white supremacists may have been equally invested in obscuring: despite their collective political and vigilante actions, there was no encompassing intimate white unity to be violated. Indeed, the drive of these narratives, in their depictions of both white domesticity and racial war, is to create a persuasive image of such unity.

Birth of a Nation mobilizes the threat of interracial sex precisely as it serves to displace the history of white disagreement, both within and without the narrative frame. As the Reconstructionist Stoneman is converted to the Klan's cause by Silas Lynch's pursuit of his daughter, the sequence between Gus and Flora follows an intertitle that claims the Klan "saved the South from the anarchy of black rule" but sardonically adds, "not without the shedding of more blood than at Gettysburg, according to Judge Tourgée of the carpetbaggers." It is interesting that this film should cite, even dismissively, a white man who supported African American enfranchisement, not only through writing against southern white supremacy but also as an attorney for Homer Plessy.[134] This oblique acknowledgment that not all whites sought to create a racially particularist nation yields immediately to a plot featuring black and mulatto attempts to "steal [white] enjoyment," a fantasy that accords with Žižek's account of nationalism: this narrative misrepresents African American history and further conceals "the traumatic fact" that white Americans "*never pos-*

sessed what was allegedly stolen from" them.¹³⁵ As Michelle Wallace argues, *Birth of a Nation* insists from its early scenes on the "poetic, gleaming beauty of the young, delicately boned white Camerons and Stonemans and how cruel it will be for them to be divided by the war."¹³⁶ It emphasizes also that their union is predestined, as, merely glancing at Elsie Stoneman's photograph, Ben Cameron "finds the ideal of his dreams." The film compensates for their setbacks by apocalyptic antiblack violence and the final union of Ben and Elsie as they embrace by the sea, juxtaposed with a "City of Peace" overseen by an Aryan Christ. But despite the intensity of the film's fantasy and the history of avidly defended white political and economic privilege, neither national nor regional whites were, or could ever be, bound by such passionate, automatic, and divinely guaranteed affiliations.

In sum, as *Birth of a Nation* claimed to present a transregional racial union in support of a regional white collective, it promoted, at a more basic level, the centrality of passionate racial affiliation to political collectivity. This film, so prominent in U.S. cultural and aesthetic history, converged with increased segregation and racial conflict, and preceded the predominant nativism of the 1920s.¹³⁷ Nonetheless, its racially particularist nationalism did not dominate all discussions concerning the principles of U.S. citizenship and affiliation, and African Americans' opposition to *Birth of a Nation* proved significant in mobilizing an activist community to combat white supremacy.¹³⁸ Political use of civic and racial nationalisms during this period was largely opportunistic; though the patriotic rhetoric disseminated to fuel U.S. support for participation in World War I emphasized liberal values, the U.S. occupation of Haiti two years earlier was legitimated through paternalistic rhetoric that argued that "the African race [is] devoid of any capacity for political organization and lack[s] genius for government."¹³⁹

During the 1930s, as I argue in chapter 2, competition between these dichotomous nationalist visions gathered energy. Confronted with an economic crisis that threatened one of the primary aspects of national identity, thinkers and artists sought ways of imagining passionate national affiliation that would better coincide with democratic liberalism. In many of these visions, the region maintained an important role. But these attempts to renegotiate the role of regional cultures in a liberal nation continued to compete with the plantation narrative of southern exceptionalism. Though Margaret Mitchell's South is less insistently white than Dixon's or Griffith's, as her ex-slaves claim to share in "Confedrut" identity, its popular fantasy of a closely bound group maintaining strict racial hierarchies staged profound ambivalence toward a more inclusive nationalism and prompted the African American essayist Melvin Tolson to argue that, in shaping national values, "The South Won the Civil War!"[140]

CHAPTER TWO

Economy Crisis

IN 1932, W. BÉRAN WOLFE, translator of Alfred Adler's *Understanding Human Nature* (1927) and author of *How to Be Happy though Human* (1931), described the U.S. economic depression as the source of a sweeping identity crisis, explaining that its effect "on the average American man and woman has been almost identical with the collapse of a romantic notion in the life plan of a blustering, overly aggressive adolescent."[1] Published in *Forum and Century*, his essay "Psycho-analyzing the Depression" argues that this phenomenon "exploded . . . the great American myth"—"the never-before-questioned rightness of unrestrained competitive individualism" (209). Observing ten neurotic responses to this "complete invalidation of formerly unquestioned shibboleths," he also notes evidence of a "normalizing tendency," which consists of a desire for more cogent and inclusive principles of social and political affiliation. Accordingly, he notes a "widening of social horizons and intensification of interest in the problems of other workers and other sections and types of Americans" (210, 213).

Emblematic of much Depression-era discourse in its contempt for the role of "Big Business" in U.S. nationalism, Wolfe's recommended responses are similarly typical. Citing the need for both structural and ideological change, he suggests approaches that were already underway in the regionalist movement. These include the "science" of "community planning," which examined how the geographic and social category of the region might provide a basis for more vigorous political and economic structures, and also the cultural effort to promote "social coöperation" and avert "the epidemic spread of neuroses"—in part, through encouraging awareness of the commonalities and differences across the whole of the national public (209, 214). In presenting these developments as remedies for broadly shared psychological crises, however, Wolfe suggests the degree to which Depression-era regionalism responded to a crisis in how the nation-state was imagined.

Local cultures had long been considered to impart much of U.S. expressive and communal life, but by the 1930s, both intellectual and popular culture configured the larger nation as the source of a potentially damaging set of values, one that required amelioration, perhaps through greater emphasis on U.S. regions. In this decade, liberal regionalism provided one vehicle for imagining a form of integrative pluralism, in which appreciation of cultural diversity could provide shared ballast against the domination of capitalist values in national life.[2] But, as I have shown, the values invoked in the history of U.S. regionalism are not inherently amenable to liberal nationalism. Accordingly, in seeking to model a passionate commitment to democratic governance on purportedly regional forms of attachment, even such liberal narratives as Frank Capra's *Mr. Smith Goes to Washington* (1939) tended to embrace essentialist and restrictive models of affiliation. But where the idealistic Mr. Smith, from his unnamed western state, seems to bumble naively in accordance with gendered understandings of political virtue and agency, southern plantation fictions still served in this decade to model overtly disfranchising delineations of social roles. Thus *Gone with the Wind,* in both novelistic (1936) and filmic (1939) versions, depicted a cohesive nineteenth-century South that, in its hierarchical but mutually binding interracial culture, provided precisely the sustaining anticapitalist values often called for in contemporary discourse.

On the whole, however, discussions of the South differed significantly from other manifestations of Depression-era regionalism. Only through historical romance, which evaded the circumstances of the Depression-era South, could this region be posited as an unproblematic resource for nationalists who sought greater balance between tradition and modernization. In contrast, assessments of the region's contemporary poverty and injustice vividly raised the possibility that not all forms of cultural collectivity could be assimilated into a modernizing and liberal nation-state. In 1930s discourse, ideas of southern exceptionalism were stretched to their limit as southern backwardness, which had long been accepted as a fundamental regional trait, was increasingly described as a threat to national politics, economics, and culture.

New Nationalisms

Discussing "Americanism and Localism" in the *Dial* in 1920, John Dewey disputed an idea that would later become a prominent theme in theorizing national affiliation: he contested the nationalist function of the newspaper. In Benedict Anderson's more contemporary and influential model, the newspaper reader "is well aware that the ceremony he performs is being replicated simultaneously by thousands (or millions) of others" of unknown other citizens, a perception that creates confidence in the anonymous community of the nation.[3] Dewey supports Anderson's later assessment of newspapers as "one-day best-sellers" by proclaiming them "the only genuinely popular form of literature [the U.S. has] achieved" and suggesting that newspapers are attuned to "the feeling of the mass of the readers."[4] Dewey does not, however, assume that the "imagined communities" of newspaper readers share the boundaries of the nation. Instead, he argues that a local newspaper models two thresholds and styles of representation. The one used to print " 'national' news," though it makes "much on provocation of its 'national' circulation," nonetheless bears "a thin and apologetic air" (686). In their treatment of "localisms," in contrast, these papers "fairly shriek" (684).

But while this emphasis on local life may diminish the degree to which the United States "is taken . . . as an entity," it nonetheless, in Dewey's assessment, enriches national culture with both depth and diversity (684, 687). In this argument, Dewey's essay exemplifies pluralist liberal nationalism, suggesting that a political system based on abstract principles of affiliation—mandating no cultural, racial, or religious homogeneity—should facilitate diverse, deeply felt affiliations among the citizenry: "The wider the formal, the legal unity, the more intense becomes the local life" (686). In a moment of hyperbole, Dewey applies this belief so broadly as to contravene his own staunch anti-imperialism, suggesting that "a United States of the World" would cultivate "local independence and variety" (686). This quip (he mentions the possibility of "federat[ing] with other planets") reflects a hope seen also in contemporary pragmatist nationalism, which is that such an approach to political affiliation might prove more broadly useful.[5] More directly, Dewey challenges the argument that "internationalism" would produce sweeping homogeneity, explaining that efforts to create national conformity oppose the values of both editors and readers.[6]

But despite Dewey's tendentious confidence, both concerns about national homogenization and attempts to increase it were proceeding apace in 1920. As the historian Desmond King demonstrates, the "one hundred percent" Americanizers' cause had already enlisted the systematic and cooperative participation of numerous independent, state, and federal agencies during World War I.[7] As Dewey argued, the national ideals promoted by this movement were very vague, and its goals appear to have been chiefly exclusive—to restrict ethnic loyalties and racial heterogeneity.[8] But critics of national culture suggested that vagueness in describing

U.S. beliefs and values was unavoidable; Waldo Frank, for example, complained that the national collective lacked "personality" because it was focused chiefly on change—"the material March."[9]

Such concerns were exacerbated during the 1920s, as, in the historian Warren Susman's words, the nation "self-conscious[ly]" questioned the effect of broad transformations—"natural, technological, social, personal, and moral"—on collective bonds and individual characters.[10] Frank's suspicions seemed to have been confirmed with the 1929 publication of *Middletown,* which held that residents of this midwestern locale (Muncie, Indiana) were "learning new ways of behaving towards material things more rapidly than new habits addressed to persons and non-material institutions"; commodity oriented and alienated from older value systems, Middletowners' lives were said to be utterly pervaded by "the money medium of exchange and the cluster of activities associated with its acquisition."[11] As one reviewer noted, the resemblance between the Lynds' Middletown and the fictional setting of Sinclair Lewis's *Babbitt* (1922) could lead one to believe that preexisting alarms shaped the sociologists' method and conclusions.[12] Instead, for many readers, the later work seemed to confirm the insights of the novel, in which the protagonist, "whose god was Modern Appliances," is, after a series of doubts and divisions, restored to membership among the town Boosters, who celebrate the view that "American Democracy did not imply any equality of wealth, but did demand a wholesome sameness of thought, dress, painting, morals, and vocabulary."[13] By the end of the decade, Lewis's novel had become a touchstone for critiques of the nation's insubstantial and materialist culture, as both journalistic and more narrowly intellectual discourse routinely invoked the specter of "Babbittry."

Nor were these concerns restricted to discussions of white midwesterners. Though it has been justly argued that, during this period, liberal intellectuals' focus on the pernicious cultural effects of capitalism superseded their attention to racial oppression,[14] urban black communities also struggled over the question of conformism. Where Americanizers and boosters targeted white ethnic groups and middle-class residents, established middle-class African Americans in northern cities sought to revise the cultural norms of recent migrants from the South, a stance against which Langston Hughes famously complained.[15] By the 1930s, writers from multiple locales tended to link efforts to promote U.S. homogeneity both with the effacing of cultural diversity and the flattening of individuals' personalities, holding that such ideologies produced "100 percenters"—xenophobic "go-getter[s] . . . whose ideas of progress are limited to increase of wealth and population."[16]

Anxieties about national culture also became increasingly prominent among policy makers, who feared public ambivalence concerning the nation's structure, values, and principles of affiliation. Charles Merriam, vice chairman of Herbert Hoover's Committee on Social Trends, reported in 1933, "We may safely forecast that in the next period it will no longer be found possible to escape full and free discussion of the fundamentals of democracy and capitalism alike."[17] Such concerns would expand throughout the decade amid struggle over controversial New Deal policies, which were understood to alter the nation-state fundamentally. But these fears emerged from global politics as well as domestic developments: having long expressed anxiety that communism might develop appeal in the United States, political thinkers in the 1930s also feared that the public might embrace fascism. European fascisms were, after all, understood as "movement[s] of the middle class in those countries where the events of the post-war years have left it poor in pocket as well as in spirit," a crisis often diagnosed in U.S. political culture as well.[18] This is not to dismiss the degree to which the threat of U.S. fascism was located in political figures and business interests; further, increased federal experimentation with social planning drew numerous analogies to the practices of the Soviet Union.[19] But discourse from across the political spectrum also targeted the public's shifting political allegiances as a potential threat and thus sought to cultivate affective ties between the populace and its system of governance—both the nation-state as a political unit and the principles of capitalism and democracy.

While such writers differed substantially in how they interpreted the national crisis and in their recommendations, they shared a tendency to posit nationalism itself as an object of desire.[20] Thus, for example, James Truslow Adams, author of *The Founding of New England* (1921) and *America's Tragedy* (1934), a southern-leaning Civil War history, warned in *Scribner's* about the political dangers of "the mass mind" and urged continued attention to "our national habit of thought," which he described as intensely individualistic.[21] Echoing regionalist complaints, a series of *Good Housekeeping* articles claimed that "the old dream of America" had "crumbled" because of the advent of industrialization and argued that the nation must "develop a society, a culture, a way of life, that can do more for common man than the Soviets can ever do."[22] Henry Wallace, Roosevelt's secretary of agriculture at the time, argued that the failure of U.S. national ideology—which Wallace described as an amalgam of individualism, Calvinism, and capitalism—was largely self-induced, as it had led to development of "an extraordinary opportunity of exploitation first by corporations and second by other organized class groups."[23] Where Wallace argued for "evolving a concept of the general welfare grounded in both political and economic democracy," the leftist V. F. Calverton called for rejuvenation of the "American revolutionary tradition" to provide "symbols of challenge and advance" and to unite radicals with the masses.[24] Notably, while all these thinkers argued that U.S. nationalism was inchoate or even dangerous, it nonetheless provided the language through which they expressed the sorts of collective affiliation and agency they wished to promote.

This tendency was not, of course, universal. Ralph Bunche, for example, represented Depression-era nationalism as symptomatic of the "significant upsurge of the middle classes of the Western world, whose claim to national leadership is predicated on their assumed ability to reconcile these conflicting class interests . . . in a higher national purpose."[25] Noting that the agenda of such classes was typically to maintain conditions amenable to capitalism, he argued that this trend in U.S. politics held little promise for social justice, particularly for African Americans.[26] But as Michael Denning demonstrates, many leftists and working-class movements during this period embraced nationalism as an important organizing locus.[27] Finally, the nation-state avidly and expertly supported Depression-era nationalism, as New Deal architects sought to legitimate their policies by illustrating the needs of the nation they sought to govern.[28]

This state-sponsored nationalism cultivated a largely liberal and non-ascriptive image: while Roosevelt's compassionate and populist political style insisted upon the responsiveness of the state to individual needs and famously emphasized the need to cultivate collective feelings, his speeches emphasized economic and political opportunity and fairness.[29] The federal government's arts projects sought both to demonstrate and to model the workings of a flexible national community, including a focus on diversity in the work of the Federal Writers' Project.[30] Efforts in this vein often sought to generate common tropes or themes, such as labor and domestic life. Roy Stryker, for example, directed Farm Security Administration photographers to represent "not the America of the unique, odd or unusual happening, but the America of how to mine a piece of coal, grow a wheat field or make an apple pie."[31] Nonetheless, these images encompassed many races and diverse landscapes: populist, in that they sought to characterize "the people," they were also effectively pluralist, in that they allowed for and even valued diversity within that group.[32] In some cases, particularly that of the Federal Theatre Project, artists succeeded in using New Deal institutions to convey radical perspectives.[33]

Regionalism constituted a vital part of this pluralist liberal nationalism, as liberal regionalists saw their project as a means of celebrating and cultivating the nation's cultural heft without attempting to impose cultural uniformity. While Depression-era regionalists echoed Dewey's invocation of the local as the site of the nation's most meaningful cultural life, they diverged from his correlation of the nation with "seats of government."[34] Combating the ideas that national culture was thin and abstract and that local culture was not directly relevant to national life, these regionalists insisted that the region "must be a *constituent unit in an aggregate whole or totality.*"[35] Thus this movement diverged from the pluralist nativism of the 1920s elucidated by Walter Benn Michaels: where the earlier approach to cultural politics "involve[d] the repudiation of any attempt to blur differences, which is to say, the repudiation of any effort of Americanization," liberal regionalism sought to create more meaningful exchange between local and national identities, rendering each less monolithic.[36] Constance Rourke exemplified its tendency to present national fragmentation as a resource for the continuing nationalist project: her *American Humor* dismissed criticism of "the American character" by arguing that study of diverse local, racial, and ethnic cultures revealed "a tradition which is various, subtle, sinewy, scant at times but not poor."[37]

This variant of cultural regionalism, like sociological and planning movements, strongly influenced New Deal nationalism; the National Resources Committee, for example, argued that "regional consciousness arising from more settled and self-conscious local communities [would] ... have a ... civic educative effect," "enhanc[ing], in the long run, the quality of [individuals'] citizenship and of [their] Government."[38] This belief—that local cultural attachments, if cultivated and contextualized, could lead to a more productive sense of national affiliation—enabled New Deal regionalists to combine "romantic nationalis[m], cultural pluralis[m], and cosmopolitan[ism]," as Jerrold Hirsch argues of the Federal Writers Project.[39] These writers represented the nation as a venue in which the particularities of local cultures served not to impede national affiliation but rather to enrich national dialogue.

Depression-era regionalism was, of course, diverse, with political tendencies ranging from reactionary to nostalgic to proletarian. As demonstrated in Robert Dorman's thorough history of the movement, many regionalists "develop[ed] their own ethic of pluralism ... on behalf of the survivals of older-stock and indigenous folk-rural cultures"; while allowing for cultural diversity, this pluralism implies substantial cultural segregation by asserting temporal difference.[40] Carey McWilliams, whose later regional studies would address contemporary class and racial conflicts, complained in 1930 that "the new regionalists reveal a typical modern tendency in their attempt to escape from the tumultuous present into the glamorous past"—a past said to be maintained, by some cultural groups, even in the present.[41] But McWilliams's later work demonstrates a countervailing tendency in regionalist studies—seen also, for example, in some analyses of southern agriculture—to examine and critique local forms of oppression in the hope of encouraging more just forms of modernization. Studying regional responses to economic and cultural change, as well as regional use of natural resources, such scholars hoped that their focus could create a greater "balance and equilibrium" for the nation—providing rural areas with productive access to modernization and cosmopolitan approaches to social life, and urban areas with access to ecological and cultural values that might counter the overwhelming influence of capitalism.[42]

Shifts in how local and national times were understood appear to have facilitated this perspective. As I have shown, in the late nineteenth century, local color fiction and even Populist regionalism tended to associate regions with roots and stasis; these were posed against a national economy and culture that were identified with changing metropolitan centers. Such associations were not absolute, but they did reflect a prominent way in which modernizing societies understood temporality during this era—the belief that distinct cultures have their own relationships to time and space, perceptual and structural differences that could not easily be negotiated in the formation of a larger collective.[43] But while this understanding of time has persisted into the present day, it has coexisted with the expansion of technologies that decrease the effect of spatial distance and increase the dissemination of commodities and expressions. By the 1930s, the spread of radio and film was already creating perceptions of a more unified national culture. Describing the effects of modernization in one Iowa town, for example, a 1935 *Scribner's* essay explained, "Just as hill billy music and Will Rogers invaded New York City, so also do Walter Winchell and Mae West carry the wit and wickedness of Broadway out to Oskaloosa."[44] Accordingly, liberals in the regionalist movement attempted to manage changes that were already proceeding, seeking to integrate—without simply effacing—the economic and cultural differences of locales that were already coalescing through mass media and consumer culture.

For while uneven economic development began, in some cases, to appear to be a more flexible process, the ideology of modernization was now widely believed to require mitigation. Following a period of particularly convulsive economic fluctuation, social scientists and government officials sought to weigh the benefits of economic expansion against those of economic stability and other types of social goods. They were often explicit concerning their hope that a focus on regional space could influence national time. The regionalists Howard Odum and Harry Estill Moore, for example, situated their comprehensive account of the movement against a background of an intensely accelerating U.S. temporality—"faster, faster, further, further, more, more, new, new, now, now."[45] American exceptionalists, in that they considered the United States "the testing grounds" for democracy and for "western civilization," were also regionalists who felt that national and global crises had arisen from the pace of change: "The demands and sweep of artificial society and of supertechnological processes exceed[ed] the natural capacity of the people or of a living culture to absorb and adjust."[46] Odum and Moore hoped to check this overwhelming rapidity by conceptualizing communities as embedded in particular geographies and histories, urging residents to attend to their pasts and present as well as their futures. Similarly, complaining of cycles of "pioneering, exploitation, and obsolescence," the urban planner Carol Aronovici argued that observers should "[find] a contemplative moment to look at the city as a medium for social relationships"; he hoped that a regionalist approach, which would situate metropolitan areas in relation to broader cultural and environmental networks, would encourage planners and residents to balance their pursuit of change with a regard for maintaining beneficial social and geographic resources.[47] Such regionalists sought to integrate not only the spaces but also the temporalities of the nation in order to create not broad conformity but finely tuned ecological and cultural balances.

In sum, the idea that locales could maintain specificity and simultaneously participate in a diverse and modernizing nation was vital to what regionalists called "the new pluralism of the American nation"—a national culture exemplifying greater equilibrium between modernization and multiple cultural traditions.[48] Interest in the possibility that local cultures could provide a needed counterbalance for the national collective appeared across a broad range of Depression-era cultural phenomena: the development of the National Folk Festival; the proliferation of local historical societies, folklore scholarship, and documentary; the popularization of folk music and handicrafts; the development of regionalist movements in painting and literature; and the focus on small-town and rural protagonists in comic strips, periodicals, novels, and films.[49] In a decade when many expressed their longing to promote a simultaneously grounded and flexible national community, regionalism seemed to provide a model for encouraging both connectedness and diversity. B. A. Botkin, for example, hoped that regionalism could promote "cultural values derived from tradition as 'the liberator, not the container.' "[50]

But Botkin's "Regionalism: Cult or Culture?" also exemplifies a conflict that plagued leftists and liberals in this movement—the tendency of onlookers to interpret all regionalisms through the principles of more conservative groups, particularly the southern Agrarians, who avidly presented regional culture not as a supplement but as an alternative to that of the United States. In their manifesto, in articles in the *American Review* and other journals, as well as in contributions to *Who Owns America?* (1936), these southern regionalists wrote explicitly against the "American industrial ideal," offering alliance only to "other minority communities . . . wanting a much simpler economy to live by."[51] As interested in temporal differences as other regionalists, the Agrarians were, in contrast, opposed to compromise. In a debate with V. F. Calverton published in *Scribner's,* the Agrarian John Crowe Ransom presented the South as a "stubborn and substantial . . . bulwark" against economic and cultural progress, whether it be capitalist or communist in aim.[52] In their determination "to defend the traditional Southern life," such writers claimed a position antithetical to that of liberal regionalists; insistently backward looking and avowedly provincial, they exemplified an approach that many observers were more inclined to associate with regionalism.[53] Botkin argued that leftists erred in assuming that all regionalists were uninterested in modernization; he claimed the movement could be, if "properly controlled," part of a trend "toward a social and cultural art," an "adjunct to literature, along with ethnology, folk lore, and Marxist economics."[54] But conservative southern regionalism suggested the kind of secure and grounding relationship with place and culture for which local cultures had long been celebrated in U.S. nationalism and with which they were still associated in some of their most popular 1930s representations. Where analytic prose could delineate between emancipatory and oppressive traditions, narratives promoting regional models of affiliation were, as I argue in the next section, less readily able to address the question of whether all locally embedded social relationships could be consistent with the principles of pluralist liberalism.

Regional Affiliations

Nowhere was the desire for a regional culture to infuse sustaining values into national life more evident than in Frank Capra's *Mr. Smith Goes to Washington* (1939), in which a naive young senator from the West fights the corruption of politicians, businesses, and media. Though Jefferson Smith's lack of political experience renders him vulnerable to deception, his work with the western Boy Rangers has protected him from the cynicism that affects others in the capital; like many films from earlier in the decade, *Mr. Smith* pits a deeply nationalist hero against a treacherous government in order to rescue an easily swayed public.[55] Also, as in other films, this hero is identified with a nonmetropolitan locale and culture—through his protection of the environment, as he is first recognized for extinguishing a forest fire; his talent for bird calls and "Indian signs," practices that Washington reporters immediately solicit and misrepresent; and his initial estrangement from the pace of urban life.[56] Smith is flummoxed by the city's train station, asking, "Things sure happen fast around here, don't they?" As Lawrence Levine argues, Capra's narratives bring "nineteenth-century small-town values and expectations to bear on a crisis involving twentieth-century modern bureaucracies"; chief among these old-fashioned traits is Smith's experience and understanding of affiliation.[57] Though the politics of this film oppose those seen in *Birth of a Nation*—as Smith insistently touts the values of civic nationalism, the protection of "human liberties . . . no matter what [a man's] race, color, or creed"—it similarly offers a locally embedded form of attachment as a model for national collectivity. Written by a Communist, and embraced as a resource for renewing nationalist and democratic feeling, *Mr. Smith* conceptualizes nationalist affiliation through regionalist logics, providing insight into a popular left and liberal "erotics of region."[58]

Like much regionalist rhetoric of the period, the film manifests a desire for balance between possible antipodes—tradition and modernization, authentic and mediated experience, innocence and shrewdness. Upon arriving in Washington, Smith has only one political talent—the ability to model and potentially stimulate passionate attachment to the nation. Though Jim Taylor's political machine tries to direct him from the moment of his arrival, Smith ignores Taylor's henchmen while, in his words, "just naturally" following his contemplative gaze from one national memorial to another. This extended montage conveys the values that Smith is supposed to embody, comprising patriotic images, words, and music that seem designed less to advance the plot than to elicit patriotic affect.[59] As the Capra scholar Leland Poague argues, this avowedly nationalist sequence can be read as ambivalent, since the "star-spangled spectacle" that accompanies images of Civil War monuments attests to the repression of national division.[60] To recognize this ambivalence, of course, one must resist propaganda, which the film, by its end, suggests that an audience should do. Given that the montage nonetheless validates the ability of these symbols to evoke virtuous inspiration, however, it also reflects the film's deeper concerns regarding both knowledge and innocence, each of which can be politically dangerous. To be "wised up," like Smith's assistant Saunders, is to succumb to corruption and alienation, and to be idealistic—"an infant with little flags in his fists," as Saunders describes

Smith—is to be vulnerable and ineffective—in Smith's later assessment, a "sucker."

The film formulates its nationalist ideal when the naive Smith inadvertently seduces the knowledgeable Saunders to his ideals by describing his region. Smith's plan to create a National Boys' Camp in his western state provides this opportunity; he seeks to "get the poor kids off the streets, out of the cities for a few months in the summer, and let them learn something about nature, American ideals." The possibility that rural experience might create a nationalist collective from a group of diverse boys—one Smith later argues will be composed "of all creeds, kinds, and positions"—is affirmed by Saunders, a "pure city dweller." While Saunders listens to Smith describe his western landscape, the camera traces her progress from doubt to longing. As Poague argues, "Capra emphatic[ally] shift[s] from key-and-fill medium-shots to gauzy soft-focus close-up, as if to mark the woman's desire to merge into the liquid space evoked by [Smith's] fantasy of a singularly unified nature."[61] Smith reveals that his father instructed him in a sense of primal connectedness: "'Son, don't miss the wonders that surround you, because every tree, every rock, every anthill, every star is filled with the wonders of nature.' And he used to say to me, 'Have you ever noticed how grateful you are to see daylight at the end after coming through a long dark tunnel? Always try to see life around you as if you've just come out of a tunnel.'" In this oddly Oedipal nationalism, Smith, through his identification with his father, learns to feel as if he has only just exited the womb. Typically, such a sense of plenitude is considered pre-Oedipal, characterizing infants' experience before their relationship with their primary caretaker has been disturbed.[62] But despite Smith's many infantile qualities, the film insists that this attribute—a sense of unmediated sensory experience and of intimacy with nature—can be cultivated through identification with a beneficent paternal figure, much as Smith continually refreshes his nationalist idealism: "Liberty's too precious a thing to be buried in books, Miss Saunders. Men should hold it up in front of them every single day of their lives and say, 'I'm free, to think and to speak.'"

Saunders is fascinated by this mode of experience, confessing, "I guess I've always lived in a tunnel"; where Smith's attachment to the nation has led to feelings of both an independent identity and union with a collective, Saunders uses his metaphor to suggest that she has experienced neither—has not been fully born. Here, too, the film echoes regionalist thinking, as the urban planner Aronovici, for example, argued that neither the "dweller of the city slum" nor "the suburbanite running for his train" can develop "civic identity"; he hoped that creating stronger ties between diverse types of regional space—rural, urban, and suburban—would enable nonrural residents to forge such a sense of agency and connection.[63] Because Saunders becomes attached to Smith's mode of attachment, she is able to help him when he feels he must abandon his ideals—upon learning that Senator Paine, who had joined Smith's father in his fatal struggle against corruption, works for Taylor's machine. Without Saunders's inspiration and aid, Smith's idealistic nationalism would be futile, as it very nearly is anyway: he passes out on the floor of the Senate after a lengthy patriotic filibuster, upon learning that the citizens of his state, on whom he had counted for support, have condemned him at the prodding of corrupt newspapers. Smith is redeemed only when Paine, moved by Smith's struggle, attempts suicide and confesses.

The film's notoriously abrupt ending suggests a problem in its regionally grounded model of heroic nationalism, for the only person sufficiently naive to fight corruption lacks the power and knowledge to succeed. Smith refuses publicly to acknowledge this as a liability, continuing, as Lauren Berlant argues, to suggest that "infantile citizens" constitute the hope of the nation: "And if [compromise is] what the grown-ups have done with this world that was given to them, then we've gotta get those boys' camps started and see what the kids can do."[64] In a sense, Smith and the film itself already serve the function of this proposed western camp, as they seek to inculcate passionate idealism in the face of broad corruption. Capra's desire to inspire virtue in his audience—"plain decent everyday common rightness," as Saunders says of Smith—was already famous, and Washington politicians and reporters were initially affronted by the film's portrayal of their professions.[65] But despite its critical stance and pedagogical project, the film seems reluctant, in Berlant's words, to advocate "a critical consciousness," preferring the "patriotism [that] the official national culture machine seeks to inculcate"—as in the film's relentless obeisance to national symbols and monuments, its patriotic tunes, and its near consecration of the Declaration of Independence and the Constitution.[66]

Accordingly, the film begs the question of who will take care of these passionately affiliated but unknowledgeable boys, and its answer is consistently, if implicitly, women. For women can also be attracted to Smith's affiliative vision—not through such institutions as the camp but through their affection for boys. This is demonstrated not only in the skillful Saunders's support of the boyish Smith and Smith's mother's direction of the Boy Rangers' attempted media blitz but also in the governor's wife, who, aware at the beginning of the film that "Happy" is under Taylor's sway, encourages him to "listen to [his] children"—Boy Rangers themselves—rather than simply appoint a stooge. Though the women's efforts are devoted to nurturing political actors, this film nearly reverses the nineteenth-century "cult of domesticity," suggesting that boys guide (or fail to guide) virtue—Susan Paine copies her father's corruption—while women provide practical direction. Still, some such division of labor seems crucial to this film's idealized nationalism; relying for its reproduction on people untainted by modern politics, it must also mobilize knowledgeable people who are bound by affection to help these innocents negotiate a potentially corrupting system.

The problem with this model of nationalism is not that it seeks to promote exclusion and restrictiveness, as it overtly seeks the opposite; despite its reliance on racial stereotypes, it suggests that a celebration of infantile attachment to diverse landscapes and values can lead to a unifying appreciation of democracy and liberty. But its *model* of affiliation—grounded in intimate affection and unmediated experience—renders the question of political values effectively moot: Saunders loves Smith because of his passion, not his politics; Smith loves democracy because it moves him, like the sight of the "capital dome... all lighted up" or of the prairies. Accepting the traditional dictum that U.S. regions produce more binding communal ties than the nation, *Mr. Smith* contemplates how one might learn to extend those ties to a political ideology through the experience of regionally grounded patriotic institutions (the camp), erotic encounters (Saunders and Smith), or arousing media (the film). But it ignores the vital problem of whether its political values can be reliably supported by the kind of passionate affiliation that it promotes, a particularly vexing question given that these collective bonds rely on the willingness of agents to cede intellectual and moral authority to people for whom they care. This antiliberal understanding of affiliation was celebrated far more explicitly by another film released in 1939—David O. Selznick's *Gone with the Wind*.

The extraordinary popularity of this plantation romance, in both novelistic and filmic forms, was not the only indication that such narratives, previously an influential model of cultural affiliation, retained a hold on popular attention. Even the Agrarian Ransom, complaining about the limited influence of southern conservatism in national culture, acknowledged the "glamour" ascribed to a "popular tradition" of southern history.[67] The Agrarian Stark Young's *So Red the Rose* (1934), described by the author as a "monument... of a certain quality of [antebellum] society... in the planting class," was a best-selling novel, even if the subsequent film was admired chiefly in southern states.[68] Two Shirley Temple vehicles featuring Bill "Bojangles" Robinson—*The Little Colonel* (1935) and *The Littlest Rebel* (1935)—were set in the Civil War–era South; as Ann DuCille argues, these films worked to present Robinson as "more mammy than man" and to construct Temple's "snow-whiteness .. against... racial difference made ridiculous by the stammering and shuffling of the 'little black rascals,' 'darkies,' and 'pickaninnies' who populated her films."[69]

But both intellectual and popular culture of this period also exemplified critical attitudes toward such accounts of southern cultural coherence.[70] The African American press did not consistently criticize romantic representations of the plantation South, sometimes admiring the role of such African American performers as Robinson and sometimes dismissing these narratives' national significance.[71] Hence Alain Locke, noticing the increasingly critical trend in southern fiction, wrote of *So Red the Rose,* "Who would begrudge the old plantation tradition this beautiful but quavering swan-song?"[72] Nonetheless, in 1935, W. E. B. Du Bois vigorously countered neo-Confederate historiography in his massive *Black Reconstruction*. Before that, Sterling Brown debunked a series of biographies that celebrated Confederate figures, arguing that "in their glorification of the Old South and in their regret for its passing" such texts suggested dangerous portents for "the future of liberalism in America"; published in 1928 and 1929, these included volumes by the Agrarians Allen Tate and Robert Penn Warren.[73] Liberal white southerners also disputed such Confederate myth making. Responding to one of Ransom's early Agrarian salvos, for example, an essayist in *Outlook and Independent* claimed that, though he had been indoctrinated by "professional Southerners" "since boyhood," he could not "realize just what this fabulous contribution to culture made by the ante-bellum South was."[74] Finally, William Wyler's *Jezebel* (1938), famously made to compensate Bette Davis for the studio battle that cost her the part of Scarlett O'Hara, is considerably more ambivalent in its representation of antebellum southern culture than its rival. Where even the regional critics in *Gone with the Wind*—Rhett and Scarlett—eventually long for "the genial grace of days that are gone," the residents of Wyler's antebellum Louisiana come to regret the code of dueling and the "fever mist" rising from undrained swamps—a situation explicitly contrasted to northern engineering.[75]

But the plantation romance still provided a prominent, popular, and fundamentally antiliberal mode of narrating the role of race in southern history. These accounts were updated for the 1930s, however. Where Dixon and Griffith represented division, Wyler, Selznick, and Margaret Mitchell suggest connection, consistently valuing intensely dehumanizing forms of affection. The greatest similarities between *Jezebel* and *Gone with the Wind*—aside from headstrong protagonists and emplotment of red dresses—may be their attempt to configure their otherwise marginalized heroines' relationships with slaves and ex-slaves as indications that these women can be rejoined to a community of white southerners. Julie Marsden, the "Jezebel" of that film, offends her community—and in so doing, her fiancé, Preston—in a fit of pique; after Preston then marries another woman, her manipulations lead to a duel for Preston's brother and another of her ex-beaux. When her friends and family express horror at her recklessness, she leads the plantation slaves in a sing-along, implicitly retorting that her slaves will continue to embrace her. The extended focus on group harmonizing suggests a stereotypical slave community to which Julie formally announces her attachment—"I'm being baptized." Her purported ability to evoke slave affection, along with her newfound willingness to use this skill in the interest of other white people, is vital to the film's conclusion. The perversity of this logic, which demonstrates the ability of a white woman to support communal bonds by focusing on her relationship with people who are legally bound to her, is matched by Margaret Mitchell's presentation of Scarlett as a white woman with, as Linda Williams argues, an impressive ability for labor previously performed by slaves.[76] Furthermore, in the novel, Scarlett, who largely rejects southern gender norms, reidentifies with the region when she observes "Yankees" insulting an ex-slave: "She had listened with calm contempt while these women had underrated the Confederate Army, blackguarded Jeff Davis and accused Southerners of murder and torture of their slaves. If it were to her advantage she would have endured insults about her own virtue and honesty. But the knowledge that they had hurt the faithful old darky with their stupid remarks fired her like a match in gunpowder . . . They deserved killing, these insolent, ignorant, arrogant conquerors" (465).

It is in this insistence on a mutually binding but rigidly hierarchical culture that *Gone with the Wind* delivers its most sustained attack on liberalism. Asserting her commitment to historical realism over paternalist racial romance, Margaret Mitchell claims to have "sweat blood to keep [her novel] from being like Uncle Remus," and despite her admiration for Thomas Dixon's work—which extended, apparently, to borrowing the plot point of the dress made from curtains—her novel hardly replicates his insistence on the necessity of a pure racial community.[77] It contains numerous and vicious stereotypes, depicting the ex-slaves of the Reconstruction era as "lazy and dangerous" and denigrating Mammy even as it celebrates her insight and flexibility: "A realist more uncompromising" than Scarlett, Mammy sees "deeply . . . clearly, with the directness of the savage and the child" (452, 412). But the novel also, as Tara McPherson argues, "exhibits a desire for [cross-racial] commonality or connection"—often through insisting that such feelings suffused nineteenth-century southern life.[78] Crucially, however, this desire is as hierarchical and restrictive as any stereotype. After the war, ex-slaves are said to be helpless and confused, desperate for "kind-hearted white people" to help them (452). As Uncle Peter, an ex-slave who continues to work as Aunt Pittypat's servant, complains of "Yankees . . . mixin' in [the] bizness [of] us Confedruts," Scarlett determines that her own feelings for Mammy exemplify white southern knowledge of "black hands, how dear and comforting they could be, how unerringly they knew how to soothe, to pat, to fondle"; Mammy, also valuing this role, insists that emancipation means that she can follow and nurture Scarlett even when unwanted (465, 464, 587).

Thus, though ambivalent regarding interracial violence (unlike other white southern characters, Scarlett criticizes the "hot-headed doings" of the Klan, a word excised from the film for its fascist implications), *Gone with the Wind* insists on the value of interracial affection based on African American *enjoyment* of radically restricted freedom.[79] And though the filmmakers sought to render the narrative more liberal than the novel, this later version oddly foregrounds its refusal to imagine autonomous lives for its black characters.[80] In a scene where Scarlett's beloved Ashley—her sister-in-law Melanie's husband—is temporarily home from the Civil War, Peter—who is not even provided a name in the film, let alone an actual family in which he provides a role other than selfless service—congratulates the "last chicken in Atlanta" on his opportunity for self-sacrifice. Explaining to the escaping rooster that his "wives" and "little chicks" have all been eaten, Peter urges: "You got nobody to worry your head about bereaving. Come on. Now you just stand still so you can be Christmas gift for the white folks. Hold on. Hold on! Don't go getting so uppity!" The character could as well be describing his own role in this narrative, which demands that slaves defy emancipation and remain in subjugation to their previous owners. In flaunting its defiance of the filmmakers' purported prohibition on the explicit dehumanization of black characters, the film replicates the pattern of the novel. For while early plantation romances routinely disavowed interracial sex—a pattern famously challenged by Alice Randall's *The Wind Done Gone* (2001)—*Gone with the Wind* openly flirts with this taboo, not only in Rhett's gift to Mammy of a scarlet petticoat but also in making Peter a black uncle to Pittypat's white aunt.

Insisting on vital and dehumanizing attachments while denying the possibility of sexual or political tension, these narratives are infantile in their depiction of interracial affiliation, presenting African Americans, in psychoanalytic terms, as magical part objects that automatically respond to infant desires; such early conceptualizations of other human figures, in the work of D. W. Winnicott, are further characterized by ruthlessness.[81] (Notably, *So Red the Rose* also includes a scene in which the white children of a plantation beg the mammy to recite the story of how her favorite charge had once tricked her and burned her with a hot potato; she refuses out of continued loyalty to the young man.[82]) The effect of these narratives, which depicted African American subjugation as the corollary to interracial emotional attachments, was to promote, as Melvin Tolson argued, the segregationist refrain that "Southern whites understand Negroes; that's the reason they treat them as they do."[83]

While this Civil War–era romance did not directly address contemporary southern race relations, such a temporal transposition was supported by the contemporary relevance of its other narrative themes. While Scarlett, as Linda Williams argues, is a "representative American heroine . . . [as] a product of cultural and racial mongrelization," she is also emblematic, in her unqualified commitment to economic advancement, of values viewed in this decade by left and right alike as a danger to national culture.[84] Though her materialism is often discussed in relation to the New South of the late nineteenth century, it also resembles that of a notorious midwestern character from the 1920s, the period when Mitchell began her tome. Like Babbitt before her, Scarlett places inordinate value on "advertised tokens of financial and social success" and consumes in a "wave of vulgarity"; entranced with commodities, each protagonist is far less interested in personal relationships, and neither is concerned with integrity in business.[85] The dangers of this value system for its contemporary audience are accentuated by Scarlett's being a mother; the historian Ruth Feldstein argues that, in the 1930s, "experts in various disciplines came to a consensus that mothers were not only responsible for the physical, educational, and religious well-being of future citizens, but also were responsible for their children's *psychological* well-being."[86] In a decade anxious about the familial effects of mothers working outside the home, Scarlett complains vehemently that motherhood interferes with her business duties; Rhett later insists—and the novel supports him—that his parenting skills are superior to Scarlett's, as her younger children fear her.[87] But she is blamed also for her husband's failures: directing his unrequited love for his wife toward his child, Rhett refuses to discipline Bonnie, and as a discredited mother, Scarlett lacks sufficient influence to intervene (684–85). The narrator and, in the film, Mammy note the dangers of this situation; Bonnie ultimately dies because her parents cannot restrain her recklessness.

Crucially, the conventional southern culture against which Scarlett rebels provides recompense for precisely the threats that she embodies—a balm for the alienation created by her profit-oriented principles and a network of women, particularly Mammy and Melanie, who are willing to provide Scarlett's children with nurturance and affection. As an individualist and a capitalist, Scarlett feels isolated from the region's traditional culture, even her adored mother; she disdains the mannerisms of upper-class white southern women and associates "gentility" with "wealth, not breeding" (55, 419). But while Scarlett feels "alien" around Ashley and others who long "for the slow beauty of our old world that is gone," the soil of her home is "very dear" to her; this feeling is central to the film's conclusion, which echoes the insistence of Henry Ford, in a series of early Depression-era public interest advertisements, that "The land! . . . is where our roots are."[88] By the end of the novel, Scarlett realizes that she has depended on Melanie, who embodies "all the qualities [that Atlanta's] embattled remnant prized, poverty and pride in poverty, uncomplaining courage, gaiety, hospitality, kindness and, above all, loyalty to all the old traditions"; Scarlett turns in the final page toward Mammy, who has already renounced emancipation (508, 587). Through their absolute disinterest in individual rights and freedoms, Mammy and Melanie provide continuity amid change and attachment amid loss; however vividly it portrays its transgressive heroine, the narrative, as critics agree, venerates cultural conservatism.[89]

In this way, *Gone with the Wind* popularized a history for precisely the understanding of southern culture that apologists for regional apartheid were still promoting. Gunnar Myrdal, who began interviews for his *American Dilemma* in 1939, found that white southerners would often "defend . . . the suppression of the Negroes by saying that they are satisfied with their status and lack a desire for change."[90] (He noted that they might continue by asserting the contradictory position that "Negroes must be kept down by all means.") The Agrarian Donald Davidson exemplified the romanticizing view of southern race relations when, in critically reviewing Arthur Raper's *A Preface to Peasantry* (1936), he argued that "the old feeling of white responsibility and of black loyalty and devotion seems to have carried over, partially at least, into the modern régime."[91] *Gone with the Wind* popularized this image of the region's "old feelings" at a time when arguments concerning interracial attachment, so prominent in the history of segregationist rhetoric, were increasingly irrelevant to the southern social structure. For while it has since been argued that, in addition to violence and exploitation, there was "a degree of [interracial] human contact and association" in the South before 1900, Depression-era writers suggest that such social patterns were largely eradicated by decades of apartheid, which enforced spatial separation as well as highly codified and regimented behavioral norms in circumstances of social contact.[92] Hence Tuskegee president Robert R. Moton argued in 1929, "The white man's knowledge of Negro life is diminishing and the rate is accelerated by the present-day policy of segregation. This operates practically to make an ever widening gulf between the two races which leaves each race more and more ignorant of the other."[93]

In popularizing the image of a holistic southern society that attracted cross-racial loyalty, then, plantation romances of the 1930s supported the cultural beliefs that underwrote apartheid; further, like much of the decade's regionalist commentary, they suggested that the South could be a cultural resource for the nation. But the latter proposition could be popularized in this decade only by narratives chronologically removed from the contemporary United States, for at this time, the South was widely seen as an oppositional culture, perhaps even a dangerously destabilizing one. Contemporary studies of plantation culture routinely presented it as spectral and deadening; the sociologist Charles S. Johnson, in his *Shadow of the Plantation,* and the journalist Clarence Cason, in his chapter of nearly the same name, agreed despite substantial differences that sharecropping uncannily reproduced "southern slavery in these modern times."[94] By the time Selznick's film appeared, the South had been proclaimed the "Nation's No. 1 economic problem," and southern white supremacists were regularly compared to European fascists.[95] *Gone with the Wind* appeared to constitute the last stand of the plantation romance, as, despite the popular appeal of this narrative, few intellectuals believed that a romanticized approach to southern history and culture could provide a plausible or compelling model for national affiliation.[96] The more pressing question, by the end of this decade, was how the United States could incorporate the South at all.

A Region in Space and Time

Practicing the quintessential Depression-era genre of documentary—more specifically, the "'I've seen America' book"—Sherwood Anderson's *Puzzled America* (1935) collects individual stories in order to demonstrate a shared "willingness to believe, a hunger for belief, a determination to believe" among the national public.[97] But in his careful, halting descriptions, Anderson also demonstrates the difficulty facing those who attempted to write about the South in the 1930s:

> "Look what we Northerners did to the South," he kept saying. . . .
>
> Men were plowing in the Southern fields. There was the thing, always a new wonder to the city man, the patience of men with the earth, the way they cling to it. We were in a poor district. They are not hard to find in the back country of the deep South. There were these miles of back roads, deeply rutted, even dangerous, bridges fallen into decay.
>
> "It is a kind of inferno," my friend kept saying.[98]

In short, Anderson stages the difficulty of comprehending that these southerners, who seem to exist "pretty much outside the modern world," are nonetheless American (29, 8).

To Anderson's friend, the South constitutes a sort of national inferno—a place understood to be part of the U.S. cosmology yet invisible and perhaps unfathomable to other residents. Anderson resists this position, to an extent, arguing that the "separation of the country into the North and South . . . is false" and pointing to the existence of intraregional variation and transregional commonality (128). But he also acknowledges that both sides believe in this regional difference, and his own relationship to that division is ambivalent: amid his protestations, he states a belief common to many nonsoutherners in their investigations of the South, which held that to write about it, one must somehow belong, for southern society is too fundamentally anomalous for outsiders to understand. (Anderson resolves this problem through his genealogy: "It is intangible and illusive—this feeling for the South and all it stands for. . . . It must be born in you or come down into you from a grandfather or a grandmother" [23].) Anderson's concern about whether it was possible for a writer to negotiate the cultural difference between the South and the larger nation suggests how poorly ideas about the South fit with the integrative paradigm of liberal regionalism.

For however nostalgic U.S. culture may have been in the midst of its erratic and difficult modernization, this interest in recuperating and maintaining certain traditional practices and attitudes was linked with an equally widespread concern that the cultural forms of the past might be incompatible with the progress still highly valued during this period of U.S. history.[99] Thus, despite the interest of regionalists in folkloric cultures, many argued that these expressions and practices must be preserved in ways that would also facilitate economic and social change. Botkin, for example, was equally determined that the beauty and utility of African American and white southern folklore must be preserved as hardy and elemental cultural components and that they must be "integrat[ed] . . . with literary and scientific education," because, to the extent that they had been preserved through cultural isolation, they were accompanied by "poverty, a low standard of living, illiteracy, prejudice, lack of enterprise, subjugation, etc."[100] Where the folklore itself might contain values that could enrich national culture, it was associated with traits believed to be painful for the "folk" themselves and resistant to cosmopolitan strains in the larger society. The more conservative Thomas Hart Benton typically argued that rural cultures maintained values elsewhere corrupted by modernization, but even he was ambivalent concerning the South's "old-time" manifestations; describing the region as the nation's "romantic land," he depicts southern time as extraordinarily slow, marked not only by a removal from "hurried northern activity" but also by "deep-set prejudices."[101] People not attracted to regionalism lacked any ambivalence in assessing southern backwardness; V. F. Calverton, for example, claimed that the South had "been brought to an abrupt standstill" and was "scarcely more progressive than a medieval village."[102]

Concerns about the South were in part economic: in a period of widespread loss, the extremity of southern poverty was both embarrassing and challenging to the nation. The idea that southern economic problems might be the fault of the greater United States—long promulgated by those seeking greater regional autonomy—was granted both federal and social scientific authority when Roosevelt's National Emergency Council, in its *Report on Economic Conditions of the South*, described the use of the region's natural resources and the development of its industry by using the paradigm of intranational colonial exploitation.[103] Though this report, which proclaimed stark economic differentiation a threat to national planning and recovery, was not issued until 1938, Secretary of Labor Frances Perkins famously raised the idea in 1933 that southern poverty exacerbated U.S. economic difficulties. Southern journalists and politicians raised an outcry over her assessment that "the whole South of this country is an untapped market for shoes. . . . We haven't yet reached the end of the social benefits and the social goods that may come from the further development of the mass-production system on a basis of consuming power of the South. . . . A social revolution will take place if you put shoes on the people of the South."[104] But in so avidly linking southern economic alterity—its differences in production and consumption—to a troubling cultural alterity, Perkins voiced an anxiety prominent in both intellectual and popular culture.

Finding it difficult to comprehend how the circumstances of southern laborers could exist in a modern nation, observers also feared the potential political effects of this population. Anderson, for example, amid his shock that such a lack of economic development could exist in the United States and his guilt at the possibility that the nation might somehow be responsible, also exhibits fear of the political proclivities of people seemingly so different—"primitives"—yet potentially equal in terms of democratic representation; he expresses particular concern that poor southerners might be attracted to "the Fascisti thing," the idea of "America *über alles*" (10). And though the Agrarians continued to maintain that traditional southern farming provided the nation's only defense against the "collectivism" that would emerge from industrialization and modernization, both popular documentaries and sociological analyses described tenant farming and sharecropping through the profoundly antidemocratic social structures of peonage and peasantry.[105] (The idea of state-supported subsistence farming did attract some support from sociologists and even from the New Deal, but Ralph Bunche noted that such a movement would so counter dominant trends in U.S. social and economic development as to constitute a path to permanent vocational segregation: it would involve not only "stay[ing] on the land" but also being "lifted out of the mainstream of our economic life and laid up on an economic shelf to dry [rot].")[106] Meanwhile, both the Agrarians and the Louisiana populist Huey Long were perceived to embrace fascistic tenets, and the latter, through the success of his radio addresses and his nationwide Share Our Wealth society, seemed poised to elicit national support for such positions.[107]

The association of the region with fascism was centrally fueled, of course, by southern racial practices and policies, which developed increased notoriety in the 1930s. This publicity resulted largely from the work of African American and leftist activists—groups that, in their variety of political approaches, overlapped and conflicted. Both the NAACP and the International Labor movement, for example, conducted anti-lynching campaigns, and they competed for the support of the African American working class.[108] But their multiple efforts garnered extensive public attention to problems of both mob and "legal" lynching, such as the Scottsboro, Alabama, trial in which eight young African American men were sentenced to death by an all-white jury for allegedly raping two white women. This case, which began in 1931, provided the topic for a volume of poetry and drama by Langston Hughes and elicited not only critical editorials and national journalistic coverage but also criticism of such reports by southern apologists.[109] Despite their opposing political positions, all such articles contained evidence of southern racial injustice and hatred, linking the region with fascist nations.

Though southern white supremacy and injustice had long been presented as an aberration reliably contained by spatial boundaries, discourse from later in the 1930s explicitly argued that southern racial oppression implicated the nation, impugning its claims to oppose fascist racism.[110] The reasons for this shift were multiple, including the significantly more widespread alarm at fascism that developed as the decade progressed.[111] But also, as the Nazis' racial agenda became more apparent, southern white supremacists—including the KKK and Mississippi senator Theodore Bilbo—announced their support for Hitler's policies, confirming Melvin Tolson's claims that the United States harbored "anti-Negro fascists."[112] In his struggle against southern congressional conservatives, Roosevelt himself equated "the feudal system," language widely used to describe the southern social structure, with "the fascist system."[113] This is not to say that Roosevelt supported antiapartheid measures, but his increased criticism of the southern social structure and, especially, the Supreme Court's increased willingness to support the Fourteenth and Fifteenth Amendments in southern cases did suggest a developing federal conviction that southern states could not be exempted from national laws.[114] Increasing African American support of the Democratic Party and changing party rules encouraged Roosevelt's administration to challenge powerful conservative southern Democrats more boldly; where, in the early years of the New Deal, the belief that southern racial policies could not be changed by legislation was convenient for a Democratic administration in need of congressional support, these political changes rendered challenges to that belief more viable and even strategic.[115]

All these shifts demonstrate an increasing tendency to examine more thoroughly the relationships between the southern states and the larger nation and to acknowledge the diversity and interconnectedness of each. Such movements included broader political organization by southern and national African Americans, leftists, and liberals seeking workers' rights and voters' rights and challenging racial violence.[116] The initial meeting of the interracial Southern Conference for Human Welfare, famously attended by Eleanor Roosevelt and interrupted by local police seeking to enforce racial segregation, demonstrated both transregional cooperation and intraregional conflict. Southern liberals also testified to such division in the national press. Virginius Dabney, for example, announced to readers of the *Nation* that the "bulk of Southern opinion appears to be definitely favorable" to federal antilynching legislation and that the regional members of Congress who were decrying the measure did not speak for their publics.[117]

By the end of the 1930s, then, numerous cultural and political groups were working to efface the purported temporal boundaries isolating the South from the larger nation. This changing approach to the parameters of U.S. and southern cultures may have been facilitated, however, by earlier and more spectacular accounts of southern cultural difference. The popular and critically acclaimed film *I Am a Fugitive from a Chain Gang* (1932), for example, depicts the South as an almost gothic region. After James Allen's unjust incarceration and second escape, he appears not only hunted but haunted, as, at the end of the film, his image fades into a dark, empty screen. This film supports not only the idea of southern alterity but also, quite possibly, the desire to reinforce regional boundaries: observing a life-destroying space might not lead audiences to imagine stronger ties between region and nation. In juxtaposing southern and national legal systems, however, and by presenting the South as a confusing and initially innocuous space into which the unsuspecting national traveler might inadvertently step, this film also suggests the difficulty of containing regional problems.

In sum, during the 1930s, as U.S. discourse demonstrated uncertainty concerning the nation's own relationship to time and the effectiveness of its central affiliative ideologies, what had once appeared a stable southern alterity was broadly perceived as a threat—a site from which antimodern and antidemocratic beliefs and practices could spread, as they had in Germany and Italy. Thus discussion of southern culture from the early to the late 1930s demonstrates two somewhat conflicting shifts—a sharpening perception of a dangerous southern difference and an increased desire for greater interregional understanding. Accordingly, where many liberal regionalists sought to reform the nation by expanding the role of regions in understandings of national culture, liberals and leftists focused on the South sought chiefly to reform the region by increasing its cultural, economic, and legal integration with the larger United States. But, particularly early in the decade, because southern backwardness was considered both acute and menacing, such a change was thought to necessitate the bridging of a difficult cultural gap, one long considered both inherent and immutable.

Even as Sherwood Anderson's *Puzzled America,* for example, participated in representing a temporal distance between the South and the rest of the nation, he argued for the importance of transcending that breach. He suggested, for example, that spatial proximity might enable citizens to overcome cultural differences, arguing that "[a] man must go into the little shacks, churches, lodge halls" in order to seek "a different notion of government from what we have had" (34). Explaining that interregional communication is necessary in a context of national political and economic crisis, he called for "a new realism that may help" counter tendencies of "putting [poor whites] aside" from national dialogue; his argument that "just now the Southern problem centers more about the poor whites . . . than about the Negro" inadvertently highlighted the need for further analysis. As formulated here, Anderson's literary ideal suggests the pluralist and nationalist hopes of the nineteenth-century literary critic William Dean Howells, who argued that fiction should "speak true American, with all the varying Tennesseean, Philadelphian, Bostonian, and New York accents."[118] But it also raises the question of how to identify realism, the mimetic claims of which depend not only on representational technique but also on reading conventions.

This is the topic of the next section of this book, in which I examine how experimental southern writers of the 1930s explored regional reality in part through testing the texture of southern time—representing perceptions or experiences of the relationship between southern stasis and southern change. Their claustrophobia-inducing repetitions, their lyrical and folkloric alienations, and their literally haunting remembrances suggested to many readers that southern culture was incommensurable with that of the nation. Accordingly, these works are often still discussed through literary rubrics identified strictly with the region—southern grotesque, southern folklore, and southern gothic. But examining this literature in the context of national debates about time makes clear how these writers' aesthetic choices responded to broader ideological and formal problems, including the question of whether and how time could be disarticulated across space, the degree to which the linear progressive time so vigorously asserted by a capitalist modernity could coexist and interact with other forms of temporal experience, and the degree to which collectives can or must be defined by a shared temporality. As I demonstrate in the final section of this book, by the end of the 1930s, as national perceptions of the South changed, southern writers became far more explicit in mapping connections between southern, national, and international cultural and political forms. But texts from earlier in this decade demonstrate the extraordinary influence exerted by perceptions of an inherent and uncanny regional backwardness, as residents of a region broadly described as the site of the past struggled over how to understand their present and future.

PART TWO

Modernist Mappings

CHAPTER THREE

Erskine Caldwell and the Abject South

ERSKINE CALDWELL is not often included in the annals of literary modernism, perhaps in part because of the broad audience that embraced his works. His most popular and arguably best novels—*Tobacco Road* (1932) and *God's Little Acre* (1933)—were long-lasting best sellers; Jack Kirkland's dramatic adaptation of the former, after struggling initially, ran for seven years on Broadway.[1] And though overtly influenced by the proletarian literary avant-garde, Caldwell rarely promoted his aesthetic innovations as such, insisting instead that his fictions realistically represented southern social conditions. Nonetheless, Caldwell's work contains many methods and themes noted in modernist writing. Using repetition worthy of Gertrude Stein, for example, his otherwise spare prose style was initially compared to that of Ernest Hemingway.[2] Because they reveled in the burlesque, these fictions provoked multiple attempts to restrict their circulation; to explain this aspect of his work, Caldwell expressed the typically modernist desire to challenge dominant sexual norms and renew attention to the body.[3] Seeking to characterize Caldwell's literary experimentation, Kenneth Burke compared him to Dadaists, superrealists, and symbolists.[4] Most important for my purposes is that Caldwell was centrally concerned with the social and characterological effects of uneven development—the radical geographic divergences within the process of U.S. modernization.

Functioning, in Susan Hegeman's useful term, as a "*peripheral* modernist," Caldwell focused on apparent temporal distinctions within the United States, particularly those posed by southern poverty.[5] Thus, for example, his recursive narrative style is said to mimic effectively the psychological and experiential effects of economic stagnation.[6] In much of his fiction, a static temporality constitutes an almost tangible barrier enclosing the actions and even the psyches of his characters; their resolute repetitions suggest—to the point, it has been argued, of inducing—a kind of psychomotor disturbance. (Regarding this aspect of Caldwell's work, Kenneth Burke confessed, "Sometimes when reading Caldwell I feel as though I were playing with my toes."[7]) Caldwell proclaimed this theme of stagnation explicitly in the photodocumentary *You Have Seen Their Faces* (1935) on which he collaborated with Margaret Bourke-White; it presented the South as "a retarded and thwarted civilization," and he argued that "the pain and indignity of it is beginning to tell."[8]

Thus the effect of Caldwell's work was less to undercut ideas of a distinct southern temporality than to stage them in a particularly startling way. Though his fiction focused on differences within regional culture—between the rural and the urban, for example, or between agricultural and industrial labor—it also represented a social order so fundamentally opposed to his contemporaries' dominant cultural ideals as to elicit profound anxiety among his audience. Caldwell's representations of economic and cultural marginalization appeared amid a period of proliferating nationalist discourse—when both New Deal propaganda and leftist protest represented the United States as a collective that could be mobilized to produce a more just and flexible socioeconomic structure. Precisely as national membership was presented as a potential source of agency, Caldwell's stagnating regional grotesques enabled audience members to manage fears of their own economic and social decline by projecting them onto the bodies of a spatially and temporally distanced population. This fantasized South was thus isolated from an idealized national temporality.[9]

Reviews of these works demonstrate the difficulties facing writers who sought to create a more sophisticated dialogue between understandings of southern and national time during this period. This purported opposition is revealed, in critical responses to Caldwell's work, to have provided a potent component in formulations of collective—and, accordingly, individual—identities. Caldwell's narratives serve as something of a foil in this section of my argument; in subsequent chapters, I argue that Hurston's innovative explorations of folkloric practice and Faulkner's gothic modernism included tropes and themes better suited to investigating the purported temporal divide between the South and the larger nation. These more subtle and difficult works were also read far less widely than Caldwell's. Nonetheless, all these novels were critically interpreted according to dominant perceptions of southern time, and reactions to Caldwell's use of the literary grotesque vividly demonstrate how southern modernists' experimental representations were collapsed into hegemonic understandings of a backward South. Despite Caldwell's progressive intentions, his representation of the "Southern Extremity of America" tended to support the widespread belief that the South constituted an essential aberration from national culture.[10] Here, as elsewhere, this formulation not only marginalized the region but also defined disfranchisement of African Americans as a regional, rather than national, concern.

The Mappable Grotesque

In 1935, Kenneth Burke questioned how Erskine Caldwell's "extravaganzas, imagined in a world essentially as fantastic as Swift's[,] should ever have passed for realism." Pronouncing Caldwell's novels "distinctly grotesque," he explains that though the characters are placed in "complex social situations," they lack the ability to cope with such situations and accordingly "act with the scant, crude tropisms of an insect."[11] The realism of these novels, in other words, consists of their setting, which mirrors that of the Depression-era United States, including crushing rural poverty; the injustice and failure of the southern agricultural credit system; the racism exercised in the sharecropping system; the unprosecuted killing of African Americans; the juridical control of the state; the broad influence of the market; the incongruous wealth in certain areas of the city; the recreational economy of the city, spanning theaters to brothels; the labor exploitation of cotton mills; and the disempowerment of striking workers. But within these recognizable worlds, the characters act unrecognizably, apparently driven, as Burke suggests, solely by the body.

Caldwell reduces these characters to their physicality by granting them particularized physical features or notably repetitive behaviors. The stereotype of the fat southern sheriff, for example, is vividly represented in *God's Little Acre*. While suffering from the heat, even Pluto Swint agrees that his "eyes are so small and [his] face is so red, that [he looks] exactly like a watermelon with two seeds showing."[12] Sister Bessie of *Tobacco Road* covers her face when she travels to town in order to prevent people from staring at her collapsed nose, which is said to resemble "the end of a double-barrel shotgun."[13] Ellie May Lester's harelip is said to "ma[ke] her look as if her mouth were bleeding profusely," a characteristic that was dramatized as well (*TR* 102; Kirkland 19, 81). The bodies of other Lesters exhibit spectacular torpor. When Dude, for instance, is not trying to procure a car (his one overwhelming desire), he spends his time "throwing a lopsided ball at the side of the house, and catching it on the rebound," an activity he continues despite his father's repeated objection that it is "chunking weatherboarding" at the family members (*TR* 6–14; Kirkland 5–9). Dude stops only to watch Ellie May and Lov have sex, after which he "s[its] down to watch the red wood-ants crawl over the stomach and breasts of his sister" (*TR* 35).

In accordance with Caldwell's desire to challenge sexual repressiveness, his characters, dominated by the body, demonstrate few inhibitions. Ellie May attempts to seduce her brother-in-law in her front yard with her family's support, and Will Thompson claims that there is no injunction against sex that is "all in the family" (*TR* 16–17; Kirkland 34–43; *GLA* 49). Under the sway of Sister Bessie's preaching, Jeeter Lester suggests that he should resist the sex drive but claims that he is helpless to do so, arguing that the only solution is "to go ahead and cut [him]self off so [he] won't do it no more" (*TR* 100). (Even as he later admits that his sexual urges are no longer so overwhelming, he announces, paradoxically, his lack of self-control: "A man feels like he ain't got no control over his tongue—and don't want none" [*TR* 49; Kirkland 124].) The characters of *God's Little Acre*, in contrast, are content to be ruled by the sex drive, a power they come near to worshipping. Other characters believe Will to be "a real man," or "the male man," because he complies with the physical urge, when he sees a beautiful woman, to "get down on his hands and knees and lick something"; some men, they explain, are too "dead inside" to feel this impulse, having listened to too much preaching (*GLA* 190, 193–95, 157). In this novel, the lack of mental agency is apotheosis: to live "like God made us to live," one must obey the body, the "feeling down inside of you" (*GLA* 183).[14]

Such representations could be understood to counter and critique the bodily alienation typical of late modernity, in which physical functions and pleasures are increasingly codified and regulated by economic and political power.[15] Caldwell's representation of labor was, after all, directly influenced by his acquaintance with Mike Gold, a prominent proponent of proletarian fiction.[16] Further, Ty Ty Walden of *God's Little Acre* and Jeeter Lester of *Tobacco Road* refuse to subordinate their bodies to a deterministic socioeconomic system, which mandates that their work shift to support changing economic trends. Rather, they respond to a bodily directive: Ty Ty has the "real honest-to-goodness gold fever," which prompts him to dig holes all over his farm in his search for a lode, and Jeeter has farming "in [his] blood" (*GLA* 11; *TR* 15; Kirkland 40). Both their choices and their practices are driven by sensation. Ty Ty can feel "in [his] bones" whether he is near the lode or not (*GLA* 2), and Jeeter, when he senses the "smell of newly turned earth," "want[s] to go out right away . . . and plant a crop" (*TR* 71; Kirkland 40). Though neither of these drives is economically productive, they do suggest a form of labor driven by the body rather than the corporation, and this configuration of intimacy with one's own labor offers a form of authenticity often longed for in Depression-era discourse.[17]

But Caldwell also represents human desire and agency in ways that do not readily accord with such critiques. In *God's Little Acre,* for example, sexual freedom and pleasure in labor are attained through a form of human sexuality oriented toward the machine. The female mill workers are said to be "in love with the looms and the spindles and the flying lint," and after work, when the machines are not accessible, they substitute by running "back to the ivy-covered walls [of the mill] and press[ing] their bodies against it and touch[ing] it with their lips."[18] This mechanistic sexuality is presented even more vividly in what may be the novel's climactic scene.[19] When Will Thompson, Ty Ty's son-in-law, finally escapes the control of the mill's owners—when, that is, he determines to start up the mill himself, thus subverting the system of timed wage-labor—he feels "as strong as God Almighty himself" and indulges this power by mimicking and reversing, with his body, the action of the mill: " 'We're going to start spinning and weaving again tomorrow, but tonight I'm going to tear that cloth on [his sister-in-law Griselda] till it looks like lint out of a gin.' . . . Piece by piece he tore like a madman, hurling the fluffy lint in all directions" (156). Despite Will's critique of capitalism, his power and determination—attributes widely ascribed to workers in proletarian fiction—are linked with a robotic sexuality that, desiring access to the machines of the mill, wishes less to alter the economic structure than to find a release in labor.

The grotesque is, in any case, a notoriously ambiguous representational mode, which can be justly criticized for its hegemonic divisiveness and also vaunted for its subversive "political fierceness."[20] By definition, grotesque literature alienates readers by challenging their sense of human ontology. But, ideally, it leads them to recognize a circumstance of their social surroundings that they might reflexively disavow when they encounter it in a more straightforward form. Caldwell's novels, for example, render literal the metaphors that mechanize human workers in Fordist modernity and could thus be said to demonstrate what Michael Denning, following Kenneth Burke, has called the "proletarian grotesque," the style of Depression-era avant-garde that seeks "to wrench us out of the repose and distance of the 'aesthetic.' "[21] Precisely because the grotesque seeks to disrupt the psychological structures through which audiences reconcile themselves to their surroundings, however, readers or viewers may seek ways to deflect its insights, often through projecting onto others in their society any disturbing qualities that might implicate themselves.

Noting this problem, two prominent theorists of the literary grotesque—Wolfgang Kayser and Mikhail Bakhtin—agree that such works require a distinct kind of setting, one that, while alienated or inverted from the world of the audience, nonetheless suggests some ineffable correspondence as well.[22] Theoretically, when encountering such a space, audiences cannot imagine a stable object on which to project whatever disgust or outlandish delight they might feel; accordingly, our fear, derision, or celebration implicates us as well. Such a potentially self-effacing response is exemplified by Ralph Ellison's retrospective account of his viewing of *Tobacco Road*, particularly the scene in which Ellie May attempts to seduce her brother-in-law Lov in the sandy front yard of the Lesters' home. Describing his "*extravagance* of laughter" at their "bizarre choreography of 'frustrabation,' " Ellison contemplates his own feelings of uncertainty amid a largely white audience during his first weeks in New York; the degree to which Caldwell's characters embody "a carefully screened assemblage of anti-Negro stereotypes"; Ellison's own biographical encounters with such stereotypes as well as with the class that Caldwell's characters also represent; and finally the degree to which this couple's desire is "embarrassingly symbolic" of Ellison's own adolescent sexuality, which was sufficiently regulated by public observation and norms that it had few and awkward opportunities for expression.[23] Arguing that the "intentional outrageousness" of *Tobacco Road* was "deeply rooted in the crazy-quilt life I knew," Ellison suggests that the "wisdom" he developed in his viewing of the play depended on his "willingness to make or withhold a human identification," generously adding that the art of the play left the viewer "no choice but to identify."[24]

For many readers and viewers, however, Caldwell's narratives *did* allow them to choose whether to identify with these representations of economic failure, irrationality, casual brutality, publicly denigrated appearance, and highly wrought sexuality, and they did so precisely in insisting on the realistic representation of their setting—Depression-era Georgia.[25] Accordingly, reviewers tended to describe Caldwell's fictional worlds not in the demonic or utopian terms of Kayser and Bakhtin but in terms of the material space of the nation. Such interpretations were encouraged by discourse surrounding the work, including Caldwell's nonfiction. Arguing vociferously that the conditions seen in his novels matched those found in the rural and industrial South, Caldwell followed the novels with a series of documentary articles for the *New York Post* on the degradation of southern poverty, including one that the *Post* headlined "Starving Babies Suckled by Dogs in Georgia Wastes."[26] These claims challenged the complacency of southern elites—a project to which Caldwell was committed.[27] Also, they served to legitimize and promote Caldwell's fiction. Caldwell argued, for example, that libraries refusing to circulate his novels, or cities seeking to ban the traveling production of *Tobacco Road*, were effectively proclaiming that "the people of Tobacco Road in Georgia are not worthy of thought or notice."[28]

In urging readers and viewers to interpret these narratives through the rubric of realism, however, Caldwell limited their ability to function in the grotesque mode.[29] As several critics have suggested, Caldwell's goal of attracting attention to southern poverty may have been incompatible with his penchant for grotesque humor and his desire to challenge repressive attitudes toward sex and physicality.[30] Though the popularity of his work seems to have derived, in large part, from its prominent display of sexuality,[31] audience members were regularly informed that these uninhibited characters existed in a world utterly unlike their own. As Peter Stallybrass and Allon White argue, privileged subjects have often attempted to manage those sensations they consider disgusting by ascribing them to bodies without money—people who cannot, because of their difference in dress and residence, be mistaken for members of the upper classes, and who are carefully policed to see that they remain in bounded spaces.[32] Such representations allow bourgeois subjects to avoid the sort of self-reflection otherwise encouraged by the grotesque, which implicates the viewer in its shameful or exciting frisson. Thus, by insisting on the poverty and difference of his characters, Caldwell enabled his audience both to engage and contain discomfiting desires. Readers and viewers who might otherwise feel uncomfortable about seeking out sensational entertainments could assert that they valued these representations for their social realism, thus demonstrating their own sense of compassion and social responsibility.[33] Advertisement for the play courted precisely such responses.[34]

But in this decade of widespread economic loss and insecurity, responses to Caldwell's work—often extending even to "nausea"—imply that the feelings evoked by his particular grotesquerie may have emerged from fears already potent among his audience.[35] Reviewers' physical revulsion suggests an encounter with the psychoanalytic abject, described by Julia Kristeva as an aspect of human physicality or experience that individuals wish to disavow, a substance or image that disrupts the psyche's sense of "identity, system, order."[36] Debates concerning efforts to close the traveling production of *Tobacco Road* explicitly argued that, by identifying with the "inexcusable degradation" it depicted, audiences would reveal their own divergence from national standards.[37] Opponents of such censorship suggested that the people the Lesters were presumed to represent had already suffered from a national repression and that these "forgotten people" should no longer be subjected to the nation's "policy of concealment, of covering up."[38] But while such writers advocated the spread of documentary knowledge concerning southern poverty, they agreed with would-be censors that audiences should not experience, or subsequently repress, any empathic identification with these characters.

Indeed, the critics argued, normal audiences would not be inclined to do so. Accordingly, responses to this play featured images not only of a Caldwellian South but also of other potentially abject regional audiences. The Chicago judge who ruled against the local opening of the play suggested that only New Yorkers could so cavalierly find it entertaining, because that city was the "front doormat" of the nation. The *Nation* responded by suggesting that midwestern officials must suspect that their citizenry would identify with the Lesters, and it argued that, among normative audiences, "no one who observes the goings-on between the turnip-eating youth and the harelipped imbecile is likely to be impelled to go and do likewise."[39]

In projecting this abjection onto spatially distanced regions, audience members rejected the possibility that, in their encounter with Caldwell's work, they might be imagining such figures for their own entertainment. Even those reviewers who dwelled on the aesthetic pleasure of the work expressed surprise that such grotesques could be entertaining; as the *Nation*'s theater critic exulted, "Perhaps it is difficult to believe that this play . . . which involves the almost continuous presence of a rutting female monstrosity with a hare lip . . . can be funny. Yet funny it was."[40] More often, reviewers explained the audiences' willingness to endure such representations through the hope that, with their increased awareness of the abjection in the rural South, they might better be able to eradicate it: "We feel . . . that we ought to know . . . we wish very violently that we could do something about such things."[41] Thus many audience members preferred the belief that, in another part of the country, people routinely killed and slept with their nonspousal family members to the belief that such activity was, at least in this case, restricted to a fictional realm. The latter explanation would place the abject not only in Caldwell's imagination but also in their own, thus violating a topographical rule of abjection—that it must be "hemmed in and thrust aside," not repressed but ejected, perhaps most effectively projected onto another, spatially distanced body.[42]

Such responses sought to contain the abjection represented in Caldwell's work both in the distanced space of the South and in a specifically regional time, one distinct from that of the modernizing nation. In other words, these responses placed Caldwell's characters not only "there" but also "then," in a society said to constitute absolute alterity.[43] Ida Gruber, for example, argued that the dramatic version of *Tobacco Road* was an "indubitably" realistic portrait of the rural South, "a section of this country that has never grown up."[44] This stasis marks a failure of both social development and human evolution: viewing the Lesters' behavior, Gruber complains that "the things that upset most human beings—births, marriages, deaths—do not disturb the even, filthy tenor of their way." Though these terms, in reconceptualizing the life cycle, suggest precisely the sort of productive reconsideration of materiality and the body that Bakhtin finds in the carnivalesque grotesque, Gruber's derision of the Lesters does not affect his understanding of his own humanity. Locating these grotesques in a clearly demarcated physical space existing outside the time of his own "grown-up" modernity, Gruber is confident that such people would not share his temporal or cultural coordinates. Other critics also suggested that the characters of the theatrical *Tobacco Road,* and the living people they were presumed to represent, had either failed to evolve or were devolving, having lived "for so long so close to the land itself as to become a part of it . . . sink[ing] to a level that was barely human."[45] The novel's characters, too, were taken to be realistic representations of people who had "sunk far, far, below the animal level," effectively removed from the national "civilization that contains them."[46] Those of *God's Little Acre* were said to be "isolated from the main trends and struggles . . . that inevitably make deep impressions on all of our lives."[47] Thus these grotesques were distanced from the audience in time—existing, it was said, elsewhere in evolutionary progression—as well as in space.

As the encounter with these fictional characters seems to have provoked a sense of abjection within many individual subjects, an abjection that could be contained and expelled by projecting it onto the extradiegetic white southern poor, the image of this supposedly abject population also provoked anxiety concerning both the status of the nation and that of the white race. If such devolving bodies actually constituted a segment of the population, they would challenge the nation's representation of itself as an economically and politically progressive democracy, revealing "a section so primitive that it is mockery almost to point with pride to our cultural advancement."[48] Furthermore, they would mark, in the drama critic Stark Young's words, a site "where our Anglo-Saxon race has found an isolated occasion for degeneration and decay."[49] As I argue in the next section, Caldwell's work supported an exclusionary response to these anxieties—the logic of spatial segregation. Despite his aspiration to encourage national intervention on behalf of the southern poor and to challenge racial norms, his fiction encouraged the belief that white poverty constituted an essential demarcation within the white race, such that poor whites gravitated toward geographic spaces isolated from national culture. In doing so, it also presented the segregation of African Americans as a practice specific to spaces already outside U.S. cultural boundaries.

Peripheral People

By containing its imagined grotesques in a restricted space understood to exist outside national time, Caldwell's work may have provided some popular resolution for an anxiety that plagued writing about the southern poor white during this decade—the concern that membership in this category might not be biologically determined. In representations of the South, poor whites had for centuries been distinguished from other financially troubled white people by their supposed psychological and physical degeneracy.[50] In the late nineteenth and early twentieth centuries, these accounts of cognitive and bodily difference were often racialized, based on the argument that poor whites were descended from convicts and indentured servants, people said to be of inferior genetic quality; this deficiency was said to be exacerbated by continued isolation and endogamy.[51] Rupert Vance found this logic prominently displayed in metropolitan journalistic accounts of the 1925 Scopes "monkey trial," as it was in H. L. Mencken's influential critique of southern culture.[52] By the 1930s, however, historians had debunked this account, positing instead a homogeneous ethnic background for southern whites.[53] Vance himself defined the category of poor white in terms of lack of access to information and education—factors readily recognizable as socioeconomic in origin.

Given that the status of "poor white" placed people, in Robert Penn Warren's words, "beyond the pale of even the most generous democratic recognition," the collapse of this category had the potential to disrupt dominant accounts of both region and nation.[54] At the most basic level, it would challenge hegemonic distinctions among the many white southerners who lacked money, suggesting that, even in the South's racially delimited democracy, white families with a history of poverty merited rights to education, economic opportunity, and economic justice—rights many such subjects were already seeking to claim. But the southern designation "poor white" is only the most famous categorization of white poverty, a phenomenon widely studied and catalogued in the United States beginning in the 1870s.[55] The genetic basis of this broader discourse was also shifting in the 1920s because of the decline of Lamarckianism; where previously it was argued that poverty's deleterious effects could be absorbed by the "germ plasm" and passed on to descendants, it now appeared that the class status of the poor could not be explained through their biologically determined character.[56] Such questions were tied to understandings of national culture through the prominence of eugenics discourse, as debates about immigration policy, for example, suggested that only individuals who could contribute to the development of an "American race"—an ability measured by health and whiteness (a term applied, by different users, to diversely delimited sets of European ethnicities)—should be admitted to citizenship.[57] But the corresponding emphasis on "Americanization" of immigrants insisted that "fit" white people could assimilate U.S. economic and political values.[58]

In sum, by the 1930s, the racializing logic that had previously located the explanation for white poverty in the bodies of the poor was losing its scientific and historical moorings, leaving in its place the explanation urged by an increasingly outspoken labor movement, which argued that poverty resulted from unjust social and economic structures. As one social scientist looking at the southern context explained, the difference between genetic and environmental accounts of identity could determine whether people labeled poor whites might be expected to function in a modernizing environment; currently, he explained, they lacked numerous qualities that are "important if not requisite for economic success and social esteem in the modern world," but if this difference were the result of "cultural—rather than racial—heritage," it could be altered.[59] (This scholar, A. H. Den Hollander, stopped short of such an explanation, repeatedly reverting to the suspicion that the causes of poor white backwardness, as well as the effects, resided in their bodies [426, 430].)

But already another argument, similar to the previous one in its effects, was arising to classify and contain the white poor by explaining that isolation in peripheral spaces produced populations of notable biological homogeneity by limiting the available genes. In other words, to the extent that the lower classes were segregated into distinct spaces, observers such as Aldous Huxley feared they might develop into a "distinct and degraded species."[60] In the U.S. context, Arthur Estabrook, writing in a 1929 issue of *Eugenics: A Journal of Race Betterment,* offered Appalachia as a case study, explaining that "the more isolated sections" were "depleted genetically by the migration of the more energetic" and are subsequently home to a "population of low intellectual level," one that posed, furthermore, "a social and economic liability to the country."[61] In this analysis, though environment does not alter biology at a cellular level, as it could in Lamarckian accounts, it still functions as a external signifier of biology: in Estabrook's analysis, those who live in a "country slum" demonstrate their genetic inferiority by living there, because "citizens of social and genetic value" would have migrated.[62]

Such arguments exemplify a prominent solution to the problem of explaining poverty in a nation that defines itself as an engine of economic progress and a wellspring of individual opportunity—the strategy of claiming that something about the poor is distinctly un-American.[63] The political economist Thomas Nixon Carver, writing in the same issue of *Eugenics,* argued explicitly that, in a nation of social and economic opportunity, only the genetically inferior could be reduced to poverty:

"In a highly democratic country . . . where there is not only an open road to talent but a good system of universal and popular education . . . the individual who shows no aptitude for anything except the lowest and most unskilled occupations is naturally of poor stock."[64] In combination, these spatializing formulations indicate that the poorest of the nation's spaces, though unworthy of the United States, serve as a sign of its progressiveness, because only in the most modern of nations could the most backward of people be isolated in unmediated poverty.

This spatializing account of white poverty is central to *Tobacco Road,* which rigorously situates the degradation of the Lesters in the type of circumscribed space and fixated temporality now said to yield genetic decline. The narrative distinguishes Jeeter's fictional world for its temporal, as well as economic, stagnation, representing this attribute through both the characters' repetitive dialogue and actions and reiteration of the narrative itself. During a two-chapter interlude from the primary narrative, for example, the novel relates the history of the Lesters in an analepsis that, like Jeeter's characteristic behavior, seems constituted by "false start[s]" (71). We hear the story of how Captain John, Jeeter's landlord, moved to Fuller, taking Jeeter's store credit with him, and then we hear it again, this time as the end point of a story that began seventy-five years earlier.[65] The novel also repeats the story of how most of the children moved away and never tried to communicate with their parents, focalized first through Jeeter and then both Ada and Jeeter. In the second of these instances, it is difficult to tell whether this is merely analepsis, or also iterative narrative, narrating once what happened many times: though the tense of the dialogue begins in past perfect ("Jeeter had told"), it concludes with an iterative description ("Ada had talked several times") (60–62, 68–71).

This repetition does not suggest, however, that the narrator is part of the Lesters' world. This voice is forcefully distinguished from the characters, not only through dialect but also through speaking directly to the reader; the narrator notes, of Captain John's tenants, that "co-operative and corporate farming would have saved them all" (57). The Lesters, in contrast, cannot imagine any solution to their problems, and so their story is told in a narrative that slips ceaselessly into the past, both repeating itself and suggesting endless repetition. The first chapter (nine pocket paperback pages) contains at least thirteen analepses and seventeen usages of iterative narrative, suggesting that the character's actions are either predicated on long-standing problems or are instances of habitual behavior. Thus the temporality of *Tobacco Road* distinguishes it from realism, in which the linear progressive time of the narrative corresponds to the social time of capitalism and emphasizes individual and societal progress.[66] The narrator's explicit invitation to readers to join in imagining a once possible, now lost opportunity for the Lesters' rehabilitation further emphasizes the alterity of this fictional space by suggesting an extradiegetic world in which individuals are capable of exercising agency and resolving problems.[67]

If the fictional Lesters, and the people they were presumed to represent, were isolated from their early readers through the temporal distance implied in the narrative, the theatrical Lesters were distanced by the arrangement of the stage itself. As Loren Kruger argues, in realist drama, the stage conventionally resembled contemporary "middle-class interiors," encouraging "bourgeois audience[s]" to empathize with the play's " 'rounded' characters."[68] While *Tobacco Road* was hardly unique in violating these conventions, the forms of its divergence, like that of the novel's narrative, encouraged audiences to understand that, in observing the Lesters, they observed a world immeasurably removed from their experience. Far from representing a bourgeois interior, the stage presented the exterior of a dilapidated shack and the fender of a disintegrating car amid piles of actual dirt.[69] Here, Jeeter pronounces his own temporal distance from modernity.[70] Informed by a banker that "times have changed," a difference constituted in the play by the banker's intent to put the land of the tobacco road under "scientific cultivation," Jeeter announces, "That's no concern of mine" (Kirkland 132–33). The text's description of the setting encouraged people involved in production of the play to accentuate the impression of temporal distance: "Poverty, want, squalor, degeneracy, pitiful helplessness and grotesque, tragic lusts have stamped a lost, outpaced people with the mark of inevitable end. Unequipped to face a changing economic program, bound up in traditions, ties, and prejudices, they unknowingly face extinction" (3).

In both novelistic and dramatic representations, the Lesters do not simply reside in a world that is peripheral to the modernity of their audience; they are also resolutely of that world, sorting themselves out so that those who might best assimilate to normative national culture leave the tobacco road, and others stay to die.[71] Thus, though Jeeter claims to have fathered perhaps dozens of children in his youth, many of them demonstrate their greater flexibility, productivity, and, hence, normativity by moving to work in the cotton mills. As Jeeter is told, "even your children has got more sense than you. . . . They didn't stay here to starve."[72] Much of the play's plot involves just such a conflict, as Ada helps her "prettiest" daughter, Pearl, a young woman who demonstrates her desire to participate in the consumption of market goods, escape her marriage to the "dull, slow" Lov, an escape conducted more quietly in the novel (23). By the end of the novel, Dude determines to take Jeeter's place on the tobacco road, and in the play, he preaches with Sister Bessie in a denomination of her own design, one that seems tailored to Lesters and their like. Lov and Ellie May, who seem likely to live together in Pearl's absence, are unlikely to move to the city: Ellie May is too embarrassed by her appearance to attempt such assimilation. The Lesters, in sum, are essentially peripheral.

As these works configure poor white alterity in terms more spatial than racial, the Lesters' self-chosen seclusion would reassure those who feared that such a population might threaten the biological and cultural integrity of the nation, a concern that seems to have influenced both the writing and the reception of *Tobacco Road*.[73] Erskine Caldwell's representation of the Lesters is based in part on his father's family study, "The Bunglers: A Narrative Study in Five Parts," published in *Eugenics* magazine in 1930.[74] Ira Caldwell's pseudonymous "Bunglers" are in many ways less threatening than his son's fictional characters. Although Ira Caldwell details the Bunglers' unproductiveness and irrationality in labor, spending, health care, hygiene, education, and religion, he points out that they also maintain close familial relationships and stick to themselves, staying away from the "criminal dockets" and impressing neighbors with their honesty (part IV:333 and elsewhere). Nonetheless, he argues, the extremity of their isolation makes them unfit to interact with the rest of the world, which they regard with suspicion, when they consider it at all (II:248). Unfortunately, their rapidly increasing numbers lead them to swarm into surrounding counties and states "like bees."[75] Ira Caldwell notes that the Bunglers do not intermarry. Though some genetic theories might commend such genealogical diversity, he explains the error of such thinking: that so many Bunglers have found willing partners in exogamous marriages suggests that "we have hidden away in the social order, a vast number of people who are a source of weakness rather than of strength" (IV:335).

Lacking any experience of the nation's flow of time and communication, the Bunglers are the antithesis of the normative rational and productive citizen: they are "indescribably filthy" and "highly emotional" (I:207); they never feel "the thrill that comes from individual success" (II:249); clinging to "ancient time-worn ruts," they fail to find new opportunities for productive and materially rewarding labor (III:299); and they maintain a devotion to "a God that no intelligent being could worship" (IV:334). Ira Caldwell does not consider the possibility that his own faith in national norms may be misplaced. When an uneducated woman tells him that educated people are rascals who make a living "by cheating honest, hard-working people out of all they make," he cites this example of what he calls prejudice as a reason for the "lamentable condition of these people as regards education," without noting that his own description of local labor conditions supports the woman's statement (III:293). Estimating that only "40 or 50 percent [of the Bunglers] could be rehabilitated," he argues that the rest should be sterilized before such people begin to outnumber the middle class, warning, "Ignorance, stolid stupidity, thick necks and low brows are the greatest perils of a republic."[76]

But though Erskine Caldwell's characters, like Ira Caldwell's Bunglers, are reduced to their physicality, the former, if they existed, would be unlikely to alter the nation's demographics or distribution of power. No longer reproductive or mobile, and lacking both rationality and agency, they appear ready to decline into nonexistence—to succumb, as one reviewer argued, to "slow starvation and economic and social stupefaction."[77] Thus, where Ira Caldwell's fears of the fecund Bunglers led him to an alarming policy recommendation, critics responded to Erskine Caldwell's work by restricting their understanding of white citizenship. In their vague calls for action and their horror at the "squalor that exists in hidden corners," critics never imagine a population that could or would exercise agency within a democratic framework.[78] Though such people were presumed to reside within the borders of the nation, they were not considered *of* the nation; essentially peripheral, they were believed to exist only beyond spatial boundaries that national culture could not penetrate.

This understanding, that spatial identification is essential to identity, is emphasized even further in *God's Little Acre,* despite the increased mobility of its characters. As Ty Ty explains, "God made a man to work the ground and a man to work the machinery," and each such man must stay where he is intended to be. Thus Will Thompson, in his own mind as well as Ty Ty's, is essentially "a mill man," and Ty Ty is a "man of the land" (181). Ty Ty's sons are "countrymen" as well, though one, Jim Leslie, moves to Augusta and marries a wealthy woman. After he has inhabited the space of the normative nation, however, his Walden sexuality leads him back to the family farm, where he is punished and destroyed: determined to have sex with his sister-in-law, Jim returns to Ty Ty's farm and is shot by his brother. And though the Walden women are not contained by this spatial logic,[79] the women of Horse Creek Valley are figuratively rooted to the mill; with their "eyes like morning glories," these "girls" spend their time in "the ivy-walled mill" looking "like potted plants in bloom" (69). Thus the characters of *God's Little Acre,* like the Lesters, are designed so that, despite their divergence from national norms, they cannot be taken as an actual threat; even readers who see them as representative of real people must also see them as people who were and would remain spatially segregated from the nation.

Of course, the logic of spatial segregation was familiar from both laws and practices of racial segregation. But the understanding that poor whites were spatially segregated from the normative nation did not merely extend the logics of apartheid; rather, it supported them. Southern apartheid was, from its early institution, justified through an understanding of temporal distance. White southern elites represented the region as unable to accommodate "social equality" because of the continuing influence of its antebellum folkways. This account of a distinct and immutable regional culture became increasingly strained, however, in the face of growing mass culture and, later, the New Deal's plans to integrate the South into the nation's economy. In this context, poor whites were represented as particularly nonsynchronous, an unpredictable and unreformable population whose virulence rendered apartheid a necessity for the safety of African Americans.[80]

Writers who sought to reform race relations challenged this claim, arguing both that white racial violence was not restricted to the poor and that elites exacerbated lower-class racial antagonism in order to secure greater influence over all people in poverty.[81] Robert Penn Warren, in contrast, maintained that no one exercises agency in the racial violence of poor whites—not even them. Writing in the southern agrarian manifesto *I'll Take My Stand,* he argued that the poor white was "just as much the victim of the slave system as the negro" but comes to understand this history through no group or individual volition. Instead, poor whites respond to their circumstances haphazardly, their violence emerging from an innate "attitude." If no one wills such actions, how social policy could prevent them is hard to imagine, and, indeed, such is Warren's point. He concludes that "a slow way, but the readiest and surest way," to ensure African American economic development and safety is for "the Southern negro" to remain "a creature of the small town and farm . . . where he still chiefly belongs, by temperament and capacity" (260–61).

Such understandings of poor white and African American identity underwrote racial segregation by distancing from national culture both the people who supposedly necessitated segregation and the people who were most restricted by it. Insisting on the alterity of the "poor white" and the "Southern negro," this explanation of southern apartheid elides its defiance of the purportedly liberal nation-state by questioning whether the populations said to be most intimately involved in racial segregation could, in any case, participate in national democracy. Caldwell's early work implicitly supported such interpretations by locating the region's nonsynchronicity not in its racist social structures but rather in the bodies of his characters. Responding to his work, audiences pictured a poor white society that was retrogressing in devolutionary time, a belief that would also exclude from the nation-state the African Americans who share these peripheral spaces.

The spatial logics of his writing tended to support apartheid despite Caldwell's investment in progressive social change. This author was vociferously opposed to the South's racial practices, and his representations of poor white grotesques did challenge existing understandings of racial hierarchies. In *Tobacco Road*, for example, the Lesters' African American neighbors are seen to institute segregation on their own behalf, watching Ellie May's seduction of Lov from a distance. Though the narrator assures us that these spectators like to talk with "other white people," including Lov himself, they rarely "had anything to say" to the Lesters (25); "straining their necks to see everything," the neighbors, like the reader, recognize the Lesters as grotesques.[82] Nonetheless, these characters share the space of the Lesters, and it seems noteworthy that, in this novel, only African Americans and Lesters get killed. Although, in the brief period covered by the novel, Dude and Jeeter spread a considerable amount of destruction through the countryside, they pose no harm to the merchants, brothel owners, or bureaucrats of Augusta or Fuller, who, on the contrary, successfully exploit the Lesters for entertainment and money. In other words, the Lesters are dangerous only in their own milieu, and though African Americans suffer from their proximity to these people, it seems the inevitable cost of existing in that space.

God's Little Acre implies that the Waldens and the African Americans who farm their land belong together, even though this relationship is clearly exploitative. The Waldens would have no money at all if it were not for sharecroppers. While Ty Ty and his sons dig futilely for gold, Black Sam and Felix farm the rest of the land, the harvest of which provides the Waldens' only income. But Ty Ty is unable to recognize either the sharecroppers' needs as human beings or their value to him as laborers. When Black Sam tells him that he and his family are starving, Ty Ty responds by arguing, "What in the pluperfect hell do you mean by . . . bothering me[?] . . . I'm going off to rope an all-white man tonight [to aid in divining the lode], and I've got to give all my thought to that" (32). In a widely racist nation, then, Ty Ty is further distinguished by his inanity, a trait that Black Sam turns out to share. When Ty Ty's son Shaw assures Black Sam that he will be fed if he "come[s] around to the back door" after the men leave, Black Sam is unable to comprehend his words, overwhelmed by his fear of the "conjur-man" that Ty Ty is bringing to the house (33). The text repeatedly undercuts Ty Ty's suggestions that, as a white person, he possesses greater knowledge and understanding than the sharecroppers, but it does so only to suggest the similarity between them; each, in other words, occupies a similar position of alterity in relation to national norms. While Ty Ty's pretensions to scientific rationality and racial superiority are thus debunked, this move serves only to further the novel's logic of segregation according to cultural difference: "lint-heads" belong in Horse Creek Valley; the Waldens and sharecroppers belong together on the farm; and others, people who can and wish to identify themselves with the national pedagogy of rationality and restraint, belong somewhere else.

This understanding—that those most victimized by these problems were incapable of exercising agency—had high stakes. Southern mill employees had already been neglected by the United Textile Workers' union because it perceived the region as a foreign land in which the relationship between mills and workers was paternalistic,[83] and the New Deal's Agricultural Adjustment Administration, in the belief that its policies could best be administered through landowners, as opposed to laborers, often worsened the economic problems of tenant farmers and sharecroppers.[84]

And yet, with local leadership, both southern agricultural laborers and southern mill workers participated in unionizing themselves and, in some cases, in racially integrating local union meetings.[85]

The forms and sources of these movements might have seemed particularly surprising in light of Caldwell's representations. The relatively deinstitutionalized Holiness Church, for example, obliquely represented in *Tobacco Road* by the inane and self-serving Sister Bessie, served as a site for unionization and protest in the mill town of Elizabethton, North Carolina, and the Southern Tenant Farmer's Union (STFU) found the forms of religious services conducive to increasing union solidarity.[86] Though Caldwell's Will Thompson leads the men of *God's Little Acre* in turning on the mill, the women in that novel—the "girls in love with the spindles"—are figured in sharp contrast to the actual women of Elizabethton, who led the strike in 1929.[87] By 1933, when *God's Little Acre* was published, the women and African Americans who worked in the textile mills were regularly petitioning the National Recovery Administration for assistance in their efforts to procure just pay and working conditions from their employers, and as *Tobacco Road* cemented its hold on the national stage, the multiracial STFU and the allied largely African American Alabama Sharecroppers Union were arguing for the enforcement of labor, interest, and assembly laws; an agricultural minimum wage; the redistribution of old plantation properties; and the establishment of cooperative farms.[88]

These laborers, in their transregional and transracial goals and perspectives, seem inconceivable in relation to the essentially peripheral and unabashedly racist Lesters and Waldens. Unfortunately, the belief that southern agricultural and industrial laborers amounted to Caldwellian grotesques proved an effective tool for those who sought to oppose such reforms. Even an attorney for members of the STFU professed that the sharecropping system destroys the "character" of its laborers, such that they lack "intelligence and force" and "must look outside their ranks for leadership and help."[89] He argued that this social and economic problem—"the most important domestic question before the American people"—could be best resolved through a government-sponsored distribution of property—"a new homestead system"—but his assessment of sharecropper characteristics rendered his position vulnerable; one respondent, writing from a landowner's perspective, mocked the idea that these laborers could become "honest, intelligent, and independent citizen[s]."[90] Conservatives repeatedly mobilized such assessments in political and journalistic venues, insisting that many white and African American farmworkers did not have the capacity for landownership and should rather be subject to compulsory sterilization; the historian Donald Grubbs suggests that this campaign succeeded in deleting provisions for land reform and farmer education from New Deal legislation.[91]

American Abjection

In much psychoanalytic theory, the development of an individual identity depends upon asserting an impossible singularity, denying both the permeability of the body's boundaries (hence Kristeva's emphasis on how certain foods as well as vomit and excrement come to be seen as abject) and the dependency of the infantile body (what Lacan described as humans' "*specific prematurity of birth*").[92] Seeking to mimic the form of others—loved people and even the infant's own reflected image—the infant imaginatively and even physically "break[s] away" from the people and things that necessarily constitute repeated points of contact with the body: "Even before being *like*, 'I' am not but do *separate, reject, abject*."[93] The abject, then, is less a consistent and identifiable substance or object than the source of an affect that is, in Kristeva's argument, never more than partially at bay—the fear of desubjectification. Though this theory of abjection is based on early infant development, it emerges also from social contexts where ideology supports the sense that the boundaries of identity must be maintained, or even "fortified"; accordingly, the abject's threat to identity is "anchored in the superego," which Kristeva, like Freud, links to "Religion, Morality, Law."[94]

Scholars have recently argued that U.S. ideology activates this psychological mechanism in a distinct way. Observing the nation's history of immigration law, for example, Karen Shimakawa notes that the imagined boundaries of the United States are, like those of the psychoanalytic subject, impossible to maintain. Shaped by restrictive cultural norms and a history of racist legal exclusions, as well as an ideology of democratic assimilation and a history of immigration, ideas of U.S. national identity are neither flexibly open nor capable of being securely sealed.[95] Accordingly, "for U.S. Americanness to maintain its symbolic coherence, the national abject continually must be both made present and jettisoned."[96] Where Shimakawa theorizes U.S. abjection through examining Asian American history and experience, Lauren Berlant finds this dynamic at work more broadly, as every encounter with "negatively invested social phenomena" can stage the possibility of exclusion—the loss of a sense of being securely "normal."[97]

Abjection in such accounts is not solely symbolic—occurring at the level of hegemonic national culture and law—but also affective. It transpires, as Berlant argues, in the desires and fears of the individual who longs for and identifies with "abstract America, which foundationally authorizes an elastic language of love and happiness"—much as one loves, in Freudian theory, one's ego ideal, the idealized self-image that serves as the source of group identification and offers itself as compensation for the loss of primary relationships.[98] But just as the loved ego ideal is simultaneously the continuously castigating superego, U.S. national identification, in Berlant's theory, holds a promise perpetually belied by experience of the "abject lived-in United States where suffering takes place and survival is decided locally."[99] Thus abjection is not solely, or even primarily, an action one takes against others: people treated as abject may or may not accept that assessment of their identities.[100] Rather, abjection reflects one's own feeling that the idealized identification to which one clings cannot be secured. This is not to dismiss the damaging effects of symbolic abjection but rather to emphasize that this dynamic is both public and private, taking place at the level of broad cultural and legal representation and at the level of subjective feeling. Abjection constitutes one hinge between U.S. nationalism and the individual psyche, one psychological pattern in which national affiliation offers itself as a source of desire and anxiety.

Writing on the occasion of Caldwell's eightieth birthday, Ralph Ellison described in "An Extravagance of Laughter" the dramatic *Tobacco Road* as a source of his own insight concerning precisely this dynamic (193). In his response to the play, Ellison not only articulates the role of abjection in U.S. social status and social violence but also refrains from participating in that process—an accomplishment in which, as I have shown, he was very nearly alone.[101] Though he argues that Caldwell's comedy provided its Depression-era viewers "with a rationale for locating the irrational both in themselves and in their society," his account of this experience demonstrates why audiences might resist such understanding: he depicts it as "a nightmare in which my personality was split in twain, with the lucid side looking on in wonder while the manic side convulsed my body" (187). Describing his attendance of the play in 1936, Ellison explains that he did not identify with any "civilized humanity" in the Lesters, of which, he argues, they are "denuded," but rather identified with that loss, comparing it to victimization at the hands of white supremacists (184, 186). But in identifying with the abject, he experiences both self-division and concern that he has "demonstrate[d] . . . social unacceptability" (188). Arguing that these dynamics of shame and self-protection constitute "a most American realm of the absurd," Ellison elucidates how the ideologies that seem to secure national identification—spatial, temporal, racial, or cultural—obtain such power in the psyches of citizens.

Ellison argues that U.S. identity requires individuals to produce not an ego but a mask, a performative identity through which to negotiate cultural norms that shift throughout both the geographical space and the chronological time of the nation (163–65). He first attests that such masking is crucial for African Americans, who must use it in order to defy racist stereotypes; here, masking allows subjects to attain greater freedom and assert their individuality. But he then extends this term to describe it as a central aspect in U.S. nationalism: "The American creed of democratic equality encourages the belief. . . . Change your name and increase your chances" (165). In this process, the mask effaces traits that diverge from racialized, regionalized, and gendered models of nationality, such that the individual becomes "Jay Gatsby" instead of "James Gatz," "New Yorker" instead of "Tuskegeian," and gendered in a manner instructed by advertisers. Thus this process of self-creation becomes a process of self-effacement, the success of which is always indeterminate, since one can never know how that "second self" will be valued in "a swiftly changing society" (164).

U.S. cultural norms, then, provide the promise of greater opportunity through conformity, but this compulsion to conform provokes both anxiety and avoidance concerning non-normative traits and interests. For example, reflecting on his efforts in New York to procure maximum freedom of movement—"I found that my air and attitude could offset the inescapable fact of my color"—Ellison argues that this process, though effective and somewhat rewarding, required "a constant state of wariness" (163). And at a further remove, it raises a "more troublesome question" regarding his previous lack of interest in the cultural experiences offered by segregated southern black communities, which, for many of his peers, facilitated "a certain verve and self-possessed fullness." He asks, "To what extent had I overlooked similar opportunities for self-discovery while accepting a definition of possibility laid down by those who would deny me freedom?" (156).

The impossible quest to ensure social status leads not only to individual pain and loss but also to socially destructive behavior, as individuals seek to allay their insecurities through symbolic abjection of others. Ellison argues that, especially "during periods of intense social unrest," privileged subjects attempt to protect the status of their mask through producing "a national mythology in which Negroes were the chief scapegoats" (162). He explains that he witnessed this practice most vividly in the South, where he was "surrounded by whiteness, and it was far from secure in its power"; he argues that "poor and unambitious Southern whites" disavowed this insecurity by denying the humanity of African Americans through intense rhetorical and physical violence, and he presents lynching as an abjectifying ritual (172–78). Ellison describes the southern "god of whiteness" as "insatiable": only through continuous vigilance and violence, in which its worshippers destroy their "identification with the basic *humanity* of their victims," can they ensure their separation from the abjection they feel they may embody, and project it onto their image of other bodies (178). Noting that post–Civil War white southern political power "was used to foil the progress of Negroes in areas far from the geopolitical center of white supremacy," Ellison insists that "American life is of a whole" and represents 1930s southern white supremacy as a ritualized and especially violent form of U.S. identity, in which subjects attempt to eject their own fears of potential nonentity into bodies policed and segregated into clear distinction from their own (175–76, 185).

But Ellison's project, in this essay, is both to recognize this logic of abjection and to challenge it. He demonstrates that, by identifying with abjection, one reveals the indeterminacy through which the abject is defined in the first place. Describing his "cloud-and-dam-burst of laughter" as "violating a whole *encyclopedia* of codes that regulated proper conduct," he claims that his hilarity created an entirely new scene of abjection, as everyone in the theater—audience and actors—paused to look at him (186, 188). His self-consciousness is intensified as he remembers a Tuskegee joke concerning a small town in which, if African Americans felt moved to laugh, they were required to thrust their heads into barrels provided for that purpose (187). The laughing barrels are meant to hide from white southerners the possibility that an oppressed population might have something to laugh about, but the barrels fail to conceal this subversive laughter, which bursts out from all corners of the public square with its Civil War memorial; further, the laugher's amusement at his own circumstances provokes an uproar so intense as to compel white southerners to join in (190, 191). This simultaneous amusement disrupts precisely the assumption that the segregation law was instituted to uphold—the belief that "whites and blacks," because of their essential and ontological difference, "could by no means be expected to laugh at the same things" (192). Thus, as he describes contemplating and engaging in such laughter, Ellison amplifies his theory of abjection with the crucial observation that, though the source of violence and oppression, it does not successfully effect an understanding of the world. Those who wish to believe themselves the embodiment of social norms are continually confronted with challenges to that view. Such defiance arises even from their own recognition that the abjection they seek to project onto others may circulate back to them. Accordingly, the white people of the town suspect that "the Negro involved was not only laughing at *himself* laughing, but was also laughing at *them* laughing at his laughing against their own most determined wills" (191).

Ellison's retrospective response to *Tobacco Road* is a virtuoso performance, situating the play in relation to its performance context, Ellison's biographical experiences of racial oppression and regional immigration, his feelings about his own process of self-fashioning, a social and psychological analysis of both apartheid and consumer culture, and African American folklore. It demonstrates, with extravagance, a possibility that Kenneth Burke suggested in regard to Caldwell's fiction: "Precisely by omitting humaneness where humaneness is most called for, he may stimulate the reader to supply it."[102] (Burke nonetheless "suspect[ed] that, in putting the responsibility upon his readers, [Caldwell] is taking more out of the community pile than he puts in."[103]) But while the insights provided in "An Extravagance of Laughter" are decidedly Ellison's own, they suggest the degree to which Caldwell's depiction of isolated and abjected southern whites resonated with a range of anxieties and experiences in the Depression-era United States.

Ellison does not participate in the chorus proclaiming southern poor white alterity, though he acknowledges that, while living in the South, he was "tempted to armor [him]self against their threat by denying them *their* humanity as they sought to deny" his (166). Instead, he focuses on the degree to which abjection is indeterminate and reversible, such that people who have been deemed peripheral to national culture reinterpret the norms of that culture for their own entertainment. Accordingly, Ellison imagines himself back at an Oklahoma barbershop, listening to people who "insist[ed] upon being themselves . . . engage in a long discussion of Mr. John D. Rockefeller Senior's . . . whiskey . . . fancy women . . . and 'yard chillun' " (164, 195). In the historian Nikhil Pal Singh's terms, Ellison represents "a black counter-public" with "its own *independent* frameworks of normative judgment, lines of debate, and social action."[104]

But while Ellison represents this scene as an admirable moment of creativity and cultural pride, he also emphasizes its status as a cultural form that is emerging from the periphery, explaining that storytellers were, in these tales, seeking "to make the world conform to the narrow compass of their own hopes and dreams" (196). Though he values such expression, Ellison seems to have difficulty imagining how it could exist in anything but isolation from the ideological center that it critiques, a tension that, as I suggest in chapter 7, emerges also in the critical, playful, and folkloric grotesquerie of *Invisible Man*. In "An Extravagance of Laughter," Ellison represents this sense of incompatibility between African American vernacular culture and national norms as vital to the "conflict" he felt regarding his own regional background; considering the possibility that the desire to escape apartheid might necessitate forgoing attachments to southern African American culture, he describes feeling "unease" (197). In the next chapter, I argue that this tension powerfully influenced African American aesthetics during the 1920s and 1930s, particularly the response to and the concerns of Zora Neale Hurston.

CHAPTER FOUR

Zora Neale Hurston and the Chronotope of the Folk

WIDELY CELEBRATED FOR resisting racism by depicting holistic, communal values within southern African American culture, Zora Neale Hurston has also been denounced for representing the "folk" in a way that accommodated a nation quick to exploit people who had been marginalized from economic development. But despite their opposition, both of these interpretations tend to situate the worlds inscribed in Hurston's work outside national modernity. Instead, critics characterize the space of her fictions as "mythic," "spiritual," "nostalgic," or "antihistorical."[1] This chapter argues that such debates demonstrate a difficulty that Hurston herself confronted as she sought to negotiate the imagined divide between national and regional African American cultures. She wrote about communities depicted in much U.S. discourse through racist stereotypes, and her white audiences were all too ready to consider as primitive the settings that she represented.[2] Northern African American readers, though deeply concerned about the political and cultural effects of such beliefs, also doubted the contemporaneity of the South, which was notorious for its racial oppression. Even as much African American writing from the 1920s and 1930s suggested that folk culture offered the attraction of an authentic racial community, that allure was often represented as uncanny—a dangerous nostalgia for an experience inaccessible to modern subjects and, furthermore, inextricably linked to racist exploitation.

Thus Hurston encountered a problem shared by many nonmetropolitan modernists—the question, as Andreas Huyssen describes it, of how to represent "the modernity of the geographically 'non-modern.'"[3] Further, Hurston did so in a national context in which beliefs concerning southern backwardness underwrote African American disfranchisement. *Mules and Men*, Hurston's 1935 collection of southern African American folklore and hoodoo practices, implicitly addresses this problem by representing the possibility of reconciling folk and modern cultural forms in individual experience. However, in suggesting the viability of the former within modernity, Hurston devotes no attention to the requirement that, for black southerners to receive political and economic justice, the region's social structure had to change, a process that might alter segregated African American communities. This tension emerges in Hurston's 1937 novel, *Their Eyes Were Watching God*, which suggests that black southern culture was increasingly influenced by bourgeois U.S. ideology. In representing this transition, Hurston provides for the preservation of folkloric values by incorporating them into the modern self-fashioning of her individuated protagonist. Through this logic, however, the novel displaces the enforced racial segregation of the South with the voluntary isolation of folkloric practice.

"The Old and the New Negro"

In the foreword to his influential *New Negro* anthology, Alain Locke claims that the "essential forces" responsible for "social change and progress" are to be found "in the very heart of the folk-spirit"; he thus mobilizes the concept of a traditional and stable population—the folk—in order to suggest the depth, or "inner life," of an "emergent nationalit[y]."[4] Despite his celebration of African American heritage, however, his teleology is resolutely focused on contemporary and coming changes—the increased demand and opportunity for African American "self-expression" and "self-determination" (xxv, xxvii). In describing this national movement, the anthology as a whole describes the temporality of a capitalist modernity, in which time is understood as the dimension of progress.[5] From Locke's description of the "New Negro"—a "new figure on the national canvas" with a "new vision of opportunity, of social and economic freedom"—to W. E. B. Du Bois's account of the "modern black American" who was leading the efforts to "give black folk a knowledge of modern culture," writers emphasize that African Americans are experiencing a "hectic period of transition," a "constant growth of group consciousness," a "rapid development . . . of the race life," and the increasing influence of the "typical spirit and push of modern industrialism in America."[6] Furthermore, these writers depict the simultaneity of these developments across such distinct spaces as Harlem; Durham, North Carolina; and Tuskegee, Alabama; in this way, the anthology inscribes a modern national community in which individuals, though unacquainted and spatially distanced, recognize themselves as working together in homogeneous linear time to pursue shared goals.[7]

In describing the rapidity of this modernization, however, the anthology also demonstrates the paradoxical nature of modern time: though it may be understood to be uniform across space, not all subjects in all spaces are understood to participate in it uniformly. One feature of late modernity is the fascination of modernizing societies with their own newness and speed; concomitantly, such societies tend to understand cultures in which change occurs more slowly as fundamentally different from their own.[8] In his contribution to *The New Negro*, for instance, Charles S. Johnson depicts the Great Migration as a movement toward modernity by people bearing the "marks of backward cultures."[9] He argues that the space of the South is characterized by both a different developmental era and a different experience of time: in contrast to the ever-modernizing city, where life is experienced as "feverish struggle," rural life is constituted by "slow move[ment]" and a lack of change (278, 291). This account understands certain spaces to exist outside modernity and outside the progress described elsewhere in the collection. Even Locke, though he sought to describe a national, unified African American community, could not avoid the inscription of temporal difference. He argues that "the migrant masses, shifting from countryside to city, hurdle several generations of experience at a leap," a leap that signifies "a deliberate flight . . . from medieval America to modern."[10]

Such analyses reflect an anxiety that Kenneth Warren has detected in African American writing of this era—the difficulty of maintaining an "imaginative contemporaneity" between urban, educated elites and rural societies.[11] This problem is exemplified in W. E. B. Du Bois's contribution to *The New Negro*, "The Negro Mind Reaches Out," a study of transnational capitalism and imperialism, which single out for exploitation cultures characterized by both a slower tempo—allowing time for "leisure" and "contemplation"—and an absence of Western science and technology—an education "far behind modern knowledge" (410). Suggesting that transnational economic and social analysis vitally supports efforts to redress the injustices facing colonized peoples, Du Bois also points to a factor that mitigates against such inquiry—the sense that "the modern black American" and the global "black folk" inhabit different temporalities (385, 413). Emphasizing the importance of spreading "a knowledge of modern culture," he seems motivated not only by the belief that such knowledge is useful in challenging capitalist exploitation but also by a conviction that shared temporal references are needed in order to construct a global racial community from which defiance might arise—a "great human force . . . reaching out hands toward each other to know, to sympathize, to inquire" (412–13). In contemporary theoretical terms, we might say that, for this sharing to occur, participants must be able to envision a coeval community, one whose members "share the same Time."[12]

But many African American writers were unable to imagine such a racial community's extending even across the United States; rather, they perceived a temporal distance separating the North and the South. George S. Schuyler, for example, complained that African America could not be articulated strictly through reference to the folk because such formulations elided the modernity of northern African Americans. Arguing in a 1926 essay that the culture of the "peasantry of the South" is foreign to other members of the diaspora, he anticipates present-day theories of nationalism by explaining that northern African American life is not only similar to, but also simultaneous with, that of northern white Americans: "The Aframerican" turns off his "Connecticut alarm clock" and sits down to "a breakfast similar to that eaten by his white brother across the street," before going to work "in mills, mines, factories, and commerce," responding "to the same political, social, moral, and economic stimuli . . . as his white neighbor."[13] In his representation of a racially integrated national community, however, Schuyler is unable to include members of the "southern peasant class," who, in his discussion, exemplify temporal alterity (52).

It is not surprising that writers would find it difficult to conceive of the South as participating in national modernity. During this period, white southerners vigilantly enforced laws and social practices that perpetuated a pre–Civil War social structure, a policy that further contributed to the South's notorious economic stagnation. Nonetheless, these formulations of northern modernity and southern medievalism are notable for their rigidity. In contrast, Du Bois's 1903 *The Souls of Black Folk* had argued that all African Americans experience multiple temporal forms, both because African Americans' political and economic activities are restricted and because, particularly in the South, many African Americans maintain traditional cultural forms. But while Du Bois represents this doubled temporal identification as a painful result of racist oppression, he also suggests that it offers some benefits—most notably, for him, a perspective from which to critique the excesses of modernization (8, 57). As the century progressed, however, writers seem increasingly to have doubted that individuals could productively manage the experience of temporal multiplicity. Thus, while discussions of black aesthetics often "had at their foundation the valorization of some notion of the African American folk," as J. Martin Favor argues, this attraction to southern black cultural forms and expressions did not necessarily constitute a sense of transregional political and social affiliation.[14]

Instead, many black intellectuals suggested that the differences between folk and modern culture were so great—in terms of values, practices, and experience—that the shift between them could prove confusing, or even devastating, to the individual subject. Thus discourse concerning migrants' alleged "social pathology" was rooted in beliefs about temporal difference; Charles S. Johnson, for example, held that southern African Americans who moved to northern cities would eventually engage in criminal and self-destructive behaviors because they could no longer rely on the "packets of stored up memories marking out channels of conduct" that had served them before they moved to northern cities.[15] Because he understands southern African American identity to be constituted by the continuing influence of individual and cultural pasts—memories and "assorted heritages and old loyalties"—he imagines that, once separated from the sensory landscape and social reminders of these pasts, migrants will be overwhelmed by their "totally new experiences" (291, 293). Not only are migrants separated from the signs of their individual and cultural heritage, in Johnson's argument, but they are also forced to experience the flow of time differently: "temperament[ally]" adjusted to rural life, southern African Americans are newly exposed to the "tension of city life," which produces "growing nervous disorders" even among those accustomed to urban culture.[16] He fears that "disillusionment" must "inevitably" result (288).

Historians have since argued that northern African American elites overstated their differences from migrants.[17] This choice has been attributed to bourgeois elitism and racial assimilationism, as well as to concerns that, in a white racist logic of association, black northerners' status would be diminished by proximity to people who maintained southern cultural forms distorted and mocked by minstrel stereotypes and who had experienced southern forms of oppression.[18] The latter qualms were justified. While studying the effects of the Great Migration on northern cities, for example, Louise Venable Kennedy noted that when African American children from underfunded, segregated southern schools were placed in lower grades to catch up with northern schoolchildren, white school officials cast the southern children's difficulties as evidence of a "high rate of retardation among Negro children" and of the necessity of northern racial segregation.[19] But in developing theories of migrant "pathology," black urban elites may also have been expressing anxieties that emerged from their own encounters with cultural differences.

The Great Migration placed African American migrants and northern residents in contact with a regional difference that appears to have seemed, on occasion, difficult to negotiate—not least because it was so often subsumed under the banner of racial similarity. As Hazel Carby argues, "The twenties must be viewed as a period of ideological, political, and cultural contestation between an emergent black bourgeoisie and an emerging urban black working class," many members of which had migrated from the South and vigorously promoted their own "conceptions of the physical and social world."[20] As southern African Americans began to reshape northern cities, long-time residents may have feared not only the loss of their social position but also disruption of the cultural frameworks through which they understood and experienced self and society. In certain fictional representations from the 1920s, at least, "folk-time" seems dangerous, both as one component of a white supremacist regional temporality and as an uncannily pleasurable experience of time, one that compensates so precisely for the alienating effects of modern individualism and urbanization that it might lure northern African Americans into temporarily overlooking the more threatening aspects of southern life.

Even Jean Toomer's *Cane*, a 1923 work that celebrates folk culture as a medium through which to contemplate African American heritage, suggests that too deep an immersion in this contemporary manifestation of the past must prove destructive to a modern, urban subjectivity. Ralph

Kabnis, recently arrived in Georgia from New York, is both fascinated by the time of the South, which he understands to be infused with a religious and historic African American culture, and troubled by its experiential difference from that of the northern cities he knows: "hours, hours north, why not say a lifetime north? . . . New York? Impossible. It was a fiction."[21] He attempts to forestall his confusion by arguing that the difference between contiguous regions cannot be so great but learns he is mistaken from the story of Mame Lamkins, a pregnant woman whose lynchers, removing her fetus and finding it still alive, "stuck it t a tree" (92). Situated in a society terrorized by white supremacist violence, Kabnis is doubly alienated because he believes he is immersed in a temporality incommensurable with his own. When he fears that he, too, has been threatened, Kabnis first loses his understanding of measured, calendrical time, believing that he has been transposed into a nineteenth-century scene (94). Soon his sense of social time is displaced by a subjective, imaginary time: he begins to see the South itself as a dream (105). Ultimately, Kabnis is trapped in his own subjectivity, in which he is tortured by the sense of both stagnation and incessant craving. Fixated on a form "burned int [his] soul" and demanding endless attention, refusing to "stay still unless [he] feed[s] it" (111), he identifies with both Mame Lamkins and her lynched fetus. Unable to withstand this metaphorical pregnancy that can never come to term, Kabnis "wish[es] t God some lynchin white man ud stick his knife through [his soul] an pin it to a tree. An pin it to a tree."

A similar danger, emerging within Harlem, is represented in Nella Larsen's 1928 novel, *Quicksand*, in which the modern, cosmopolitan Helga Crane is paralyzed by an encounter with southern migrants' cultural practices. At the moment when she encounters a folk religious service, Helga has reached a crisis: having suffered a "tantalizing oppression of loneliness and isolation" all her life, she has recently been rebuffed by a man whose presence had always produced in her a "longing for sympathy and understanding."[22] Wandering the streets of Harlem until a storm drives her into a migrants' revival (137), she is initially repulsed but becomes fascinated by the way the migrant women's bodies seem to evoke past temporalities. She is first greeted by a mammylike "grotesque ebony figure" who "croon[s]" over her, saying, "Yes, chile, yes, chile" (140). This figure constitutes an Old South stereotype, but as the service progresses, a "wild, ecstatic fury" develops, until the women's "writhings and weepings" become "almost Bacchic"; at the peak of the service, they seem "like reptiles" (140, 141, 142). These women embody not only the African American past that Kabnis sees in the soil of *Cane* but that of all evolution. Observing these folk, whose songs remind Helga of a song she heard "years ago—hundreds of years, it seems," she fears she may become entangled in, or infected by, their atavism: "She remained motionless, watching, as if she lacked the strength to leave the place . . . with its mixture of breaths, its contact of bodies, its concerted convulsions, all in wild appeal for a single soul. Her soul" (139, 141). Both her fears and her desires for a communal experience are realized: "She felt herself possessed. . . . Time seemed to sink back into the mysterious grandeur and holiness of far-off simpler centuries" (142). Helga loses her sense of self in her attraction to this promise of serenity and abandons the independence and love of "nice things" previously so important to her (41); she marries a southern minister she meets at the service and returns to the South, where she is "used up" by childbearing, housework, and the duties of a minister's wife (150, 148).

Critical writing from the early 1930s suggests that northern African Americans' anxiety concerning folk culture was impeding efforts to theorize a politically active national-racial community. Literary critics urged writers to challenge perceptions that a temporal distance separated northern and southern African Americans. Sterling Brown complained that African American intellectuals avoided southern and rural topics, and Alain Locke called for representations that would enable readers to imagine the possibility of bridging the apparent temporal divide between North and South—revealing "a common denominator between the old and the new Negro."[23] Concerns about southern African American culture were fueled by the many sociological reports on southern sharecropping released at this time. Charles S. Johnson, for example, argued in 1934 that the "Black Belt" constituted a peasant society and described as "fixed" and "complete" folk "accommodation" to both African Americans' economic status and to local white supremacist practices.[24] Faced with such representations, writers for African American periodicals located in New York began to wonder whether poor southern African Americans were prepared to seek political and economic equality or whether the circumstances of their lives had rendered them "too apathetic to condemn and rend apart the system which has kept them shackled."[25]

Notably, some Harlem Renaissance writers charged Hurston herself with accommodationism and associated her with minstrel stereotypes, a representation to which she referred decades later while taking a truly controversial stand against southern school desegregation.[26] But while she was accused of portraying, in performance and prose, "darkies [who] always smiled through their tears," Hurston described such representations, still prominently influenced by the tradition of the plantation romance, as misleading.[27] And though some of Hurston's work from the 1930s seems determined to defend southern African American culture against a potentially corrupting modernization, such concerns acknowledge the influence of material and social change.[28] Contradicting Alain Locke, who described "folk traditions" as the "deep resources of the past," Hurston famously argued, "Negro folklore is not a thing of the past. It is still in the making."[29] In contrast to many of her contemporaries, then, Hurston repeatedly insisted on the coevality of southern African American culture. Finally, though Hurston's political beliefs were unquestionably complicated, they comprised not a consistent conservatism but rather a continuing and dynamic ambivalence concerning the effects of modernization in southern African American communities.

Folklore's Temporalities

Debates about *Mules and Men* often reflect anxiety regarding the role of folklore and its representations in a rapidly changing capitalist society. As the folklorist Roger Abrahams argues, romantic celebrations of folklore often depict it as the cultural expression of "simple conservative agrarian peoples," individuals who might not seem to share modern cultural experiences and interpretive frameworks.[30] As I have shown, such dynamics were already prominent in representations of the poor in the southern United States. Even writers sympathetic to the plight of sharecroppers and tenant farmers described their circumstances in terms of peonage and peasantry, language that suggested the uncanny existence of past social structures—slavery and feudalism—within a modernizing nation. However aptly such terms described the oppression confronting southern laborers, authors who used such language did not encourage their readers to imagine possibilities for such workers to participate in shared political protest or alliance. Thus progressive folklorists, if not carefully attuned to the political valences of their work, ran the risk of supporting poor southerners' temporal marginalization.

Such concerns were particularly important in relation to Hurston's work, as racist stereotypes of southern African Americans labeled them primitive or backward, suggesting that they were unbothered by political and economic discrimination. Such representations were rife in some white southerners' collections of purported African American folklore. For example, Roark Bradford's *John Henry* (1931), which was published while Hurston was working on *Mules and Men*, denied both the difficulty of the labor performed by black southerners and the desire to challenge injustice. The protagonist ludicrously proclaims, "Efn they's nigger blood in yo' fingers de cotton will stick and follow," and further refuses to complain when he is jailed, and all his friends sentenced, as part of whites' efforts to secure more workers.[31] Noting that Bradford's earlier work served as a source for Marc Connelly's Pulitzer-winning play, *Green Pastures* (1930), yet another popular but stereotypical representation of African Americans, Sterling Brown remarked that "the author [was] considered, in some circles, a valid interpreter of *the* Negro"; complaining of this dangerous trend in U.S. literature, Brown argued that *John Henry* "ma[de] over a folk-hero into a clown."[32]

Hurston's work combated such representations in many ways. Most important is that the folkloric performances in *Mules and Men* challenge the political implications of Bradford's work, as Hurston's workers repeatedly describe—often using the plots and tropes of folklore—economic exploitation and competition. David Nicholls, examining the frames and the tales themselves, argues that Hurston depicts folklore as a form of "everyday resistance . . . in the Jim Crow South."[33] But she also implicitly challenged Bradford's authority by disputing the role of "John Henry" in African American tales. Bradford's collection, though it contains no contextualizing information, presents this figure as an icon, but *Mules and Men* argues that "*John Henry* . . . occupies the same place in Negro folklore that Casey Jones does in white lore and if anything is more recent."[34]

Notably, this single reference presents folklore as a highly mobile cultural form, one that traverses not only racial groups but also cultural media.[35] Believed to have been written by an African American engine worker, William Saunders, after a 1900 train wreck, the ballad "Casey Jones" demonstrated a point that Hurston made elsewhere—with some disapprobation—concerning the cross-racial influence of African American culture.[36] The folklorist E. C. Perrow, who collected numerous versions of this ballad from southern areas in the early twentieth century, identified some with "mountain whites," some with "negroes," and several with question marks.[37] But "Casey Jones" also traveled further via the recording industry: many of Hurston's readers may have been familiar with the version recorded in 1927 by the popular "hillbilly band" called "The Skillet Lickers," whose styles and repertoires further reflected influences by white and African American folk music as well as blues, jazz, and Tin Pan Alley.[38]

But though *Mules and Men* rebutted Bradford's work through content, form, and historicization, several of Hurston's contemporaries argued that she lacked awareness of the period's racial politics. Sterling Brown, for example, complained that her work lacked the "bitterness" inescapable in southern African American life and labeled the work "pastoral."[39] Praising her knowledge of the "rare native material and local color," Alain Locke nonetheless argued that the locale, as she presents it, is "too Arcadian," even "extinct."[40] Since Hurston's subjects often, through their folktales, describe the impact of white supremacist oppression on their lives, these interpretations seem to depend on the narrator's lack of political commentary. The Marxist folklorist Harold Preece complained, for example, that Hurston did not "cast [her] lot with the folk."[41] But discussion of Hurston's own political agenda would not necessarily have led critics to recognize the contemporaneity of Hurston's Floridians. On the contrary, as Rosemary Hathaway argues, "if Hurston had wielded her anthropological authority more overtly," she might more readily have been accused of denying southern African Americans' coevality.[42] When Preece, for example, argued that southern African Americans must transform their "archaic" cultural forms for political activism, he precluded the possibility that they already share the temporality of those researching their lore.[43]

Much of *Mules and Men*, in contrast, challenges the depiction of the folk as backward. Despite the narrator's stated interest in "old-time tales," Hurston represents folk cultural forms as flexible and vital (8). As Brian Carr and Tova Cooper note, Hurston seems to raise the concern that it might soon be too late to collect folklore threatened by social change only so that she may repeatedly affirm that there is "no danger of that."[44] Rather, in accord with her statements elsewhere, she represents a form of cultural expression that was changing so rapidly that no collector could keep up with it. Of the songs included in *Mules and Men*, one, "Ella Wall," is so new as to be based on a character in the text itself (150). Many tales are hotly contested, as audience members accuse the tellers of creating "the lie" themselves or indicate that they heard it differently (30, 69, 96, 98, 105). Because this lore is framed in a context of conflict, interchange, and alteration, it cannot be understood to comprise finished artifacts.

Compared with the stagnating peasantry of Johnson's *Shadow of the Plantation*, in fact, Hurston's folk appear to be surprisingly modern: where Johnson focuses strictly on the sharecroppers and tenant farmers of a county in the Alabama Cotton Belt, Hurston's folklore comes mainly from wage laborers in a lumber mill. Nor are her folk strictly rural: the second section of the book takes place mainly in New Orleans, and Hurston's narrator claims that her subjects in central Florida came from "all over the South" and that they often move between city and country (60). Hurston's southern African Americans differ further from Johnson's in that they do not rely on the "paternalism" of a "protecting white family"[45]; Hurston's sawmill workers recognize the white "boss" as wielding undue legal and economic authority, and find it "noble" when one of their number stands up to "dat cracker" (152). Perhaps most important, these folk are linked to the national economy through both production—the log train around which labor in the Polk County lumber mill is organized (69)—and consumption—the "mail-order dresses" worn by southern African American women at social events (63).

And yet the text does not emphasize the modernity of these southern African Americans; on the contrary, the opening frame of the narrative implies that Eatonvillians themselves would deny the coevality of other regions. Hurston, as narrator, suggests that if she were to flaunt her college education, the townspeople she had known from childhood would criticize her inauthenticity, sending her "word in a match-box that I had been up North there and had rubbed the hair off my head against some college wall, and then come back there with a lot of form and fashion and outside show to the world" (2). In many ways, this statement seems typical of Hurston's approach: always scornful of those who prefer the "Glee Club style" of spirituals to that sung in "some unfashionable Negro church," or of those who prefer the Broadway productions with African American casts to the "real Negro theatre" in the "Jooks and the cabarets," here she represents a community that turns such values on their heads.[46] Still, this formulation from *Mules and Men* seems to place the folk in a different typological time from that of the North; rejecting its "sham-polish," and uninterested in education, they seem isolated from the modernizing nation (2). As Hazel Carby points out, the text ignores the Great Migration, at a time when movement to the North and to cities constituted one of the largest factors of change in African American life; this omission further emphasizes the isolation of Hurston's folk.[47] *Mules and Men* contains no mention of the many residents of Eatonville who probably had left; on the contrary, Hurston's narrator expresses "delight" on crossing the township line into Eatonville and seeing that "the town had not changed" (7).

But despite these temporally isolating tendencies, Hurston's text is nevertheless structured to emphasize experiences in which she and other Floridians share in the same time. Though much of the early narrative represents the attempts of Hurston the anthropologist to fit in with the communities she is studying, the later "lying sessions," framed in the context of work, relaxation, or fishing, are rendered with a nearly transparent narrator, so that the reader can experience a sort of vicarious contact with Hurston's ethnographic subjects.[48] By representing her participation in the lives of the folk, then, Hurston shows the intersection of multiple temporalities in her own experience. In the narrator, we see the temporality of the folk mapped onto that of the highway—the simultaneous, cross-space time in which Hurston speeds from New York to Eatonville (4). In addition, we see the unclocked time of the lying session, which ends only when one participant has "mumbled down into his shirt bosom and [gone] to sleep" (19, 3); the ambivalently marked time of the "shack rouser," who gets paid to see that workers do not miss a minute of labor and yet announces, instead of the hour, the time of the breaking day, hoe-cake, and rooster (66–67); the clearly transregional clock time of the laborer who is a "half hour behind schedule" (68); and the exaggerated lying time of "forty o'clock" (10). Most notable, perhaps, is Hurston's juxtaposition of clock time with the transcendent timelessness of hoodoo, when she lies naked, facedown, on a snakeskin, waiting "sixty-nine hours" while her "spirit went wherever spirits must go that seek answers never given to men as men" (199).

Here, Hurston describes the spectacle of herself in what seems an incommensurable intersection of temporalities—the modern social scientist in a hoodoo trance. She does not allow the reader to discount either of these temporal frames: her prose here is particularly detailed and objective, yet she assures us that, during this episode, she had "five psychic experiences." Such narrative is largely absent from "Hoodoo in America," her *Journal of American Folklore* article on which she based the second part of *Mules and Men*; this earlier work includes more anthropological commentary—comparing, for instance, hoodoo and obeah—but far less of Hurston's own experience with hoodoo—describing even the ceremony of the Black Cat Bone as if she had never seen it.[49] In *Mules and Men*, however, Hurston represents this ceremony as the most uncanny experience of her study—producing "indescribable noises, sights, feelings"—but she is not so overwhelmed as to reject the results—"a small white bone for me to carry" (221). In depicting her own reconciliation to even this "unearthly terror"—a reconciliation impossible to imagine in, for instance, the work of Toomer or Larsen—Hurston suggests that the widely perceived temporal distance between northern and southern experience is not, in fact, such a radical disjuncture.

In this way, Hurston's ethnography quietly disrupts notions of an unbridgeable southern temporal difference. In *Mules and Men*, she shows both the South as a region and the cultures of its African American residents to be comprehensible, if not automatically open, to modern subjects. Hurston does not stress the political possibilities inherent in this understanding of a permeable folk culture already influenced by and commensurable within the framework of modernization; instead, she focuses on the sharing of folkloric expression. However, by contradicting earlier representations that suggested such pleasures must necessarily unsettle the temporal frameworks of modern subjects, and offering in their place a model of subjectivity that allows for the interaction of multiple cultural forms, she provides an understanding of southern African American culture that could enable readers to imagine transregional interaction and, accordingly, transregional political activism.

This reading of *Mules and Men* is not easily reconciled, however, with Hurston's 1937 novel, *Their Eyes Were Watching God*, which often seems to represent modernization as inimical to folkloric practice. It is notable that Hurston wrote this novel in Haiti, where she was conducting research for *Tell My Horse: Voodoo and Life in Haiti and Jamaica* (1938), a volume that suggests a shift in Hurston's thinking about modernization.

Where *Mules and Men* represents communities that participate in modernity while deriving pleasure and sustenance from folk culture, *Tell My Horse* associates folkloric practice with isolation and the lack of political and economic resources. Even when visiting the Maroons at Accompong, whom she described to the Guggenheim Foundation as "exactly the kind of isolated community many folklorists hope to discover," Hurston asks about their attitudes toward "education, transportation, public health and democracy"; describing their government as "very primitive," she explains that their leader "wished to bring things up to date" and depicts her own contribution to this process in building the society's first stove.[50] Invoking rhetoric recognizable from Locke's contributions to the *New Negro*, she speaks of societal problems as holdovers from the past that are not yet removed— the Ku Klux Klan and Sect Rouge "still" linger in the United States and Haiti, respectively (483).

I argue in the next section that, as Hurston's anthropological work began to promote modernization in African Caribbean contexts, her fiction explored the emotional responses that might emerge from concomitant cultural change. A direct opposition between these nearly simultaneous texts highlights this difference: where *Tell My Horse* argues that a focus on past glories can inhibit needed political change in the present, distinguishing "dreamer[s]" from "heroes" and claiming that the latter are "m[e]n of action," *Their Eyes Were Watching God* opens with a meditation on the former.[51] The novel suggests that most people have little control over whether they will ever possess the objects of their desires and claims that individuals seek to locate such goods in the realm of their own imaginations. Men watch the "horizon" for their "ship" to come in, and women arrange their pasts to suit themselves, so that "the dream is the truth."[52] This passage configures both space and time in a way that displaces their social and historical dynamics, focusing instead on a stylized subjective view. Such an emphasis can yield apolitical interpretations, fueling the charges of accommodationism that have trailed Hurston's reputation. Accordingly, reminding readers of the need to recognize time as a venue for social and political change, Hazel Carby has argued influentially that Hurston's oeuvre "attempt[s] to stabilize and displace the social contradictions and disruption of her contemporary moment" by "privileg[ing] the nostalgic and freez[ing] it in time."[53]

But the novel's psychological focus should not be mistaken for a denial of social change. On the contrary, *Their Eyes Were Watching God* is centrally concerned with modernization, and its folkloric representations, as Daphne Lamothe argues, constitute a "means of comprehending transformation."[54] But Hurston's attitude toward such changes is ambivalent: despite her history of embracing liberal nationalism and her increasing interest in economic development, Hurston was deeply aware that each incorporated practices especially discriminatory to southern African Americans.[55] Further, though *Their Eyes Were Watching God* does explore possibilities for preserving folkloric expressions and practices, it also manifests considerable concern that oppressive institutions and ideologies could use folk cultural forms to further their own ends. Rather than imagining that a culture could remain static in time, then, *Their Eyes Were Watching God* seeks to imagine and inscribe a way to manage the losses that social change must entail. Paradoxically, it retains a vision of folkloric pleasure, typically associated with social performance and sharing, within a bourgeois form given to individual consumption—that of the novel.

Modernization and Mourning

Their Eyes Were Watching God not only represents the transformations that occur in its protagonist, Janie Crawford Killicks Starks Woods, but also focuses on changes in physical environment and societal structure. Several critics have noted the novel's allusions, in plot and imagery, to tropes from Vodou, Yoruba, Egyptian, Greek, and Babylonian cultures that describe transition, loss, and regeneration; as Henry Louis Gates argues, Hurston's novel also contains numerous metaphors that she elsewhere described as characteristic of African American "oral narration."[56] In some cases, her mythic and folkloric tropes describe a natural environment responsive to characters' moods and desires. As Janie describes her harrowing experiences to her friend Pheoby, for example, "the kissing, young darkness became a monstropolous old thing"; famously, Janie's intimacy with nature is so powerful that she learns about human sexuality from observing a pear tree in bloom.[57] But more uncanny transformations often imply changes involved in modernization. For example, when Joe Starks, as the mayor of Eatonville, begins acquiring bourgeois status symbols, the narrative, focalized through the townspeople, argues, "It was like seeing your sister turn into a 'gator. A familiar strangeness. You keep seeing your sister in the 'gator and the 'gator in your sister, and you'd rather not" (48). Later, the movement of Lake Okeechobee suggests the natural world's retribution against a society that sought to "chain" it: in the perception of the laborers farming its floodplain, it becomes a "senseless monster" "roll[ing] and complain[ing] like a peevish world on a grumble" (158). Incorporating multiple folkloric traditions, then, the novel critically engages modernization.

Critics have not consistently noticed the prominence of this theme, in part because the novel's chronotope—literally, time-space—often appears allotemporal, existing outside that of the nation and its economy.[58] Where *Mules and Men* represents the intersection of multiple temporal forms within an encompassing chronotope, *Their Eyes Were Watching God* imagines more limited spaces, and even these diverge from the spatial interests most common in African American literature of this time; unlike protagonists of Great Migration narratives, Janie, in pursuing the horizon, generally goes south.[59] The communities in which she lingers are discrete and somewhat insular; for example, the residents of Eatonville, in central Florida, seem utterly uninformed of the disastrous effects of the hurricane on southern Florida.[60] Even more than the spaces in which Janie resides, her cyclical conception of time seems removed from the linear time of the nation-state; at the beginning of her story, for instance, she waits "a bloom time, and a green time and an orange time."[61] Thus the novel seems strenuously to separate southern African Americans from the political institutions that restricted their rights, a move for which Hurston has often been criticized. Richard Wright, for example, argued that Hurston's characters "swing like a pendulum eternally in that safe and narrow orbit in which America likes to see the Negro live: between laughter and tears."[62] In other words, to the extent that readers accepted the novel as a realistic representation of southern African American life, they would see a culture utterly removed from that of the nation-state and so focused on its own interactions (and, in Wright's account, emotions) that it might have little interest in political and economic justice.[63]

Despite her folkloric ideals, however, Janie is not uninterested in her rights or the larger world; after waiting a year in an oppressive marriage, for example, she "look[s] up the road" (25). But even as the novel depicts Janie's travels to the "big 'ssociation of life," it isolates the wisdom she has gained from the community to which she returns (6). Although she tells her story to her friend Pheoby (and, in part, to the reader), Janie ultimately avows that "you got tuh *go* there tuh *know* there . . . nobody else can't tell yuh and show yuh" (192). This final speech suggests, in Carby's argument, that the folk might be incapable of learning about "what is outside of its social consciousness."[64] Indeed, Janie's isolationism at the close of the novel can hardly be questioned: eschewing the communities of both Eatonville and the "muck," she creates a chronotope of the self, one in which she negotiates time and space to her own satisfaction, "pull[ing] in her horizon like a great fish-net," creating an individualized, imaginative space in which events from her past return to "sob and sigh, singing and sobbing" (192–93).

This metaphor may suggest one reason why Hurston's approach to folklore is so individualistic and psychological here: observing references to the horizon throughout Hurston's oeuvre, Claudia Tate argues that they suggest desire for reunion with Hurston's mother, who died "at sundown" when her daughter was only thirteen.[65] Though Lucy Potts Hurston appears to have encouraged her daughter's creativity and ambition, her death left Zora without a reliable supporter, advocate, or even home. Accordingly, Tate explains that, in pursuing a career as a folklorist and writer, Hurston sought both to fulfill her mother's wishes for her success and to "preserv[e] the folklore of her mother's speech community."⁶⁶ But as Tate notes, Lucy Hurston's stance toward folkloric traditions was ambivalent; the younger Hurston wrote that for years after her mother's death, she agonized about her inability to prevent others in the community from enacting the final rituals that Lucy had not wanted.⁶⁷ These feelings may help to explain the confining metaphor that Hurston used to describe her early relationship with folklore—"it was fitting me like a tight chemise"—and why she welcomed "the spy-glass of Anthropology" as a tool for investigating her "garment."⁶⁸ Her mourning may have required—as Freud held it always requires—preservation with a difference; rather than internalizing an unchanged relationship—fetishizing the folklore of her youth or maintaining hostility toward traditions that once seemed inflexible—she sought new perspectives on the cultural expressions that she loved in childhood.⁶⁹ Such a process would align with her choice of the horizon as a metaphor for her mother, which implies that one must journey to reunite with the person who once constituted home.

Though Hurston's interest in folklore appears to provide, then, a method of mourning her mother, that affective impulse does not render her attachment strictly nostalgic; while she presented folklore as "that which the soul lives by," her writing suggests continuing awareness that its effects can be positive or negative and, further, that it functions in a changing world and constitutes a shifting cultural form.⁷⁰ But given that the importance of folklore to her was simultaneously cultural, psychological, and memorial, it stands to reason that she would not be willing to tolerate the potential loss of African American folklore. In this novel, which describes the cultural effects of modernization in southern African American communities, she seems determined to create a protected space for folkloric enjoyment—preserving this form of expression amid cultural changes presented as potentially destructive. In what Tate aptly describes as a "novel of overdetermined mourning," Hurston imagines a private, individualized form of folkloric preservation—one that, though perhaps ultimately conservative, constitutes a formal innovation in response to social change.⁷¹

Their Eyes Were Watching God depicts a southern African American culture in which bourgeois ideology was vital even at the turn of the twentieth century. Janie's grandmother Nanny wishes her to be distinguished by class and property—to claim, for example, the "onliest organ in town, amongst colored folks" (23). Nanny's narrative mirrors Kevin Gaines's analysis of "uplift ideology's romance of the patriarchal family": speaking from the knowledge of her own and her child's sexual victimization, Nanny argues that Janie needs protection.[72] But Nanny believes this safety is best achieved through property and class differentiation, both of which are inimical to Janie's own desire, which dictates a "great journey to the horizons in search of *people*," a quest based on a folkloric understanding of human desire (89). The novel represents Nanny's determination to procure a bourgeois class identification for her granddaughter as an oppressive reification of Janie's more folkloric desire: Nanny "pinch[es the horizon] in to such a little bit of a thing that she could tie it about her granddaughter's neck tight enough to choke her." Furthermore, the novel explicitly links this reification and discipline of individual desire to capitalist values and practice. Nanny's efforts commodify Janie herself, as she is "set in the market-place to sell" (90). In short, Nanny obtains property and status for Janie through the discipline of Janie's own body. Because critics correctly think of Hurston as an artist devoted to the representation of folk culture, they occasionally overlook the extent to which her critique of patriarchy connects it with bourgeois, as well as folk, ideology.[73] But Nanny's understanding of gender and desire, which centers on status and property, ultimately shapes every community that Janie encounters.

The linkage between bourgeois and patriarchal values is particularly clear in the portrayal of Janie's second husband, Joe Starks, whose eventual conflict with Janie emerges not only from his sexism but also from their opposing views of modernization and folk practices. Joe is Eatonville's most explicit proponent of modernization: upon his arrival, he buys land to create a larger housing market, begins construction of a store, and establishes a post office—an official connection between the town and the nation.[74] "Uh man dat changes everything," Joe creates a committee for the construction of roads and argues that the town must incorporate (49, 40–43). Helping Eatonville conquer nature, he procures a street lamp for the town, arguing that, faced with the limitations of natural light, "us poor weak humans . . . [must] make some light ourselves" (45). Throughout this process, Joe limits Janie's interactions with the community in order to assert the couple's bourgeois social status. In Janie's words, "Jody classed me off" (112). Under these restrictions, Janie feels isolated and lonely; though Joe tells her that he wants to make "uh big woman" out of her, to her mind, his incessant activity keeps them in a "kinda strain" (46). With differing evaluations of capitalist and folkloric practice, their understandings of how everyday life should be spent also diverge. Joe criticizes the more folkloric, less acquisitive, conceptions of time common in Eatonville when he first arrives, arguing that those in the community who "don't want nothin' but uh full belly and uh place tuh lay down and sleep afterwards" are merely "playin' round de toes of Time" (63, 54). Janie, on the other hand, finds Joe's insistence on precise mathematical calculations in trade to be "a waste of life and time."[75]

But the novel does not simply suggest that modernization will displace folkloric values; rather, though it holds that these two systems of thought could be "so different it put you on a wonder," it goes on to demonstrate that the two can be reconciled when capitalist modernization puts folkloric forms to its own use (48). Joe's insistence on his own class status initially alienates others in the community as well as Janie. Eatonvillians compare Joe's "golded-up" spittoon, as well as the "little lady-size spitting pot" that he buys for Janie, to the ostentatious objects of white people; residents feel a mixture of respect for Joe's ability to procure such items and hate for his investment in them (47–48). Ultimately, however, Joe acquires the affection of the community through his participation in folkloric entertainment. First, inspired by Janie, he buys Matt Bonner's mule, an overworked and underfed animal that has become the star of many original folk performances. Eatonvillians respect that Joe intends to let the mule rest and eat well for his remaining years; as a "free-mule," the animal is an even more celebrated figure (58–59). The community also "love[s]" Joe's eulogy for the mule after its death, a performance that makes Joe's reputation "more solid than building the schoolhouse had done" (60). Joe explains that he must participate in the mule funeral because of his gender—"Ah'm uh man even if Ah is de Mayor"—but argues that his wife, unlike the other women of the town, should not go near such a "mess uh commonness"; in this way, Joe is able to participate in, and even dominate, a folkloric activity while still signaling his own elevated class status. This imbrication of folkloric activities in the development of a bourgeois hegemony is further suggested by the emergence of the store porch as the site of folkloric performance.[76] Joe builds the store both to profit and to define the space of the town as a civic entity, as opposed to "a raw place in de woods," but he allows members of the community to conduct their "eternal arguments" there (34, 63). Though he disapproves of these activities, they further both his causes: the store becomes, in the perception of the community, "the center of the world," and when the talk turns flirtatious, his business increases dramatically (64, 67).

Written during Hurston's trip to Haiti, a context in which Hurston became particularly sensitive to the kind of myth-making propaganda practiced by Haitian president Sténio Vincent—whom she called "a king with a palace"—and Dominican dictator Rafael Trujillo, *Their Eyes Were Watching God* characterizes the leader of its modernizing community as exploitative but also suggests that folkloric communities cannot easily defend against such influences.[77] The narrative is, on occasion, explicit and cynical regarding the emergence of hegemony: Eatonvillians "bow down to [Joe] . . . because he was all of these things [positions and possessions], and then again he was all of these things because the town bowed down" (50). The corruption of folkloric values by Joe's bourgeois ideology is made clear in the townspeople's changing attitudes toward class and gender from the turn of the century to the 1920s. When Joe and Janie arrive in Eatonville, Sam Hicks and Lee Coker argue about whether women are attracted by money or "co-talkin'," "pleasurin' and givin' pleasure" (36). By the time of Janie's romance with the "co-talkin'" Tea

Cake, however, the townspeople are united in their belief that women should "stay in [their] class" (2). Further, they seem increasingly inclined to grant authority to powerful but self-interested figures: when Joe first has his "committee" dig a drainage ditch, its members "murmured hotly about slavery being over," but by the end of his life, they seem content to perceive him and Janie as "Emperor" and "Empress" (47, 88, 93). Even Tea Cake, though he invites Janie to violate this restriction, seems to enjoy her transgression less because it challenges the dominant ideology than because it increases his status within it: he assures his friend Sop-de-Bottom that Janie is a "high time woman" and that he "got her outa uh big fine house" (148).

Representing a southern African American culture that has already accepted many aspects of modernization, *Their Eyes Were Watching God* denigrates that development through the figure of its protagonist, who repeatedly demonstrates her determination to prioritize folkloric pleasure over social status. Violating class and gender restrictions in her marriage to Tea Cake, Janie enjoys the fact that, having moved to the "muck," she is allowed to participate in "woof[ing]" and dice games (134). Exceeding even other members of the Everglades community in her enthusiasm for folkloric entertainments, she is the first to seek out the Bahamian "Saws," who are "laugh[ed] . . . to scorn" by other workers for their drumming and dancing (139). Most notably, when she joins the bean pickers at work, she is the one who gets "the whole field to playing off and on" by setting an example of "romping and playing" with Tea Cake as she works (133). This combination of play and labor, as opposed to the strict separation of work and leisure, is, according to Victor Turner, one of the chief differences between the "expressive cultures" of preindustrial and industrializing societies; conflict over this issue is also one of Janie's chief dissatisfactions in her marriage with Joe.[78]

But as the protagonist is linked ever more closely to folkloric values, her communities are increasingly distanced from them, particularly during the trial scene, in which the narrative relentlessly separates Janie from the other muck workers. Janie briefly ponders her being tried for murder by an all-white jury—a critique of apartheid injustice that Depression-era readers would remember for its centrality in the political outcry over the Scottsboro trial (185). She displaces that critique, however, with her observation of "all the colored people" in the courtroom, who are standing "packed tight like a case of celery, only much darker than that" (185). This objectification of the workers, though it seems to unite Janie's perspective with that of the court, could be understood as sympathetic in its acknowledgment of the dehumanizing aspects of segregated southern courts, which did not allow African Americans seating in the courtroom of their friend's trial, isolating them in a white supremacist juridical system. The narrative undercuts such a reading, however, by immediately describing Janie's conviction that the black community is against her, "pelting her with dirty thoughts." The narrative triangulates the scene so that the workers' community is understood to be restricted in "the presence of white folks" and is further suggested to be in favor of Janie's "[h]anging"; thus the novel insists on Janie's belief that she should fear not a sentence of death from an unjust white court but rather the "lying thoughts" already attributed to the African American community (186, 187).

By emphasizing both Janie's engagement in folkloric practice and her separation from the community of workers, Hurston seems to be shifting the role of folklore from that of public cultural enactment to private cultural consciousness. As social categories, neither folk nor modern is sufficient to account for Janie: though she seems, in many ways, the most folkloric of the novel's characters, she is also an individualist, not only, as Carby notes, because of her class status but also because of her tendency to reject demands for conformity.[79] She is, in important ways, ambivalent concerning folklore. Although, in her early days in Eatonville, Janie finds it "nice" that "people sat around on the porch and passed around the pictures of their thoughts for others to look at and see," by the end of her travels she rejects such forms of communication, in part because the porch talk has become so hierarchical (51). Despite her love of folkloric performances, Janie views the local "root-doctor" as a scoundrel, arguing that her husband should see a medical doctor (82). (In her conviction that Joe's illness has scientific causes, she seems less ambivalent than the plot, in which Joe starts to become "baggy . . . all over" immediately after Janie has publicly announced that, naked, Joe looks "lak de change uh life"; this devastating pronouncement, as Lamothe has noted, links this protagonist with the Vodou *lwa*, or deity, Ezili Danto.[80]) Upon her return to Eatonville, Janie chooses to contemplate only mental pictures from her own past and then only in isolation or with her closest friend.

Creating an imaginative chronotope linked with mourning, both through the plot of the novel and in intertextual relationship with Hurston's other writings, the novel distances Janie from the community but presents her private spaces—her yard and bedroom—as sustaining sites of folkloric values to be enjoyed with Pheoby or by herself. And while property defines the boundaries of this space, it could also be considered through the anthropologist Victor Turner's concept of the liminoid, a quirky space that exists "apart from the central economic and political processes" of a society, allowing "ludic" experiences that may incorporate "a plurality of alternative models for living" or "freewheeling, experimental cognitive behavior."[81] This is a text, after all, that figures the liminoid through the funeral of Matt Bonner's mule, the ceremony in which the community leaves the space of its everyday life to engage in play at subverting the social structure. For while Joe uses this event to consolidate individual power, the ceremony imagines the reversal of hierarchies: "Out in the swamp," Eatonvillians talk of a world in which "mule-angels would have people to ride on," a rhetorical subversion echoed in the performative elevation of women—"the sisters got mock-happy . . . and had to be held up by the menfolks."[82]

This playful moment serves to support the community in the face of cultural changes paradoxically enabled through the funeral itself, and also to liberate the narrative, which, though it presumably relates information from Janie's perspective, moves from the telling of an event that she did not attend but could have heard of to the telling of an event that no one in the community witnessed—the buzzards' ritualistic consumption of the mule's body. Embedded in the text in this way, the buzzard funeral suggests the vitality of folkloric knowledge while also signaling its marginal role in the town. Outside the space of the community, buzzards dance and "stand" funerals for men, mocking human pretensions to immortality such as Joe's characteristic expression "I God," but the sign of this folkloric wisdom is "gone from the town except for the porch talk, and for the children visiting his bleaching bones now and then" in a perhaps liminoid "spirit of adventure" (62). But while the folkloric understanding forged by the memories of the mule funeral may be marginalized on the return to Eatonville, the continued relevance of these memories can be gathered not only from the momentary expansion of Janie's narrative but also from the change in Janie herself, as she becomes increasingly skeptical of Joe's authority.

It is possible to see the novel, a form generally experienced in isolation, as providing a similarly liminoid site for its readers. In other words, readers might see Janie, and her final chronotope, as a figure through which Hurston inscribes a form of understanding that is not meant to be incorporated into the public sphere but rather to be preserved in its position at the margins of a community. Thus, even as Hurston argues for economic and political modernization for the rural communities of *Tell My Horse*, *Their Eyes Were Watching God* models a strategy for preserving folklore in changing southern African American communities. Hurston suggests that public folkloric practices are too easily made to serve the agendas of people in power and chooses to preserve an altered form of folkloric experience, one that emphasizes individual consciousness over communal exchange. In doing so, she also makes such an experience accessible to her readers: the space of Janie's bedroom is, after all, not unlike the spaces in which they may be reading *Their Eyes Were Watching God*, and Janie's experience of manipulating space and time to create an imaginative chronotope of the self is similar to what Hurston's readers experience, with Hurston's help, in visualizing Janie's world. Thus the novel enables its readers to create an imaginative space in which to incorporate multiple forms of cultural knowledge into their own subjectivities.

I am suggesting that, rather than aestheticizing folkloric culture chiefly for the pleasure of bourgeois subjects, Hurston may have done so in order to preserve aspects of that culture at a time when bourgeois ideology seemed already to be broadly ascendant.[83] But this difference is, in effect, a small one. In considering the way in which readers might imagine their connection to Janie's world, it is also important to consider the way in which they might map that world in relation to their own. And though *Mules and Men* tacitly encourages readers to understand that southern African American communities are accessible to modern subjects, *Their Eyes Were Watching God* hints at such a possibility only to efface it. Although Hurston represents these communities as being increasingly permeated by national modernity, the novel privileges, in the place of these communities, the world of the imagination, isolating folkloric practice for individual pleasure. But this is a move, as Carby argues, to which only the fictional Janie and privileged readers have substantial access, as the residents of southern African American communities were often forced to interact with others in oppressive circumstances.

Thus, in celebrating Janie's ability to preserve a folkloric selfhood, the conclusion of the novel evades a problem that the narrative nonetheless does not deny: however much the citizens of Eatonville and the workers on the muck may regret the decreasing prevalence of folkloric practice in their own communities, they suffer much more directly from the abuses that they encounter through their labor in neighboring white communities, where Tea Cake, for example, is forced to dig graves at gunpoint and where Eatonvillians are reduced to "earless, eyeless conveniences all day long" (169–71, 1). In the face of such problems as these, Janie's chronotope of the self may provide individual sustenance, but it is not readily conducive to thinking about social or political solutions for the community. The close of the novel displaces the enforced racial segregation of the South, which denied African American economic and political rights, with a voluntary segregation of the self, which preserves African American folkloric culture. This self-segregation is largely what allows Walter Benn Michaels, for example, to mistake a novel that often seems skeptical of group affiliation as a "rewriting of the people as the race"; Janie's cultural authority is so profound by the narrative's end that she might seem to figure the race in herself.[84] And this insistence on Janie's autonomy is what so frustrates Carby, who urges readers to remember the impact of systematic racial disfranchisement on the communities of the novel, the South of the 1930s, and the metropolises of our contemporary period.

Hurston herself remained ambivalent in her treatment of racial segregation, complaining vehemently, in later essays, about both the denial of political and economic rights to African Americans under racial segregation and the efforts of the federal government to enforce desegregation.[85] She was hardly unique among southern African Americans in valuing economic and political opportunities over school integration, and her commitment to cultivating African American institutions appears particularly compelling in light of late twentieth-century educational history.[86] But her "Court Order Can't Make Races Mix" (1955) misstated the case in suggesting that there was "nothing different" between black and white southern schools "except the presence of white people"; the states' fiscal neglect of segregated African American schools was notorious.[87] (Surveying the findings of a special issue of the *Journal of Negro Education* in 1947, the editor claimed that "elimination of disparities in Negro and white common schools has been so slow that, even if equality of expenditures assured equality of opportunity, it would take . . . 100 years to attain parity."[88]) Perhaps even worse, in linking the antiapartheid movement with "Moscow" in the immediate wake of McCarthyism, Hurston supported beliefs on which southern white supremacists since at least Thomas Dixon had relied—the idea that, however flagrantly they might contravene the Constitution's Fourteenth Amendment, they were the most avid protectors of U.S. cultural values.[89] Segregationists would exploit such ideas throughout their resistance to the civil rights movement.[90]

Support of such sophistry is surprising from a writer who had so incisively criticized U.S. racial nationalism just a decade earlier, arguing that "President Roosevelt could extend his four freedoms to some people right here in America" and stating satirically that "democracy is a wonderful thing, but too powerful to be trusted in any but purely Occidental hands."[91] In the early 1940s, this writer, who would later become conservative, shared the critical language of black diasporic radicals, describing racial oppression and exploitation as systematic and global capitalist practice.[92] Where her editor excised such statements from her autobiography, white southern newspapers eagerly circulated her attack on desegregation, such that her political reputation was shaped for decades by publishers' decisions as well as by her own vacillations.[93] But the latter were acute in themselves, suggesting, perhaps, the intensity of her struggle to assess the political options available to people experiencing entrenched and systematic disfranchisement in a nation that proclaimed itself the vanguard of democracy. These efforts, duly eliciting concerns about the political, economic, and cultural effects of modernization, may also have prompted the preservationist desire that critics find in Hurston's work. And yet early approaches to this desire, filtered through other discourses' relentless iteration of southern backwardness, overlooked the temporal complexity of her writing and the formal innovations required for her even to imagine a carefully demarcated space of stasis. As I demonstrate in the next chapter, such interpretive practices also informed the critical reputation of her contemporary William Faulkner, whose analytic exploration of the "presence of the past" has often been read as testimony to southern temporal isolation.[94]

CHAPTER FIVE

William Faulkner and the Haunted Plantation

AMONG THE "high" modernists of Britain and the United States, Faulkner is widely considered the most gothic—the inadvertent exemplar, even, of the school of southern gothic.[1] In the modernist context, this combination of regionalism and gothicism can seem provincial. Where Faulkner is famous for fictionalizing familial and regional stories, Ezra Pound and T. S. Eliot combed diverse cultural histories, searching for alternate myths and traditions that might, in Pound's words, "free [the audience's] . . . perceptive faculties . . . from . . . set moods, set ideas, conventions."[2] And where James Joyce, another modernist famous for his scrupulous attention to the local, nonetheless represents cosmopolitan protagonists whose minds are occupied with national and international political and cultural events, many of Faulkner's characters find it difficult to concentrate on anyone outside their immediate familial or romantic interests (or, notoriously, the combination of the two). Finally, the gothic novels to which Faulkner's work so prominently alludes are characterized by precisely such an enclosing and anomalous space and time, a site where supernatural forces escape the temporal logics of a purportedly rational world. Early responses to Faulkner's work suggest that, during this era, the logic of the gothic novel also provided U.S. intellectuals with a way to understand southern culture and to distance it, both spatially and temporally, from national culture. Accordingly, the pathologies represented in Faulkner's characters were seen as endemic to southern subjectivity, the inevitable results of the interaction between an individual mind and a stagnating, aggressively backward culture—a condition said to paralyze the author himself.

Among the modernist writers who influenced Faulkner, however, gothicism provided a formal mode through which to explore not a monolithic temporal alterity but, rather, temporal fragmentation. Though Faulkner's inspirations in European modernism have been well documented, the role of gothicism in this movement merits further analysis.[3] This chapter situates Faulkner's writing in relation to a literary history in which gothic tropes were mobilized to represent individuals' anxieties as they perceive that the temporal uniformity in which they wish to believe is fissured by both substantial cultural differences and by uncontrollable psychological responses. But while Faulkner's gothicism facilitated his broader exploration of modernity's temporal multiplicity—a pattern that helps to explain his popularity among Latin American writers interested in how psychological and social times intersect and diverge—it also provided him with an analytic tool through which to investigate ideas of southern collective memory.[4] As they develop through his career, Faulkner's representations of haunting memories belie the idea that his characters participate in a shared white southern cultural identity. Rather, they suffer individualized mnemonic disorders presented in the novels as sources of pain, cultural misrecognition, and ethical failure.

Modernist Gothic

In 1935, when Ellen Glasgow complained of the "inflamed rabble of impulses in the contemporary Southern novel," she urged newer writers of the region to pursue more "realism" than "romance."[5] The term she coined to lodge this protest—*southern gothic*—has since been associated with grotesquerie in plot and image, a legitimate emphasis, given her description of "moral and physical disintegration" and her analogy of "spoilt meat."[6] But Glasgow's use of the term *gothic* reflects her particular interest in temporal relations: she argued that such writing constituted an attempt "to run away from the past," an effort as "useless" as it would be "to run away from what we call life." Explaining that "not the South alone, but the whole modern world, after its recent bold escape from superstition, is in fact trembling before its own shadow," she suggested that the problem with southern fiction of the era, and of contemporary writing more generally, was its inability to place present and past in a meaningful relationship.[7]

Many of Faulkner's initial reviewers felt he exemplified such a failure; as a "romantic" engaged in a "flight from reality," he was said not even to represent time as a dimension in which public activities are conducted but rather to inscribe it as a subjective and variable medium.[8] Reviewers recognized his challenge to the tradition of the plantation romance, still active and popular in *Gone with the Wind* (1937) and *So Red the Rose* (1935).[9] Nonetheless, leftist critics in particular complained that Faulkner seemed unable to engage the material conditions of either history or contemporaneity in a productive way. Because of their emphasis on change and collective progress, these critics valued narratives that, in describing developments through linear time, could both model and reflect cultural advances.[10] In contrast, Faulkner's *Absalom, Absalom!*, in the words of Philip Rahv, represented an "ideological dream . . . of history" and functioned to "mystif[y]" the "historic process"; it further suggested that the author himself was "hemmed in by his own consciousness, . . . beat[ing] his fists against its walls, finding a forced release only in violence and melodrama."[11]

Such reviews suggested that Faulkner not only created but actually inhabited a gothic space, one hostile to more rational forms of social life and tending to isolate and madden its denizens. Describing southern culture as categorically different—in both its age and its rapid process of dissolution—from that found elsewhere in the nation, such critics suspected that, amid such conditions, the artist or intellectual might be overwhelmed by emotional attachments to the past and trapped in a purely subjective realm, incapable of interaction with or understanding of contemporary social life.[12] Thus Faulkner's gothicism was understood less as an aesthetic choice than as a reflection of the temporal alterity in which both author and subject matter were submerged. Malcolm Cowley, for example, argued that because Faulkner was recording a perception of a contemporary region in a "state of catastrophic decay," his romanticism was "social as well as personal or pathological."[13]

It is true that Faulkner's interior monologues often represent subjectivities that seem detached from linear time. In *Absalom, Absalom!* for example, Quentin Compson describes his fictional world as "the deep South dead since 1865 and peopled with garrulous outraged baffled ghosts."[14] These apparent ghosts are not utterly removed from the nation's history, as attested by their relationship to its cultural forms: Rosa Coldfield, whose "static rage" renders her the most spectral of the novel's living characters, nonetheless supports herself for years through her contributions to the county newspaper, and the dead Sutpens, materializing "out of the biding and dreamy and victorious dust," appear much as they would if their image had been preserved by more technological means, "arranged into the conventional family group of the period . . . [a] fading and ancient photograph" (3, 6, 4, 9). But though their world can easily be mapped in national time and space, the characters do not seem to progress in that time: even Quentin, though ostensibly "preparing for Harvard," believes that his life promises no forward development because he, too, is already a "ghost . . . since he was born and bred in the deep South same as [Rosa] was" (4). These ghosts share fictional space with such earthy folk as *Light in August*'s Lena Grove; people who, like *The Sound and the Fury*'s Benjy Compson, seem incapable of comprehending the causal connections implicit in an understanding of linear time; and people who, like *Sanctuary*'s Temple Drake, lose their sense of time in the course of devastating experience. Such subjectivities seem diversely incapable of participating in the linear time of the nation, even though Faulkner represents that time, and the nation's development, as crucially transforming the region's economy and institutions.

But while Faulkner's representational style was typically attributed to the strangeness of his subject matter, such temporal multiplicity was prominent in much modernist writing—certainly, as I have shown, in black modernism in the United States, and also in the European and Anglo-American expatriate modernism that overtly influenced Faulkner's early work. Glasgow's complaint, after all, echoes one of this movement's most prominent figures; T. S. Eliot, in "Tradition and the Individual Talent," also insists on the importance of cultivating a particular sense of time, one capable of comprehending "the timeless . . . and the temporal together."[15] Eliot allows for the importance of linear time, arguing that culture undergoes continual development and rejecting aesthetic repetition, but he also claims that the writer must inhabit "not merely the present, but the present moment of the past" (51, 49, 58). But while he seems to advocate historicist knowledge of "what is already living," this focus, when manifest in his poetry, is often expressed through gothic tropes.[16] Allowing "dead poets" to "assert their immortality" in *The Waste Land*, for example, Eliot describes a cityscape in which ghosts walk amid the public.[17] Voicing Baudelaire, the poem speaks to a "cité pleine de rêves / Où le spectre en plein jour raccroche le passant."[18] In this "Unreal City," the very instrument that measures the flow of linear time has a "dead sound," and the poem's voices repeatedly avow their equivocation between life and death, inhabiting neither (lines 60, 6).

The Waste Land thus exemplifies how even metropolitan modernism could be permeated by gothic imagery, representing the era as one in which discordant temporal frameworks uncannily coincide. This gothicism generally differs from that of the eighteenth-century novel, in which the borders between haunted and habitable chronotopes were more stable. As Maurice Lévy argues, conventional gothic spaces cannot be measured by the spatial and temporal dimensions of the realist novel's "l'espace diurne" (everyday space).[19] Rather, be they castles or catacombs, gothic realms are endless and labyrinthine, confronting the linear time of modern society with that of an uncanny other: narrow rooms open into unexpectedly vast and haunted hallways or vistas, and the wilderness either suggests, in its density, the absence of human civilization, or opens up to present an uncanny civilization—a gathering of Satanists or a city that belongs in another time or on another continent. These novels represent spaces that defy the laws of biographical, chronological time and demonstrate how such ontological shifts could overwhelm the individual personality. But by containing their horrors in distinct chronotopes, they also tend to normalize the social space and linear time of the public sphere, which appears, in contrast, to be a potential site for rational human development. In contrast, modernist texts represent gothic emergences—sudden perceptions of haunted or shifting time, spectral or vertiginous space—within a recognizable, even mimetic, social space.

Thus objections initially leveled against Faulkner's work have been echoed in scholarly accounts of literary modernism more generally. Observing such innovative representations of time, many critics have argued that these writers produced subjectivities and spaces that made no distinction between past and present, absorbing all temporalities into an omnivorous and subjectivized contemporaneity.[20] Despite the great diversity of this writing, its rejection of linear time—the typical temporal form of history and of nineteenth-century realism—is taken as a constitutive feature: modernists sought to augment or even replace linear time (in representation or, in the case of some avant-gardes, in life) with a spasmodic and accelerated, or spiritualized, or folkloric, or subjective, or internally diverse and fragmented time.[21] And while modernists often suggested that their formulations provided necessary supplements to linear time, critics have argued that such representations ineffectually retreat from social life, creating an isolated realm in which to contemplate anomie, angst, defeatism, and alienation.[22] From this perspective, Faulkner's gothicism exemplifies modernism's most subjectivist tendencies. He repeatedly describes the fall of isolated "dark houses" in which characters unleash and encounter their haunting pasts, seemingly mobilizing what Fredric Jameson describes as a "private language" to describe "those serried ranks of monads that are the ultimate result of the social fragmentation inherent in our system."[23]

More recently, however, scholars have begun to argue that modernism provided a way of exploring how and why individuals' temporal perceptions diverged from pervasive and hegemonic accounts of the era. As Andrew Hewitt argues, it appears that, for many writers in the early twentieth century, "time seems to 'go spatial' "—not in the sense of mappable "culture gardens," as described in Johannes Fabian's study of anthropology, but in the sense that local spaces and even individual subjectivities were increasingly recognized as sites incorporating temporal alterity.[24] Sources of such perceptions included the continuing influence of old beliefs as well as the effects of uneven economic development, in which capitalist and imperialist centers were tied to peripheries that they nonetheless represented as belonging to another—primitive or backward—time. During this period of increasing globalization, the nationalist idea that cultures and identities could reliably be attached to bounded spaces was increasingly challenged by flows of media, markets, objects, and people.[25] But while such changes encouraged new ways of thinking about space, time, and culture, modernizing nations were also consumed by images of and efforts toward progress. Thus the recognition of temporal multiplicity within local spaces reinforced perceptions of how exclusive the nation's linear time might be: it suggested that one might inhabit national space while nonetheless contravening its temporal norms. The idea that people living in contiguous space might inhabit different times emerged also from developments in psychological theory, which had become particularly interested in the temporal displacements of the individual mind.

As scholars of gothic modernism have noted, these particular forms of temporal multiplicity were well suited to investigation through reformulating a genre that had long confronted modernity with resistant and powerful temporal alterities.[26] John Paul Riquelme notes that the emergence of British modernism coincided with the striking literary reclamation of gothic motifs in Oscar Wilde's *Picture of Dorian Gray* (1891) and Henry James's *The Turn of the Screw* (1898), which brought the confusion and violence of gothic space "much closer to home"; this convergence is particularly apparent in Bram Stoker's *Dracula* (1897) and Joseph Conrad's *Heart of Darkness* (1899).[27] Representing how temporal differences cannot be restricted by spatial boundaries but rather emerge within cultures and consciousnesses, these narratives demonstrate why gothic modernism might powerfully influence a writer interested in the psychological effects of identifying with a culture considered backward. Given Faulkner's interests in lurid tales, uneven modernization and its effects, and, not least, the aesthetic experimentation of Joseph Conrad, these narratives provide an important aesthetic backdrop for Faulkner's mobilization of gothic tropes; they help to demonstrate how the gothic provided him with a vocabulary for representing temporal multiplicity and the anxieties it elicited.[28]

Both *Dracula* and *Heart of Darkness* initially appear to record encounters between modern British subjects and a timeless alterity, only to undercut that dichotomy as they progress. The former famously maps the emergence of an ageless evil in the modern cityscape, inscribing the distance between social and gothic space not as a temporal or metaphysical fissure but as a traversable distance between nations or between colony and imperial seat.[29] Stoker further compromises the temporal and ethical alterity of the gothic in that the count shares the tools and the purposes of the British Empire. Having spent centuries in "a ruin tomb in a forgotten land," the vampire nonetheless uses modern devices to his own ends, "learn[ing] new social life; new environment of old ways, the politic, the law, the finance, the science, the habit of a new land and a new people who have come to be since he was," in order to establish control over the British population by creating a group "to do [his] bidding and to be [his] jackals."[30] Though Conrad's novella does not represent supernatural characters, his storytelling protagonist relies heavily on gothic descriptors to describe his experience. Marlow compares Africa to "an overheated catacomb," describes its rivers as "streams of death in life," and claims its wilderness is as "quiet as the ruined house on the hill"; he seems to believe that he has arrived in gothic space.[31]

But the perception of nonsynchronicity is not what fuels Marlow's "creepy thoughts" so much as his increasing suspicion that his own consciousness might not be steadfastly instantiated in European time: referring to Africans on the riverbanks as "prehistoric man," he nonetheless acknowledges a "remote kinship with [their] wild and passionate uproar" (62–64). For Marlow, the realization that the absolute temporal difference in which he has previously believed may be false—a "cloak" in which "time" has been dressed by imperialist ideology—is "the worst of it": the European "man" must confront that possibility with "his own true stuff," a "deliberate belief" that may be abetted by "surface-truth"—in other words, colonialist practicalities. Marlow's cultural identity depends on attachment to the linear progressive time that he believes is characteristic of his contemporary England; to challenge his relationship to that temporality is to disrupt his very sense of self. *Dracula* also stages the concern that an encounter with what one considers an impossible or oppositional temporality might destabilize individual consciousness; after escaping Dracula's castle, "where the devil and his children still walk with earthly feet," Jonathan Harker succumbs to "brain fever," an illness brought on by a "fearful shock" that leaves him weak and subject to delirium (58, 113, 107). Having lost or denied his memories, Harker undergoes his gothic experiences again in nightmare, as weeks later he still "sometimes starts out of his sleep in a sudden way and awakes all trembling," his nightmares suggesting that he continues to suffer the earlier shock in his unconscious state (107). Marlow also endures a severe illness marked by continuing fever and subsequent mnemonic disorders; his memory of Kurtz, unlike "other memories of the dead that accumulate in every man's life," has a tendency to emerge, in hallucinatory fashion, against his will (117).

In sum, these narratives use gothic tropes not only to explore perceptions of cultural difference but also to represent the effects of psychological trauma. In the words of Mina Harker, her husband has suffered a "wound" to the consciousness (245). The adaptation of the word "trauma" from discussions of physiological to psychological injury was contemporary with these works, occurring during the 1890s. As early as the 1850s Jean-Martin Charcot had studied the potential for a psychological shock to produce recurrent symptoms; this phenomenon became an object of intense psychological study during the late nineteenth century, particularly in the work of Charcot's students Pierre Janet and Sigmund Freud.[32] In their work, as in *Dracula* and *Heart of Darkness*, psychologically traumatic experiences are unassimilable to the conscious mind—in Marlow's words, "monstrous, intolerable to thought and odious to the soul."[33] Subsequently, the memory of such events is not narrativized but visceral, reproducing the originating traumatic sensations and emotions without the participation of the conscious mind; until patients can "work through" their relationship to the originating trauma, to which they often feel they did not respond adequately, they simply reexperience its pain and horror.[34] Because such patients contain pain and knowledge in a region of the mind over which they have no conscious control, they are said to experience "splitting"; with the encoding of these theories, it became reasonable to imagine that one might be traumatized without consciously realizing it.[35] Such symptoms are readily represented through gothic conventions because traumatized subjects are, in effect, haunted by the traumatic event, either through hysterical symptoms or through hallucinations and nightmares.

Through their confluence of gothic imagery and the logic of psychological trauma, these narratives suggest that the encounter with a temporality perceived as nonlinear might itself be sufficient to detach subjectivity from the time of capitalist modernity, leaving individuals isolated and confused by memories that manifest precisely the sort of temporal multiplicity that they first sought to disavow. Jonathan Harker is ultimately restored to his community: by joining the hunt for the vampire and sharing the narrative of his traumatic experiences, he participates in a psychotherapeutic cure, such that his traumatic memories never invade his waking life. Mina

Harker, who recognizes the importance of a discursive community in her husband's treatment, refuses exclusion from the group of vampire hunters even after she has been bitten. Marlow, however, is preeminently concerned that he no longer fully "fits" in his society; he complains repeatedly that his English peers cannot understand him and that he cannot explain his experiences to them, because they are firmly entrenched in English space and time (81–82). It is not only the content of his memories that alienates him but the way in which the memories have altered his consciousness, which cannot fully participate in linear time because it is fixated on his past confusion, a distress it still experiences. This haunting is described through both visual hallucinations and the continuous presence of perhaps metaphorical noise, a surrounding incomprehensibility—"one immense jabber, silly, atrocious, sordid, savage, or simply mean" (80). Notably, it is largely the qualities that represent Marlow's incurability—his circular and dissatisfied narrative, his alienation from his peers and his society, his recognition of what he still perceives as nonsynchronicity within himself—for which *Heart of Darkness* is canonized as a modernist text.[36]

The influence of these narratives may be suggested by the work of a later modernist—James Joyce—who also sought to describe the fears of a character wishing to identify with a hegemonic modernity and fearful that his residence in a colonial culture may thwart him. Stephen Dedalus worries, in *A Portrait of the Artist as a Young Man* (1916), that he might be caught in the "nets" of Irish or Catholic traditionalism, but by his young adulthood in *Ulysses* (1922), he is more profoundly threatened by a manifestation of the past that assaults him from within—the repeated invasion of his consciousness by a hallucination of his dead or dying mother, whom he angered on her deathbed in a scene that appears to have traumatized him.[37] Stephen feels compelled to differentiate himself absolutely from his mother, whom he sees, in her compliance with religious and social traditions, as entrenched in a temporality that he does not wish to occupy. He believes that their opposition is as extreme as that between life and death; in his assessment, each is, to the other, a resident of a different kind of time, a "ghoul," a form of alterity that cannot be negotiated.[38]

But Stephen cannot escape her gothic image: when he sees his mother in a dream, she is bathed in "ghostly light"; in the "Circe" section, she materializes, "green with gravemould" (9, 473).

Crucially, these individuals with differing temporal identifications share contemporary social space; here, as I have shown in regard to the gothicism of Stoker and Conrad, temporal differences cannot be mapped effectively along spatial lines. But precisely this impossibility of containing what he perceives as backwardness is what creates Stephen's anxiety: there is no space from which he can be sure he will escape it. And his fixation on this danger and his own destructive responses to it force him repeatedly both to relive his own past and to confront the cultural and familial voices of tradition that he fears. In his discussion of Shakespeare, Stephen argues that trauma can enable artistic production by compulsively producing narratives that seek to understand the event and to discharge the emotions it caused, but Joyce's representation of Stephen suggests that some relationships to the past may be neither pleasurable nor productive (155–75). Despite the efforts of others, particularly Bloom, to engage Stephen in new relationships, the young man is fixated on the image of his mother; still believing he must differentiate himself from her utterly or "not at all," Stephen "run[s] amok," into the street, into a confrontation with British soldiers that he is ill equipped to handle (475–76). Thus the plot supports Stephen's fear that his inability to transcend the past—either personal or cultural—will render him unable to negotiate his contemporary world.

Faulkner, in a sense, reverses this story: where Stephen vigorously struggles against the perceived threat of gothic entrapment by familial memories and local culture, Quentin Compson, in *Absalom, Absalom!*, is convinced that he is already barred from linear time, "his very body" serving as a "barracks" for the region's "stubborn backward-looking ghosts" (7). Even when he leaves his home for Massachusetts, he arrives only through "a sort of geographical transubstantiation" and is followed by "unratiocinative djinns and demons" "attenuated up from Mississippi" (208, 142). But while, as I have shown, early critics fairly fixated on the novel's gothicism—its "drama of . . . diabolism . . . with clouds of sulfur smoke"—scholars have since devoted little attention to Quentin's insistent haunting.[39] Rather, they have tended to interpret his strange sense of space and time through psychological and cultural paradigms, effectively interpreting Faulkner's metaphors but not scrutinizing his specters as such.[40] This ready acceptance of such images reflects, in part, the degree to which white southern fixation on the past has been naturalized in critical discourse, such that Quentin's hauntings seem unexceptional. As Michael Kreyling argues, Quentin's belief that white southern identity must maintain a fixed relationship to regional history was long celebrated by a "legion of white males who have assumed responsibility for inventing a style for thinking of the South."[41] More critical readers have tended to find Quentin's mode of identification symptomatic, for example, of white southerners' "madness," traumatization, or consent to their ideological positioning as the nation's anomalous backward-looking population.[42]

But while white southerners in the 1930s were said to be profoundly attached to the region's collective memories, such representations, as Jon Smith argues of such statements in present-day contexts, were often offered in "bad faith."[43] As I have shown, despite the region's increasing interaction with national and international economic and social forms, arguments for southern cultural immutability were used to justify southern apartheid, and ideas of southern traditionalism were often promulgated through white southerners' memorial practices and narratives.[44] Young William Falkner (born in 1897, and later to change this spelling) grew up amid still rampant regional commemoration of the Civil War, including institutionalization of Confederate memorial days, building of Confederate memorials, publication of periodicals devoted to Confederate narratives, preaching on Confederate themes and by Confederate veterans, and the development of a southern school of historiography.[45] Where traumatic memories are typically private, alienating, and confusing, these "invented traditions" and public remembrances staged contemporary white southern solidarity through reference to a shared history.[46] Thus Confederate commemoration was mobilized in the transition to a "New South," reconciling white southerners to sectional reunification and economic reform by providing them with an identity narrative tied to the past.[47] Arguing that both black and white southerners were inherently attached to the patterns of antebellum culture—even generations after the war had ended—public memorialization cast purportedly traditional values, including white supremacy, as immutable elements in a culture that maintained an anomalous relationship to time. Faulkner's novels have often been cited in support of this narrative of backward-looking white southern identity, which forever attempts to justify and recuperate the South's role in the Civil War.

I argue later in this chapter, however, that when examined in relation to gothic modernism, Faulkner's novels suggest not a simply backward culture but one in which individuals damage themselves and others by avowing an absolute split in time and refusing to engage in more nuanced investigation of the relationship between past and present. As his career developed, he began to represent his characters' hallucinatory images of the southern past less as valued interlocutors and more as manifestations of a destructive pathology, offering not a sustaining memory but a taunting reminder of their beholders' inability to function in their contemporary world. Early in his career, Faulkner appears to have found white southerners' memorial traditions and narratives of collective identity compelling. But his exploration of more individualized mnemonic disorders, particularly those created through trauma, seems to have led him to question the etiology of white southerners' relationships to the past—whether they were psychologically inevitable, culturally dictated, or varying and potentially flexible. In this effort, gothic tropes provided him with a method to estrange characters' belief in a distinct southern temporality, presenting such ideas as sources of distress, passivity, and isolation and also as a strategy that enabled white southerners to disavow their knowledge of racial injustice.

Identity and Gothic Memory

By the 1930s, even some celebrants of southern tradition suggested that ossified commemorative practices and narratives could not provide a meaningful sense of continuity with the region's past.[48] When Allen Tate, for example, famously argued in *I'll Take My Stand* (1930) that "the Southerner [must] take hold of his tradition . . . by violence," Tate did not suggest that Civil War memorialization might constitute one strategy for such "recovery and restoration."[49] Tate's poetry from this period opposes this idea more directly, linking such practices to both intergenerational and psychological alienation. The speaker of "To the Lacedemonians," a Confederate veteran on the eve of a publicly celebrated reunion, expresses both distance from and distaste for the younger generation "crowding round"; complaining that these "Men . . . / Put the contraption before the accomplishment," he asks, "Where have they come from?"[50] Tate's "Ode to the Confederate Dead" (1928, 1937) takes the contrasting perspective of a young man who seeks to forge connection with "the immoderate past," but rather than valuing that connection as a source of meaning, the poem flaunts the speaker's marginality and morbidity.[51] Accordingly, the speaker warns other potential observers that the spectral veterans' "orient of the thick-and-fast . . . Smothers you, a mummy, in time."[52]

This poem demonstrates tensions evoked in much southern gothicism of this era in which images from the past often appear *both* inevitable and appropriate *and* strange and alienating. This strategy for representing Civil War memorial practices reflects the lingering influence of the "New South" creed, which argued that homage to the region's past provided a strategy through which southerners could adapt to economic and social change; simultaneously, however, it invokes the contemporary psychological and social theories that associated such attraction to past times with cultural and psychological dysfunction. Thus, in the "Ode," the fascination with the region's past is hardly shared and nourishing, as Tate elsewhere argued it should be. Rather, it allows at best for a dispersed community demarcated by members' desire for access to what seems a gothic realm, as they ponder whether to "set up the grave / In the house . . . the ravenous grave."[53] Although I have shown that gothic tropes were often associated in this period with traumatic memory, Tate did not believe white southerners born after the war to be traumatized; on the contrary, his contribution to the Agrarian manifesto expresses uncertainty as to whether the past should even be expected to influence contemporary generations.[54] Nor does he present the speaker's fixation on the southern past as an empty ideological gesture, however devastating its results. Rather, for the contemporary southerner of the "Ode," the actions and beliefs of past generations provide a seductive *promise* of fulfillment, contemplation of which ultimately may prove hallucinatory and paralyzing.

This concern with mnemonic pathology, which appears even in the poetry of an Agrarian who wished to invigorate white southerners' sense of tradition, is even more overt in Faulkner's work. Still, because many of Faulkner's characters, like the speaker of the "Ode," accept their spectral perceptions as an inexorable element of white southern heritage, the shock typically occasioned by the gothic is displaced from their narratives. Where Stephen Dedalus, for example, is horrified by hauntings that seem to isolate him from others, Quentin Compson in *Absalom, Absalom!* believes his to be shared by all who are "born and bred in the deep South" (4). This strange conjunction in which gothic hauntings are both expected and uncanny helps to explain Depression-era critics' response to *Absalom, Absalom!* Early reviewers—observing Quentin's fatalism and understandably alarmed by many white southerners' continued romanticization of plantation life—read this novel as evidence of the author's mnemonic pathology, one shared by the whole of his region. Like other modernist gothic texts, *Absalom, Absalom!* begins with a world in which ghosts emerge, suggesting that the borders between past and present are unstable, but such formal strategies did not quickly become legible as a way of exploring temporal multiplicity; indeed, as I have suggested, that work is still proceeding. Accordingly, initial interpretations of Faulkner's texts were more profoundly influenced by the trope of the backward South, which was, in this period, supported by southern elites and by regional critics alike. But while Faulkner's novels from the late 1920s through the mid-1930s—novels characterized by increasing experimentation with gothic form—were read as evidence of a monolithic regional abnormality, they move with ever greater conviction toward aligning Confederate commemoration with individualized psychopathology.

Faulkner's first novel set in Yoknapatawpha—which he called, at the time, Yocona County—contrasts these two forms of memory, though it already explores some similarity between them. As Bleikasten argues, *Flags in the Dust*, published in edited form in 1929 as *Sartoris*, equivocates between irony and "sentimental allegiance" regarding the Sartoris family's memorialization of their departed Civil War heroes.[55] The novel does suggest the need to question the romanticization of the white southern past, as the chief purveyor of Confederate memorialization—eighty-year-old Virginia Du Pre—complains vehemently about the tendency of Sartoris men to die violently and young, even as she promulgates stories of Civil War adventures.[56] Using language that, with its imagery of swamps and superhuman beings, provides a precursor for Rosa Coldfield's narrative in *Absalom, Absalom!*, the narrator further mocks du Pre's telling of such tales: "As she grew older the tale itself grew richer and richer . . . until what had been a hair-brained prank of two heedless and reckless boys wild with their own youth, was become a gallant and finely tragical focal-point to which the history of the race had been raised from out the old miasmic swamps of spiritual sloth by two angels valiantly and glamourously fallen and strayed, altering the course of human events and purging the souls of men" (14). Like the later and better-known Rosa (also variously titled "Aunt" and "Miss"), Jenny seeks to implant her memories, and her romantic understanding of them, into later generations. However, where Rosa is said effectively to have "died of outrage in 1866 one summer," Jenny is not traumatized but nostalgic in her memories, her voice "proud and still as banners in the dust."[57] Thus, while mocking Jenny's narrative, the novel celebrates her "indomitab[ility]" and "steadfastness"; she is, further, actively engaged in the contemporary lives around her (410). The novel's ambivalence on this question of commemoration is compounded because Jenny shares fictional space with other survivors of the Civil War whose sense of agency is dampened by their attachment to the past, as "old man Falls" and "old Bayard" are "cemented by deafness to a dead time and drawn thin by the slow attenuation of days" (5).

This novel's most overt exploration of traumatic memory is seen in its depiction of young Bayard Sartoris, who witnessed the violent death of his twin, John, in World War I. Given Faulkner's fascination with this war, it is likely that the widespread discussions of veterans' susceptibility to traumatic memories influenced his interest in mnemonic disorders; when, as Ruth Leys argues, many soldiers began to experience "shell shock," its treatment became a medical and a strategic priority.[58] Much of Faulkner's earlier prose depicts soldiers confused about the reality or unreality of their memories or seeking to repress memories that seem to return against their will.[59] His representation of Bayard suggests both traumatization and repression. The character seems compelled to repeat life-threatening behaviors and circumstances, experiences nightmares from which he awakes groaning, and is unable to discuss his wartime experiences except when drinking or just awakened; when his inhibitions are lowered, however, he routinely "f[alls] to talking of the war" (133). Where his grandfather is haunted by a patriarch killed almost fifty years earlier—a haunting rendered with an almost palpable ghost, in exterior social spaces such as rooms and porches—young Bayard is haunted in more metaphorical ways, in mental, largely unconscious, space, by a presence he cannot bring himself to acknowledge.[60] Notably, each has observed the destruction of a figure vital in constituting his "ego-ideal"; the novel suggests that young Bayard's twin, like a father, served as a primary identification, libidinal object, and guide.[61] But where old Bayard is able to maintain a sense of connection to his father while comprehending that he died, young Bayard feels utterly severed from his twin and remembers his death only through physical symptoms, barely repressed memories, and repetition. Bayard dies in an accident as similar to John's as a postwar plane wreck could be.

Thus the novel contrasts two forms of memory. Of these, Civil War memorialization may either alienate or energize its practitioners in relation to the contemporary world, but it consistently provides them with a way to mourn their losses and preserve their lost objects; it is, further, "glamourous" (93). Although Civil War memorialization is closer to conventional gothicism in its representational logics, it is nonetheless not horrific. Contemporary traumatic memory, however, seems purely destructive, isolating young Bayard from those who care for him, preventing him from mourning losses that he cannot fully acknowledge, and leading him to repeat the dangerous behaviors and painful affects associated with the initiating event. These two forms of memory are not absolutely opposed, as old Bayard shares some of his grandson's symptoms; the novel acknowledges that each of these wars had traumatic losses. And yet the commemorative community produced by the Civil War appears, in this novel, to produce some compensation for that conflict's effects. The elder Bayard is a less "definite presence" in life than his father is in death, but he nonetheless leads a lengthy life that includes substantial relationships (5).

This relatively positive representation of white southern collective memory coincides with a generally uncritical assessment of southern racial oppression: as other critics have noted, the novel both stages and encodes white supremacy. In *Flags in the Dust*, as in so many plantation romances, ex-slaves share in white southerners' reverence for Confederate patriarchs. Simon, now a servant of the Sartoris family, continues to talk to the "arrogant ghost" of the elder John Sartoris, encouraging him to instruct his progeny "how ter conduck deyselfs in de gent'mun way" (121). Simon's son Caspey has, at the book's opening, just returned from World War I, and Jenny, who so celebrates the efforts of Confederate soldiers, allows Caspey "a day to get over the war" (54). The novel's one historical insight—Caspey proclaims, "War unloosed de black man's mouf"—is paired with insidious propaganda: the narrator claims that his European experience rendered Caspey "a total loss, sociologically speaking" (62). The novel does diverge a bit from the plantation formula, in which scenes of white-on-black violence are generally depicted without further comment. When old Bayard, upon realizing that Caspey does not intend to return to work for the Sartorises, picks up "a stick of stove wood . . . and knock[s] Caspey through the door and down the steps at his father's feet," Faulkner closes the scene with Simon's commentary, which emphasizes Caspey's lack of economic options and implies that Simon's lack of interest in civil rights results from cultivated cynicism (87). Overall, however, *Flags in the Dust* naturalizes southern apartheid through ideological tropes lifted directly from the romantic plantation tradition, representing an "organic society" in which all residents—aside from those, such as young Bayard and Caspey, who have been disoriented by their war experiences—are accustomed and attached to their social roles.[62]

Given that this first novel set in Mississippi tends more toward a nostalgically romantic than a critically gothic tone, Faulkner may have made an aesthetically and intellectually beneficial choice to forgo such direct engagement with Confederate commemoration in the novels that immediately followed.[63] As other critics have noted, his subsequent novels before *Light in August* (1932) situate characters' values and obsessions in intimate, private, and personal concerns. Philip Weinstein argues that *The Sound and the Fury*, for example, "cannot afford Pierre Bourdieu's disturbing suggestion that the unconscious is not 'in here' but 'out there': 'The "unconscious" is never anything other than the forgetting of history which history itself produces.' "[64] But given that this "genesis amnesia" was produced by a mystifying memorial narrative that Faulkner seems initially to have found attractive, it is noteworthy that these intervening novels focus so closely on mnemonic disorders.[65] Often unable even to imagine a sustainable and productive relationship to time, Faulkner's characters from this period, like Breuer and Freud's hysterics, "*suffer from reminiscences.*"[66] In *The Sound and the Fury*, the Compson sons perpetually return to scenes from their past, and *As I Lay Dying* depicts the difficulties of the Bundren children as they attempt to comprehend the death of their mother, an event that leads some of them briefly to deny their experience of linear, progressive time. *Sanctuary*'s Temple Drake, unable to comprehend, in the context of her previous life, the traumatic events following her abduction, falsifies her history. While she lies about her past in an effort to make it conform to a present image, the Compson family, particularly the mother, perpetually seeks to describe its present circumstances in a way that supports its self-aggrandizing account of its past (a pattern concerning which Quentin's brother Jason unceasingly complains).

These narratives about individual and familial trauma and mythification generate both thematic and formal elements that Faulkner later used in his gothic representations of characters who attribute their temporal confusion to a regional past.[67] For example, the ghostliness that Quentin attributes to white southern culture more generally in *Absalom, Absalom!* is explored in more individualistic and familial terms in *The Sound and the Fury* (1929). His father, Jason, inculcates Quentin, for example, in a patrilineal time of futility, conferring on him his grandfather's watch while calling it "the mausoleum of all hope and desire."[68] Certainly, Quentin's difficulties are shaped in this novel by his identification with regional norms, which produce both psychological shame and social expectations that he is often unwilling or unable to meet; these gendered stereotypes are generally modeled in plantation fiction as well. Quentin cites, for instance, his sense that he must engage in sexual conquests—"in the South you are ashamed of being a virgin"—and is overwhelmed by memory in a fugue state precisely as the mother of one of his southern classmates begins to describe a familial ancestor who was "as crotchety about his julep as an old maid" (78, 148). But Quentin is less concerned with the source of these stereotypes than with the loss that they have caused members of his family and with his own uncertainty concerning their aptness; in effect, the novel refuses comment on such beliefs and rather imagines how they might emerge in the consciousness of someone who finds them both influential and painful. Accordingly, the novel's most gothic image is explicitly used as an analog for a state of consciousness, as Quentin, uninterested in attributing his confusion to definite causes, simply describes how it feels[69]: "I seemed to be lying neither asleep nor awake looking down a long corridor of gray halflight where all stable things had become shadowy paradoxical all I had done shadows all I had felt suffered taking visible form antic and perverse mocking without relevance inherent themselves with the denial of the significance they should have affirmed thinking I was I was not who was not was not who" (170).

After these explorations of trauma and mnemonic distress, Faulkner represented a character obsessed with regional memories that he falsely considers collective—images from the past that prove to be a mechanism for masking unbearable confusion concerning his familial relationships and that ultimately prevent his establishing a full contemporary existence. In *Light in August*, Gail Hightower's idealization of his grandfather mobilizes a collective framework of memory, the icon of the valiant yet foolhardy Confederate found in so much of Faulkner's work. But Gail's memories occur in isolation and are gothic in form: every evening, he experiences again the hallucination of the cavalry galloping toward the spatial and temporal scene of his grandfather's—and, in his odd temporal logic, his own—death, a haunting he claims to be all he knows "of life."[70] This memorial practice is associated in the novel with an overwhelming childhood experience: while growing up with parents rendered "phantoms" by their experience of the Civil War, Gail felt nausea, as well as "horrified triumph and sick joy," upon finding in the attic his father's Confederate uniform, with its single dark blue patch (474, 468–69). Unable to ask directly whether his father killed the Union soldier from whom the patch came, Gail suppresses these threatening emotions by focusing on the grandfather he never met but who he knew had killed many Yankees (468–70). Gail believes that this commemoration both gives his life meaning and provides commonality with other southerners. Convinced that they share his haunting, he seeks to relate to them by proclaiming, "You can see it, hear it" and by exulting that God would share the dead with the living as he does in Jefferson, Mississippi (484–85). But because Gail misunderstands his own memories as collective, his efforts to interact with others reveal, to them, a shockingly narcissistic lack of awareness of their lives. He ultimately comes to believe that such an identity formation is unethical, determining that, though he has "bought [his] ghost . . . with [his] life," that is not, as he had thought, his "privilege," for it implicates him in the destruction of others as well—people with whom, because of his temporal dislocation, he has been unable fully to interact (490).

Hightower, like Quentin, remembers a past in which he did not participate; further, like post-traumatic memory, this purportedly collective memory disrupts both characters' relationship to time and impedes their ability to constitute their own lives in the present. Approaching his death, Hightower claims, "I have not even been clay: I have been a single instant of darkness in which a horse galloped and a gun crashed" (491). But in strict terms, this is a screen memory and a vicarious one at that.[71] Hightower's hallucinations, which conceal events of his childhood that he could not comprehend at the time, are idealized and fictitious, mobilizing tropes from plantation romance. If readers consider their knowledge of Quentin from *The Sound and the Fury* in reading *Absalom, Absalom!*—as John Irwin, among others, has argued they should—the Sutpen family history that Quentin seems compelled to revisit could be seen as providing a sort of screen trauma; explaining his affect as the result of regional identification provides Quentin with a diagnosis that does not require him to acknowledge the pain resulting from his familial past.[72] But where Gail feels pleasure in his commemoration, and Quentin believes that at least his sense of futility and isolation is shared by others in a memorial community, the novels' gothic representations emphasize the temporal distortions enacted by this memorialization, the characters' alienation from contemporary social networks, and the deformation of the events supposedly remembered. Gail imagines his grandfather's raiding party to have comprised "a tide whose crest is jagged with the wild heads of horses and the brandished arms of men like the crater of the world in explosion," and Quentin sees Sutpen as a "man-horse-demon . . . faint sulphur-reek still in hair clothes and beard."[73] These images are not horrifying to their viewers, who greet their hauntings with irony, but their passive identification with these purported memories allows Gail and Quentin neither agency in their contemporary world nor insight into the actual past.[74]

Absalom, Absalom!, following *Light in August*, not only subverts the idealized view of the antebellum South presented in plantation romances but also criticizes the very idea that white southerners should feel compelled to memorialize this past.[75] For despite Quentin's protest that his hauntings constitute an irrevocable cultural inheritance, he proves unreliable concerning the effects and forms of his regional identification, as the novel demonstrates by finally allowing him to explore his relationship to the past in a revisionary way. As Quentin re-creates the local history of the Sutpen family from the distance of Harvard with his Canadian roommate, Shreve, the novel suggests both that Quentin need not passively acquiesce to the memories of a southern community—he and Shreve change their understanding of the story to fit their own desires—and that interest in the story need not isolate Quentin from other people and spaces.[76] As Alison Landsberg argues, the roommates' shared narration creates a "transferential space"—their interactions and creative interventions providing, in the words of Laplanche and Pontalis, "the ground on which intra-subjective conflicts . . . can once more find expression in a relationship where communication is possible."[77] Where Quentin has previously felt overwhelmed in his identification with a regional past—one he believes to isolate him in a distinct and deadened southern time—he finds, in his conversation with Shreve, that he can exercise critical agency in his approach to this history and that he can intimately contemplate it without being irrevocably detached from his contemporary world. Quentin's difficulty in overcoming painful beliefs about time and southern identity is represented as a sort of psychoanalytic "working through"—initially resisted and ultimately aborted when Shreve reasserts the primacy of spatial identities—but briefly a source of "peace."[78]

The gothic tropes of *Light in August* and *Absalom, Absalom!* thus serve to represent Civil War commemoration as an exaggerated view of history and even, more profoundly, as an uncanny relationship to time; this damage is further linked in each novel to an inability to comprehend the menace and injustice of southern racial hierarchies. This theme is particularly central in *Light in August*, which also attributes other characters' dangerous beliefs about racial and cultural identities to pathogenic memories. Joe Christmas, for example, comes both to see himself as black and to associate that affiliation with vulnerability and abjection through an episode at his orphanage in early life, and Joanna Burden absorbs her father's racist and paternalist ideology along with a traumatizing image of infanticide (119–22, 114–18, 156–57, 225–26, 252–53, 258). Gail's attachment to the past corresponds with that often used to justify southern apartheid, as his weekly sermons, unable to untangle from religion tales of the Confederacy's "galloping cavalry," exemplify the most conservative accounts of southern culture (62). Although Gail is appalled at and victimized by white supremacist violence, he comes to believe that his fixation on his grandfather's past has encouraged his passivity in the face of injustice. At the end of his story, he visualizes the faces he has encountered in his life in an "inextricable composite" that gradually resolves into the images of Joe, the man so recently castrated and killed in Gail's own kitchen, and Percy Grimm, the perpetrator of the crime. Gail determines that, in his refusal to offer direction to the "children" around him, he has been one of those who allowed Percy to grow into a violent racist, just as surely as he waited too long to try to save Joe (491–92).

If the suggestion that inflexible and uncritical attachments to the regional past serve to blind white southerners to truths about their society that are "hidden in plain sight" is less overt in *Absalom, Absalom!*—in which the very idea of "plain sight" is problematic—this theme resonates in the novel's intertextual citation of *So Red the Rose* (1935).[79] Walter Benn Michaels has described many of the parallels between the children of Thomas Sutpen and the protagonists of *So Red the Rose*, a popular plantation romance written by Stark Young, another writer from Oxford, Mississippi, and a member of the Agrarians.[80] However, he omits the fact that Young's narrative places Edward McGehee in precisely the position held by Henry Sutpen in Jason Compson's account of that family's history—that of a young white plantation owner troubled by his friend's relationship with an octoroon. In Young's novel, as Jason says of the story he tells, "something is missing," but this element is hardly the elusive insight into motivation that Faulkner's narrators seek (80). Rather, *So Red the Rose* diligently disavows racial oppression, presenting the antebellum South as a culture in which slaves eagerly provide "birthday surprise[s]" for their owners, who do not "believe in the system" of slavery but see no "way out"; in this society, slaves are punished only when their background renders them "savage," and the sale of their family members provides them with desired opportunities to commit adultery.[81] Edward's encounter with Charles Taliaferro's lover, however, produces a small crisis in this narrative's strategy of repression by raising issues of interracial exploitation and intimacy, neither of which the novel seems able to name; Edward is here rendered especially inarticulate, saying, "By God, man! . . . And so on and so on" (134).

Notably, this refusal to analyze his feelings is the quality most valued in Young's representation of Edward, who elsewhere in the novel is celebrated chiefly for his love of the "Southern country" (103). This form of affiliation is purged of reason and consists strictly of a "feeling" of "tru[th]" and the appearance of "glamour"; Edward thus exemplifies the kind of "peculiar devotion" to a region that Young explicitly celebrated elsewhere.[82] In championing such affiliative feelings over analysis, Young encourages a pattern of disavowal, such that the racial injustice everywhere apparent in the antebellum South and also in his novel may forever be overlooked. This pattern seems to be parodied in Faulkner's representation of Jason Compson, who concludes that, if his account of the Sutpen history seems unreasonable, "the only possible" explanation emerges from "the old virtues": he could not have overlooked any facts, but he may have underestimated the strength of the feelings binding these antebellum protagonists (96). In *Absalom, Absalom!*, however, such assessments of white southern cohesion are consistently inaccurate, whether ascribed to an active antebellum society or to a postwar collective of ghosts.

In contrast to Jason's conservative interpretation of the Sutpen family history, and in sharp opposition to Young's novel, Quentin, with Shreve, delineates a narrative that takes more seriously the desires of and discriminations against people of African ancestry (94). This shift is particularly notable in comparison with the Quentin of *The Sound and the Fury*, who is persistently unable to acknowledge the fullness of African Americans' subjectivity and experience. To cite only one example, even at the moment when Quentin remembers how Dilsey rightly explained why Quentin's mother rejected his younger brother Benjy, Quentin separates himself from both the knowledge and the pain evoked by this memory through denying Dilsey's personhood: "They come into white people's lives like that in sudden sharp black trickles that isolate white facts for an instant in unarguable truth like under a microscope; the rest of the time just voices that laugh when you see nothing to laugh at, tears when no reason for tears" (170). In contrast, the Quentin of *Absalom, Absalom!* cannot so readily produce such disavowals; though his recognition of racial injustice remains limited, these constraints are produced less through verbal dismissal of African American humanity than through retreat into an isolated subjective realm. Accordingly, as Shreve mocks Jim Bond, the "one nigger Sutpen left" without family or home following the burning of the plantation house, Quentin returns to his notoriously fixated regard of his own regional identification: "*I dont hate [the South] . . . I dont. I dont!*" (302, 303). As other critics have noted, the roommates' narrative remains limited, focusing on miscegenation in a way that obscures systemic racial oppression.[83] Nonetheless, as Richard Godden argues, this recital of southern history reveals that such "repressed knowledge . . . lies [close] to the surface."[84] Through gothic form and parodic content, *Absalom, Absalom!* presents a world in which purportedly determinate affiliations serve only to mask more individualized sources of suffering and to belie a history of oppression and division.

My narrative about Faulkner's development is, in one sense, hardly surprising, suggesting as it does a shift from a regional romanticism to a more cosmopolitan modernism, a pattern that would seem to support accounts of delayed but eventual cultural development. But for Faulkner, this movement was facilitated by intensifying his use of a literary form identified with the peripheral and the backward. Rather than simply altering his aesthetic project to demonstrate his attachment to a more progressive culture, Faulkner's use of gothic tropes, like that of other modernists, challenged monolithic and spatializing constructions of local time, exposing the temporal multiplicity that shaped both metropolis and hinterland. After *Absalom, Absalom!* Faulkner appears less attracted to gothic imagery; though later white characters remain interested in the region's past, as exemplified in Ike McCaslin's genealogical research in *Go Down,*

Moses (1942), they are not formally haunted. It may be that the gothic strategies employed in earlier novels enabled Faulkner to explore ideas of a backward-looking white southern identity to his satisfaction; it is also likely that his writing was influenced by a more general shift in representations of the South. As I argue in the next chapter, by the end of the 1930s, southern writers sought to bridge understandings of national and regional time through less spectacular representational forms.

This project coalesced with the beginnings of the civil rights movement, which insisted both that southern apartheid constituted a national problem and that racial injustice permeated the United States. *Go Down, Moses* participates in this "temporal mapping," exploring the extent to which the residents of Jefferson, Mississippi, do and do not participate in national and global models of modernity.[85] For example, in the story "Go Down, Moses," a young man's identity is discovered by a (presumably federal) census taker just before the young man is executed in Chicago, and news of his death reaches Mississippi through a national press association. His grandmother, and the white woman who intercedes on her behalf, walk to town or travel by buggy: their relationship, and the grandmother's understanding of the young man's suffering, are directly shaped by their experiences in the postslavery South.[86] Similarly, in "Delta Autumn," Ike McCaslin learns of miscegenation in another generation of his family and exhibits affective responses as pronounced, if not as gothic, as Quentin's—both denying linear time and compressing space; on the way to this encounter, however, Ike and his nephew also discuss their value conflicts in relation to the New Deal and fascism (361, 364, 338–39).

In suggesting that gothic representations of memory no longer served Faulkner's purposes in the same way after *Absalom, Absalom!* I do not mean to deny his continuing interest in how history affects contemporary life, a view apparently encapsulated in his famous line, "The past is never dead. It's not even past."[87] Spoken by Gavin Stevens (whose opinions often merit critical scrutiny) in *Requiem for a Nun* (1951), these words encourage Temple Drake Stevens (who is married to Gavin's nephew) to acknowledge her feelings of loss and guilt and perhaps even to use her knowledge of history to pursue greater justice in the present.[88] Here, as in so much of Faulkner's work, the narrative seeks to imagine ways in which history and contemporaneity can be placed in productive dialogue, one that avoids two prominent dangers. On the one hand, the past should not displace the present through a gothically alienating and politically oppressive renunciation of change. On the other, the damaging and continuing effects of an unjust history should not be denied through a triumphalist insistence on incessant and unquestionable progress. Where the former still constituted the more influential and dangerous paradigm in the 1930s, the two coexisted by 1951. In the years that followed, these polarized perspectives on racial injustice continued to impede recognition that apartheid constituted not merely a recalcitrant holdover from the past but rather a broadly dispersed element of regional and national modernity. The development of this trend is the topic of my final chapter.

PART THREE

The Shifting "South"

CHAPTER SIX

Provincial Cosmopolitanism

THE PHRASE "provincial cosmopolitanism" may appear simply oxymoronic. As Tom Lutz argues, "Regionalism may seem an odd place to look for an ethos of cosmopolitan openness to difference."[1] Where cosmopolitanism is typically associated with spatial mobility and detachment from any particular locale, the region or province would seem to be defined by spatial boundaries and disarticulated, in meaningful ways, from the nation or larger world.[2] But recent work in both the humanities and the social sciences has disrupted such understandings, insisting on the need to recognize more limited, varying, and contingent forms of local affiliation, including the ways in which people in nonmetropolitan areas may be nonetheless interested in or attached to diverse broader social networks. Thus prominent cultural theorists have urged scholars to be "archivally cosmopolitan"—to "look at the world across time and space and see how people have thought and acted beyond the local."[3] Such analysis can be challenging when studying a region insistently represented, by both residents and observers, as a cultural monolith, or closed society. But while such representations often serve strategic purposes, they may also suggest the difficulty of recognizing cosmopolitan trends in one's own contemporary province.

Certainly, such appears to have been the case for leftist and liberal southern writers during the late 1930s and early 1940s. While the historical record demonstrates that the region was influenced by such broad political affiliations as unionization, black internationalism, and white southern fascism, these movements coexisted with and were often obscured by the perception that the South existed in a distinct and isolated time, comprising one of many global spaces left behind in the march of capitalist modernity. In contrast, the writers discussed in this chapter—Richard Wright, Lillian Smith, Carson McCullers, and James Agee—could be identified as avant-garde: each explicitly sought to disrupt readers' established patterns of thought and to promote experimental or radical trends in artistic and intellectual work, and each further participated (not without discord) in social networks committed to cultural innovation. This chapter examines how assessments of southern temporal seclusion affected such writers' efforts to articulate and advance southern cosmopolitanism during the early years of the civil rights movement. On the one hand, these writers vigorously situated the image of the South in relation to other spaces, demonstrating the ways in which aspects of regional life considered backward were comparable to cultural forms seen elsewhere and, accordingly, exemplified prominent patterns in global modernity. On the other, their narratives demonstrate how perceptions of backwardness could intervene in attempts to imagine regional activism, as characters question whether their cosmopolitan impulses might demonstrate their own temporal divergence from their local peers.

Temporal Mapping

In assessing southern and U.S. history, it is important not only to recognize the effects of the South's comparatively delayed economic modernization and dominant political conservatism but also to observe how perceptions of southern backwardness were mobilized to support political and cultural agendas. As the geographer Edward Soja argues, "Geographically uneven development is an essential part of capitalist spatiality": in the growth of a capitalist economy, both capital and various types of labor become concentrated in geographic areas, producing new differences in power, landscape, and daily experience.[4] Though these spaces are unquestionably coeval—existing at the same time and embroiled in encompassing economic and cultural dynamics—modernization discourse has tended to describe these differences as both spatial and temporal, distinguishing modern capitalist centers from their premodern peripheries.[5] But such rhetoric does not issue solely from hubs of capitalist growth. Soja argues that regionalism, a discourse asserting the cultural specificity of other spaces, often constitutes a response to capitalist regionalization. This "reaction formation" seeks to resist, manage, or exploit capitalist development.[6]

Often cast as the work of a minority group seeking to protect cultural traditions threatened by an advancing and adversarial modernization, regionalism may also protect existing forms of oppression, ensuring that they will be maintained amid processes of economic and cultural change. Developing through history, such social structures are nonetheless dynamic components of the present. Their apparent backwardness emerges not simply from their incongruity with other elements in contemporary life but, more importantly, from the ways in which they are described by both celebrants and critics, who seek either to preserve or to eliminate what they describe as inheritances from the past. Such temporal coding is exploited, as Arjun Appadurai explains, to obscure the role of modernization in stimulating oppression and violence as well as the ways in which dynamics labeled "primordial" support modern nation-states.[7]

During the 1930s, logics of temporal preservation and isolation were vital both in justifying southern apartheid within U.S. discourse and in sustaining the practice within the region. Examining southern history, Immanuel Wallerstein argues that its formulations of cultural continuity and stasis have often served purposes more persuasive than descriptive: "Groups, in seeking to pursue their interests . . . [argue] that the desired behavior is normal, 'traditional,' hallowed by time and therefore expected in the present."[8] Many Agrarians, who promoted resistance to modernization, were explicit about this strategy. John Crowe Ransom, for example, complained that "the urban South, with its heavy importation of regular American ways and regular American citizens, has nearly capitulated to these novelties"; for precisely this reason he urged "Southern leaders to arouse the sectional feeling of the South to its highest pitch of excitement in defense of all the old ways that are threatened."[9] The social psychologist John Dollard argued during this period that white southerners' commitment to the local social structure was upheld by an aggrandizing understanding of the relationship between the region's past and its present—the belief that white supremacist ideology "comes to them through sacred tradition" such that "exercising independent perception against it is unwise and even impious."[10] Dollard, who understood southern racial hierarchies as deeply embedded in the region's institutions and beliefs, nevertheless insisted that these ideas were defensive, cultivated in social discourse as well as in individual thought and feeling amid prevalent recognition that southern traditions existed in a rapidly changing society.

The widespread belief that southerners of all races lived in sway to a backward social structure also marginalized the political opinions and analyses of black southerners. Though the sociologist Charles S. Johnson, for example, altered his assessment by the end of the decade, he argued in *Race Relations* (1934) that "Negroes who are practical psychologists in racial situations know very well . . . that if [they make] the mistake of expecting certain privileges which go with an advanced occupation or status, something very unpleasant may occur. These are well grounded in the mores and are seldom questioned by Negroes."[11] Johnson, who here portrays southern African Americans as acculturated to oppression, acknowledged in the same volume both evidence of changing attitudes and the difficulty of assessing African American political thought, an analytic issue raised by the diversity not only of opinions but also of expressive styles.[12] Contrasting the "articulate group" and the "inarticulate group," he expresses some uncertainty regarding the opinions of the latter, whose "chief symptom of disaffection" he describes as "various patterns of escape from the situation, by direct withdrawal or by dissimulation" (534). The latter reading suggests Zora Neale Hurston's famous theory, published the following year in *Mules and Men*, concerning the complex communicative strategies employed by disempowered African Americans. Hurston argued that "the Negro . . . is particularly evasive. You see we are a polite people and we do not say to our questioner, 'Get out of here!' We smile and tell him or her something that satisfies the white person because, knowing so little about us, he doesn't know what he is missing"; she noted here and elsewhere that she also experienced such "featherbed resistance."[13] But what Hurston represented as opposition was often interpreted as capitulation by sociologists, both white and African American, who were influenced by what Oliver Cox critically described as "the modern caste school of race relations." This theory suggested that both black and white southerners were so acculturated to racial segregation that "the white caste and the black caste [must] remain indefinitely intact"; as Cox argued, such studies suggested that all southerners were inherently isolated from "western society."[14]

Because southern apartheid was sustained among practitioners and protected against opposition by perceptions that it constituted an immutable tradition, it was not effectively challenged by complaints about southern backwardness. Thus, though *The Mind of the South* (1941), W. J. Cash's prominent and influential critique of the region, overtly supported the "great and real changes" taking place there, its detailed attention to such forces was superseded by its certainty that the "old pattern['s] . . . power over the body of the South would remain tremendous, even conclusive."[15] Cash's purpose was to describe how a certain formulation of affiliation—in this case, a "vastly ego-warming and ego-expanding" racial identification and hierarchy—was mobilized to elicit lower-class whites' support for southern elites, obscuring the "economic and social focus" that might have facilitated interracial working-class alliances; as Houston Baker points out, such analysis was vital for southern culture and politics and could usefully be extended to the nation as a whole.[16] But as Michael O'Brien argues, though Cash effectively demonstrated that "a dialectical process had helped to create an influential southern myth," he also "accepted the myth as true": Cash depicts white southerners as so intimately identified with their "proto-Dorian" compact that its perpetuation hardly requires agency or manipulation.[17] And while Cash observes such psychological dynamics in the recent history of multiple capitalist nations, his insistence that the South maintained particular "violence, intolerance, aversion and suspicion toward new ideas, an incapacity for analysis, an inclination to act from feeling rather than from thought, an exaggerated individualism and a too narrow concept of social responsibility, attachment to fictions and false values, above all too great attachment to racial values and a tendency to justify cruelty and injustice in the name of those values, sentimentality and a lack of realism" tended to support existing perceptions of southern backwardness.[18] Thus *Mind of the South* suggested, in a quite familiar way, that apartheid constituted not a broad pattern of modern social organization but rather an anachronistic cultural trait distinct to the region.

In contrast, civil rights activists were at this time emphasizing spatial and implicitly temporal continuity: they insisted both that southern apartheid must be recognized as a national problem and that racial segregation constituted a national practice. World War II provided particular motivation for national audiences to recognize southern racial oppression as an urgent concern, as this transnational conflict pitted the United States against enemies known for racist brutality and for articulating racism as a central aspect of their political philosophy—a focus explicitly shared by southern white supremacists. While the nation's intensified global awareness provided a broader framework through which to view southern beliefs and practices, the war further encouraged the federal government to attend to African Americans' demands, because it needed their support for the war effort. These negotiations highlighted the national and even federal parameters of apartheid, as activists, journalists, and potential soldiers repeatedly emphasized the injustice through which African Americans were placed in segregated units of the armed forces and denied employment at defense companies that were filling federal contracts.[19] This movement also increased national awareness of activism and political diversity within the South, as the NAACP and the Southern Conference for Human Welfare began more actively to challenge southern disfranchising policies. The bill to abolish the poll tax, for example, was cosponsored by Florida senator Claude Pepper in the same year that Cash's book was published, demonstrating, in Congress, both the effects of southern apartheid in limiting national citizenship rights and the efforts of many southerners to alter the region's social structure.[20] By configuring southern apartheid as an urgent national problem and a source of controversy within the region, these movements defied the idea that it existed in a monolithic and isolated time.

In debunking this previously predominant understanding of regional difference, civil rights activists revealed an antinomy that ideas of southern backwardness had long served to mask—that the United States practiced apartheid while insisting on its status as a vanguard of liberal democracy. In other words, by illustrating the coevality of southern apartheid—its existence and potency within the time of the nation—activists interrogated and sought to redefine U.S. nationalism, which had long embraced both liberal and white supremacist principles of affiliation. As the historian Nikhil Pal Singh argues of civil rights activism and discourse during this period, "the political stakes were high as the imperative to include blacks within the nation was increasingly linked to the struggle to imagine the world-system and the future U.S. role within it.... The great promise of World War II was that black aspirations for justice and the interests of American world-ordering power would coincide" to alter the practices and strategies of U.S. governance.[21] Though these hopes were not realized—as evidenced by increased violence against African Americans and the internment of Japanese Americans—they did effect a significant shift in U.S. political thought, which manifested an "intense, racially inflected struggle over the meaning of American freedom."[22]

As the 1940s progressed, the policies and practices of the nation-state were examined in relation to those of collectivities both within and without U.S. borders, forcing discussions of national citizenship to consider its forms of exclusion. Thus, for example, the President's Committee on Civil Rights situated its 1947 report in relation to both notorious global systems of governance, particularly the communism with which the United States was embroiled in intensifying conflict, and notorious local practices. Claiming that "we abhor the totalitarian arrogance which makes one man say that he will respect another man as his equal only if he has '*my* race, *my* religion, *my* political views, *my* social position,'" the committee's report generated recommendations for the institution and protection of civil rights in the southern states as well as throughout the nation, extension of citizenship to residents of Guam and American Samoa, reimbursement for material losses to Japanese Americans who had been placed in internment camps, redress of racism in naturalization laws, self-government in the District of Columbia, and supervision of state practice in order to end, for example, police brutality and military segregation.[23]

For avant-garde southern writers during this transition, such agendas were often expressed through efforts at temporal mapping—challenging the belief that the South existed in a distinct and premodern time, such that its practices and structures could be assessed separately from those of the nation. Temporal mapping also included the project that Robert Brinkmeyer finds in southern literature of this era—one of exploring the relationships between European fascism and southern conservatism.[24] Though fascism itself was often coded as backward, its emergence alongside socialist and democratic states rendered formulations of its temporal isolation doubtful. Thus, as writers and thinkers increasingly explored modernity's political diversity, they necessarily began to explore the mutual influences of its seemingly oppositional times. Describing the South in terms that served to negotiate its apparent temporal seclusion, writers from the late 1930s and early 1940s positioned stereotypically *southern* and *national* traits and experiences as coexistent in bounded locales, and they further situated these locales in relation to broader spatial networks.

Thematically, these works exhibited continuity with narratives that I discussed in the second section of this book; all these probe, to varying extents, the power of individual as opposed to communal desires, the relationship between governmental and vigilante justice systems, the pull of modernization against tradition, and the difficulties of atomization as against those of conformity. But when these differing value systems, associated with differing temporal frameworks, collide in such works as *Their Eyes Were Watching God* and *Light in August*, they are described through literary forms that foreground temporal disjuncture. Thus, for example, Hurston's narrative suddenly gives way to the surrealistic buzzards' funeral, and Faulkner's repeatedly loops back to an often indeterminate past in order to understand contemporary fragmentation and conflict. In contrast, as civil rights discourse increasingly emphasized the connections between southern and national practices of apartheid, creative writers also began to represent U.S. temporal multiplicity in ways that did not require such formal complication. Creating dialogue among diverse temporal forms, they demonstrated that, despite its differences and specificities, the South was nonetheless coeval with the nation—was, as one of Richard's Wright's characters asserts in his first novel, "a part of" the nation.[25]

Such methods were particularly important to Wright, whose early work probed what the critic Robert Stepto calls the nation's "symbolic geography" and its relationship with capitalist modernity.[26] Wright's configurations of the link between the time of the South and that of the larger United States were ambivalent and shifting. Nonetheless, they represent an enduring effort to comprehend relationships between southern-rural and northern-urban experiences as well as the ways in which diverse formulations of southern time could restrict or support antiapartheid activism. His oeuvre from the late 1930s through the early 1940s contains many representations of intransigent southern backwardness; these include notorious assessments of southern African American culture, such as his autobiographical complaint concerning "the strange absence of real kindness in Negroes . . . how bare our traditions, how hollow our memories, how lacking we were in those intangible sentiments that bind man to man."[27] This claim was explicitly written to criticize the effects of apartheid, which, he argues, separates African Americans from "Western civilization," but while this project suggests temporal distance, his work from this period also manifests an alternate perspective. Wright's fiction, particularly, often undercuts or reframes such perceptions describing African Americans' explicitly *modern* experience—both the ways in which racial oppression constituted a distinctly modern system of economic and political exploitation, and the ways in which African Americans positioned themselves in time.[28] These conflicting conceptions emerged from multiple influences.

Wright's focus on southern backwardness was fueled, for example, by his study of sociology, which routinely described southern agriculture as "a plantation-feudal economy," a phrase reiterated in Wright's "Blueprint for Negro Writing" (1937).[29] The Chicago School social scientists whom Wright credited with providing his "first concrete vision of the forces that molded the urban negro's body and soul" often viewed folkloric and rural cultures with nostalgia, but this desire itself imposed temporal distance, promoting the thesis that people affiliated with such cultures might not be able to withstand their inevitable transition to modernity.[30] Like many African Americans and leftists of the era, Wright expressed substantial concern about how such a temporal lag might affect the consciousness of the people it affected. Though he argued that folklore—"the channels through which the racial wisdom flowed"—contained perspectives demonstrating "the emergence of a new culture in the shell of the old," he also suggested that some elements of southern African American culture—such as "reactionary nationalism" and "the archaic morphology of Christian salvation"—could be antithetical to political progress.[31]

Wright's interest in Communist politics and theory proved an ambivalent influence on his approach to temporal difference. Wright moved to Chicago before 1930 and does not appear to have shared directly the experience of black southern Communists, who created, as described by Robin D. G. Kelley, a political culture that drew on preexisting African

American expressions.³² Rather, Wright's autobiography describes his initial attraction to communism as distinctly textual: though he is cynical concerning the speakers he sees and the faction-ridden groups he encounters, the "revolutionary words" he reads suggest "the possibility of uniting scattered but kindred peoples into a whole."³³ As Bill Maxwell notes, at least one of these texts bolstered Wright's hope that folk culture could be mobilized for political change: his autobiography avows a "total emotional commitment" to Josef Stalin's *The National and Colonial Question*, which "encouraged . . . forgotten folk . . . to see in their ancient customs meanings and satisfactions as deep as those contained in supposedly superior ways of living."³⁴

But communist theory also offered a quite opposite influence in Marx's own "The Eighteenth Brumaire of Louis Bonaparte," which argued that nineteenth-century French "small peasants," because of their poverty and isolation, developed "no unity, no national union and no political organization" and, rather, remained in "stupefied bondage" to the "old order"; as their agricultural system deteriorated, they became "troglodytes" enslaved to the bourgeoisie.³⁵ Such arguments particularly influenced leftist understandings of fascism, which was said to mobilize a specifically reactionary appeal to people isolated from the centers of capitalist modernity; Wright himself used this argument to explain African Americans' attraction to fascism.³⁶ But while he was sometimes careful to emphasize that such dynamics constituted one aspect of modernity itself, he also occasionally reinforced ideas of southern African American anachronism. Accordingly, Wright's documentary of African American life parallels Marx's depiction of nineteenth-century peasants: *12 Million Black Voices* (1941) describes the "movement of a debased feudal folk toward a twentieth-century urbanization," in which they are exploited first by the "Lords of the Land" and then the "Bosses of the Buildings."³⁷ As Farah Jasmine Griffin argues, this volume suggests that African American migrants from the South must work to "acquire the status of modern men"; to do so, in Wright's words, they must "[accept] . . . the death of our old folk lives."³⁸

Wright's tendency to depict southern African Americans as temporally isolated also appears to have been a response to interpersonal dynamics. It emerges most forcefully in his autobiography as he describes his alienation from his father, whose abandonment of his family caused painful consequences while Wright was still a young child. Describing his reunion with this "peasant" figure, which occurred after Wright migrated to the North, the son determines that his father's behavior is "chained... to the direct, animalistic impulses of his withering body" and that the two are now "forever strangers, speaking a different language, living on vastly distant planes of reality."[39] His allochronic discourse, which insists that these two contemporaries inhabit distinct temporalities, enables Wright to describe and secure their profound estrangement.[40] Accordingly, one could extend Robert Stepto's argument to say that Wright "shelve[s]" his father "in the space" *and time* that "he has created for him."[41] Qiana Whitted suggests that such personal and psychological factors may also have shaped Wright's allochronic representations of African American women and religion, themes repeatedly linked in his work.[42] But given that images of southern backwardness, so common in this era, enabled Wright to communicate so many political and personal beliefs concisely, it is noteworthy that he often resisted or disrupted such temporal logics, insisting instead that the "Southern scheme of oppression," as he described it in the essay "How Bigger Was Born" (1940), was both an organizing principle in U.S. modernity and "an appendage of a far vaster and in many respects more ruthless and impersonal commodity-profit machine."[43]

His "Big Boy Leaves Home" (1936), for example, depicts lynching not as a long-established custom, as it was often understood, but as a modern scene of mass entertainment used to create and cement oppressive political collectives. Thus this story, republished in *Uncle Tom's Children* (1940), confronted those representations of lynching that separated these forms of racial oppression from the temporality of the nation, depicting them as anachronistic anomalies rather than as contemporary systems for delimiting social power. Such allochronic understandings of southern racial violence were promoted even by liberals' studies of the region. For example, in W. T. Couch's substantial anthology *Culture in the South* (1935), which explicitly challenged conservative agrarian accounts of the region, the social psychologist H. C. Brearley's contribution attributed lynching and other forms of homicide to the "feudal spirit" inherited from the South's first white settlers, according to which "honor was esteemed more than life itself."[44] In this account, lynching exemplifies centuries-old cultural traits rather than a response to contemporary economic and political competition. Such understandings, though challenged, were pervasive and lingering. Willis Weatherford and Charles Johnson's *Race Relations* also associated lynching with "primitive communities," and Gunnar Myrdal's *An American Dilemma* (1944) described lynching as one element in the South's broader resistance to modernity; Myrdal linked racial violence with "isolation . . . and the general boredom of rural and small town life" as well as "denunciations of modern thought, scientific progress, and all kinds of nonconformism."[45]

Ideas of a premodern South do appear in Wright's novella, but here they are invoked with heavy irony. The narrative foregrounds pastoral description in the scene in which Big Boy, who is hiding, hears the lynching party singing while torturing his friend Bobo: "There were women singing now. Their voices made the song round and full. Song waves rolled over the top of the pine trees. . . . Sometimes cricket cries cut surprisingly across the mob song."[46] Wright's account of the setting, even aside from the events that are transpiring, evokes a somber rural scene: "The sky sagged low. . . . A dog had gone to the utmost top of the hill. At each lull of the song his howl floated full into the night." But while the narrative situates this practice among local flora and fauna, the representation of the mob suggests a population motivated not by tradition or by strictly primitive traits but rather by demand for modern excitements; thus their violence is marked by visual excess—"MO WOOD!" and "MO GAS!"—and desire for lasting signs of their participation in this spectacle—"SOURVINEERS!" (56–57).

Read through Wright's theory that diverse global political movements expressed the inchoate desires of publics simultaneously excited and marginalized by capitalist development, this lynch mob appears less resistant to modernity than symptomatic of its conflicts. In "How Bigger Was Born" (1940), Wright describes Bigger Thomas—both the protagonist of *Native Son* and a more generalized "symbolic figure" who is experiencing a "deep sense of exclusion"—as a young man struggling to negotiate competing temporalities. Wright's essay explains that Bigger is "estranged from the religion and the folk culture of his race" and "trying to react to and answer the call of the dominant civilization whose glitter came to him through the newspapers, magazines, radios, movies, and the mere imposing sight and sound of daily American life"; Wright further suggests that such "emotional patterns" facilitated both communist and fascist revolutions.[47] Arguing that rhetorics from both "the side of the Fascists" and the "side of the oppressed" resonated with his understanding of Bigger, Wright explains that the numerous dislocations of modernity—particularly its "national and class strife" and nullification of "metaphysical meanings"—created the desire for "a highly ritualized and symbolized life" as well as "violence . . . extreme action and sensation."[48] These ideas appear also in "Big Boy Leaves Home." Although distinct in its public torture and murder, the lynching's status as a politically unifying entertainment for white families suggests comparison to fascist celebrations of national pride, and in doing so, the scene invokes an increasingly prominent understanding of southern racism. Big Boy's own imagining of the lynching before it takes place reinforces the story's temporal multiplicity. Despite the rural tropes of his life—as he skips school, for example, to visit the "swimming hole" with close friends—his imagination suggests the influence of contemporary media, particularly the violent urban pulp fictions for which Wright describes his early fondness in *Black Boy*.[49] Fantasizing about what he might do if caught, Big Boy imagines newspaper representations of his fighting off the mob with a shotgun: "N the newspapersd say: NIGGER KILLS DOZEN OF MOB BEFO LYNCHED!" (50).

Uncle Tom's Children, which comprises several novellas concerning racial conflict in the South, explicitly argues that the region's continuing white supremacist oppression occurs in a new social context: the epigraph describes "a new word from another generation which says:—'Uncle Tom is dead!'" Accordingly, though the religious African American protagonist of "Fire and Cloud," Dan Taylor, romanticizes "the good ol days" when there was "plenty to eat [and] the blessings of God had been overflowing," he recognizes the hypocrisy of the mayor, who suggests that the town has maintained a beneficent stasis (159). This white official argues that "its [sic] our job to keep order among the whites, and we would like to think of you as being a responsible man to keep order among the blacks" (184); the mayor's invocation of "good old Dixie" demonstrates what the literary critic Scott Romine, examining southern literature, has described as the "first law of community . . . insofar as it is cohesive, a community will tend to be coercive."[50] Taylor, however, rejects the mayor's attempt to impose such stagnation; reexamining the meaning and purpose of his work and his faith, he determines that his mission is for "the *people*," as expressed in political protest (250). The social and individual changes depicted in this collection reveal the texture of southern time to be multiple and uneven. Thus the work insists that southern apartheid and racial violence must be understood through their relationships to numerous temporal frameworks. As Maxwell argues, it "flaunts leaks in the rural/urban, South/North opposition."[51]

Where *Uncle Tom's Children* linked southern apartheid to a broader temporality of change and modernization, Wright's novel *Native Son* (1940) linked Chicago's racial oppression to that of the South, arguing that these seemingly disparate spaces shared white supremacist practices and that northern elites mobilized avowedly southern images and rhetorics to justify apartheid elsewhere. The de facto segregation of Bigger's Chicago is absolute: his attorney, Max, describes it as the effect of agreements shared by "every school teacher," "authorities," and "all real estate operators" (394). Like the African American defendants of Scottsboro, Alabama, whose fame persisted through the decade as their lawyers pursued multiple appeals, Bigger would face a jury "not of his peers, but of an alien and hostile race!" As protestors argued of the historical case, Max exclaims, "An outright lynching would be more honest" (384). In "How Bigger Was Born," Wright explained, "In Dixie there are two worlds, the white world and the black world, and they are physically separated," but he noted that Chicago's Black Belt was equally "locked-in" (437); his fictional attorney generalizes such treatment to all African Americans (390).

Max's discourse is temporally ambivalent, insisting on both the specific modernity of segregated African Americans—"a new form of life"—and their temporal isolation (391). He suggests that, in their segregation, they maintain "emotions and impulses and attitudes as yet unconditioned by the strivings of science and civilization" (387). His tropes are, on occasion, gothic: evoking Marx's representation of French peasants "on the margins of existence" after being eviscerated by the "vampire" of capital, Max describes the entire populace of the Black Belt as a "corpse."[52] Max seeks to place the seeds of this destruction in the past: predicting that the nation's Black Belts will revolt in "a wild cataract of emotion that will brook no control," he understands this potentiality as the eruption of "old" emotions—"guilt" and "hate" (392, 387). But the larger narrative situates Bigger's desire and frustration more directly in his relationship with new technological and cultural forms, as he longs to fly airplanes, go to the movies, disseminate his own image, and feel a sense of connection with multitudes he has never met (17, 28, 130, 361–63). Marginalized from the central forces of capitalist change, Bigger is vitally influenced by its marketing and, more interestingly, its tendency to forge connections among dispersed populations. Thus, while the novel associates primitivist tropes with modern racism—vividly demonstrated, for example, as Bigger views the film *Trader Horn*—it unambiguously situates its protagonist within modernity.

Within this modernity, as Houston Baker has since argued in *Turning South Again* (2001), southern white supremacy provides institutional models as well as support for the oppressive practices of other regions. Accordingly, a *Chicago Tribune* editorial quotes a Mississippi newspaper that advocates "public and dramatic" execution, apartheid, and regulation of African Americans' "speech and actions"—practices to which Bigger has felt vulnerable throughout the novel (280–81). But Wright goes beyond his description of Bigger's life and his representation of this editorial to link Chicago's racial structures to those of the South. Ultimately, Bigger's trial replicates the court decision that instantiated southern apartheid in U.S. law. In determining Bigger's punishment after he has pleaded guilty, the judge argues that his "duty . . . is clear" because "of the unprecedented disturbance of the public mind," and he endorses the prosecutor's assessment that the law is concerned not with liberal conceptions of rights but with "all our cherished values," including white supremacy (417, 408). Accordingly, this fictional ruling supports the verdict of *Plessy v. Ferguson* (1896), which held that federal authorities could not intervene in "the established usages, customs and traditions of the people" and must support "public peace and good order."[53] By foregrounding this particularist facet of U.S. governance, the novel thus challenged the political self-representation of a nation that, preparing for war against fascism, described itself as a bastion of liberal democracy.

But while Wright's narratives often seamlessly explore how temporal multiplicity traverses national space—observing especially how the idea of backwardness is often mobilized to support people in power—he was more tentative, as I have shown, in attributing such multiplicity to southern communities and individuals. His persistence in this effort, however, may suggest its importance in his thought concerning social and political change. In the course of expanding *Uncle Tom's Children*, for example, he shifts from depicting folk consciousness as essentially removed from that of modern subjects to showing how a woman deeply cathected to traditional views develops new frameworks of understanding and belief.

In "Long Black Song," a novella included in the first edition of *Uncle Tom's Children*, Wright depicts time as the central element in the contrast between a southern African American woman and a white traveling salesman. After hearing that the woman, Sarah, has no clock and that her family "get[s] erlong widout time," the salesman, shocked, exclaims, "This beats everything" (131). He then shows her his graphophone clock, and upon hearing, from the graphophone, that *"time shall be no more,"* Sarah's body begins to enact a radical compression of her own temporal framework, such that she experiences the seasons of the year in a heartbeat: "Her blood surged like the long gladness of summer. . . . Her blood ebbed like the deep dream of sleep in winter" (132–33). This reaction prefigures her helpless response to the salesman's sexual predation and to the apocalyptic violence that follows, destroying her husband and home.[54] Here, by representing national commerce in a heterogeneous local setting, Wright indicates the connections between regional and national culture but only to suggest that, however corrupt the ambassadors of capitalism may be, they will inevitably overcome those dependent on folk consciousness, even though the latter maintain more humane values. In Zora Neale Hurston's critical account, Wright offers only "the solution of the PARTY. . . . And march!"[55]

But in "Bright and Morning Star," which was added to the 1940 edition of *Uncle Tom's Children*, this solution—as Sue sacrifices herself for the local Communist Party—is less imposed than carefully and tentatively adopted through the protagonist's shifting thoughts and identifications. This novella depicts a position of which Wright was often harshly critical, as Sue found it "a great boon . . . to cling to [Christ], to be like Him and suffer without a mumbling word," but here Wright ascribes a political meaning to that faith. Imagining "the white folks and their laws" as "temptation, something to lure her from her Lord," Sue sees her rejection of white supremacy as a religious protest and obeys the laws "with a soft smile of secret knowing" (224–25). When her sons become Communists, she maintains the structures of her previous faith in her zeal for this new one: "Her sons had ripped from her startled eyes her old visions, and image by image had given her a new one, different, but great and strong enough to fling her into the light of another grace" (225). But this faith continues to feel "strange" and "new," and she realizes late in the narrative that her love of Christian hymns demonstrates a continuing attachment to the distrust of white people that had informed her religious faith (252). Crucially, this distrust proves correct: where her sons see such racial judgments as outdated, Sue's belief that she knows "*all*" local African Americans "from way back" and that such knowledge provides an important guarantee of loyalty is legitimated when a white Communist Party recruit turns out to be a mole (234). Confused by these differing beliefs, and weakened from a brutal police beating, Sue reveals important information to this informer and then, seeking to redress her mistake, seeks "another hope, one more terrible vision to give her the strength to live and act" (252). The story concludes when she creates a new identity for herself from more narrow and stereotypical social roles, presenting herself to the mob as a folk mother who is seeking only to preserve her dead son's body; she uses that opportunity to kill the traitor (253, 261). As Cheryl Higashida argues, the Popular Front mobilized the figure of such mothers to symbolize how working-class women could use Communist activism to provide expression and communal support for their existing beliefs and needs.[56] Through the figure of Sue, then, Wright compresses both old and new and southern and leftist-national, suggesting that none of these divisions need constitute the absolute communicative and affiliative barriers they appeared to be in many of his other works.

Wright was hardly alone in struggling to imagine the subjective transcendence of such barriers. Like his work, Lillian Smith's *Strange Fruit* (1944), described by the literary critic Richard King as "a sort of tract," traced connections among diverse sites of racial violence and cultural conservatism.[57] Grace Elizabeth Hale argues that Smith "spoke out with increasing and unparalleled white directness in the late 1930s against the culture of segregation and the damaging effects of racial separation on southern whites themselves"; using the title of the haunting and popular song about lynching first recorded by Billie Holiday in 1939, Smith's novel also challenges celebratory images of the "gallant South."[58] But it does so, in part, by situating regional politics in relation to contemporary global and national movements. For example, in the mill town area of the novel's Maxwell, Georgia, one resident wants to start a union and is accused of "talking like them Russia folks!"[59] A white southern character, Tracy Deen, goes to France in World War I, where a soldier from Newark expresses his belief that the war is being fought for democracy and could result in a "new world" of egalitarianism. The southerner speaks up to say, "You don't understand us," and is seconded by someone from Chicago, where residents would "never let the Jews in," and a Californian, who would "never let the Japs and Chinks in" (49).

Disputing the idea of absolute cultural barriers between the U.S. South and other spaces, *Strange Fruit* nonetheless insists on the experience of temporal distance in shaping one's responses to others and even one's sense of self. Ideas of "cultural lag" are most evident in the text among characters who have traveled and must confront their feelings about the South upon returning. Thus, for example, a white woman returns from a northern university and objects to the local revival's use "in this day" of "frontier methods," and an African American man returns from Washington, D.C., only to fear that his family members in Georgia are "rotting away" (66, 9). In attending to how travel forces individuals to negotiate such differences, the narrative challenges ideas of an isolated southern time. But it also suggests that perceptions of a monolithic temporal difference may make it impossible for individuals to reconcile their diverse experiences and desires. When Tracy Deen, a white southerner, returns from the war, after contemplating a life unaffected by apartheid, he feels alienated from southern culture and even materiality, as if despite his presence in the South, he finds it unintelligible: "It was as if he were the only thing real" (53).

Thus Tracy manifests in his own consciousness a problem that has been theorized in relation to social interaction. The anthropologist Johannes Fabian argues that, if one wishes to communicate with a person perceived to inhabit a different temporality, one must create intersubjective time—a form of experience that acknowledges the contemporaneity of diverse participants and thus facilitates negotiation of socially constructed temporal categories.[60] But Tracy identifies his own feelings and perceptions with distinct temporalities; accordingly, he finds it impossible to comprehend them simultaneously. Eager to visit his publicly unacknowledged African American lover, Nonnie, he finds "nothing real" in his interactions with other old friends and family members, and as he observes the landscape, though his "eye muscles resum[ed] old movements learned long before he could remember . . . no feelings returned with them" (55). With Nonnie, he reveals the experiences of his immediate past while at war and speculates about their future; on leaving her company, he feels confident of his identity and desires—secure in his "new world" (57). On his way home, however, he meets a familiar African American couple and observes that the woman, Roseanna, immediately changes her manner when she sees him, "as if she were hastily buttoning" on a mode of interaction reserved for white people (58). Immediately afterward, he feels depressed—"tired as hell . . . and nothing was worth doing"—and as if he has lost his new world, such that "the woman he loved" has become "a colored girl named Nonnie. That was all there was to it" (59). This shift is described explicitly as a return to his previous way of being: "Maybe it had been shell-shock. . . . Or plain amnesia. . . . Maybe he'd lost, not his memory, but his white feelings" (60).

In this way, Smith's work suggests that individual identifications with a seemingly isolated southern temporality could coexist, through a kind of psychological self-division, with attention to broad social changes that were already affecting the region. Tracy, for example, "knew what the world was thinking . . . what the facts were"; these include the economic and social inefficiency of southern apartheid, as well as the debunking, among anthropologists, of theories of white racial superiority (59). He feels, however, that these facts are irrelevant to his "old world," and that his desired new world could never exist in its place (61). Despite alterations in his worldview—demonstrating individuated change within the region—and also shifts in the broad social networks of which the South was a component, he is convinced that southern cultural and political stasis is immutable. Accordingly, as he seeks to change his life on his initial return, the narrative uses an image of psychological repression to describe his feelings toward his previous identification with the region: he "pushed the South from him as he went through it, pushed everything he had ever known or feared or hated or believed in, away from him" (53).

Smith's representations, like those of Wright, demonstrate that in their efforts at temporal mapping, southern writers considered not only the relationships between the South and other geopolitical spaces but also the ways in which individual residents might experience the region's temporal ambiguities. As these narratives explored continuities between the South and other areas, challenging the idea that the region was a temporally isolated cultural alterity in which all southerners were adapted to their social positions, these writers confronted the issue of how residents did understand the South's distinct social and political structures. In short, if regional culture was not essentially backward, then how and why did its elites manage to enforce political, behavioral, and economic norms that were widely recognized as, to use Ralph Ellison's word, "regressive"?[61] For Ellison, analysis of this question—"the problem of the irrational"—constituted "that blind spot in our knowledge of society where Marx cries out for Freud and Freud for Marx"; demonstrating that "the economic base of American capitalism had become dislocated from its ideological superstructure," the intransigence of U.S. apartheid suggested a need, insufficiently recognized by the "New Deal and the official left," to examine "those points where economic and psychological pressures conflicted."[62] The usefulness of such investigation was also suggested by southern literature of this period, which increasingly mobilized psychoanalytic concepts—such as repression, projection, and working through—to describe characters' responses to apartheid, change, and temporal multiplicity.

Apartheid's Psychic Structures

Scholars continue to question whether southern apartheid was experienced as a firmly established system that effectively acculturated its inhabitants or as a site of contestation. Such concerns seem implicit in historiographic debates about the agency of participants in the Great Migration—the degree to which the decision to migrate reflected political, as well as economic, goals—and in assessments of the "southern folk aesthetic."[63] While such historians as Robin D. G. Kelley and Nan

Elizabeth Woodruff have articulated rich histories of southern African American political thought and protest, some literary scholars' accounts of southern African American life from the 1920s and 1930s have tended, in Madhu Dubey's view, to produce images of a "lost racial community" that, in inhabiting a "putatively premodern era," can seem incompatible with antiapartheid activism.[64] Scholarship concerning white southerners has long held that they were complacent about apartheid, maintaining beliefs that the historian Joel Williamson describes as a specifically temporal disavowal; he argues that, during the 1920s and 1930s, white southerners "looked backward" into a mythical Old South past "and somehow felt all together, warm, and secure . . . as if . . . it had somehow stepped out of time and lost its place in the flow of the larger world."[65] More recent scholars seek to understand the psychological or ideological processes that facilitated such disavowal. For example, Patricia Yaeger, studying white southerners' disavowals in "everyday racial interactions," invokes the psychoanalytic concept of the "unthought known," Christopher Bollas's term for the "countless rules for being and relating" that the infant incorporates during early relations with caretakers and that are generally inaccessible to subsequent intellection.[66]

This topic was vital to southern writers of the late 1930s and early 1940s, who both explored impediments to the development of broader political awareness and often sought to imagine how these could be worked through. Thus Wright and Smith, as I have shown, explored the ways in which perceptions of temporal fixity or multiplicity—local and global—affected both individual consciousness and communities. Their work describes the power of temporal ideologies to obstruct communication between people who might otherwise, for political, social, or psychological reasons, desire to affiliate. In a society where, to use Appadurai's term, the "production of locality" involved rigid segregation, mandated behaviors, and near incessant surveillance, the quest for a "reliably" hierarchical social structure also involved "the socialization . . . of time," an insistence on stasis, tradition, and inherently backward people.[67] This is not to deny that many southern individuals desired change, and that regional life also included economic and institutional transformation, as well as vital cultural influences from other states and nations. But when, for example, visual and aural media brought images of other locales to southern neighborhoods, they also, as I have shown, often bore portrayals of a temporally isolated South. Thus residents observing their region in print, radio, or film may have been, on occasion, impressed simultaneously with the modernity of their own interests and the anachronism of their environs. Southern narratives from this era suggest the difficulties facing people who are convinced that temporal difference separates them from others in their locale, as such beliefs thwart precisely the kind of communication that might enable such individuals to reconsider these assumptions.

The degree to which perceptions of temporal distance could produce a sense of isolation and futility among would-be avant-gardists during the era leading up to the civil rights movement is powerfully suggested by James Agee's text in *Let Us Now Praise Famous Men* (1941). This work serves as a foil to others in this chapter, as it accepted prominent accounts of southern agricultural laborers' backwardness. Nonetheless, as it thematizes the difficulty of communication, it sheds light on the conceptual problems facing writers who sought to detect any form of cosmopolitanism within the region during this period. Agee is convinced that his readers could not possibly comprehend the alterity represented by tenant-farming families, and he complains that language cannot convey the "actual existence" of their lives, which he fears will seem phantasmic to his audience.[68] Cynical about others' ability to comprehend the tenants' "single, irreparable, unrepeatable existences," he often doubts his own as well, describing himself and the photographer Walker Evans as "quite monstrously alien human beings" (7, 10). Much of this difference is configured as temporal: placing the tenants at a less advanced level of what was then broadly recognized as social evolution, Agee describes them as "profoundly simple individuals" and his conversation with the elder Gudgers as that between "two plain people and one complex one."[69] As is often noted, Agee's text insistently returns to his distress about the material and educational advantages that he has in relation to the tenants; while these seem to create an inherent barrier between him and his subjects, his efforts to efface or overcome that barrier without neglectfully disavowing it are also duly famous.[70] It is also the case that he describes his commonality with them in terms both developmental—"we, human beings, at our best are scarcely entered into the post-diaper stage of our development"—and experiential—"these families, not otherwise than with every family in the earth, how each, apart, how inconceivably lonely, sorrowful, and remote!" (221, 48). But while the text suggests, as Susan Hegeman argues, that all individuals are "essentially *unknowable*" to others, that does not reduce the significance of temporal difference.[71] On the contrary, the primitivism of the tenants appears to be one of the text's few certainties.

The centrality of temporal distance in Agee's project is suggested by its role in his methodological and aesthetic meditations. As T. V. Reed has argued, Agee relentlessly foregrounds these reflections as part of his effort to "shatter . . . readers' expectations."[72] Thus he devotes many descriptive passages to the beauty of the tenants' environments—the "virtuosity" of the wooden palings that protect the Gudgers' garden, for example, and the "classicism" of their clothing—but also considers the "moral problems involved in evaluating" these aesthetic qualities (115, 234, 177): "These classicisms are created of economic need, of local availability, and of local-primitive tradition: and in their purity they are the exclusive property and privilege of the people at the bottom of that world. To those who own and create it this 'beauty' is, however, irrelevant and undiscernible. It is best discernible to those who by economic advantages of training have only a shameful and thief's right to it" (178). As John Hilgart argues, these efforts to imagine a more "liberating" relationship to the material world correspond to Agee's goal of inculcating a particular kind of consciousness in the reader, such that "everything is to be discerned . . . without either dissection into science, or digestion into art, but . . . as it stands . . . simply the cruel radiance of what is."[73] But despite the zeal with which Agee encourages such perception, he does not suggest that it will alter the tenants' circumstances. Nor is it clear that they might partake of such consciousness, as they inhabit their social position not only because of "the whole world-system of which tenantry is one modification" but also because of "other sources . . . psychological, semantic, traditional, perhaps glandular" (182). Thus, despite the intensely oppositional tone of Agee's text, it nonetheless suggests, as Hegeman argues, "that cultural strata ought to remain distinct."[74]

But while Agee did not, like other writers discussed in this chapter, seek to disrupt understandings of a distinct southern time, his approach to temporal distance does suggest why such attempts may have been so tentative and difficult. Agee foregrounds both his desperation to establish some kind of reciprocal relationship with his subjects and his belief that it is inherently impossible to do so. He argues that they lack both the knowledge and the cognitive ability of modern subjects: "No equipment to handle an abstract idea or to receive it: nor to receive or handle at all complex facts: nor to put facts and ideas together and strike any fire or meaning from them" (276). Given this assessment, it is no wonder that he so doubts their ability either to express thoughts or to comprehend his. He cannot imagine any way to communicate with Mrs. Ricketts when she appears anxious as he and Walker Evans prepare to take her family's pictures, and his inability, as well as the paltriness of his attempt, fills him with self-loathing; dismissing the possibility of verbal interaction, he regrets that she could not interpret his gaze and "tender smiling (which it sickens me to disgust to think of)" (321–23). Conversely, describing how Emma sought to make him feel welcome by saying, "You make us feel easy with you; we don't have to act any different from what it comes natural to act," he argues that he is now incapable of expressing his feelings about that moment to readers—"What's the use trying to say what I felt?"—and parenthetically asserts the limits of her ability to communicate to Evans: Agee promises to convey her sentiments, saying, "I knew she could never say it over again" (57–58). Throughout, he depicts his mental state as one of overwhelming desire and frustration, as he perpetually projects a barrier that he longs to transcend.

Often overstating the effects of differences—whether deriving from social position or the idiosyncrasies of individual experience and desire—Agee also denies them, engaging in unrestrained projective identification. He claims intimate knowledge of the tenants' bodies, for example—"I lie down inside each one as if exhausted in a bed"—and produces numerous statements that appear to originate from the tenants but could not, in many cases, have been spoken to him.[75] Agee's description of the sexual attraction between him and the tenant women has been said to counteract readers' perceptions of an impermeable class barrier between the writer and his subjects, but his unabashed projection of his desires onto others suggests the kind of invasiveness of which Agee is overtly ashamed elsewhere in the text.[76] Noting the consistency and anxiety with which Agee stages this dynamic, William Todd Schultz has argued that the text is shaped by a "primal scene schema," an unconscious paradigm providing both images and affects that the author is compelled to restage and repeat.[77] The text pervasively links, for example, its descriptions of excessive bourgeois consumption and a depleted, "trapped" working class with suggestions of incessant infantile need and a spent, rejecting maternal breast: it imagines the sky as a woman "withdrawn from us with all her strength . . . with her stars as milk above our heavy dark," the farm as "the wrung breast of one human family's need and of an owner's taking," and Annie Mae Gudger's breast as "delicately shriveled, and blue."[78] These representations could emerge from unconscious compulsion or conscious intention, as Agee cites Freud as an "unpaid agitator" in the text's front matter. In either case, however, their effect is to reinforce the idea that the tenants could not meaningfully interact with Agee in social space, as they are so decisively located in Agee's own psyche.

In sum, the barriers that Agee records in this text seem overdetermined, emerging from desire, experience, ideology, and the awareness of others' responses to his interactions. (He repeatedly describes the way others in the town observe him as he talks to tenants and, especially, African American sharecroppers.) Within this proliferation of social boundaries, however, temporal distancing plays a particularly stratifying role, intensifying both perceptions of difference and assessments of whether it can be mitigated. The centrality of allotemporal understanding in his experience is demonstrated even in the moments when he comes closest to working through his anxieties about his relationship to the tenants and describing a reciprocal, less phantasmic, exchange. As other critics have noted, and as the progression of the text suggests, Agee is consciously attempting to work through ideas of class difference that shaped his childhood experience and continue to inform his self-image. By the end of the book, he describes a late meal with George and Annie Mae Gudger in which they "seemed not other than my own parents," and at which point he imagines that his father's family lived in similar circumstances.[79] As he explains how Annie Mae apologizes for the meal she has left her bed to prepare for him and how he eats a great deal in order to dispel the idea that he might be " 'superior' to them and their food," he implicitly also suggests how so many of his communicative anxieties and his imagined invasions were related to his desire to recapture a long lost—and, it is suggested elsewhere, all too fragile—sense of familial unity (364–65). But his dream of transcending the chronological time in which he has grown to adulthood is both enabled and obstructed by his sense of the tenant farmers' temporal stasis: on the one hand, the tenants seem to maintain the time he has lost, but on the other, his education and his urban affiliations exclude him almost as thoroughly from that time as do years. Such beliefs preclude his forging a relationship with the tenants in a truly intersubjective time, as he seems unable to comprehend their coeval existence.

Such difficulties are also staged in Carson McCullers's *The Heart Is a Lonely Hunter* (1940), which foregrounds the prominence of new influences on southern residents. Rather than positing that its characters are cut off from the world strictly by the isolation of southern time, this novel suggests that desires for new forms of experience alienate these figures from local social networks, which they associate with fixity. McCullers emphasizes the removal of the novel's locale from events that attract global attention by juxtaposing a newspaper column describing the town's inability "to afford traffic lights at certain dangerous intersections" and a story reporting "on the war in the Orient." But she also describes how knowledge of a broader world affects the feelings and aspirations of the townspeople.[80] Young Mick Kelly—who is alienated from a sister who thinks of nothing but "movie stars and getting in the movies" and attached chiefly to the younger siblings for whom Mick is a major caretaker—phantasmically identifies with famous figures from Edison to Mussolini (41, 37). Though these attachments sustain Mick amid her palpable isolation, they also, in indicating her desire to transcend her current environs, perpetuate that seclusion. Although such desire is clearly shared by others, Mick feels that her longings must be kept private and secret: "With her it was like there was two places—the inside room and the outside room. School and the family and things that happened every day were in the outside room. . . . Foreign countries and plans and music were in the inside room" (163).

This secrecy reflects the shame that Mick feels concerning her transregional fantasies: she seems to fear that, because of her spatial and economic circumstances, her desires may never be fulfilled, and to admit those desires would be to risk public failure. Mick has access to media that stage the possibility of fame and of rewarding creativity through images of "DICK TRACY" and Mozart's music, but she can hear the latter only through listening to others' radios, and her daily experience is embedded in a town where a "large percentage of the population" is employed by low-paying factories, such that "in the faces along the streets there was [often] the desperate look of hunger and of loneliness" (37, 102, 6). The possibility that her circumstances will not support her desires is confirmed when she must quit piano lessons and eventually even high school because of her family's poverty. Her fear that the longing for broad attention must lead to rejection and failure is clarified by the similar experience of her friend Harry Minowitz, whose early longings to connect to a distant community become a source of shame as he develops deeper understanding of its actions: "I used to be a Fascist. . . . You know all the pictures of the people our age in Europe marching and singing songs and keeping step together. I used to think that was wonderful. All of them pledged to each other and with one leader. All of them with the same ideals and marching in step together. I didn't worry much about what was happening to the Jewish minorities because I didn't want to think about it. And because at the time I didn't want to think like I was Jewish. . . . It was a terrible transgression. A moral wrong" (247).

Each of these characters desires social attachment—the one seeking support for creative effort and aspiration, and the other passionate commonality—but believes that such desires cannot be uttered publicly. Unwilling or even unable to share their desires with others, they have no one to help them understand their overwhelming feelings of frustration and self-loathing. Refusing to listen to Mick's comments, the older Harry appears never to discuss his interest in fascism with others; though he subsequently "dream[s] of killing Hitler every night," he cannot examine his early longings in a more analytic and transformative way (249). He maintains his absolutist moral sense—"everything was either very right or very wrong"—and ultimately runs away from home in shame after having sex (248, 276). To Mick, music suggests "the greatest people in the world running and springing up in a hard, free way" and, for that very reason, music also suggests "the worst hurt there could be," because "there was not enough of her to listen" (118–19). Seeking to replace her longing for such union with somatic sensation, she hits herself and scrapes herself with rocks; she begins to feel better once she starts composing, thinking "the notes out like a problem in geometry" (119). Once she begins working at Woolworth's and no longer has time to compose or opportunities to practice playing, she feels "mad all the time," but having guarded her earlier desire so carefully, she has no one to help her comprehend her feelings of loss (354). In a novel famous for its depiction of painfully isolated characters who desperately seek connection to others—a desire encapsulated in the multiple characters who form primary attachments to a deaf-mute who does not understand them well, and is himself attached to a deaf-mute who shows little interest in understanding him—the very desire for social attachments seems a precursor of profound seclusion and ceaseless longing.[81]

Louis Rubin has argued that this quality in McCullers's fiction emerges from the social rigidity of her southern settings: "The particular vision of Carson McCullers, the capacity for recognizing and portraying and sympathetically identifying with pain and loneliness, could arise only out of a social situation in which the patterns and forms and expectations of conduct and attitude are very firmly and formidably present, so that the inability or failure to function within those patterns seems crucial."[82] The text suggests, however, that Mick and Harry have the ability to conform. Although Harry, two years younger than other students in his class, leaves school for a year after the children look at him while discussing "the Jew in 'Ivanhoe,'" he later starts to enjoy school and work, and Mick's tomboyishness is a phase that serves her well among the neighborhood children (248). But while these characters are capable of functioning and even of achieving admiration in their community, they are profoundly unfulfilled and are further convinced that their developing desires are unsuited to the social networks around them. Nonetheless, these desires, like many other aspects of the novel, testify to incipient social change.

This is not to deny the apparent rigidity of their "fairly large" town but rather to note that it exists in tension with both widespread desires for change and violent social struggle. The narrative describes a "fervid outbreak of new beliefs" and murder, as a starving woman stabs her foreman, and an African American family, moving into a white neighborhood, is attacked by their neighbors (37, 198). Thus Mick and Harry constitute not anomalous instances in which emergent forms of consciousness exist within a fixed social system but rather characters symptomatic of a town in which perceptions of nascent transformation are oddly squelched and muted. Accordingly, violence and "restlessness" are described as "incidents" in which "nothing had really changed." Suggesting that "the people" both expect change and fear to consider what it might bring, the narrative explains that "by habit they shortened their thoughts so that they would not wander out into the darkness beyond tomorrow" (199).

Meanwhile, the perception that the community is essentially not amenable to change torments and isolates the characters who most vocally desire it. The would-be Communist Jake Blount complains of "the strangled South. The wasted South. The slavish South" (155, 296). Arguing that "at least one third of all Southerners live and die no better off than the lowest peasant in any European Fascist state," Jake claims that the worst aspect of regional life is the way in which "the truth has been hidden from the people" (297). Accordingly, he feels that his understanding places him among a distinct category of people, both remote from and far outnumbered by "the don't-knows": "Us who know . . . . [are] like people from way off yonder somewhere," "stranger[s] in a strange land" (152, 151, 23). Jake travels, trying to spread his message, but feels that his mission is futile: "I been all over this place. . . . I talk. . . . But what good does it do? Lord God!" (152). Almost consistently enraged at the people around him, he believes that the only hope for any kind of change is absolute revolution in all aspects of life: "The old traditions smashed and the new ones created. To forge a whole new pattern for the world. To make man a social creature for the first time, living in an orderly and controlled society" (304).

Dr. Copeland—who is, in some respects, Jake's African American counterpart—shares Jake's attraction to Marxism, feelings of isolation, and sense of mission, but Dr. Copeland's goals change through the course of the novel; unfortunately, as this happens, he is also weakened by tuberculosis, loss, and police violence. Arguing that, early in his life, "the hopeless suffering of his people made in him a madness, a wild and evil feeling of destruction," McCullers's representation of Copeland tended to support the contemporary stereotype of the "maladjusted" upper-class African American, but it is notable that this character's anger parallels that of the white activist Jake, in comparison with whom Copeland exhibits steady dedication and love.[83] Like Jake, however, he is overcome by anger when others do not understand him or dismiss his "words of reason" in their attachment to religion, which he calls "the cult of meekness" (147, 81). He feels particularly disappointed by his children, whom he had hoped would follow in his pattern. When his daughter explains that "a person can't pick up they children and just squeeze them to which-a-way they wants them to be," his response suggests that he feels isolated from her both emotionally and temporally: as she tries to comfort him, he dismisses her talk of "hurt feelings" as "primitive" (78, 79).

This belief that the people around him cannot comprehend his thought—such that teachers and leaders are "our greatest need"—seems to underwrite the strangely accommodationist ending to his lecture on Marxism, fulfilling labor, and political affiliation. Despite the clarity of his words and the evident interest and enthusiasm of his listeners, he concludes, "The time will come when we will be allowed to serve... and our labor will not be wasted. And our mission is to await this time with strength and faith" (195). But when his son loses his legs after being tortured, Copeland forgoes indoctrination for action; going to the courthouse to protest, he is jailed and beaten. After this, he determines that an activist "must not attempt to stand alone" and that injustice necessitates not "patience and faith" but "to act and act quickly." He plans to lead more than one thousand African Americans of his county in a march to Washington to demonstrate against southern racial oppression.[84] The significance of this plan, which posits broadly shared participation, is suggested by Jake's response, which reasserts the singular role of the educated class: "What good will it do if you get them to demonstrate against a thing if they don't *know*?" (302). The absurdity of this complaint is starkly demonstrated by revelations of Jake's racism and childishness, as he proposes the castration of African American men and, more insistently, the creation of a traveling display in which he would narrate and Copeland's maimed son would comprise the spectacle. His idea suggests a politicized "freak show," a variation of a cultural form still popular in southern towns during this period and consistently associated in McCullers's fiction with oppressive social norms.[85] But Jake's dismissal of Copeland's discussion also appears inane in relation to the substantive comments that both Jake and Copeland receive as they seek to exhort their listeners, who respond by insisting on the difficult relationship between union and scab labor, questioning the role of capital in Marxist theory, and describing the attractions of militant black nationalism (66, 190, 183). Perhaps most insistently of all the texts covered here, *The Heart Is a Lonely Hunter* presents individuals' perceptions of their temporal isolation as a destructive mystification, one tending toward psychological distress and political inaction.

This brief survey demonstrates that southern writers of the early civil rights era continued to struggle with the question of how to represent regional time, which contained multiple and contradictory influences. The region's erratic process of modernization left many intellectuals uncertain about the pace of and possibilities for cultural and political change, and literature from this era suggests that fears of intraregional temporal fragmentation may have complicated even mundane social interactions. But such struggles themselves reflect the increasing difficulty of imagining the region as monolithically backward: however strange southern time, it was unquestionably contemporaneous with—influenced by and participating in—that of the larger nation and globe. This escalating recognition of the South's temporal multiplicity and, accordingly, its substantial ties to U.S. culture and governance challenged the idea that southern apartheid comprised an anomaly in an otherwise liberal nation.

The tension that such a shift created in the triumphalist model of U.S. nationalism is well demonstrated by the pressure that Richard Wright encountered when publishing his autobiography. The Book-of-the-Month Club was particularly determined that Wright cut chapters describing the racism and alienation that he experienced after migrating to Chicago and that he depict greater optimism about life in the North.[86] The complete manuscript, titled "American Hunger," corresponded to much of Wright's work in its insistence that racial oppression constituted a problem that was national in both scope and intensity. It concludes by indicting U.S. principles of collectivity: "If this country can't find its way to a human path, if it can't inform conduct with a deep sense of life, then all of us, black as well as white, are going down the same drain" (453). In contrast, the edited *Black Boy* (1945) ends with Wright's leaving the South, having long looked forward to "fle[eing]" its "terror," with no implication that his subsequent years might be narrated under a title insisting on both "Horror" and "Glory" (257). Having long treated southern racism as an anomaly, many U.S. elites were not eager to explore the commonalities between national and regional racisms, or—as also described in "American Hunger"—the difficulties of modernization in diverse U.S. locales. As I demonstrate in the next chapter, this tendency to represent conflicts about race and region as transitory problems sure to be overcome by U.S. liberalism became increasingly dominant during the cold war.

CHAPTER SEVEN

The Nation's Region Redux

I HAVE ARGUED that southern literature from the 1930s through the early 1940s participated in changing understandings of southern time. Once considered a backward region whose racial oppression was inextricable from its idiosyncratic bounded temporality, the South in this period was increasingly represented, in literature and in political discourse, as a coeval region with strained but undeniable ties to the larger nation. Accordingly, its apartheid could no longer be viewed an anomaly within U.S. governance. But U.S. historiography, as influentially manifested on each end of this book's chronology, presents a parallel so stark as to confront the foundations of my argument. These histories suggested that regional differences and, indeed, most U.S. divisions had been overcome decades earlier. In 1927, in their phenomenally popular *The Rise of American Civilization*, Charles and Mary Beard argued that the values and practices of southern slaveholders inevitably fell before the "dynamic thrust" of "northern capitalism," a force that eventually shaped "the whole scheme of American life."[1] In 1955, Louis Hartz's equally prominent *The Liberal Tradition in America* proclaimed that the "iconoclastic" conservatism of the slaveholding South had been at most "an alien child in a liberal family, tortured and confused," finally "buried by [American] democratic liberalism."[2] In each of these accounts, the early South constituted a feudal anomaly in a larger nation, one already overwhelmed by the power of U.S. liberalism and capitalism. Each of these volumes suggested that the process of national modernization had long been accomplished; Hartz's account, written at a point when the nation-state had achieved more substantial hegemony, argued that democratic orthodoxy was producing a potentially stifling unanimity.

This later volume was, of course, published one year after the Supreme Court's unanimous verdict in *Brown v. Board of Education*, a decision that, as the historian and legal scholar Mary Dudziak argues, was seen to pronounce racial segregation an un-American set of institutional practices and cultural values.[3] And yet, as the Court's subsequent verdict in 1955 confirmed, the conflict between democratic liberalism and white supremacy as guiding principles of national collectivity had hardly been resolved. Urging "all deliberate speed" in desegregation but also allowing "public and private considerations" to determine this pace, the Supreme Court, like officials in charge of enforcing the verdict, manifested apprehension over the potential intractability of local circumstances.[4] In short, even this famous liberal mandate bowed before what the 1896 Court, in the *Plessy v. Ferguson* ruling, called the "established usages, customs and traditions of the people."[5] Given this approach, southern segregationists were able to maintain apartheid through ostensibly unrelated local regulations, a practice that continues to affect court struggles over desegregation; the legal scholar Derrick Bell argues that such debates still revolve around the purportedly "vital national tradition" of "local autonomy."[6] And while U.S. institutions remained equivocal in their pursuit of desegregation, that goal itself, during the early decades of the cold war, was also labeled un-American—evidence of a Communist plot—by white supremacists.[7]

In sum, midcentury accounts of the dominance of American liberalism do not at all reflect the emergence of a liberal consensus nor solely the ideological pressures of the cold war. Rather, they reveal, as the historian Charles Payne argues, "the hegemony of a certain way of thinking about race," one that understands the presence of racial discrimination in the United States not as a facet of social and institutional structures but as a cultural and interpersonal problem.[8] Such configurations were well established, underwriting, as Payne argues, white supremacist structures since *Plessy*.[9] But where such thinking had been challenged during the late 1930s and early 1940s by accounts attending to the diverse ways in which white supremacy shaped U.S. society—including, for example, the role of racial oppression in capitalism—these broader critiques were allowed little voice as the cold war advanced. On the contrary, by the late 1940s, activists suggesting that U.S. apartheid reflected broad and intractable problems with the nation-state and its purportedly liberal structures were pronounced subversive and subjected to harassment and substantial penalties.[10] (This occurred even as events vindicated the activists' analysis: as federal discourse became increasingly focused on segregation, Congress terminated the Fair Employment Practices Commission.[11])

Marginalizing such critiques smoothed the path for the cold war's particularly uncompromising version of American exceptionalism, in which the United States presented itself as the standard-bearer for democratic liberalism and capitalist development. Touting this global role, the United States proposed to lead other nation-states, particularly emerging postcolonial nations, in pursuing models of collectivity more beneficial than that of communism. This narrative emerged early in the cold war, developing ever greater prominence. It was already apparent, for example, in the 1947 report of the President's Committee on Civil Rights. Though its recommendations addressed numerous domestic structures of racial discrimination, the committee also insisted that U.S. "achievements in building and maintaining a state dedicated to the fundamentals of freedom have already served as a guide for [other states] seeking the best road from chaos to liberty and prosperity"; it argued that the nation-state must expand its own commitments to liberalism in order to facilitate "*the final* [global] *triumph of the democratic ideal.*"¹² In keeping with this rhetoric, as Dudziak argues, the federal government tended, in the years that followed, to treat domestic civil rights reform as an exemplary narrative of democratic progress; if the United States had not fully achieved an egalitarian democracy, official documents argued, this process was well under way, as demonstrated by challenges to southern apartheid.¹³

In efforts to describe the momentum of U.S. liberalism, then, the trope of the backward South again proved useful, as it presented racial violence and disfranchisement as the distinct domain of an anachronistic region that would eventually yield to the modernizing and democratizing influences of the nation-state.¹⁴ During a period when social scientists and policy makers began to describe cultural differences overwhelmingly through the oppositions of traditional and modern societies, and associated the latter not only with capitalist development but also with democratic political participation, southern white supremacy was again labeled a temporal aberration.¹⁵ This argument had not, after all, vanished during the 1940s; on the contrary, it was prominently reasserted in Gunnar Myrdal's massive *An American Dilemma* (1944), which treated racism as a manifestation of cultural lag that would be eradicated by the processes of modernization.¹⁶ Citing a variety of social trends that were already reducing discrimination nationwide, Myrdal further claimed that, because the South was becoming more vitally tied to the nation, "the conservative white Southerner himself can be won over to equalitarian reforms in line with the American Creed."¹⁷ In this formulation, as in many from the early decades of the twentieth century, the breadth and multiple forms of U.S. racial oppression are displaced by the image of a backward region—for Myrdal argues that black southerners, as well as white ones, are only recently "permeated by the democratic and equalitarian values of the American culture"—presented as an anomaly within an otherwise liberal nation.¹⁸

Certainly, midcentury analyses of national and regional temporalities varied from those seen decades before. Where early twentieth-century texts often gazed in astonishment at the backwardness of the South, writing in the early 1950s tended to gape in equal amazement at the nation's relentless speed. Appearing to exist on the margins of this powerhouse of modernization, the South's purported temporal distance, still noted and even celebrated in cultural discourse, began in many quarters to be deprived of political meaning. The domestication of this once alarming regional alterity occurred even though southern segregationists were vigorously politicizing the idea of "local control," which Strom Thurmond, the Dixiecrat/States' Rights Democratic candidate, proclaimed in 1948 to be a vital principle of social organization.[19] Emerging as the United States was asserting unprecedented global power, however, responses to the "Second Reconstruction" hardly threatened the stability of the nation-state. Meanwhile, the idea of a distinct southern identity became popular among national elites as ballast for an increasingly conformist and progress-oriented nation.

White southern intellectuals tended to support the idea of this cultural identity. For example, the contributors to *The Lasting South* (1957), who varied from liberal to conservative, claimed to "share one underlying assumption about the South, and that is, that in an increasingly modern and cosmopolitan world, there is more than ever the need for the persistent individuality of the South."[20] Offered as a way of demonstrating commonality and continuity amid "the segregation controversy" and the editors' own disagreement about that issue, this formulation works to separate political content from cultural discussion, suggesting that shared commitment to "the South's identity" need not be affected by discord regarding the apartheid that continued to shape the region's economic, governmental, and social structures.[21] And though this attempt to separate political from cultural commentary might seem untenable, it prefigures a pervasive problem in contemporary U.S. political discourse—the displacement of debate by a focus, on the part of both candidates and commentators, on models of cultural identity depicted as immune to political negotiation.[22]

Where my earlier chapters examined how southern writers challenged monolithic understandings of regional time, this one examines novels written amid the resurgence of such ideological containment, and each stages the problem of how to articulate the political meanings that might emerge from cultural differences. In William Faulkner's *Requiem for a Nun* (1951) and Ralph Ellison's *Invisible Man* (1952), minority political beliefs are, variously, embedded in gestures concerning heritage and aesthetics, considered so futile as to be unutterable, rendered through heavy use of figurative or ironic language, or, famously, invisible—apparently only through Freudian slips, manifestations of unconscious desire that even the speaker claims not to understand. And though, in using the word *minority*, I refer to its narrow political sense—views not held by the apparent majority—these novels associate such ideas with distinct subject positions: "unvanquished" white southerners, women with traumatic sexual backgrounds, and African Americans marginalized by apartheid.[23] This is not to say that these works are committed to the presumption that a certain social position necessitates a certain political opinion, as neither social boundaries nor political views are, in these novels, ultimately stable. Rather, they explore the hypothesis that differences in experience or values could distance one so thoroughly from the field of the political, as it was broadly understood, that one might be unwilling or even unable to express one's ideas as political opinions.

To be clear, the obfuscation of political issues through manipulation of cultural symbols is often, and appropriately, associated with antiliberal politics. Theoretically, any campaign can "bundle" cultural concerns into its strategy; rarely straightforward, such campaigns rely not on discourse about the relevance of tradition or belief to the polity but rather a "symbol or code word" intended to motivate voters at an unconscious or emotional level.[24] (The political scientists who wrote *The Politics of Cultural Differences* argue that this is the pattern of the most efficient U.S. campaigns.[25]) But because such symbols are often used to mobilize voters' "dislike and distrust"—their feelings "that some groups have no right to participate in democratic politics"—such strategies seem inherently incongruous with the idea of a liberal state, in which citizenship does not depend on ascriptive qualities demarcating certain groups.[26] Accordingly, the use of covert cultural appeals to do political work is particularly effective when pursuing overtly antiliberal agendas, such as implying a commitment to white supremacy. In the post-*Brown* era, for example, Republican strategists have regularly used "implicitly racial appeals" in order to signal support for a form of political exclusivity that, if candidly endorsed, would blatantly challenge a prominent strand of U.S. nationalism.[27]

But *Requiem for a Nun* and *Invisible Man* were written during a period when this method of masking white supremacist strategies was not predominant; in the late 1940s, debates about race and civil rights were explicit. Thus, though each novel indicates that vital issues are being bracketed from discourse about the national polity—topics that included the disfranchisement of southern African Americans—these works target a different source for this problem. Rather than focusing on the manipulation of cultural symbols, *Requiem* and *Invisible Man* suggest a limitation in how the field of the political is construed. In particular, they criticize models of governance and collectivity that insist upon a progressive linear temporality as their ontological ground. In each novel, this narrow definition of time functions as an epistemic structure that limits political discussion and understanding. Individual characters, desiring to articulate or contemplate broader conceptions of justice, are left isolated and alienated, their views marginalized by the strict temporal parameters assigned to discourse about social life. Though these novels' experimentation in representing time has been widely discussed, it has not been examined in relation to this concurrent shift in understandings of the South, which deferred previous investigations of the region's and nation's multiple and overlapping temporal forms and instead classified southern anachronism as exceptional—and even, paradoxically, a national resource to be preserved. This shift depended on the idea of a nation marked by inexorable forward motion, which these novels suggest may be as mystifying as cultivated backwardness.

Though these critiques are potent and prominent in each novel, they were unrecognized in critics' initial readings. *Requiem for a Nun* was largely panned, even as critical estimates of Faulkner's early writing were newly and famously elevated, and *Invisible Man*, which had many admirers, was lauded for the universality of its themes, an interpretive paradigm generally inattentive to temporal nuances. Nor are these works typically queried for shared political critiques, as Faulkner and Ellison differed substantially in their approach to apartheid: after the publication of these novels, Ellison emerged as a powerful voice for cultural and political integration, and Faulkner notoriously advocated a gradualist approach. But their fictions share a concern with how experiences deeply rooted in social structures are nonetheless recast as private tragedies, losses with no viable link to public policy. And though contemporary commentary rightly attributes constriction of political discourse to the way in which cultural conflicts are manipulated to displace other debates, these novels point to another problem no less relevant to twenty-first-century politics—the belief that the linear temporality associated with capitalist development constitutes the only time relevant to collective life.

Time, Culture, Politics

By 1951, Faulkner, once dismissed as a pathological writer from an aberrant region, was widely celebrated as an exemplary national writer. This reversal derived, at least in part, from a revaluation of the traits according to which he was once dismissed. While reviewers had initially been frustrated because Faulkner's narratives so rarely privileged linear progressive time, by midcentury, many critics valued that tendency, suggesting that the author's interest in a traditionalist region provided him with a useful critical distance from mass culture. During the Great Depression, as I have shown, the larger nation's relationship to the ideology of progress was sufficiently uncertain that the South's developmental lag was deemed a problem and even a threat, but by midcentury, the United States was consistently depicted as the vanguard of modernization. Thus, where earlier critics were more favorably inclined toward narratives that incorporated a progressivist view of history, presenting time as a venue through which a more just, humane, and productive social order would emerge, midcentury critics were more concerned, in Philip Rahv's words, that "the past . . . [was] being ground to pieces in the powerhouse of change."[28] To quote his fellow "New York intellectual" Richard Chase, they feared that the increasing spread and prominence of mass culture was producing a temporality of "suspended animation and cultural confusion."[29] The largely conservative and southern New Critics, whose influence was rapidly gaining institutional hegemony during this period, had long argued that capitalist modernization was hostile to art. But in the face of impending homogenization, many liberal critics began to concur with these former Agrarians.[30] Although John Aldridge's claim that there were "only two cultural pockets left in America"—New England and the Deep South—quickly became notorious for its hyperbole and prejudice, the view that literary achievement relies on connection with the "indigenous and homely strains of a culture" was more widely embraced.[31] Accordingly, in the work of Irving Howe, R. W. B. Lewis, Richard Chase, and Malcolm Cowley, Faulkner's haunted southerners, like Hawthorne's haunted New Englanders, seemed to testify to the possibility of a meaningful national culture that would bridge present and past.[32]

Ironically, though *Requiem for a Nun* was not greeted as a literary contribution to critical assessment of the nation's time—and was, in fact, considered silly in comparison with Faulkner's earlier work—it explores the temporality of the United States far more overtly than his previous novels, and it tends to question the prospects for the temporal vision with which he was newly attributed.[33] The novel's locale consists of dramatic scenes and lengthy prologues that historicize these sets, and it is rigorously situated in relation to an ever-expanding United States. The description contrasts numerous styles through which the past may be recounted, from narratives of a frontier community's idiosyncratic interactions to geographic accounts that combine biblical and gynecological rhetoric (87). But each prologue demonstrates the increasing incorporative power of the nation, appearing in one instance through the authoritarian threat of a zealous mail carrier, in another as a spatially bounded collective that was "established and ordained" from the emergence of the planet, and finally as a kind of time, moving "that fast that rapid" (88, 194).

Though Faulkner's prologues encompass southern history from the Ice Age to the present, his configuration of U.S. nationalism consistently evokes cold war anxieties about time such as those published, alongside one of *Requiem for a Nun*'s prologues, in *Partisan Review*.[34] The power of midcentury modernization ideology, of course, depended in part on its resonance with an established nationalist teleology devoted to development; accordingly, *Requiem* argues that contemporary critiques of the nation's temporality could be applied to any era of U.S. development, allotting the time of the marketplace a determinate role in national history. Describing the period in which Mississippi was incorporated into the nation, for example, Faulkner depicts a form of progress that is both incessantly moving in its quest for further codification and profit and forever suspended in its values—a "boundless immeasurable forenoon" in which "men's mouths were full of law and order, all men's mouths were round with the sound of money . . . profit plus regimen equals security" (92). In this way, *Requiem* provides a predictive account of U.S. history, associating the time of the nation-state not merely with the progressive linearity of liberalism but with the more overtly restrictive and speeding time of neoliberalism, with its teleology, as Wendy Brown argues, of "*extending and disseminating market values to all institutions and social action.*"[35]

Though this temporality does not actually move toward a new epoch—"confound[ing] forever seething with motion and motion with progress"—it does "dispossess" people ascribed to purportedly "obsolete" eras (4, 89). And in this recognition, Faulkner explains how U.S. liberal and white supremacist nationalisms, though seemingly contradictory, so easily coincide; describing development in terms of capitalism ("one vast single net of commerce") and federalist democratic governance ("Mississippi: a state . . . triumvirate in legislative, judiciary, executive"), the novel observes that this temporal trajectory is nonetheless racialized (91, 92). Thus, for example, Native Americans are pronounced "obsolescent" not through an anthropological or economic rationalization but through blatant racial nationalism: "because this was a white man's land;

that was its fate, or not even fate but destiny" (35). In characterizing modernization as ultimately neoliberal—such that the state serves chiefly to extend the reach of the market into new territories and more aspects of life, a process that may eventually supplant the state—and in recognizing the ways in which modernization theory fuels profoundly destructive forms of racial stereotyping and demarcation, the novel's history of federal and frontier relations pertinently describes domestic and global elements of U.S. cold war ideology.

Critics who have observed the novel's overt exploration of U.S. nationalism, and particularly U.S. time, have not, with the exception of Barbara Ladd, noted how critically it addresses its cold war context.[36] Interpretation may have been influenced by Faulkner's assertive public nationalism during this period; as François Pitavy points out, Faulkner accepted a new role in the 1950s, writing essays and giving speeches that, in the face of his belief "that the original meaning of the American dream had been debased into meaninglessness," nonetheless enacted a "furious, and at times even shrill, reaffirmation of that dream."[37] But *Requiem for a Nun* offers no such sanguine vision, describing instead a pace of change that consumes participants and then thrusts them aside: "the next act and scene itself clearing its own stage . . . commencing the new act and scene right in the midst of the phantoms, the fading wraiths of that old time which had been exhausted, used up" (191). The incompatibility of this perpetual upheaval with the dimensions of the human body—limited in both time and space—are further emphasized as the novel describes the nation's imperialist spread and destructive power. These are granted a compulsive force that can be illustrated only by a lengthy quote:

> One nation: no longer anywhere . . . one last irreconcilable fastness of stronghold from which to enter the United States . . . one world: the tank gun [set as a monument in Jefferson]: captured from a regiment of Germans in an African desert by a regiment of Japanese in American uniforms, whose mothers and fathers at the time were in a California detention camp for enemy aliens . . . one universe, one cosmos: contained in one America: one towering frantic edi-

fice poised like a card-house over the abyss of the mortgaged generations; one boom, one peace: one swirling rocket-roar filling the glittering zenith as with golden feathers, until the vast hollow sphere of [man's] air . . . the very substance in which he lives and, lacking which, he would vanish in a matter of seconds—is murmurous with his fears and terrors and disclaimers and repudiations and his aspirations and dreams and his baseless hopes, bouncing back at him in radar waves from the constellations. (212–13)

Here, the United States appears to be an instrument of apocalypse, unstoppable in its spatial spread, unabashed in its racial nationalism, and overwhelming in its physical and psychological effects. In important ways, of course, this prose describes a stage of technological modernity that need not be identified with any particular nation-state; rather, Faulkner depicts a global era in which individuals recognize the existence of weaponry that could render the planet uninhabitable and yet also depend on technology for whatever broad and unfulfilling communication they can muster. But Faulkner was hardly alone in ascribing such modernizing agency to the United States. Aside from domestic and global cultural critics, the federal government, seeking to advance its hegemony, also encouraged such views.

In the face of such unremitting change, *Requiem for a Nun* poses one famous model of redemptive temporal experience in a passing "outlander['s]" attention to Cecilia Farmer, a nineteenth-century woman who carved her name into a jail window and has since become a treasured figure "out of the town's composite heritage" (220). Noel Polk, who calls these passages "the most eloquent in all of Faulkner," explains that they evoke "those crucial moments . . . when we transcend time"; Marnie Parsons further explains that, in "bringing the presence of himself, and thus of 'now,' and all the perceptions/knowings integral to his selfhood, to the trace of a past now obsolete, the outlander joins his unique present with an obscure past, and so enlivens that past."[38] As these apt descriptions suggest, this stranger's sudden sense of intimacy with Cecilia constitutes a respite from the preceding relentless transformations, such that the outlander, whom the narrative addresses in second person, realizes that linear time constitutes only one construction among many forms of temporal experience. Shedding narrow and restrictive understandings of time and space, "you know again that there is no time: no space: no distance" (225).

But where midcentury critics argued that Faulkner's work demonstrates how regional identification could provide ballast for a national culture overwhelmed by change, *Requiem for a Nun* suggests that this more flexible view of time is available only to a stranger—someone who lacks any fixed identification with the South. Irving Howe, for example, claimed that Faulkner's work, particularly in his representations of Quentin Compson, theorized ways "to stare at the 'old ghost times' from a preserving distance"—providing individuals with a way to contemplate the past amid modernization. But *Requiem* suggests that contemporary attachment to the southern past constitutes absolute rejection of the nation's linear time.[39] As Yoknapatawpha County is fully incorporated into the United States—"not only a new century and a new way of thinking, but of acting and behaving too"—regional identification is restricted to the "old irreconcilables . . . facing irreconcilably backward toward the old lost battles, the old aborted cause" (207, 206). Not haunted, as were Quentin Compson and Gail Hightower, these figures are simply resolute in their resistance to change.

Rather subtly suggesting the conflicts about civil rights that were taking place outside the novel's frame, *Requiem for a Nun* also insists that these Yoknapatawphans' "intractab[ility]" encompasses more than attachment to an idea of heritage or even complaint about defeat in the Civil War (216). They are also attached to the racial hierarchies that were instituted, the novel suggests, as a way of disavowing that loss. They resist modern appliances not because they value the experience of labor but because they maintain "the servants, housemen, and gardeners and handymen" who are jailed every weekend and "extracted the next morning by their white folks" (216). Furthermore and, in historical context, ominously, these Old South partisans are persuading others to their perspective: "Instead of dying off as they should as time passed, it was as though these old irreconcilables were actually increasing in number," incorporating into their ranks "the children of that second outland invasion" (217). *Requiem* neither celebrates nor devalues this intractability; in its relationship to the central tropes of white supremacist discourse, the novel is equivocal, sensitive to racial injustice and particularly economic oppression but also insistent about the affective charge of the past (216). Such ambivalence also notoriously characterized Faulkner's comments on desegregation. But *Requiem*'s figuration of this developing struggle is nonetheless instructive, as it demonstrates how narrow conceptions of time also delimit the sphere of the political.

In rejecting the teleology of the nation-state and seeking to maintain distinct forms of temporal experience, these old and new irreconcilables claim that their time itself is incommensurable with that of the nation-state. To configure the matter in this way is to preclude the possibility of political remedy or negotiation, as they disdain even the ontological premises of classical liberalism, in which, as Wendy Brown argues, the notion of "continual progress" is "fundamental."[40] In targeting their rejection toward the temporality of their opponents, of course, these malcontents may appear to assert a difference more cultural than political. This difference generates no efforts toward or even interest in social change, as the irreconcilables spend their time in celebrating and introducing visitors to their heritage. But these cultural activities are associated with a host of political issues that the prologues do not address as such, including not only the economic discrimination endemic to paternalist labor relations but also the white supremacist policing that causes both their servants and "others (what the town knew as the New Negro, independent of that commodity)" to be arrested every weekend (216).

Thus the novel stages what is today often described as a slippage between the cultural and the political, a way of narrating political opposition by, in Adolph Reed Jr.'s words, "essentializ[ing] culture as primordial identity" and suggesting that those who disagree on social "values and concerns" differ "fundamentally."[41] As Reed argues, assertions of such cultural alterity are often "hortatory as well as descriptive": they provide a carefully crafted model of cultural identity that is then mobilized as a reason for political action—one relatively resistant to debate, as such causes are said to be rooted not in opinion but rather in one's constitutive beliefs about self and society.[42] *Requiem for a Nun*'s irreconcilables pursue precisely such a strategy for declaring their beliefs. They restrict their demonstrations to a cultural expression concerning their heritage—"rising up and stalking out in the middle of *Gone with the Wind*"; their most public actions appear innocuous, as they disrupt only the showing of old movies and meanwhile preserve local history (220). But while taking their stand, so to speak, about the regional past, they quietly maintain only one declared "inten[tion]," and that concerns the town's present and future—maintaining the current role of the town jail as a way of constraining African Americans (217). Thus they seek, in cultivating a certain notion of southern culture, to shape local social structures without ever having to engage in an argument about contemporary institutions. And in depicting these quirky irreconcilables, the novel stages a prominent transition of this period, as models of an intransigent white southern identity—mobilized, in debates about civil rights, for overtly political means—were in other contexts depoliticized and further embraced for their cultural difference.

This approach to white southern identity was fueled by the intensification of cultural and political hegemony within the United States during this period—the increasing dominance of business culture and the cold war state. Paralleling midcentury critics' interest in southern literature, the idea of a distinct and unyielding white southern identity was celebrated in both intellectual and popular culture. Observing the work of such diverse cultural producers as Andy Griffith and C. Vann Woodward, Andrew Hoberek finds that the figure of the white southerner was popularized as an icon of resistance to the "organization"—big business, big government, and middle-class conformism.[43] Meanwhile, as the idea of white southern difference was acclaimed in this way, southern segregationists' supporters from outside the region—now more often Republican than Democratic—described the conflict about civil rights in terms of personality. Dwight D. Eisenhower and later George H. W. Bush, for example, argued against federal intervention against apartheid because they felt that laws could not change individuals' feelings.[44] Like regional apologists in the period from the 1890s through much of the 1930s, these politicians presented southern segregationists' political recalcitrance as a form of inherent difference. Notably, however, these cold war statements emerged during a period marked by both expanded federal power and encompassing networks of cultural and institutional interconnectedness, rendering the attribution of white supremacy to a discrete and immutable culture even more dubious than before.

While *Requiem for a Nun*'s attention to the people who preserve southern heritage serves in some ways to support this trend, the novel nonetheless complains of a constriction in political discourse that displaces disagreement into seemingly inherent cultural differences. It does so, paradoxically, from the perspective of the irreconcilables, arguing that ideas of social goods and circumstances are temporally coded, such that certain goals and problems correspond to the trajectory and time accorded political action, while others do not. *Requiem* insists that the nation-state and the forms of governance associated with it constitute the horizon of all political activity in Mississippi—"that Idea risen now, suspended like a balloon or a portent or a thundercloud above what used to be wilderness, drawing, holding the eyes of all" (92). Accordingly, it is hard to imagine what political sphere might be inhabited by people who reject the very time in which such structures exist, and such seems to be the point of these Old South partisans' choice of cultural over political protest. While their political isolation is self-chosen, it reflects the temporal logics practiced also by their opposition, which does not recognize the political implications of desires and damages that can be sited outside the "rush and roar of civic progress and social alteration and change" (213).

The novel does not explore the effects of such seemingly oppositional temporalities in broad political terms, only hinting, for example, that African Americans' political and economic disfranchisement is overlooked as an effect of history even while the "people (white people)" who can afford "electricity and window screens . . . suddenly [develop] a belief in [their] inalienable civil right to be free of dust and bugs" (208). It does, however, reveal how the beliefs and losses of individuals are rendered irrelevant, from the state's perspective, when they fail to conform to its linear time (208). In the dramatic scenes, Mrs. Gowan Stevens, née Temple Drake, responds to the death sentence rendered against Nancy Mannigoe, who killed Temple's child. Temple's sense of time is painful but sophisticated: traumatized by earlier events (narrated in Faulkner's *Sanctuary* [1929]), she both claims radical discontinuity in her life—"Temple Drake is dead"—and plays with the idea that social transactions can restore one's relationship to linear time, such that, for example, a Parisian wedding can "fumigate an American past" and a new marriage and appliances can enable a couple to "face [the shame] down . . . never to haunt us more" (80, 133, 135). Though she initially seeks to escape her immediate past by traveling with her family to California, she returns when her son suggests that spatial movement cannot alleviate one's sense of closeness to an event in time; accordingly, heeding the request of Gavin Stevens, her husband's uncle and Nancy's lawyer, Temple returns to seek clemency for Nancy from the governor. Her efforts lead her into conflict not with the law itself but, more specifically, with the time in which it is conducted.

As the prologues demonstrate the centrality of temporal constructions in U.S. nationalism and development, the dramatic scenes reveal how powerfully beliefs about time shape legal procedures and decisions. These temporal parameters are asserted through mundane rules, interpretations of what motivations are signified by individual acts in time, and qualitative requirements about how actions should be narrated and interpreted. They appear, for example, in Gavin's failure to file an appeal during the time allotted to such procedures, the governor's decision that Nancy has chosen a trajectory that the law should not interrupt, and in both men's insistence that Temple produce a linear narrative in which blame can be ascribed. Gavin, in particular, seeks to emphasize those moments in which Temple has been victimized by men, opposing Temple's sense of agency as well as her apparent belief that none of the actions or actors in her story can be properly understood if examined separately from their social networks. Most important, she recognizes Nancy's act not simply as a crime but rather as the result of profound ethical confusion—both Nancy's and her own—resulting from histories outside of which their acts cannot be properly assessed.

Requiem for a Nun's representation of Nancy vividly illustrates Ralph Ellison's claim that Faulkner tended to create black "characters embodying both" malignant and benign stereotypical traits: Temple repeatedly calls Nancy a "dope-fiend whore" and nonetheless credits her for loyal family service.[45] As Karl Zender notes, Nancy is also, in keeping with many Faulknerian portrayals of African American religiosity, utterly devoted to a faith that, in this novel, seems untenable, involving as it does the unbidden sacrifice of a child.[46] But within this representation, the novel nonetheless insists that its most disparaged qualities be traced to the abuse that Nancy suffered during her life as a prostitute, a period during which her unborn child was beaten to death while still in her body, giving her, it seems, intense sensitivity to the vulnerability of children. Temple is somewhat attuned to Nancy's perspective because of her own past experience of sexual victimization and prohibited desires, which remain so forceful that she "hired another reformed whore so I could have someone to talk to" (131). (This identification seems to fuel Temple's verbal slurs against Nancy, on whom she projects all the feelings that flout her melancholically maintained ego ideal of "all-Mississippi debutante."[47]) For both women, the tensions between their sexual desires, sexual oppression, maternal experience, and patriarchal marginalization have created a complex relationship to linear time: Temple, unable to recognize the moment of her baby's death as one of criminal culpability, argues rather that she killed the baby herself "eight years ago" when she embarked on the trip that would end in her kidnapping and rape (215).

But in persistently resisting requests for a linear narrative, Temple suggests not only a post-traumatic perspective but also, more profoundly, that this history cannot be assimilated to the time of the state. Demonstrating that more encompassing analysis is necessary for Temple even to proceed in her life, *Requiem* also stages her frustration that such understanding is restricted to a private realm, perhaps potentially beneficial for her but irrelevant to Nancy, whose execution the governor portrays as the end point of a trajectory outside his purview. Where, in the prologues, the outlander's encounter with Cecilia Farmer's signature suggests that a broader sense of time than that of the nation-state can enrich individual consciousness, the dramatic narrative reveals that this more encompassing sense of time also provides greater insight into human relations and responsibility. But if held in isolation, this understanding does not enable one to address the injustices that one can nonetheless more thoroughly comprehend. Knowing that the governor has not commuted Nancy's sentence, and observing that her interpretation has not even influenced her family—as Gowan seems readily and bitterly to accept the blame that Gavin ascribes to him—Temple mocks the idea that her efforts could help "to save my soul" and despairs at the thought of "tomorrow and tomorrow and tomorrow" (182, 177). Ultimately, her awareness of the intersections between past, present, and a possible but unknowable eternity is neither grounded in a shared and generative regional tradition nor relevant to the polity; rather, her temporal understanding is isolating and futile in a social structure governed in linear progressive time.

In attributing such harm to the progressive temporality of U.S. political life rather than the conservative temporality of intransigent and white supremacist regionalists, *Requiem for a Nun*'s critique can appear irrelevant or even reactionary. For where the novel describes the constriction of political discourse in temporal terms, this phenomenon is at the time of this writing (2005) most vividly demonstrated as a spatial one, through robustly reproduced images of the nation's red and blue states. Though these maps denote Republican and Democratic victories in the electoral college, they are suggested, by many journalists and political consultants, to illustrate "states of mind, not actual states"; in other words, they promote the view that political differences emerge from spatialized cultural differences, implicitly raising the question of whether meaningful exchange can take place among opposing parties.[48] As I demonstrated in earlier chapters, this style of understanding and staging political difference has long influenced U.S. political thought. Tara McPherson notes that contemporary "red states," though spanning a vast area of the country, are often, in media exchanges, identified simply as "the South," but this compression reflects the nation's particular history of attributing southern political differences to an intransigent cultural divergence.[49] Contemporary discussions of the "red state/blue state" dichotomy often trace its genesis to the "southern strategy" pursued by Richard Nixon's campaign in 1968, but taking a broad view, one might argue that such practices have been used to influence the South's role—as both agent and image—in U.S. politics since at least before the Civil War; certainly, as I have shown, they underwrote the legal establishment of southern apartheid. This history amply demonstrates Kenneth Warren's claim that "southernness, as a political concept, has rarely if ever portended a broader democratization of American life."[50]

Still, as I have shown, this concept has worked its damage by asserting the contrast between an archaic regional culture and a progressive national state; in other words, conceptions of regional distinctness have wreaked such harm through their appeal to specifically *temporal* opposition. And such temporal oppositions remain portable and enervating within social debate, as strategists produce distinctions among the polity—authentic versus sophisticated, heartland versus cosmopolitan, conservative versus progressive—that suggest not simply conflicting beliefs but more sweeping and potentially nonnegotiable divergences in relationships to space and time.[51] (The contrast between conservative and progressive seems so typical as to be banal, but in an era when neoconservatism is associated with support for imperialism and deregulation of markets and progressives often argue for the importance of local protection and preservation, such titles are misleading or even dubious. In each case, temporal terms are used to signal moral virtues—old forms of social cohesion or individual agency, or the liberal value of continuing improvement. But such moral claims are far too vague and sweeping to describe actual political agendas; further, they regularly serve to misrepresent the goals of political elites.) Describing political conflicts through spatial and temporal tropes suggests that they pose bounded populations against inherent antagonists, for such dimensions shape, as the anthropologist Johannes Fabian argues, the way in which the parameters of a people are understood: "Shared time and space are fused into identities we call community, society, civilization, and history."[52] Accordingly, people seeking to encourage more flexible, dialogic, heterogeneous, and creative political discourse might seek more nuanced understandings of both space and time—not only producing and analyzing alternative "red/blue" maps, with their varying shades of purple, but also considering how diverse political positions negotiate between past experiences and contemporary goals, and what sorts of insights may be either produced or precluded by disparate ideas of time. In the early years of the cold war, as modernization ideology produced global maps describing temporal and cultural differences, which were said to have determinate political implications, *Requiem for a Nun* provided an incisive but rather limited account of how narrow conceptions of time hamper social understanding. *Invisible Man* explored this problem in more overtly political—and also psychological—terms.

Plunging "Outside of History"

Where Faulkner's temporal insight was attributed to his regional background, Ellison was credited with "a truly heroic quality"—a trait necessary, according to Saul Bellow, for any writer who seeks, amid rapid modernization, to "resist the heavy influences and make their own synthesis out of the vast mass of phenomena, the seething, swarming body of appearances, facts, and details."[53] Ellison himself claimed a qualified southern background, asserting, for example, that "the South . . . has never left me" but also noting that Oklahoma "lacked many of the intensities of custom, tradition, and manners which 'colored' the institutions of the Old South."[54] Perhaps the clearest evidence of restraint in Ellison's identification with the South is his assessment that Faulkner was the region's greatest artist, for as Ellison's essays consistently demonstrated, he was deeply aware of the limits in Faulkner's vision.[55] But Ellison nonetheless described the older author's work as "exception[al]" in contemporary U.S. literature, because it "work[ed] the great moral theme" of the contradictions between racial oppression and the nation's democratic ideals.[56] These essays further suggest that the force of Faulkner's analysis emerged from his regional project, for Ellison argued that "the South has been the center of our national dilemma, both political and moral."[57] Accordingly, like Faulkner's later work, *Invisible Man* explores the temporal continuities and conceptual barriers between the South and the larger United States. Further, like *Requiem for a Nun*, it posits the extraordinary difficulty of the temporal transcendence with which the author was credited.

From the opening of the novel, Ellison introduces both the novel's critical project—one explicitly focused on U.S. nationalism—and the idea that concepts of temporality may be used destructively. Situating himself "in the great American tradition of tinkers . . . a 'thinker-tinker,'" the narrator warns, "Beware of those who speak of the *spiral* of history; they are preparing a boomerang."[58] As Jonathan Arac explains, though the spiral seems to align with the curving motion of the boomerang, it constitutes a philosophical figure for progress that was widely embraced in Marxist theory; in Ellison's novel, it subsumes the "arrow," which the narrator presents as a typical but fundamentally erroneous understanding of the time of the liberal nation-state.[59] Where the arrow is expected to move forward, the boomerang circles back, striking people in the polity who might otherwise be expected to exist alongside this weapon, safe from its point. This theme—that conceptions of time may be not only misleading but also dangerous—is developed throughout the novel, such that, by the end, the narrator describes his trials as a process through which he "boomeranged a long way from the point in society toward which I originally aspired" (573). He concludes that one's relationship to time—whether one is "in the rear or in the *avant-garde*"—is impossible to determine (573, 572).

Maintaining in his epilogue the nationalism for which Ellison became well known, the narrator nonetheless distinguishes this belief system from that of his youth, when he wished to participate in an idea of progress that was established by elites. Early in his life, he believes that accommodation "work[s]," enabling African American individuals to achieve success; he feeds this belief at college while observing "the black rite of Horatio Alger" (17, 111). This early investment in one version of U.S. ideology—individual success in a society offering broad opportunities—is reversed by the end of the novel's chronology; contrasting "the principle on which the country was built" to "the feudal past," he nonetheless acknowledges that economic and political liberalism has maintained an intimate relationship with white supremacy, suggesting that the *former* is "the plan in whose name we had been brutalized and sacrificed" (574). Notably, the narrator never uses the word *liberalism* to describe this "principle"; though his discussion suggests some fusion of democracy and capitalism, he appears dissatisfied with such terms, perhaps implying that the extant principle must be transformed into something rather different. But neither does he invoke a temporality of progress to describe this change; rather, he argues that people who have experienced oppression must guide this transformation because they are "older than" oppressive elites "in the sense of what it took to live in the world with others." Accordingly, it seems that one way in which the novel seeks to revise U.S. political philosophy is to defy its valorization of the new and thus to sever from modernization ideology the ideas of democracy that Ellison routinely championed.

In this way, the narrator's critique addresses a cold war context in which a fixed model of national liberalism was used in efforts to induce postcolonial nations to ally with the United States. The narrator, in contrast, argues that the "others in the loud, clamoring semi-visible world . . . were tired of being the mere pawns in the futile game of 'making history,'" and insists that beneficial political practices cannot be imposed through "exploitation" or "condescension" (574–75). Rather, they must emerge from attending to the critical perspectives of those previously excluded from political participation, even in the nation proclaiming itself liberalism's vanguard. The narrator also subverts the idea that a society's insight will be centered in the sites it promotes as banners of achievement. Mocking the idea that Broadway or the Empire State Building might be "bright[] spot[s]" in "our whole civilization—pardon me, our whole *culture* (an important distinction, I've heard)," he positions his discussion in a rather complex cold war transition. Where *civilization* had once been used to describe a teleology of human development against which various societies were measured, it had, by the 1940s, largely yielded for comparative purposes to *culture*, a term that allowed for more diverse trajectories. With the emergence of modernization theory, however, *culture* became a crucial rubric for area studies and was once again used to position various societies—particularly postcolonial nations—within predetermined patterns of capitalist or communist economic and political development.[60] Through emphasizing the significance of the term *culture*, the narrator notes the return of restrictive teleology to the dominant schools of U.S. social thought while simultaneously criticizing this spatiotemporal configuration, which marginalizes the perspectives of those previously excluded from capitalist development.

Acknowledging how the idea of progressive societal development affects U.S. foreign policy, the novel focuses on how it shapes domestic ideology, depicting it as a mystification central to both American exceptionalists and the purportedly radical Brotherhood.[61] Norton, a "multimillionaire," "skilled scientist," "bearer of the white man's burden," and "symbol of the Great Traditions," famously embodies a patriarchal and patronizing approach to African American uplift, a project that he presents as the solution to a national conflict (37). As Alan Nadel argues, this figure is not just a spokesperson for U.S. nationalism but an icon thereof in a novel that vigorously lampoons this ideology, even as it ambivalently recuperates it. (Accordingly, Norton is modeled on a nationalist vision of Ralph Waldo Emerson, one particularly important during these early days of American studies.[62]) Norton's understanding of progress does not stipulate apartheid but promotes it nonetheless, as he supports Dr. Bledsoe; this university president is considered the leader of "a fast-rising . . . people" but sends the narrator after a "promise which, like the horizon, recedes ever brightly and distantly beyond the hopeful traveler" (133, 191). In sum, to be "Bledsoed" is to be told that one is moving up (progressing along a trajectory) when, in teleological terms, one is moving laterally, which is to say, static. Despite significant differences from that of Norton, the temporality posited by the Brotherhood shares the former's forward momentum and limited scope, such that, as Jack argues, history poses "new questions . . . for the living" but "passe[s others] by" (306, 291).

Given that each of these ideological positions has a predefined trajectory that allows neither input nor critique from African Americans, the novel suggests the arguments emerging during the early cold war—that the battle between communist and capitalist states constrained the political options of both African American activists and emerging postcolonial nations.[63] This position is influentially delivered by Ras the Exhorter, who refuses the belief that "everything between black mahn and white mahn can be settled with some blahsted lies in some bloody books written by the white mahn in the first place" (375–76). After listening to Ras, Tod Clifton acknowledges disquiet concerning not only the Brotherhood but also progressive teleologies more generally, speculating that "sometimes a man *has* to plunge outside history" (377). The narrator, however, rejects such critiques for much of the novel. Having experienced time as convulsive—such that he is hurled from one physical and emotional crisis to another, and even loses his memories at the hands of the factory's electroshock experimenters—the narrator is deeply attracted to the idea of a linear, predictable time: "The Brotherhood had both science and history under control. . . . Life was all pattern and discipline" (381–82).

But this attraction is not based solely on the narrator's previous painful experiences, as he also seeks to evade exclusion from an overwhelmingly hegemonic progressive time. Such exclusion, as Ellison implies in "Harlem Is Nowhere," functions through both racial and regional vectors, particularly targeting southern African Americans.[64] As Riché Richardson demonstrates, *Invisible Man* further explores temporal hierarchies within the South.⁶⁵ As a student in Bledsoe's school, for example, the narrator "hate[s]" the black farmers living nearby who are occasionally invited to sing "what the officials called 'their primitive spirituals' " to entertain visitors; calling these local singers "peasants," the narrator argues, "We were trying to lift them up and they . . . did everything it seemed to pull us down" (47). But the narrator's participation in this dynamic only heightens his awareness of the influence and rigidity of temporal demarcations. Excluded people are imagined to lie outside the teleology promoted by the school because of their practices, living conditions, culture, and perhaps biology; Norton invokes the latter cause, at least, to describe the white southern "stock" that descended from slaveholders and is now "degenerat[ing]." These oppositions are so absolute as to defy the animation and humanity of backward people, and the temporal distinctions asserted outside the South are equally degrading. Jack describes the Provos, the elderly couple in whose eviction the narrator has intervened, as already "dead," "agrarian types . . . being ground up by industrial conditions. Thrown on the dump heaps and cast aside" (290).

In addition to describing economic and social change, this dynamic has profound psychological implications. People identifying with a teleology of progress distance themselves from those regarded as incompatible with that temporality in powerful terms—emotional (hatred), ontological ("stock" as opposed to humanity), and spatial—in a metaphor that also suggests physical violence (the Provos' bodies are pulverized and then forcefully ejected into a space designated for trash). As Richardson argues, the novel is suffused with representations of abjection, in which people focus their attention on a body with which they vigorously disidentify; this process is consistently performed through spatial, racial, and temporal distancing. Given the intensity of this abjection, and the regularity with which it is exerted, it is not surprising that the narrator fears becoming vulnerable to it.

Profoundly sensitive to the temporal stereotyping that he repeatedly encounters, the invisible man seems to fear above all else that he might, in the eyes of those who view him, seem to exist "outside of history." This concern underlies his continuing confusion about how to position himself in relation to not only his individualized southern past but also the history of racial oppression and the contemporary segregated South. The novel criticizes this perplexity through a series of episodes that reiterate this perplexity; the veteran doctor at the Golden Day, for example, argues that the young narrator suffers from his disregard for "such things as most peasants and folk peoples almost always know through experience" (91). Certainly, the narrator disavows any identification with knowledge or people not associated with progress, a pattern that, for a time, renders him "ashamed of my grandparents for having been slaves" (15). This distancing tendency is apparent also in his more casual interactions; considering Peter Wheatstraw, for instance, whose figures of speech he had known "from childhood," the narrator nonetheless configures Wheatstraw's carnivalesque lyrics as the expression of an external group—"they're a hell of a people" (176, 177). Upon moving north, he determines to "slough off my southern ways of speech" and associates purportedly southern foods such as pork chops and chitterlings with abjection and embarrassment, though he famously reconciles himself to the pleasures of the hot buttered yam (164, 178, 313, 264–65). He further separates himself from his family and seems unable to reconcile the history of slavery with his own sense of chronology.

In deepening its analysis of how temporal ideologies limit understanding, the novel suggests that the narrator's adherence to progressive time interferes not only with his ability to comprehend history and his ability to affiliate with people purportedly excluded from it—two difficulties serious enough in themselves—but also with his ability to accept his own memories. The novel is centrally concerned with the porous boundaries between the individual unconscious and the social world; the narrative is suffused, as Deborah Cohn argues, with "subjective visions, hallucinations, and dreams that conflate time and space and blur the boundaries separating exterior from interior reality."[66] Thus, as Houston Baker has famously explicated, Trueblood's dream partakes of prominent ideological tropes and constitutes, in its telling, a performance so seductive as to be ambiguous—almost calculated to stage the dreams of his listeners.[67] But for much of the novel, the narrator, despite vivid dreams and surreal experiences, seems unable to recognize connections between the notoriously timeless realms of memory and desire—feelings and impressions that manifest in subjectivity with little regard for chronology or timing— and the rigorously timed world of social interaction. Crucially, the latter is defined, in this period, not only by the temporal demarcations of activities said to be distinct but also by an insistence on progressive time. Seeking always to protect his position *inside* history, the narrator represses any idea or affect—whether a critical approach to history or contemplation of his own mental images—that might lead him to question dominant accounts of time.

His encounter with Primus Provo's manumission paper, for example, provokes a chronological confusion represented as a disavowal of ineffable personal knowledge:

> My hands were trembling, my breath rasping. . . . *It has been longer than that, further removed in time,* I told myself, and yet I knew that it hadn't. . . . A bitter spurt of gall filled my mouth and splattered the old folk's possessions. . . . [I was] no longer looking at what was before my eyes, but inwardly-outwardly, around a corner into the dark, far-away-and-long-ago, not so much of my own memory as of remembered words, of linked verbal echoes, images, heard even when not listening at home. (272–73)

Replete with descriptions of psychosomatic response, expressions of sharp and inarticulate fear and anxiety, and images of escape and shock, and also pointing to a mnemonic realm comprised of unprocessed words and images, this passage insistently evokes psychoanalytic formulations of the unconscious and of repression. But while the narrator's initial response to the Provos is abjectifying, this encounter seems to initiate a limited working through of his internal division, such that he can both briefly imagine identifying with those located "outside of history" and also, for a moment, accept some of his memories. Thus, as he observes the Provos' "dispossession" from their apartment, the narrator realizes that he is being "dispossessed" of his psychological resistance—"a painful yet precious thing which I could not bear to lose." This shared terminology reflects a form of identification quite new for this narrator.

This emerging sense of alliance with the Provos disrupts the narrator's mystifying identification with institutional power, which Ellison described, in "Harlem Is Nowhere," as "one of the bulwarks which *men* place between themselves and the constant threat of chaos."[68] The narrator is thus able, as Warren argues, to replace the sense of shame that he announces early in his narrative with "understand[ing of] how it feels to have been treated shamefully."[69] And it is at this moment that the narrator, who is isolated from his family and has purportedly lost his memories, receives an image of his laboring mother: "*And why did I, standing in the crowd, see like a vision my mother hanging wash on a cold windy day?*" (273). The narrator first finds this vision threatening, but it appears, in the context of this narrative, to constitute a kind of psychological breakthrough, suggesting the possibility of a renewed sense of continuity and connection.

The novel suggests that its narrator is too invested in his identifications with power, which he understands as typically white and wealthy but consistently heterosexual, masculine, and attached to linear time. Certainly, he forges no meaningful relationships with women in the novel, with the brief exception of Mary Rambo, who begins their relationship by speaking to him of his potential for leadership (273, 255). By the conclusion, he has, in a hallucinatory state, imagined himself to be surrounded by a number of male role models, from Norton to Bledsoe to Jack to Ras, who threaten to "*free*" him of his "*illusions*" and ultimately castrate him (569). Despite his pain, the narrator claims that he can "*now see that which I couldn't see*"—that the "*drip-drop*" of his blood, or the torment of those sacrificed to ensure the domination of others, constitutes "*all the history*" that these men have made or will make (570). Through this horrific vision, the narrator finally severs himself, as Anne Anlin Cheng argues, from the very idea of or desire for "political or masculinist identities"; despite the centrality of identity in this novel's plot and rhetoric, its "political thesis" turns out to be "identificatory renunciation."[70] It seems remarkable, however, that even as he expresses this relinquishment through the most famed bodily metaphor for hegemonic masculine identities, and even as this symbolic abnegation openly describes a practice used repeatedly to torture and kill African American men, Ellison continues to reiterate his concern with ideas of history. The narrator does not thoroughly challenge ideas of progressive time until the moment that he imagines sacrificing not only all other illusions but also, in both senses, his phallus. Thus, though he feels briefly bereft of his claim to a stake in the nation's time as he stands in front of the Provos' apartment, and even tells Jack afterward, "I like them. . . . It's taken me a long time to feel it, but they're folks just like me," he quickly succumbs to Jack's assertive temporal ideology, with its easy dismissal of "those old ones" (291).

I return to the moment with the Provos, however, because in its status as a missed opportunity for a more complete working-through, it suggests what is at stake in the ability to view time differently—to accept and even value memories pronounced marginal to the polity, to recognize how the nation-state's oppressive practices exist in a time simultaneous with its triumphalist liberal narrative, and to imagine alternate trajectories from those preestablished by elites. The invisible man does not speak, on this earlier occasion, from such a broad temporal perspective; he seeks only to intervene in the potential violence of the crowd in order to stave off his own psychological turmoil, and his speech has little effect on the outcome of this scene, other than to attract the attention of the Brotherhood. But during this speech, he is able, for the first time, to imagine and articulate affiliations—with his mother and grandparents, with the Provos, and with other African Americans in both North and South. As Danielle Allen argues, Ellison argued elsewhere that "intimate and personal practices such as love and friendship hold resources for dealing with democracy's difficulties," but such qualities are painfully absent from his narrator's life; in this one scene, we are given a suggestion that such has not always been the case, and this is, notably, a moment when the narrator spontaneously finds his voice.[71] But this ability to imagine broad affiliation does not return until the events of the novel are concluded; even in his first speech for the Brotherhood, during which he claims to feel "more human," he cannot see others, for he is blinded by the spotlight, and after it is finished, and he seeks to understand his feelings, he "quickly dismiss[es]" thoughts of his grandfather, arguing, "What had an old slave to do with humanity?" (354).

In showing the narrator's inexorable tendency to revert to the very forms of temporal elitism through which he fears being marginalized, the novel suggests the extraordinary difficulty of resisting an ideology of progress that is manipulated by left and right alike. In contrast, isolated in an unknown basement, the narrator contemplates how one might counter an "opponent's sense of time," a reflection that also fuels exploration of his own relationship to time through jazz, "reefer"-enhanced hallucination, memory, and narrative (8). As this memoirist project concludes, the narrator acknowledges that his hesitancy to emerge from this secluded space arises from the outside society's intensifying conformism, according to which his rejection of "progress . . . is very much against the trend of the times" (576). But the novel suggests that this denunciation is one of the narrator's most important accomplishments: he insists that "the mind that has conceived a plan of living must never lose sight of the chaos against which that pattern was conceived. That goes for societies as well as individuals" (580). Ultimately, his story suggests that a rigid sense of progressive time can be both pathogenic and politically destructive, leading individuals to misunderstand themselves and the world around them.[72]

Ellison made this argument explicitly in "If the Twain Shall Meet" (1964), his review of Howard Zinn's *The Southern Mystique* (1964). Invoking the "spiral" that he so thoroughly critiqued in his earlier novel—the "swift and tightly telescoped continuity" through which nationalist histories are narrated—he links it even more explicitly to tendencies of repression and unconscious return (88). To the extent that the polity believes in the region's perpetual progress—embraces, in Ellison's words, "our well-known 'American innocence' "—it accordingly fails to recognize that "our unresolved issues persist" and are left vulnerable to ideological manipulation. Presenting the civil rights movement as the "resumption of . . . Reconstruction," Ellison argues that "the point of maximum tortuosity" in the nation's disavowal of its white supremacist practice "is once again the South." To an important extent, this was Zinn's argument as well, for he argued that, rather than constituting "an abnormal growth on the national body . . . the South crystallizes the defects" of the United States, thus posing an opportunity for "candid self-recognition by the nation."[73] But while Ellison praised Zinn's interest in such a psychologically inflected approach to social change, he criticized the temporality through which Zinn conducted this analysis—an understanding of time directly in opposition to that of *Invisible Man*.[74]

Rather than exploring the relationships among multiple temporal forms—the linear progressive time of U.S. nationalism, the conflicting histories within it, the "boomerang" of the returning repressed (both social and individualized), and the immeasurable *durée* of the unconscious—Zinn, in explicit opposition to "orthodox Freudianism," argues that the behavior of societies and individuals should be interpreted and predicted through a quite strict focus on their "immediate environment" (27, 31). He does so in part to dispute the old and invidious argument that " 'state-ways' cannot change 'folkways,' " an effort that Ellison supports (33). But Ellison nonetheless insists that "human beings are creatures of memory and spirit, as well as of conscious motivation," noting that "words, even Mr. Zinn's words, are rooted deep in the realities of the past" (94, 97). Demonstrating the need for social theorists to consider how their metaphors might emerge from repressed associations, Ellison repeatedly refers to Zinn's description of experiences in "what is often thought to be the womb of the South's mystery: the Negro community of the Deep South."[75] This metaphor, which Zinn does not go on to refute, serves to represent southern African Americans as a monolithic and feminized group; the womb, an organ of capacious nurturing, has no means of articulating political critique. More than an unfortunate turn of phrase, this idea recurs in the conclusion that Ellison singles out for his most forceful critique: Zinn rejects the idea that southern African American history and experience might have facilitated development of distinctly valuable expressive forms and perspectives, a political and cultural resource that Ellison had posited not only in the epilogue of *Invisible Man* but also in numerous essays before and after.[76]

Ellison demonstrates that Zinn's purportedly synchronic approach to psychology and politics serves neither effectively. Though overtly well intentioned, Zinn's approach to African American communities is clearly problematic; more broadly, his fascination with the mystery of the South exemplifies what is, as I have shown, a quite venerable analytic error—the idea that segregation comprises chiefly a set of social and cultural habits. For where Zinn focuses his critique on ideas of racial difference, which he represents as "the most vicious thing about segregation" and also the main impediment to social change, Ellison argues that this presentation "makes too much mystery of what, in its political aspects, is really a struggle for power, as white and Negro Southerners understand very well."[77] Zinn seeks to assimilate both race and region to his preferred temporal framework, such that all people in the United States should discount the past and focus on the transformations of the present, but Ellison argues that such a rigid approach to time prohibits analytic thought, explaining that Zinn "underplay[s] the influence of the past—ironically, a tendency that reformers share with reactionaries and conservatives, who would repress all details of the past that would unmask their mythologies" (100). To be clear, Ellison argues not for the perpetuation of Zinn's "southern mystique" but rather for an approach to southern and U.S. society that attends seriously to history, culture, and psychology, one that neither accepts conceptual boundaries established in the past nor seeks merely to dismiss them without understanding how they have functioned (103). In doing so, he targets a tendency particularly prominent in cold war–era U.S. liberalism, which, in dismissing its past struggles and failures, tended to yield extraordinary testaments to its power and beneficence. Zinn's study is no exception, arguing "that we are powerful enough today, and free enough, to retain only as much of the past as we want. We are all magicians" (13).

As Kenneth Warren argues, Ellison's insistence on the importance of the past requires a difficult negotiation, for commitment to heritage had long been the province of southern segregationists, and even the resistance to a triumphalist and market-oriented form of liberalism is often associated with the conservative and white supremacist southern Agrarians.[78] But Agrarian arguments sought to retain a stark temporal division between the South and the larger United States. Characterizing national culture as "urbanized, anti-provincial, progressive, and mobile," and, most damning, "in a condition of eternal flux," John Crowe Ransom, in the manifesto *I'll Take My Stand*, described southern regional life as "backward-looking, intensely provincial . . . [and] stable."[79] This approach was antithetical to Ellison's, which sought to track correspondences and commonalities between region and nation and also to understand how mystifying accounts of both southern and national time impede political affiliation and understanding.

Unfortunately, as red state rhetoric and political southern strategies attest, the trope of the backward South—positing a sharp cultural dichotomy between the region and the nation—has been far more influential, as it produces images of implacable cultural divides primed for implicit political manipulation. And though this strategy is notorious for its use in supporting distinct campaigns, it has also proved portable, such that contemporary debate about the central goals and principles of the national collective is routinely curtailed and misdirected through recourse to perceived temporal divisions, which also, more broadly, serve to constrain or marginalize debates about globalization. As the nation-state bids to enter an era of ever more concentrated wealth extraction and perhaps fundamentally determinate market rationality, Republican politicians who vigorously support these policies rally their publics with images of more contained "cultural threats"—women getting abortions, same-sex couples forging long-term partnerships—paradoxically describing these quite aged phenomena as urgent threats to traditional values. Meanwhile, in another paradox, similarly neoliberal Democratic leaders argue that voters should be guided by their "economic interests," hesitating even to acknowledge the significance of value systems that are not centered in capitalism.[80] The temporal flexibility advocated by Ellison—in which ideologies or perceptions about time signal targets for analysis rather than parameters limiting thought or identification—remains elusive, in part because knowledge production seems increasingly to be driven by diverse institutions' economic goals. Thus, though they focus on a national/regional divide that (however often reasserted in relation to U.S. politics) might seem outmoded in a context in which the role of nation-states themselves appears to be shifting, these novels, in their concern with how temporal ideologies affect political understanding, raise problems that are not only intractable in contemporary politics but are also only beginning to be theorized.[81]

It may seem odd for a book on southern literature to posit fiction as a site for forms of analysis and understanding that resist constraining ideologies. This particular literature has long been identified as the source of "hooded vision[s]," narratives and images that seek to naturalize, celebrate, and preserve a white supremacist social order.[82] But southern literature both presents the efforts of segregationists to evade political protest by insisting that apartheid constituted a vital cultural trait and testifies to the efforts of others to create a venue for more democratic and radical visions. Its formal experiments and constitutive ambiguities testify to the difficulty of this latter project. Because, for several decades, studies of this literature tended to support hegemonic accounts of southern backwardness, its investigations of spatial and temporal ideologies have yet to be understood in relation to their deeply political context. But while the efforts of southern modernists to challenge the purported division between national and regional temporalities initially lacked a receptive audience, that circumstance has now been reversed, and this has occurred in a period in which the need for more nuanced and flexible understandings of space and time is broadly apparent in political discourse and action. It is my hope that this investigation and what is now known as "the new southern studies" may develop together. Exploring a region long situated at the center of triumphalist disavowals of the nation's political and temporal multiplicity—the coexistence of liberalism and white supremacy, and the relationships between supposedly modern and supposedly backward cultural forms—this field may ultimately offer insight not only into how such mystifications function but also into strategies for rebutting them.

Notes

Introduction. American and Southern Exceptionalisms

1. See, for example, Rorty, *Achieving Our Country*; Hollinger, "Authority, Solidarity, and the Political Economy."
2. Kammen, "Problem of American Exceptionalism," 26–33.
3. R. Smith, *Civic Ideals*; Gerstle, *American Crucible*.
4. Recent monographs on this topic include Grant, *North over South*; Baker, *Turning South Again*; Graham, *Framing the South*; McPherson, *Reconstructing Dixie*; and Greeson, *Our South*. For examinations of the way in which beliefs concerning regional backwardness or tradition and national modernity have inflected formulations of African American identity, see Favor, *Authentic Blackness*; and Richardson, *Black Masculinity*.
5. L. Griffin, "Why Was the South a Problem?" 13, 12–13. Another relatively early analysis of this dynamic appears in Ladd, *Nationalism and the Color Line*. I

make this chronological distinction because these studies predate the recent scholarship concerning the relationships among liberalism, cultural nationalism, and cosmopolitanism in U.S. nationalism.

6. Said, *Orientalism*, 55, 95, 54, 22.

7. Ellison, "If the Twain Shall Meet," 88.

8. Lipsitz, *Possessive Investment in Whiteness*, 216.

9. Although, as Rita Barnard notes, the transposition of the word *apartheid* into other national contexts must be conducted with care, I use it to redress a lexical deficiency of U.S. English that she also concedes; see Barnard, "Of Riots and Rainbows," 400–401.

10. The common name for U.S. racial segregation—*Jim Crow*—may have exacerbated this disavowal, appropriated as it was from the popular minstrel song and character. Serving as the name of what came to be an elaborate system of legal codes, Jim Crow evoked the image of a stereotypical figure quite rigorously dissociated from state practice.

11. B. Anderson, *Imagined Communities*, 26; Hegeman, *Patterns for America*, 22–24.

12. For a description of capitalism's temporality, see Osborne, "Modernity," 70–75. For the linkage between ideas of capitalist expansion and U.S. identity during the late nineteenth century, see Trachtenberg, *Incorporation of America*.

13. Bender and Wellbery, *Chronotypes*, 3–4.

14. Holt, *Problem of Race*, 19.

15. *Plessy v. Ferguson*, 163 U.S. 537, 551 (1896).

16. Osborne, "Modernity," 75. See also McClintock, "Angel of Progress"; T. Mitchell, "Stage of Modernity"; Goldberg, *Racial State*, 38–73.

17. W. Williams, "United States Indian Policy." For the role of temporal distancing in racist discourse, see Lloyd, "Race under Representation," 249–59.

18. Grady, "New South," 532.

19. Payne, " 'Whole United States,' " paragraphs 3–12.

20. Guérard, "Southern Memories," 493. Explaining that he lived in the South for eleven years, Guérard argues that southern white supremacy is too widely understood as a feeling that is "in the blood" (492); as Sartre later would, he situates southern race relations in a global context by comparing them to colonial relations in Algeria (497–98; Sartre, introduction to *Colonizer and Colonized*, xxi). Guérard also, however, recapitulates tropes of the backward South, assuring his readers that "the Southern Mammy is no myth" (493). Demonstrating how such ideologies were valorized amid acknowledgement of southern social change, *Scribner's* published, one year later, a lengthy tribute to the mammy that warned

of this figure's imminent obsolescence but reproduced the stereotype in lengthy and vivid detail (Vaughan, "Exit Mammy").

21. Brinkmeyer assesses white southern writers' accounts of parallels between European fascism and southern social structures in "Fourth Ghost."

22. Singh, "Culture/Wars," 473; Sitkoff, *Depression Decade*, 59.

23. Bakhtin, "Forms of Time," 84–85. For the importance of affect in transmission of cultural representations, see Westen, "Beyond the Binary Opposition," 33–43.

24. For the centrality of temporal representation in modernist innovation, see Calinescu, *Five Faces of Modernity*, 5; Müller, "Identity, Paradox, Difference"; Cohn, *History and Memory*, 22–34. For discussion of these coexisting temporal experiences, see Castoriadis, "Time and Creation," 49; Benjamin, "Storyteller," *Illuminations*; Bhabha, *Location of Culture*, 1–13; Breuer and Freud, *Studies on Hysteria*, 1–18, 183–305; Bergson, *Time and Free Will*, 125–39.

25. For discussion of exchanges among modernism, popular culture, and diverse academic disciplines, see North, *Reading 1922*.

26. Ellison, "Extravagance of Laughter," 156.

27. For the importance of shared assumptions in shaping readers' understandings of a text, see Fish, *Is There a Text?* 332–42.

28. Dubey, "Postmodern Geographies"; McPherson, *Reconstructing Dixie*, 9–10.

29. See, for example, R. King, *Southern Renaissance*; Singal, *War Within*.

30. T. Davis, "Expanding the Limits"; Romine, *Narrative Forms of Southern Community*; Kreyling, *Inventing Southern Literature*; Yaeger, *Dirt and Desire*.

31. Handley, *Postslavery Literatures*, 13–40; Ladd, "Dismantling the Monolith," 53–56; Smith and Cohn, introduction to *Look Away*. For the importance of similar concerns in American studies, see Radway, "What's in a Name?"

32. C. Tate, *Psychoanalysis and Black Novels*, 16, 5–21. Other critics who seek to correct and expand psychoanalytic approaches include Spillers, "'All the Things You Could Be Right Now,'" and Cheng, *Melancholy of Race*.

33. Scott, "Fantasy Echo."

34. Freud, *Ego and the Id*, 643, 637–58; Freud, *Group Psychology*. Though related in that each involves identification and may be said to derive from the child's efforts to overcome powerful ambivalence toward a parent, their political implications differ in that Freud associates the former with sublimation and morality, as well as guilt and the inverted death instinct, while the latter is characterized more prominently by jealousy and impairment of intellect.

35. Rose, *States of Fantasy*, 8–11.

36. For an extended such account of U.S. cultural dynamics, see Fisher, *Still the New World*, 153–87.

37. Sullivan, *Days of Hope*, 1–168; Denning, *Cultural Front*.

38. For an optimistic reading of regionalist possibilities, see Kroes, *Them and Us*, 26–27. For an explanation of scholarly skepticism, see Dubey, "Postmodern Geographies"; Dainotto, *Place in Literature*. Celebration of holistic regional communities—as opposed to national fragmentation—is often associated with white conservatism, but such valuation of the regional is also prominent among African American discussions of segregated black southern communities. Dubey argues that "the utopian dimensions of such projects . . . are fraught with political risk" (367); see also K. Warren, *So Black and Blue*, 77–82.

Chapter 1. Region, Race, and Nation

1. Odum, *Race and Rumors of Race*, 15–16.

2. Woodward, *Strange Career of Jim Crow*, 117; Klinkner, *Unsteady March*, 135.

3. Klinkner, *Unsteady March*, 125–32.

4. J. Johnson, *Negro Americans, What Now?* 13.

5. Klarman, *Jim Crow to Civil Rights*, 108.

6. Kirby, *Media-Made Dixie*, 44.

7. G. Johnson, "The Ku-Kluxer," 16; S. Anderson, *Puzzled America*, 63; Benton, *Artist in America*, 109; Pinckney, "Bulwarks against Change," 44.

8. Freud, "Uncanny."

9. Rose, *States of Fantasy*, 2–12; Scott, "Fantasy Echo," 285–92; Volkan, "Psychoanalysis and Diplomacy."

10. A. Smith, "Origins of Nations," 113.

11. B. Singer, "Cultural versus Contractual Nations."

12. R. Smith, *Civic Ideals*, 1–39; Gerstle, *American Crucible*, 1–9. Though individual relationships to these categories can be variable and shifting, nation-states that exclude on the basis of such ascriptive traits typically disavow or ignore such fluidity. Accordingly, Aihwa Ong argues that exclusionary and restrictive norms of ascriptive citizenship affect both individuals' relationships to the state and their processes of identity formation; see Ong, "Cultural Citizenship as Subject Making."

13. *Plessy v. Ferguson*, 163 U.S. 537, 550 (1896).

14. Ring, "Problem South."

15. D. Davis, "Free at Last."

16. Mencken, "Sahara of the Bozart," 70.

17. Odum, *Race and Rumors of Race*, 15.

18. Williamson, *Crucible of Race*, 475–82.

19. See, for example, Vance, *Human Geography of the South*, 61–62; C. Johnson, *Shadow of the Plantation*; Burns, *I Am a Fugitive!*; "Shoes for Southerners?"; Beard and Beard, *Industrial Era*, 3–121; Twelve Southerners, *I'll Take My Stand*; Dollard, *Caste and Class*, 61–96.

20. Bishop, "*Plessy v. Ferguson*," 128–29.

21. *Plessy*, 163 U.S. at 551.

22. Bishop, "*Plessy v. Ferguson*," 126; Woodward, *Strange Career of Jim Crow*, 103–4.

23. Sumner, *Folkways*, 79.

24. Ibid., 78.

25. Ely, "South, the Supreme Court, and Race Relations," 127–29.

26. Gerstle, *American Crucible*, 82–122, 128–55.

27. Myrdal, *American Dilemma*, xlvii, 20, 33.

28. Boles, *South through Time*, 471. Boles reports that the trial was recorded on movie cameras and broadcast live on WGN radio, in addition to being covered by print journalists.

29. See, for example, Moran, "Reading Race."

30. Barnard, *Great Depression*, 17–31. For the role of country music in transregional consumer culture, see Mancini, " 'Messin' with the Furniture Man.' "

31. Cripps, "Myth of the Southern Box Office."

32. D. Merritt, "Democracy and the South"; Burt, "Democracy and the Broken South"; Crabités, "White South, or Black?" The last, which is stridently white supremacist, testifies nonetheless to southern change, warning that "education and thrift have made such progress among the Blacks of the South that menacingly large numbers of them can now legally answer to any Constitutional provisions that the Courts would declare valid" (279). Though it may seem more than usually absurd that African American achievement would be mobilized as an argument against African American voting rights, Crabités insists that racial segregation is the only preventative against racial violence. For the prominence of such arguments in the creation and defense of southern apartheid, see Cell, *Highest Stage of White Supremacy*, 172–91.

33. Doyle, *Etiquette of Race Relations*, 145, 158; C. Johnson, *Preface to Racial Understanding*, 178; J. Johnson, *Negro Americans, What Now?* 83.

34. See, for example, Gellman and Quigley, *Jim Crow New York*.

35. Rable, "South and the Politics of Anti-Lynching Legislation," 201–9. During the 1930s, southern congressional strategies shifted to citing nonsouthern hate crimes such as urban "race riots" (210).

36. Balibar, "Racism and Nationalism," 39.

37. Klinkner, *Unsteady March*, 72–118.

38. Du Bois, "Segregation." David Theo Goldberg notes that official state racisms leave few other options for social transformation; see *Racial State*, 115.

39. Du Bois, *Darkwater*, 524–32.

40. Du Bois, *Souls of Black Folk*, 142.

41. Du Bois, "Scottsboro."

42. Baker, *Turning South Again*, 21–22; Baker and Nelson, "Preface," 234–37; Ayers, "What We Talk About," 66; L. Griffin, "Why Was the South a Problem?" 17–28; Tindall, "Benighted South," 291; Williamson, *Crucible of Race*, 497–99; Zinn, *Southern Mystique*, 218.

43. Loewenberg, "Construction of National Identity," 46–52; Norton, *Reflections on Political Identity*, 1–94; Said, *Orientalism*, 54–55, 94–95; Scott, "Fantasy Echo," 288–92; Shimakawa, *National Abjection*, 2–17; Volkan, "Narcissism of Minor Differences," 175–91.

44. Berlant, *Anatomy of National Fantasy*, 4–16; Butler, "Subjection, Resistance, Resignification," 229–49; Castoriadis, *Imaginary Institution of Society*, 117–64.

45. Among prominent psychoanalytic accounts of this process, Freud held that the child's ambivalence toward the parents is resolved in the creation of an ego ideal, the sedimentation of identifications with social authority figures; Lacan, who describes this aspect of Freud's theory as "the joint of the imaginary and the symbolic," explains the subject's investment in societal beliefs as the effect of entry into language, through which "symbols in fact envelop the life of man with a network . . . so total that they provide the words that will make him faithful or renegade," a defiance that would itself be transindividual in its sources. See Freud, *Ego and the Id*, 638–45; Lacan, *Seminar of Jacques Lacan, Book I*, 137; Lacan, *Écrits*, 67. In each case, identification with nationalist societal norms results from a combination of psychological and social forces that produce a somewhat alienating version of selfhood to which the subject is nonetheless attached. As Lauren Berlant argues, "The modern nation installs itself within the memory and the conscience of citizens" (*Anatomy of National Fantasy*, 225n3).

46. Greenfield, *Nationalism*, 484.

47. Blight, *Race and Reunion*, 251, 211–12, 216–27; see also Hale, *Making*

Whiteness, 51–84. For information on writers of these romances, see Censer, *Reconstruction of White Southern Womanhood*, 269.

48. Brennan, "National Longing for Form," 51.

49. Harris, "William Henry," 334; Page, *Red Rock*, 344.

50. Cooper, *Voice from the South*, 101.

51. Ring, "Problem South," 1–39; Blight, *Race and Reunion*, 221–31, 234–37.

52. Hale, *Making Whiteness*, 284.

53. F. Turner, "Sections and Nation," 316, 321.

54. Ibid., 318, 338, 338–39. The development of fixed printable versions of "administrative vernaculars" is a prominent feature in the history of nationalisms (B. Anderson, *Imagined Communities*, 40–46). Thus, in citing the language through which political functions are performed, Turner indicates that the national community had distinguishing characteristics. He also insists, however, on the relative cultural importance of regional vernaculars, apparent not only in "pronunciation, idioms, and so on, but also in the mental attitude that underlies the expressions" (328).

55. F. Turner, "Sections and Nation," 323, 324, 326, 328.

56. Ibid., 326.

57. Ladd, *Nationalism and the Color Line*, 44–45; Franklin and Steiner, "Taking Place," 7–9; Conforti, *Imagining New England*, 1–7.

58. Dainotto, *Place in Literature*, 1–33.

59. Greenfield, *Nationalism*, 422–40; Onuf, "Federalism, Republicanism," 11–31.

60. B. Anderson, *Imagined Communities*, 163–85, 26–36; A. Smith, "Origins of Nations," 120–21.

61. See, for example, the ambitious if short-lived effort of the National Endowment for the Humanities to encourage development of regional studies centers across the United States (Southwick, "Humanities Centers").

62. Hechter and Levi, "Ethno-Regional Movements," 186–88.

63. Conforti, *Imagining New England*, 83–104; Nissenbaum, "Inventing New England," 116, 113–18; Greeson, "Figure of the South"; Dawson, "Puritan and the Cavalier."

64. Greenfield, *Nationalism*, 433–34; Onuf, "Federalism, Republicanism," 27–30; Wrobel, *End of American Exceptionalism*, 5–9.

65. Garland, *Crumbling Idols*, 53.

66. Bramen, *Uses of Variety*, 125, 154.

67. Brodhead, *Cultures of Letters*, 177, 120–21.

68. Bhabha, *Location of Culture*, 145.
69. B. Brown, "Regional Artifacts," 211, 210–15, 195–97.
70. Ibid., 214–15; Brodhead, *Cultures of Letters*, 177, 135–37.
71. For accounts of the complexity of such arguments, see Howard, "Unraveling Regions"; Zagarell, "Troubling Regionalism"; Evans, "Object-Life of Books."
72. Pryse, "Writing Out of the Gap," 22.
73. Fetterley, " 'Not in the Least American,' " 44.
74. Limerick, "Region and Reason," 84–85; Armitage, "From the Inside Out," 32.
75. Sumida, "East of California."
76. Appiah, "Cosmopolitan Patriots," 99–106.
77. R. Smith, *Civic Ideals*, 37; Berlant, *Queen of America*, 4. Berlant cites specifically the "fantasy of the American Dream," a model of U.S. belonging that is particularly cogent to this period but that has existed, in varying forms, since the inception of the nation (Cullen, *American Dream*).
78. R. Smith, *Stories of Peoplehood*, 76.
79. For this understanding of supplementation, see Derrida, *Of Grammatology*, 144–45.
80. Slavoj Žižek suggests that such fundamentalist dynamics may be inherent in liberal nationalism (*Tarrying with the Negative*, 200–225).
81. Balibar, "Racism and Nationalism," 54. Nikhil Pal Singh criticizes as "too simple" the idea that "racial ascription" responds to "an invariant need to constitute a compelling collective identity for the nation," noting that "racism has also been central to the constitution and defense of material investments and market inequalities (in the United States and globally)." He acknowledges, however, that the pursuit of national hegemony and capital accumulation have been mutually supportive in U.S. history. See his *Black Is a Country*, 28, 31.
82. Balibar, "Racism and Nationalism," 60.
83. Lott, "Love and Theft," 25.
84. Rogin, "Two Declarations of American Independence," 16.
85. Žižek, *Tarrying with the Negative*, 201–2, 212–13; Rose, *States of Fantasy*, 2–15; Volkan, "Psychoanalysis and Diplomacy," 35.
86. K. Warren, *So Black and Blue*, 78–80.
87. Baker, *Turning South Again*, 23.
88. Balibar, "Racism and Nationalism," 53; Rogin, " 'Sword Became a Flashing Vision,' " 153–54.

89. Sommer, "Irresistible Romance," 81.

90. Hahn, *Nation under Our Feet*, 442–43.

91. Kaplan, "Romancing the Empire," 221, 238; Hale, *Making Whiteness*, 75–76, 81.

92. Michaels, "Local Colors," 741, 744.

93. "Bush and McCain"; Riskind, "Gore Calls Bush." The Republican candidate John McCain later recanted his position, explaining that his Confederate ancestors "fought to sever the union of our great nation, a cause that would have terribly harmed America, perhaps irreparably, and, for a time at least, perpetuated the grave injustice of slavery" ("McCain Flag Apology Extraordinary").

94. Polman, "If Democrats Look Away"; Marlantes, "Make or Break?"; Liasson, "Impact of Gay Marriage."

95. K. Warren, "Appeals for (Mis)Recognition," 57–59.

96. Ellison, "Extravagance of Laughter," 164.

97. For this account of how U.S. identity is experienced, see Berlant, *Queen of America*, 1–3. The metaphor of "scarification" suggests both the degree to which a sense of marginalization from the nation may cause affective pain and the degree to which individuals may feel that this status can be seen, thus assuring the perpetuation of this condition. Accounts of citizenship as abstract and broadly accessible deny the importance of the visual register in its presentation and experience. Freud argued that the "ego is first and foremost a bodily ego," suggesting that individuals conceptualize identities as substantial, visible, and potentially decipherable to others (*Ego and the Id*, 636).

98. M. Wallace, "Good Lynching," 94–95.

99. Du Bois, *Black Reconstruction*, 723.

100. Rogin, "'Sword Became a Flashing Vision,'" 151; J. Gaines, "Birthing Nations," 299.

101. Michaels, *Our America*, 67. See also Rogin, "'The Sword Became a Flashing Vision,'" 153–56. For a discussion of "Americanization" discourse, see D. King, *Making Americans*, 86–126.

102. Cited and reproduced in Everett, *Returning the Gaze*, 92–93.

103. Ibid., 60–106.

104. M. Wallace, "Good Lynching," 93.

105. L. Williams, *Playing the Race Card*, 114.

106. Dixon, *Clansman*, 277, 219–22, 233–36. One such ex-slave is tortured by the northern military, and another single-handedly succeeds in attaining the release of his former owner from the military through negotiation, as opposed

to Griffith's multiracial and vaudevillian rescue. Though Dixon's representation of ex-slaves who maintain loyalty to their former owners could constitute an inheritance from earlier, more paternalistic, plantation romances, that possibility is unlikely, because his previous novel, *The Leopard's Spots* (1902), thoroughly rejected even paternalistic interracial relationships by insisting that ex-slaves were inevitably treacherous (Michaels, *Our America*, 19). In *The Clansman*, Dixon appears to have sought to avoid the charges of crudity leveled against the previous work (Clark, introduction to Dixon, *Clansman*, v–vi).

107. Dixon, *Clansman*, 186–87. Subsequent references are cited parenthetically. For the importance of the mythic history of a *Staatsvolk* in affective or "proto-" nationalism, see Hobsbawm, *Nations and Nationalism*, 73. Scott Romine observes that Dixon's *The Leopard's Spots* (1902) similarly places the idea of southern Anglo-Saxonism at the center of a U.S. nationalist—and more overtly imperialist—project; see Romine's "Things Falling Apart," 186–95.

108. For discussion of the instability of racial categories in Dixon's prose, despite his obsession with racial purity, see Magowan, "Coming Between."

109. L. Williams, *Playing the Race Card*, 104–7.

110. To clarify, I use the word *complement* rather than *supplement* here because, in this articulation of nationalism, racism is an overtly necessary component of national affiliation.

111. Michaels, *Our America*, 10.

112. Freud, *Civilization and Its Discontents*, 55, 51.

113. Freud, *Group Psychology*, 81–82.

114. Ibid., 53, 41–51; Freud, *Civilization and Its Discontents*, 81–92.

115. Freud, *Civilization and Its Discontents*, 61–63.

116. Bartov, "Defining Enemies, Making Victims," 778–83.

117. Freud, *Civilization and Its Discontents*, 62.

118. Žižek, *Looking Awry*, 165.

119. Žižek, *Tarrying with the Negative*, 201, 207. The semantic incongruity between an ineffable "way of life" and a material "thing" reflects the ineffability of the Lacanian Thing: a subject cannot find or describe the Thing and yet feels as if it must be there—something previously experienced, dimly perceived, and perpetually desired (Lacan, *Seminar of Jacques Lacan, Book VII*, 52–53).

120. Lacan, *Seminar of Jacques Lacan, Book VII*, 56, 67, 70. Žižek more often describes this Thing as traumatic, perhaps because it is alienation and frightfulness that designate the Thing as such (Žižek, *Looking Awry*, 167). The mother becomes "the first outside" when the infant perceives her as "strange and even

hostile," from which point the infant's previous experience of the mother seems elusive, "something missed" (Lacan, *Seminar of Jacques Lacan, Book VII*, 52). Lacan's description of the phantasmic mother is influenced by Melanie Klein, who also appears to have shaped Freud's understanding of collectivist passion in *Civilization and Its Discontents* (76–78). Although, in keeping with his earlier Oedipal theory, Freud speaks here of the central parent in the development of the superego as "the authority—the father," he had formerly argued that the earliest object of desire—the object invoked in this account—was chiefly maternal. Thus, though Freud cites Klein only on a more limited point, this conception of the superego seems deeply informed by her early work, which situates the Oedipus complex in "the frustration which the child experiences at weaning" and holds that the child, who "desires to destroy the libidinal object by biting, devouring and cutting it," fears a corresponding punishment for that desire. This fear and aggression attach to the primary object of desire—the mother—with whom the child now identifies in split and phantasmic forms, "excessive goodness and excessive severity existing side by side." Unable, at this stage, to enjoy pleasure without ambivalence, "the infant, still undeveloped intellectually, is exposed to an onrush of problems and questions," rendered all the more overwhelming because the child still lacks language; this "early feeling of *not knowing*" underlies a subsequent and lasting "feeling of being incapable, ignorant" (Klein, "Early Stages," 202–4). Of course, these two theories are mutually informing: Freud had already argued that Oedipal identification "behaves like a derivative of the first *oral* phase of the organization of the libido" (Freud, *Group Psychology*, 61). My point is that *Civilization and Its Discontents*, like Freud's remarks on maternal dread in *Group Psychology* (1921), suggests that Freud's thought on group feeling consistently returned to the perceived tenuousness of a child's relationships to early objects of desire.

121. Such theorization is not unique among scholars of nationalism. Eric Hobsbawm, for example, argues that "states and national movements . . . mobilize[d] certain variants of feelings of collective belonging which already existed and which could operate . . . potentially on the macro-political scale"; thus, the nation's "'imagined community' . . . can be made to fill the emotional void left by the retreat or disintegration, or the unavailability of *real* human communities and networks" (*Nations and Nationalism*, 46).

122. Ibid., 221; Harpham, "Doing the Impossible," 472.

123. Žižek, *Tarrying with the Negative*, 222–24, 211.

124. Ibid., 205.

125. L. Williams, *Playing the Race Card*, 110.

126. M. Wallace, "Good Lynching," 91; L. Williams, *Playing the Race Card*, 119.

127. Bhabha, *Location of Culture*, 140.

128. The dance held by slaves and attended by the Camerons and their Stoneman visitors is said to take place during the slaves' daily "extended" lunch break.

129. Rogin, " 'Sword Became a Flashing Vision,' " 181–82.

130. R. Merritt, "Griffith's *The Birth of a Nation*," 219, 227–29.

131. See, for example, Williamson's discussion of Thomas Dixon, which argues that Dixon's writing and political positions emerged from a "very deep emotional problem," exemplary of the "disorder of the mind" that engenders racism and of the "psychic plight of several million [of his] contemporary white Southerners" (*Crucible of Race*, 158, 151, 152). It is quite probable that, as Williamson argues, Dixon's obsessive concern for his mother's sexual history and menstrual dysfunction shaped other aspects of his thought; I would further suggest that his rabid post-Confederate sympathies may manifest rage at a father who never fought for the Confederacy (152–65). This focus on familial circumstance and individual psychopathology, however, elides the ability of ideological structures—even as they are shifting—to lend form and expression to idiosyncratic psychological dynamics, and leaves Williamson to protest, "It remains difficult to imagine that a vast part of the leadership in the turn-of-the-century South could actually have embraced the Radical mentality" (176). It is possible that this tendency to focus on individualized psychopathology in interpreting white supremacist discourse contributes to what Michelle Wallace describes as an "unfathomable conundrum"—the way in which "academic discussion of [*Birth of a Nation*] remain[s] so endlessly important and yet so hopelessly inadequate to the task of ameliorating the textual racism this discussion seeks to diagnose" ("Good Lynching," 86).

132. For discussion of how such rhetoric can be used to misdirect psychoanalytic investigation, see Žižek, *Looking Awry*, 52; Lacan, *Écrits*, 51.

133. Žižek, *Looking Awry*, 52–63.

134. In some respects, *Birth of a Nation* and particularly *The Clansman* could be seen as responses to Tourgée's similarly romantic novel, *A Fool's Errand* (1879), which differs unreservedly from the later works in its political implications, configuring white supremacist terrorism as an effort to impede democratization in the South.

135. Žižek, *Tarrying with the Negative*, 203.

136. M. Wallace, "Good Lynching," 92.

137. Sitkoff, *Depression Decade*, 20–22.

138. Everett, *Returning the Gaze*, 105–6; Sitkoff, *Depression Decade*, 22.

139. Gerstle, *American Crucible*, 89–91; Renda, *Taking Haiti*, 94–101; U.S. Secretary of State Robert Lansing quoted in Schmidt, *U.S. Occupation of Haiti*, 62–63.

140. M. Mitchell, *Gone with the Wind*, 465; Tolson, "*Gone with the Wind* Is More Dangerous Than *Birth of a Nation*," *Caviar and Cabbage*, 217.

Chapter 2. Economy Crisis

1. W. Wolfe, "Psycho-analyzing the Depression," 209.

2. For a similar Depression-era interest in ethnic pluralism, chiefly concerning the cultural traditions of European immigrants, see Weiss, "Ethnicity and Reform."

3. B. Anderson, *Imagined Communities*, 35.

4. Ibid.; Dewey, "Americanism and Localism," 686, 685.

5. See, for instance, Rorty, *Achieving Our Country*, 30–31; Hollinger, *Postethnic America*, 140–43.

6. His argument that internationalism will "release" localism echoes Horace Kallen's earlier claim that "Americanization has liberated nationality," that is, encouraged U.S. immigrants to renew their identification with their nationality of origin ("Democracy versus the Melting-Pot," *Nation* [February 25, 1915], cited in Weiss, "Ethnicity and Reform," 577).

7. D. King, *Making Americans*, 87–100.

8. Dewey, "Americanism and Localism," 685; D. King, *Making Americans*, 123–26.

9. W. Frank, *Our America*, 93, 225.

10. Susman, *Culture as History*, 121, 106; see also pp. 105–21.

11. Lynd and Lynd, *Middletown*, 499, 21. For the influence of this volume, see Hegeman, *Patterns for America*, 134–37.

12. Max Lerner, review of *Middletown* in the *New York Evening Post*, February 9, 1929, cited in Gerstle, "Protean Character of American Liberalism," 1062–63.

13. S. Lewis, *Babbitt*, 8, 317.

14. Gerstle, "Protean Character of American Liberalism," 1059–65.

15. Hughes, "Negro Artist." See, for example, Grossman, *Land of Hope*, 129–60.

16. W. Wolfe, "Psycho-analyzing the Depression," 210; J. Adams, "Our Changing Characteristics," 321.

17. Merriam, "Government and Society," 33. See also President's Research Committee on Social Trends, *Recent Social Trends*.

18. E. Brown, "American Road to Fascism," 392.

19. Shaw, "Fascism and the New Deal"; Pate, "Federal-State Relations in Planning," 187.

20. Gerstle, *American Crucible*, 132–55. Susman notes this era's domestication of the idea of culture as well as its "general revival of communitarian concern"; though he does not consistently stress the nation's role as a threshold of such ideas concerning affiliation, many of his examples demonstrate its importance (*Culture as History*, 154, 175, 153–80).

21. J. Adams, "Crisis and the Constitution III," 68; J. Adams, "Crisis and the Constitution V," 212.

22. Hunt, "America Must Dream Again!" 205, 206.

23. H. Wallace, "Search for an American Way," 22, 23.

24. Ibid., 26; Calverton, "American Revolutionary Tradition," 355.

25. Bunche, "Critique of New Deal Social Planning," 59.

26. Ibid., 60–65.

27. Denning, *Cultural Front*, 126–35.

28. Singh, *Black Is a Country*, 83–87.

29. Susman, *Culture as History*, 159, 179; Gerstle, *American Crucible*, 131–55.

30. Szalay, *New Deal Modernism*, 2–6, 61–69; Hirsch, *Portrait of America*.

31. Cited in Stott, *Documentary Expression*, 50.

32. Ibid., 50–58. Denning notes a diversity of populisms in this era (*Cultural Front*, 126–35).

33. Denning, *Cultural Front*, 78–80.

34. Dewey, "Americanism and Localism," 685.

35. Odum and Moore, *American Regionalism*, 16.

36. Michaels, *Our America*, 69.

37. Rourke, *American Humor*, x, 297–302.

38. National Resources Committee, *Regional Factors in National Planning*, 8, 9.

39. Hirsch, *Portrait of America*, 27.

40. Dorman, *Revolt of the Provinces*, xii.

41. McWilliams, *New Regionalism in American Literature*, 23.

42. Odum and Moore, *American Regionalism*, 3.

43. Kern, *Culture of Time and Space*, 19, 137; Fabian, *Time and the Other*, 5–69.

44. Hayworth, "New Day in Oskaloosa," 246.
45. Odum and Moore, *American Regionalism*, 624.
46. Ibid., 3, 629.
47. Aronovici, "Let the Cities Perish," 438, 440.
48. Odum and Moore, *American Regionalism*, vi.
49. Becker, *Selling Tradition*, 13–37; Steiner, "Regionalism in the Great Depression," 438–40.
50. Botkin, "Regionalism: Cult or Culture?" 184. See also Denning, *Cultural Front*, 219–20.
51. Twelve Southerners, *I'll Take My Stand*, xxxix.
52. Ransom, "South Is a Bulwark," 299.
53. O'Brien, *Idea of the American South*, 90–93.
54. Botkin, "Regionalism: Cult or Culture?" 183–84.
55. Levine, "Hollywood's Washington."
56. For the prevalence of this logic, see Levine, "Hollywood's Washington," 187.
57. Ibid., 188.
58. Smoodin, "'Compulsory' Viewing for Every Citizen." Moran and Rogin identify the screenwriter Sidney Buchman as a Communist Party member and also note that "the *Daily Worker* loved *Mr. Smith*" ("'What's the Matter with Capra?'" 112). Though *Mr. Smith* could seem to mock the New Deal—as, for example, the movie's public works bill is a vehicle for graft—Muscio shows that Roosevelt's speeches align closely with many of the political values espoused by the movie; see "Roosevelt, Arnold, and Capra," 170–85.
59. C. Wolfe, "*Mr. Smith Goes to Washington*," 315.
60. Poague, *Another Frank Capra*, 174.
61. Ibid., 173.
62. See, for example, Poague's reading of this scene, with which I largely agree. Observing how Saunders and Smith become attuned in writing the bill, Poague argues that they metaphorically mother each other, an apt psychoanalytic account of how each nurtures the other's nascent identity (174–75). This ambiguity concerning their stage of development results, I would argue, from the film's approach to how Smith's Boy Ranger identity emerged—its insistence that his sense of connectedness is both natural and a result of identification; the film thus holds that nationalist longing constitutes both an essential trait and an achievement that must be cultivated.
63. Aronovici, "Let the Cities Perish," 440.

64. Berlant, *Queen of America*, 50.
65. C. Wolfe, "Mr. Smith Goes to Washington," 305-10.
66. Berlant, *Queen of America*, 51.
67. Ransom, "Reconstructed but Unregenerate," 2.
68. Young quoted in Justus, "Enduring Modernism," 419. On the novel's popularity, see Dwyer, "Case of the Cool Reception," 12. On the film's popularity, see Soderbergh, "Hollywood and the South," 4-6.
69. DuCille, "Shirley Temple of My Familiar," 18, 21.
70. Hale notes that Mitchell herself was critical of "Old South" romanticism but argues that *Gone with the Wind* "salvaged . . . even as it criticized the myth" (*Making Whiteness*, 260).
71. For the conundrums confronting a "black press . . . founded on a principle of protecting and promoting its vested interest in the accomplishments of African Americans" when those accomplishments constituted talented portrayals of largely stereotypical roles, see Everett, *Returning the Gaze*, 193-99.
72. Locke, "Eleventh Hour of Nordicism," 9.
73. S. Brown, "Unhistoric History," 750.
74. Roller, "No More Swords and Roses," 136.
75. M. Mitchell, *Gone with the Wind*, 717.
76. L. Williams, *Playing the Race Card*, 207-14.
77. Mitchell's attitudes toward her literary forebears are quoted in Cripps, "Winds of Change," 139. Both Scarlett and Dixon's Marion Lenoir use their curtains to create postbellum finery (M. Mitchell, *Gone with the Wind*, 374-76; Dixon, *Clansman*, 193).
78. McPherson, *Reconstructing Dixie*, 59.
79. M. Mitchell, *Gone with the Wind*, 556, 517; Cripps, "Winds of Change," 140.
80. Cripps, "Winds of Change," 139-45.
81. Winnicott, "Primitive Emotional Development," 184, 185. For discussions of how the experience of having an African American caretaker in childhood may have shaped some white southerners' racial fantasies, see Yaeger, *Dirt and Desire*, 142-43. Such fantasies may have had a broader cultural influence; Hale argues that Mitchell "never described having close relationships with African American servants as a child" (265).
82. Young, *So Red the Rose*, 70-71.
83. Tolson, "*Gone with the Wind* Is More Dangerous Than *Birth of a Nation*," *Caviar and Cabbage*, 217.

84. L. Williams, *Playing the Race Card*, 214.

85. S. Lewis, *Babbitt*, 82; M. Mitchell, *Gone with the Wind*, 608.

86. Feldstein, *Motherhood in Black and White*, 6.

87. Ibid., 35–39; M. Mitchell, *Gone with the Wind*, 514–16, 474, 655.

88. M. Mitchell, *Gone with the Wind*, 418, 363, 367; Lord, "Back to the Farm?" 97.

89. A. Jones, *Tomorrow Is Another Day*, 349; McPherson, *Reconstructing Dixie*, 49–64.

90. Myrdal, *American Dilemma*, 31.

91. Davidson, "Sociologist in Eden," 178.

92. Woodward, *Strange Career of Jim Crow*, 32.

93. Moton, *What the Negro Thinks*, 5.

94. Cason, *90° in the Shade*, 33

95. Roosevelt, primary campaign speech, 198; Sitkoff, *Depression Decade*, 122–23.

96. Cripps, "Winds of Change," 148–49.

97. Stott, *Documentary Expression*, 256, 190–257; S. Anderson, *Puzzled America*, ix, xvi.

98. S. Anderson, *Puzzled America*, 63.

99. Ekirch, *Ideologies and Utopias*, 92, 106, 130.

100. Botkin, "Folk and Folklore," 592, 570.

101. Benton, *Artist in America*, 198, 172, 188.

102. Calverton, "Bankruptcy of Southern Culture," 94.

103. National Emergency Council, *Economic Conditions of the South*, 54, 8. See also Tindall, "'Colonial Economy.'"

104. "Shoes for Southerners?" See also Swint, "'Northern Interest in the Shoeless Southerner."

105. A. Tate, "Notes on Liberty and Property," 83; C. Johnson, Embree, and Alexander, *Collapse of Cotton Tenantry*; Caldwell and Bourke-White, *You Have Seen Their Faces*. The most idyllic Agrarian portrait of farming is perhaps Andrew Nelson Lytle's "The Hind Tit," which suggests that the main threats to southern agriculture are broader financial and industrial trends and ignores both economic discrimination in and experiential aspects of sharecropping and tenant farming. Such lapses were not consistent across the movement; see, for example, O'Donnell, "Looking Down the Cotton Row," 161–65. It is worth noting that many Agrarians wrote little about actual farming.

106. Bunche, "Critique of New Deal Social Planning," 64. For Couch's interest

in such programs, see "Agrarian Programme for the South," an essay presented as a response to criticism from Allen Tate.

107. Calverton, "Bankruptcy of Southern Culture," 298; Leuchtenburg, *FDR Years*, 76-100. I am not arguing that Agrarian political philosophy, diverse and often vague as it was, should be collapsed into the category of fascism, but contemporary observers were acutely aware of similarities between these agendas; furthering such concerns, the Agrarians' publisher at the *American Review* explicitly embraced fascism. See also A. Stone, "Seward Collins and the *American Review*."

108. See, for example, Kelley, *Hammer and Hoe*, 78-115.

109. See, for example, Styron, "Southern View of Northern Reformers."

110. Sitkoff, *Depression Decade*, 115-22.

111. Alpers, *Dictators, Democracy, and American Public Culture*, 15-58.

112. Sitkoff, *Depression Decade*, 117-22; Tolson, "Hitler Blitzkrieg Strikes Near White House!" *Caviar and Cabbage*, 123.

113. Speech delivered in Gainesville, Georgia, on March 23, 1938, quoted in Sitkoff, *Depression Decade*, 115.

114. Ibid., 216-43.

115. Ibid., 84-138.

116. Singh, *Black Is a Country*, 65; Kelley, *Hammer and Hoe*; Sitkoff, *Depression Decade*, 128-38.

117. V. Dabney, "Dixie Rejects Lynching."

118. Howells, *Criticism and Fiction*, 338, 340.

Chapter 3. Erskine Caldwell and the Abject South

1. Fearnow, *American Stage*, 107-8. In this chapter, I include the dramatized *Tobacco Road* in my discussion of "Caldwell's work"; though Caldwell did not assist Kirkland in adapting the novel for the theater, much of the dialogue, characterization, and plot of the novel are faithfully reproduced, as Caldwell acknowledged (Caldwell, "Note about 'Tobacco Road'"). The differences in plot and characterization are largely irrelevant to my argument, except as noted here. Subsequent references to the text of the play are cited parenthetically as "Kirkland."

2. MacDonald, "Repetition as Technique," in *Critical Essays on Erskine Caldwell*, 330-41; Sykes, "Poetry of Unfeeling."

3. For the importance of the burlesque in literary modernism, see North, *Reading 1922*, 150. Censors targeting these works included the librarians of Teachers' College of Columbia University, members of the New York Society for the Sup-

pression of Vice, and, in the case of the play *Tobacco Road*, several theater owners throughout the country.

4. Burke, "Caldwell: Maker of Grotesques," 356.

5. Hegeman, *Patterns for America*, 24.

6. Watson, "Rhetoric of Exhaustion."

7. Burke, "Caldwell: Maker of Grotesques," 360.

8. Caldwell and Bourke-White, *You Have Seen Their Faces*, 26.

9. For a discussion of normative nationality, see Berlant, *Queen of America*, 35–36.

10. Caldwell and Bourke-White, *You Have Seen Their Faces*, 25.

11. Burke, "Caldwell: Maker of Grotesques," 354–55.

12. E. Caldwell, *God's Little Acre*, 29. Subsequent references to this text are cited parenthetically, using the abbreviation *GLA*.

13. E. Caldwell, *Tobacco Road*, 40. Subsequent references to this text are cited parenthetically, using the abbreviation *TR*.

14. For a similar interpretation, see Cook, *Erskine Caldwell and the Fiction of Poverty*, 125–28.

15. Foucault, *Discipline and Punish*, 135–69; Foucault, *Introduction*, 135–59.

16. Foley, *Radical Representations*, 49, 107; D. Miller, *Erskine Caldwell*, 156–59; Mixon, *People's Writer*, 93.

17. Irr, *Suburb of Dissent*, 106.

18. Caldwell, *God's Little Acre*, 68–69. This description is focalized through the character Will Thompson, whose perspective need not be taken as a reliable vision of the world of the novel. Female characters in the novel, however, validate Will's understanding of female sexuality.

19. Other—and, I would argue, less likely—candidates for this category include the death of Will Thompson, which is narrated secondhand, and the death of Jim Leslie, which occurs after the novel's other characters have already been devastated by either Will's death or their knowledge of his adultery with Griselda.

20. Segrest, *My Mama's Dead Squirrel*, 29; Yaeger, *Dirt and Desire*, 25.

21. Denning, *Cultural Front*, 123, 118–23.

22. Kayser, *Grotesque in Art and Literature*, 179–89; Bakhtin, *Rabelais and His World*, 4–51. Notably, such dynamics have rarely been invoked in discussions of the "southern grotesque," which has until recently been undertheorized.

23. Ellison, "Extravagance of Laughter," 145, 196, 186, 196, 146, 186, 181, 166–80, 196.

24. Ibid., 196.

25. Brinkmeyer argues that the novel forces readers to recognize that they differ from Jeeter only because of their more fortunate circumstances, a recognition that creates an empathic identification. Though such a reading is certainly possible, it is rarely represented in the critical record, especially among Caldwell's contemporaries. See Brinkmeyer, "Is That You in the Mirror?" (370–74).

26. *New York Post*, February 21, 1935, cited in Mixon, *People's Writer*, 4.

27. E. Caldwell, "Tobacco Roads in the South."

28. E. Caldwell, letter to the editor, *New Republic*.

29. For the ambivalence that this duality evokes in responses to the play, see Fearnow, *American Stage*, 105–26.

30. For a survey of additional critics advancing this opinion, see R. Gray, *Southern Aberrations*, 214. See also Keely, "Poverty, Sterilization and Eugenics," 32–33.

31. Goldstein, *Political Stage*, 136; D. Miller, *Erskine Caldwell*, xi, 328–36.

32. Stallybrass and White, *Politics and Poetics of Transgression*, 125–48, 171–90.

33. Rozario argues that such an understanding of sensationalist representation was widely encouraged after World War I by promoters of philanthropic causes, for whom such images were vital to fund-raising strategies ("Delicious Horrors," 426, 420–21, 428–39).

34. Fearnow, *American Stage*, 108–13.

35. Jarrell, review of *Kneel to the Rising Sun*. See also Isaacs, "News-Reel Theatre"; J. Gray, "New Realist."

36. Kristeva, *Powers of Horror*, 1–31. Kristeva explains that, as the infantile subject begins to develop the borders of a distinct, individual identity, it undergoes a process of separation from the objects to which it is most often physically connected—the body of the mother, for example, or its own spittle and excrement. This process of ejecting the abject is never finished, however, because the material ejected from that identity comes to appear threatening, defying the subject's image of its distinct, bounded ego.

37. G. Miller, letter to the editor, *Nation*. For a brief history of the closings of *Tobacco Road*, see D. Miller, *Erskine Caldwell*, 198–202.

38. "Week."

39. "Long Road."

40. Krutch, "Poor White."

41. Jarrell, "Beyond the Cave," 36. See also J. Gray, "New Realist"; Beach,

American Fiction, 219–49; Wyatt, review of *Tobacco Road*; Cargill, *Intellectual America*, 390; Young, review of *Tobacco Road*.

42. Kristeva, *Powers of Horror*, 16.

43. For the tendency to assert sameness or difference through the identifiers *here* and *now*, see Fabian, "Of Dogs Alive," 189.

44. Gruber, "All Around the Town."

45. Isaacs, "News-Reel Theatre," 93–94. See also Wyatt, review of *Tobacco Road*; Young, review of *Tobacco Road*.

46. J. Gray, "New Realist," 13; White, review of *Tobacco Road*.

47. Rolfe, "God's Little Acre."

48. Gruber, "All around the Town," 247.

49. Young, review of *Tobacco Road*, 168. Young was both the associate editor of *Theatre Arts Monthly* and a member of the Nashville Agrarians.

50. For a famous colonial codification of this distinction, see Byrd, *History of the Dividing Line*.

51. McIlwaine, *Southern Poor-White*, xvii–xxxii; Cash, *Mind of the South*, 6; Den Hollander, "Tradition of 'Poor Whites.' "

52. Vance, *Human Geography of the South*, 464–67; Mencken, "Sahara of the Bozart."

53. Cash's sources for this view date from before 1915. Odum presented the racial homogeneity of white southerners as an uncontroversial position in *Southern Regions*, 15.

54. R. Warren, "Briar Patch," 258n1.

55. See Rafter, introduction to *White Trash*.

56. Barkan, *Retreat of Scientific Racism*, 75.

57. D. King, *Making Americans*, 128–38.

58. Ibid., 87–127.

59. Den Hollander, "Tradition of 'Poor Whites,' " 426.

60. Huxley, "Social Degeneration" (1928), quoted in Leon, "A Literary History of Eugenic Terror," 166.

61. Estabrook, "Country Slum," 12.

62. Ibid.

63. G. Jones, "Poverty and the Limits," 765, 768–70.

64. Carver, "Economic Test of Fitness," 6.

65. Caldwell, *Tobacco Road*, 57, 60. I take the term *analepsis*, or a narrative movement into the past, from Genette, *Narrative Discourse*, 49. Other descriptive

terms, such as *iterative narrative, primary narrative,* and *extradiegetic,* are taken from this source as well.

66. L. Mitchell, *Determined Fictions,* 1–33; Bender and Wellbery, *Chronotypes,* 4; Seltzer, *Bodies and Machines,* 43.

67. For a discussion of a similar structural effect in naturalist narrative, see Howard, *Form and History, Naturalism,* 104–41.

68. Kruger, *National Stage,* 18.

69. " 'Tobacco Road' "; D. Miller, *Erskine Caldwell,* 196.

70. In *Time and the Other,* Fabian explains that "temporal distance" is measured by cultures' differing relationships to such "socioculturally meaningful events" as industrialization and urbanization (23–31).

71. Richard Gray notes that southern journalists and politicians, in responding to Caldwell's representations, argued that the southern poor existed outside national and regional norms; Gray's thematic reading of the fiction does not consider how Caldwell's novels courted such a response (*Southern Aberrations,* 154–60, 215–27).

72. E. Caldwell, *Tobacco Road,* 108; Kirkland, 14–15.

73. See also Keely, "Poverty, Sterilization and Eugenics," 23.

74. D. Miller, *Erskine Caldwell,* 122–30.

75. I. Caldwell, "The Bunglers," 1:209–10.

76. Ibid., V:383. Mixon argues that Ira Caldwell "quickly passed over" the suggestion of sterilization, in order to appeal to educated people to fight "the forces . . . that created people like the Bunglers" (*People's Writer,* 17). In this conclusion, however, Ira Caldwell does not mention such forces but spends more than half the installment discussing the "evolutionary process" that destroyed the Roman Empire and its likely replication by the United States.

77. Dahlberg, "Raw Leaf."

78. J. Gray, "New Realist," 15. See also Wyatt, review of *Tobacco Road*; Young, review of *Tobacco Road*; Beach, *American Fiction*; Dahlberg, "Raw Leaf," 16–17; Conroy, "Passion and Pellagra."

79. Their circulation could hardly seem threatening from the perspective of a eugenicist, however, because, despite considerable sexual activity, they do not get pregnant.

80. "Nonsynchronism," taken from Ernst Bloch's essay on the role of the peasantry in fascist Germany, suggests the way in which elements of an earlier culture, contradictory to the "Now," can seem dangerous, because they may have the power to transfigure the "Now." See Bloch's "Nonsynchronism."

81. See, for instance, Du Bois, *Darkwater*, 530–32; Brewer, "Poor Whites and Negroes"; Bontemps, "Saturday Night," 160.

82. In this respect, Kirkland's play does differ from Caldwell's novel, as it offers no African American counterperspective to Jeeter's claim that, if Ellie May does not "get a man," then, after he dies "the niggers would get her in no time" (110). Audience members may have recognized this line as another absurd Jeeterism; given the prevalence of both racial stereotypes and challenges to them during this era, interpretations are likely to have varied.

83. Hall et al., *Like a Family*, 219.

84. C. Johnson, Embree, and Alexander, *Collapse of Cotton Tenancy*, 48–63.

85. Grubbs, *Cry from the Cotton*, 62–83; Hall et al., *Like a Family*, 218–19.

86. Hall et al., *Like a Family*, 220–21; Grubbs, *Cry from the Cotton*, 64–66, 75–77. Church support for unionization was a hotly contested issue in mill-area Protestantism; on the other hand, the tenant farmers' union garnered substantial public support by attracting the interest of national religious organizations.

87. Hall et al., *Like a Family*, 213, 219.

88. Ibid., 309–19; Grubbs, *Cry from the Cotton*, 121; Southworth, "Aid to Sharecroppers," 39–41. The STFU represented white and African American members from its inception and forged an alliance with Native American unions in Oklahoma in 1935.

89. Carpenter, "King Cotton's Slaves," 194, 198.

90. Ibid., 199; Fletcher, letter to the editor, *Scribner's*.

91. Grubbs, *Cry from the Cotton*, 126–27, 148–49.

92. Kristeva, *Powers of Horror*, 2–4; Lacan, *Écrits*, 6.

93. Kristeva, *Powers of Horror*, 13.

94. Lacan, *Écrits*, 7; Kristeva, *Powers of Horror*, 15, 16. See also Freud, *Ego and the Id*, 642–44.

95. Shimakawa, *National Abjection*, 3–17.

96. Ibid., 3.

97. Berlant, *Queen of America*, 286n5.

98. Ibid., 203; Freud, *Ego and the Id*, 641–43. See also Freud, "On Narcissism," 558–59.

99. Berlant, *Queen of America*, 203.

100. Ibid., 286n5.

101. Among initial critics, only Burke identified with Caldwell's characters, in a process he describes as both difficult and "anguish[ing]" ("Caldwell: Maker of Grotesques," 351–55).

102. Ibid., 355. Burke and Ellison raise similar themes in their reading of Caldwell, an unsurprising convergence given their lengthy debates about aesthetic and political theories. See Pease, "Ralph Ellison and Kenneth Burke."

103. Burke, "Caldwell: Maker of Grotesques," 356.

104. Singh, *Black Is a Country*, 153.

Chapter 4. Zora Neale Hurston and the Chronotope of the Folk

1. Wall, "Mules and Men and Women," 667; Baker, "Workings of the Spirit," 300–305; Carby, "Politics of Fiction," 174; Gilroy, *Black Atlantic*, 91.

2. See, for example, Tompkins, review of *Their Eyes Were Watching God*.

3. Huyssen, "High/Low," 364.

4. Locke, *New Negro*, xxv.

5. For the influence of nationalism on Locke and on "New Negro" movements more generally, see Dawahare, *Nationalism, Marxism*, 3–69. For a discussion of capitalist time, see Osborne, "Modernity," 70–75; Castoriadis, *Imaginary Institution*, 207. This temporality corresponds closely to the "homogeneous, empty time" in which, in Benedict Anderson's model, the nation-state is developed. Though Anderson considers the concept in terms of its importance in configuring a nation of dispersed people as a community, and does not link this temporality with a devotion to incessant "progress," that linkage is clear in the work of Walter Benjamin, from whom Anderson derives this phrase. See B. Anderson, *Imagined Communities*, 24–26; Benjamin, "Theses on the Philosophy of History," *Illuminations*, 260–61.

6. Locke, *New Negro*, xxv, 6; Du Bois, "Negro Mind Reaches Out," 413; C. Johnson, "New Frontage on American Life," 278; J. Johnson, "Harlem: Culture Capital," 301; K. Miller, "Howard: The National Negro University," 312; Frazier, "Durham," 340.

7. B. Anderson, *Imagined Communities*, 26–27.

8. Osborne, "Modernity," 75; Fabian, *Time and the Other*, 23–31.

9. C. Johnson, "New Frontage on American Life," 294, 280.

10. Locke, *New Negro*, 3, 4, 6.

11. K. Warren, "Appeals for (Mis)Recognition," 393.

12. Fabian, *Time and the Other*, 30.

13. Schuyler, "Negro-Art Hokum," 51, 53.

14. Favor, *Authentic Blackness*, 10.

15. C. Johnson, "New Frontage on American Life," 288.

16. Ibid., 285. Johnson's social constructionist account is influenced also by

racial essentialism, as he argues that "probably . . . the Negro is a rural type," and attributes to "the Jew" "a neurotic constitution traceable to the emotional strain of peculiar racial status and to the terrific pressure of city life" (279–80).

17. For a brief survey, see Dubey, "Narration and Migration," 298–99.

18. K. Gaines, *Uplifting the Race*; Carby, "Policing the Black Woman's Body," 741–47, 750–55; Grossman, *Land of Hope*, 140–55.

19. Kennedy, *Negro Peasant Turns Cityward*, 196–97.

20. Carby, "Policing the Black Woman's Body," 754.

21. Toomer, *Cane*, 86.

22. Larsen, *Quicksand*, 77, 82.

23. S. Brown, "More Odds," 189; Locke, "We Turn to Prose," 42; Locke, "Sterling Brown," 115. Locke often used the phrase "Old Negro" to refer to stereotypical figures (cf. *New Negro*, 3). That does not seem to be the case here, however; in his 1930s essays on folk representations, he vacillates uneasily between criticism of clichéd figurations of the "pure soil peasant"—the existence of which he, nonetheless, does not refute—and his desire to know more about "the real Negro peasant" ("We Turn to Prose," 42).

24. C. Johnson, *Shadow of the Plantation*, 6.

25. Lamont, review of *Shadow of the Plantation*, 283. See also "Scottsboro," 134; "Recovery in the South"; T. Dabney, "Southern Negroes and Politics"; Pickens, "Re-Visiting the South."

26. Hurston, "Court Order," 956. For a participant's portrayal of Hurston's role in the Harlem Renaissance, see Hughes, *Big Sea*, 238–40. Also, in Thurman's *Infants of the Spring*, a novel that clearly fictionalizes conflicts and events related to this cultural movement, a character named "Sweetie May Carr" is described as "a short story writer" and "able raconteur" who, "given a paleface audience . . . would launch forth into a saga of the little all-colored Mississippi town where she claimed to have been born" (229). Born in Mississippi rather than Florida, and "get[ting] her tuition paid" at Columbia rather than Barnard, the theatrical Sweetie May closely matches Hughes's description of Hurston, whom Sweetie May is widely believed to represent. Thurman's representation implies that Hurston may have faced some regional prejudice: another character, angered, calls Sweetie May "an illiterate southern hussy" (242).

27. Thurman, *Infants of the Spring*, 229; Hurston to Thomas E. Jones, 1934, quoted in Hemenway, *Zora Neale Hurston*, 184.

28. See, for instance, Hurston, "Spirituals and Neo-Spirituals," 869–70; Hurston, "Sanctified Church," 901.

29. Locke, "Black Truth and Black Beauty," 14–18; Hurston, "Characteristics of Negro Expression," 836.
30. Abrahams, "Phantoms of Romantic Nationalism," 4.
31. Bradford, *John Henry*, 26, 59–64.
32. S. Brown, "Negro Character," 179, 190.
33. Nicholls, "Migrant Labor, Folklore, and Resistance," 467.
34. Hurston, *Mules and Men*, 3.
35. For the importance of such arguments in contemporary scholarship, see Prahlad, "Guess Who's Coming to Dinner," 565.
36. Hurston, "Sanctified Church."
37. Perrow, "Songs and Rhymes," 165–68.
38. Cohen, "Skillet Lickers," 235, 229.
39. S. Brown, *Negro in American Fiction*, 160–61.
40. Locke, "Deep River," 291.
41. Preece, "Negro Folk Cult," 37.
42. Hathaway, "Unbearable Weight of Authenticity," 177.
43. Preece, "Negro Folk Cult," 37.
44. Carr and Cooper, "Zora Neale Hurston and Modernism," 298–300.
45. C. Johnson, *Shadow of the Plantation*, 27.
46. Hurston, "Characteristics of Negro Expression," 845.
47. Carby, "Politics of Fiction," 172.
48. Hemenway criticizes this technique because, in indicating the book to be "about" folklore, as opposed to "about" the author, it suggests "a need for folklore analysis" (166–67). In contrast, Sánchez-Eppler argues that Hurston's "dialogical mode" allows her "informants [to] remain strong interlocutors" ("Telling Anthropology," 477, 479).
49. Hurston, "Hoodoo in America."
50. Hurston, *Tell My Horse*, 23. Hurston's 1936 letter to Henry Allen Moe, administrator of the Simon Guggenheim Foundation, which provided Hurston a grant for this research, is quoted in Hemenway, *Zora Neale Hurston*, 229.
51. Hurston, *Tell My Horse*, 80, 77, 80.
52. Zora Neale Hurston, *Their Eyes Were Watching God*, 1.
53. Carby, "Politics of Fiction," 172, 174. For a discussion of "allochronic discourse," which places the "other" outside the temporal and cultural frameworks of the speaker, see Fabian, *Time and the Other*, 20–35 and elsewhere.
54. Lamothe, "Vodou Imagery," 166.

55. For Hurston's attraction to civic nationalism as suggested by her early essays, see Duck, " 'Rebirth of a Nation,' " 130–31.

56. Lamothe, "Vodou Imagery," 166–77; Pavlic, "Papa Legba"; Barr, " 'Queen of the Niggerati' "; Pondrom, "Role of Myth"; Gates, "Zora Neale Hurston and the Speakerly Text," 92–94.

57. Hurston, *Their Eyes Were Watching God*, 6, 10–11.

58. For an account of allotemporality in fiction, and in the cultural imagination, see B. Brown, *Material Unconscious*, 212, 220, 232. For the importance of the chronotope, or how the interpretation of a literary work is affected by the representation of the spatial and temporal qualities of its setting, see Bakhtin, "Forms of Time."

59. For the importance of this departure in shaping responses to the text, see Carby, "Politics of Fiction," 176.

60. Wainwright, "Aesthetics of Community," 234.

61. Hurston, *Their Eyes Were Watching God*, 25. See also Pondrom, "Role of Myth," 189.

62. Wright, review of *Their Eyes Were Watching God*, 17.

63. Wright's ideas concerning African American women may have influenced his interpretation of time in Hurston's novel; in *12 Million Black Voices*, he argued, "More than even that of the American Indian, the consciousness of vast sections of our black women lies beyond the boundaries of the modern world, though they live and work in that world daily" (135).

64. Carby, "Politics of Fiction," 180.

65. Hurston, *Dust Tracks on a Road*, 65; C. Tate, *Psychoanalysis and Black Novels*, 159–60; Boyd, *Wrapped in Rainbows*, 42. Hurston claims in *Dust Tracks* that she was nine, but her tendency to misinform regarding her age is widely noted.

66. C. Tate, *Psychoanalysis and Black Novels*, 160.

67. Hurston, *Dust Tracks on a Road*, 64.

68. Hurston, *Mules and Men*, 1.

69. Freud, "Mourning and Melancholia."

70. Hurston, *Mules and Men*, 2.

71. C. Tate, *Psychoanalysis and Black Novels*, 161. Hurston described this narrative as one in which she "tried to embalm all the tenderness of [her] passion" for a romantic interest; it has also, as I have shown, been described as a memorial to her mother. Finally, rather as Hurston wondered whether her parents were happy together, this novel's protagonist questions the relationship between her

mother and father, both of whom are inaccessible: Nanny tells Janie that her mother was raped, but Janie insists that her father tried to marry her mother (19, 10). See *Dust Tracks on a Road*, 188–89, 65–67.

72. K. Gaines, *Uplifting the Race*, 5–6.

73. See, for instance, Hemenway, *Zora Neale Hurston*, 238; Carby, "Politics of Fiction," 176–79; and Kodat, "Biting the Hand," 321.

74. Hurston, *Their Eyes Were Watching God*, 35–39. The references to modernization ideology that follow are based largely on Lears, *No Place of Grace*, 8–12.

75. Hurston, *Their Eyes Were Watching God*, 54. This moment suggests the fictional pattern, noted by Bakhtin, in which the "idyllic world," notable for the "humanity of [its] human relationships," is contrasted to a world in which "people are out of contact with each other . . . [and] greedily practical" (233–34). For Joe's investment in ideologies of "monopoly capitalism," see McGowan, "Liberation and Domination," 113–16.

76. Here, I rely on Raymond Williams's definition of *hegemony* as a process that links people from high and low social hierarchies in consensus (*Marxism and Literature*, 112–13).

77. Hurston, *Tell My Horse*, 75, 86–87, 88.

78. V. Turner, *From Ritual to Theater*, 30–33.

79. Carby, "Politics of Fiction," 179.

80. Hurston, *Their Eyes Were Watching God*, 79; Lamothe, "Vodou Imagery," 174–76.

81. V. Turner, *From Ritual to Theater*, 54, 33.

82. Hurston, *Their Eyes Were Watching God*, 61. Dalgarno also notes the importance of the liminoid in the novel (" 'Words Walking without Masters,' " 527). The novel also links mules and women in terms of labor (Hurston, *Their Eyes Were Watching God*, 14).

83. For the former position, see Carby, "Politics of Fiction," 180.

84. Michaels, *Our America*, 94; Barbeito, " 'Making Generations,' " 389.

85. Hurston, "Crazy for This Democracy"; Hurston, "Court Order."

86. Fairclough, "The Costs of *Brown*"; Carson, "Two Cheers for *Brown*."

87. Hurston, "Court Order," 956.

88. Thompson, "Editorial Note," 268.

89. Hurston, "Court Order," 957.

90. Singh, "Culture/Wars," 490–91.

91. Hurston, *Dust Tracks on a Road*, 251, 250.

92. Ibid., 248–51; Kelley, *Hammer and Hoe*, 114; Singh, *Black Is a Country*, 154–55.

93. Boyd, *Wrapped in Rainbows*, 357–59, 424.

94. C. Brooks, *William Faulkner*, 314.

Chapter 5. William Faulkner and the Haunted Plantation

1. Glasgow, "Heroes and Monsters."

2. Pound, "Wisdom of Poetry," 360. For Faulkner's use of local lore, see Blotner, *Faulkner: A Biography*, 1:vii.

3. For the emergence of this study as a critical field, see Riquelme, "Toward a History of Gothic and Modernism," 586; Smith and Wallace, *Gothic Modernisms*, 1. On Faulkner's modernist influences, see Kinney, *Faulkner's Narrative Poetics*, 53–65.

4. On Faulkner's influence among many Spanish American authors of the 1960s and 1970s, see Cohn, "Faulkner and Spanish America."

5. Glasgow, "Heroes and Monsters," 34.

6. Ibid., 35, 34. This treatment of the term is noted also by Donaldson, "Making a Spectacle," 567.

7. Glasgow, "Heroes and Monsters," 34–35.

8. Canby, "Grain of Life"; G. Stone, review of *Light in August*.

9. See, for example, Field, "American Novelists vs. the Nation," 556.

10. For the Depression-era literary-critical prioritization of realism, see Irr, *Suburb of Dissent*, 32–33, 41–42. For the relationship between the representation of linear time and nationalism, see B. Anderson, *Imagined Communities*, 24–26. For the relationship between linear time and capitalism, see Benjamin, "Theses on the Philosophy of History," *Illuminations*, 260–61.

11. Rahv, review of *Absalom, Absalom!* 210, 208.

12. See Trilling, "Mr. Faulkner's World"; Hicks, *Great Tradition*, 262–68; Kronenberger, "Faulkner's Dismal Swamp"; Kazin, "Faulkner: The Rhetoric and the Agony"; Geismar, *Writers in Crisis*, 143–83.

13. Cowley, "Poe in Mississippi," 206.

14. Faulkner, *Absalom, Absalom!* 4.

15. Eliot, "Tradition and the Individual Talent," 4. For Eliot's influence on Faulkner's writing, see Blotner, *Faulkner: A Biography*, 1:241, 307, 514, 867.

16. Eliot, "Tradition and the Individual Talent," 58, 59; Tabachnick, "Gothic Modernism," 79–84.

17. Eliot, "Tradition and the Individual Talent," 4.

18. "City full of dreams / Where the ghost in full daylight accosts the passerby." Qtd. in Eliot, *Waste Land*, n2.

19. Lévy, *Roman "gothique" anglais*, 7. Sedgwick debates this claim but nonetheless notes that crossing the boundaries of gothic space, which she describes as "originally arbitrary," provokes extraordinary violence; though she argues that gothic chronotopes "undermine the sense of inside and outside," their effect is thus to release gothic settings from any stable dimensions. See Sedgwick, *Coherence of Gothic Conventions*, 24, 31, 29. My discussion of conventional gothicism is also informed by DeLamotte, *Perils of the Night*, 15–23; Punter, *Literature of Terror*, 1–128; and Fiedler, *Love and Death*, 126–61.

20. See, for example, J. Frank, *Idea of Spatial Form*, 64, 63.

21. As concrete examples of these modernist phenomena, consider, in corresponding order, Italian futurism, Eliot's *Four Quartets*, Harlem Renaissance collections of folk art and tales, French surrealism, and Ernst Bloch's defense of German expressionism. For the centrality of nonlinear temporal logics in distinguishing modernist texts, see, for instance, Jameson, for whom the representation of linear time suggests an interest in mimesis that identifies the artist with nineteenth-century aesthetics and not high modernism ("Beyond the Cave," 120–23). See also Calinescu, *Five Faces of Modernity*, 41; Quinones, *Mapping Literary Modernism*, 30–31. An overtly nonlinear time is also often considered a constitutive feature of postmodernism. See, for example, Ermath, "Crisis of Realism."

22. Jameson, "Beyond the Cave," 122–23. See also Lükacs, "Ideology of Modernism"; Rahv, "Myth and the Powerhouse," 141–44; A. Tate, "Man of Letters," 7–8. For an account and refutation of the continuing critical complaint that modernists' temporal experimentations, often described as "spatial form," conflict with progressive politics, see Hewitt, *Fascist Modernism*, 31–45.

23. Jameson, "Beyond the Cave," 132. Both *Light in August* and *Absalom, Absalom!* were titled, in early drafts, "Dark House"; in each, an old plantation house collapses in conflagration. For Faulkner's repeated use of this working title, see Pitavy, "Gothicism of *Absalom, Absalom!*" 206.

24. Hewitt, *Fascist Modernism*, 45; Fabian, *Time and the Other*, 47. For changing perceptions of the relationship between space and culture during the early twentieth century, see Said, *Culture and Imperialism*, 189; R. Williams, "Metropolitan Perceptions," 44–47; James Clifford, *Predicament of Culture*, 13–16.

25. For the spatial ideology of early twentieth-century nationalisms, see Pollock et al., "Cosmopolitanisms," 578–79. Appadurai discusses the cultural flows of the contemporary period in "Disjuncture and Difference."

26. Punter, "Hungry Ghosts and Foreign Bodies," 21–26; Glover, "'Spectrality Effect' in Early Modernism," 32–42. These texts do not consider the convergence of critiques of imperialism with recognition of trauma in psychological studies.

27. Riquelme, "Toward a History of Gothic and Modernism," 587–88. Martín describes multiple parallels between *Dracula* and *Heart of Darkness*, though she focuses on masculinity rather than temporality; she argues that, as Conrad had not read or met Stoker, the similarities between their works suggest the broad influence of the "imperial Gothic," which, in the late Victorian era, generated "new myths about modernity." See "Meeting the Civilized Barbarian," 101–2.

28. Faulkner was introduced to Conrad's writing by his mother and claimed particular admiration for *Heart of Darkness* (Blotner, *Faulkner: A Biography*, 1:110, 388). I cannot say whether Faulkner read Stoker's narrative, but it continued to elicit broad interest during the years when Faulkner began writing fiction. Notably, Faulkner went to Hollywood to begin screenwriting in May 1932, shortly after Universal's successful release of Tod Browning's *Dracula*.

29. For the relationship between *Dracula*'s maps and late Victorian psychology and imperialism, see Mustafa, "Mapping the Late-Victorian Subject," 20–79.

30. Stoker, *Dracula*, 342–43, 329.

31. Conrad, *Heart of Darkness*, 31, 61.

32. Van der Kolk and van der Hart, "Intrusive Past," 158–68.

33. Conrad, *Heart of Darkness*, 104. For a brief summary of Janet's analyses of traumatic and "subconscious" memories during the early 1890s, see Janet, *Psychological Healing*, 1:589–96. The discussion of trauma that follows will rely more heavily on the theories presented in Breuer and Freud, *Studies on Hysteria*, 1–18, 183–305. Janet, Breuer, and Freud all note that, during this time period, they agreed to a significant extent concerning the effects of traumatic memories and the treatment of subsequent psychopathology; each also cites the investigations of several psychologists proceeding along similar lines (Janet, *Psychological Healing*, 601; Breuer and Freud, *Studies on Hysteria*, 229–33, 235–38). These early articulations of traumatic neuroses did not specify that the symptoms must be traceable to a singular event; *Studies in Hysteria* argued that "we must be prepared for *successions* of *partial* traumas and *concatenations* of pathogenic trains of thought," suggesting that repeated exposures to an incomprehensible stressor might induce symptoms now commonly referred to as PTSD (288). The appearance of this logic in *Dracula*, a narrative dominated by the discourse of fictional psychotherapists, is not surprising. Though Marlow is, through his narrative, represented as hostile to psychological inquiry, he uses Janet's language

with remarkable precision; I do not know whether Conrad, like the fictional doctor in *Heart of Darkness*, studied the clinical psychology of imperialism.

34. Freud did not theorize "working through" until the twentieth century; see "Recollecting, Repeating, and Working Through." However, in the late nineteenth century, many European therapists agreed that the assimilation of the traumatic event to narrative form might allow the patient to "discharge" the overwhelming emotions associated with it. For a history of these debates, see Leys, "Traumatic Cures." Notoriously, certain therapists prescribed rest, a conflict depicted in *Dracula*: though the doctors wish to protect each of the Harkers from discussion that would remind them of their separate traumas, Jonathan recovers only after he shares his story with Mina.

35. Janet and Breuer were uncomfortable that their early theorizing of traumatic neuroses necessitated some remapping of consciousness, a practice that, Breuer anxiously points out, relies on a metaphorical understanding of mental space (228). These theories predate Freud's more confident mapping of the mind. The classic early case of dissociation is Janet's patient Irene, who was traumatized by her mother's death, occasionally repeating, in a fugue state, her actions on that occasion but, at other moments, insisting that her mother was not dead.

36. Said, *Culture and Imperialism*, 189; Cole, "Conradian Alienation and Imperial Intimacy."

37. Joyce, *Portrait of the Artist*, 203.

38. Joyce, *Ulysses*, 9, 474.

39. De Voto, "Witchcraft in Mississippi," 146. In one important recent exception, Pitavy notes the gothic tropes that describe "the three places of narration, all dark, darkened, or darkening" ("Gothicism of *Absalom, Absalom!*" 210).

40. Rosa Coldfield's gothic rhetoric has received more attention, and it is true that Quentin's initial visualization of her "invoked ghost" seems characteristic of his repeated and passive acquiescence to authority (*Absalom, Absalom!* 8). For readings of Rosa's gothic language, see Pitavy, "Gothicism of *Absalom, Absalom!*" 220-25; R. Gray, *Literature of Memory*, 245-47; Kartiganer, *Fragile Thread*, 73-76.

41. Kreyling, *Inventing Southern Literature*, 106.

42. Sundquist, *Faulkner: The House Divided*, 23; P. Brooks, *Reading for the Plot*, 311-12; Ladd, *Nationalism and the Color Line*, 153.

43. J. Smith, "Southern Culture on the Skids," 82.

44. Woodward, *Strange Career of Jim Crow*, 103-4; Williamson, *Crucible of Race*, 478-82.

45. Wilson, "Religion of the Lost Cause."
46. On this term, see Hobsbawm, introduction to *The Invention of Tradition*.
47. Hale, *Making Whiteness*, 52–53.
48. R. King, *Southern Renaissance*, 7–8, 11–19.
49. A. Tate, "Remarks on the Southern Religion," 174, 166.
50. A. Tate, in *Poems 1922–1947*, lines 18, 16, 85, 38–39, 43.
51. Ibid., line 43.
52. Ibid., lines 48, 54.
53. Ibid., lines 85–86. This point was not lost on fellow Agrarian Donald Davidson; see R. King, *Southern Renaissance*, 101.
54. A. Tate, "Remarks on the Southern Religion," 162–63.
55. Bleikasten, *Ink of Melancholy*, 36–37.
56. Faulkner, *Flags in the Dust*, 13, 432–33, 12–20. See also R. King, *Southern Renaissance*, 82.
57. Faulkner, *Absalom, Absalom!* 142; Faulkner, *Flags in the Dust*, 23.
58. Leys, "Traumatic Cures," 622–34. For Faulkner's interest in World War I, see Kartiganer, "'So I, Who Had Never Had a War,'" 627–31.
59. Blotner, *Faulkner: A Biography*, 1:261–62, 408–9, 478.
60. Richard King rightly argues that young Bayard's compulsions also result from "the family romance with death" (*Southern Renaissance*, 83). Although I acknowledge this point, I also think it important to distinguish between the forms of memory these characters exemplify.
61. Faulkner, *Flags in the Dust*, 134. For this understanding of "ego-ideal," see Freud, *Ego and the Id*, 639–43; Lacan, *Seminar of Jacques Lacan, Book I*, 141–42.
62. For the prominence of such views among white southerners in the 1920s and 1930s, see Williamson, *Crucible of Race*, 478–82.
63. R. King also represents this as a productive and perhaps intentional decision, arguing that Faulkner's later narratives "move toward the creation of an historical consciousness *within* the narrative which will be able to comprehend and tell his story" (*Southern Renaissance*, 83). Moreland argues that, through Faulkner's career, his writing moves toward a "less compulsive, more differential, critical style of repetition and writing" (*Faulkner and Modernism*, 32).
64. Weinstein, *Faulkner's Subject*, 160. See also Sundquist, *Faulkner: The House Divided*, 5–7.
65. Bourdieu, *Outline of a Theory of Practice*, 79.
66. Breuer and Freud, *Studies on Hysteria*, 7.

67. See also Sundquist, *Faulkner: The House Divided*, 6–7.

68. Faulkner, *Sound and the Fury*, 76.

69. Godden argues that, through Quentin's day's events and contemplations, he "blunts [the] pathological edge" of his internal monologue and is here "prepared to comment dispassionately on his earlier stylistic habits" (*Fictions of Labor*, 42–43).

70. Faulkner, *Light in August*, 492, 60.

71. On "screen memory," see Laplanche and Pontalis, *Language of Psycho-Analysis*, 410–11.

72. Irwin, *Doubling and Incest*, 25–52.

73. Faulkner, *Light in August*, 493; Faulkner, *Absalom, Absalom!* 4.

74. On Quentin's attitude of irony, see Moreland, *Faulkner and Modernism*, 30–31. Gail appears to develop irony through his ostracization.

75. For comparisons of *Absalom, Absalom!* with plantation romances, including *Gone with the Wind* and *Birth of a Nation*, see Weinstein, *Faulkner's Subject*, 94–96; Railton, "'What Else Could a Southern Gentleman Do?'"; Lurie, "Some Trashy Myth of Reality's Escape."

76. On the "passionate involvement of [Shreve and Quentin] with their subject and with each other," see Kartiganer, *Fragile Thread*, 92–104.

77. Landsberg, "Prosthetic Memory," 105–12; Laplanche and Pontalis, *Language of Psycho-Analysis*, 460. N. Jones persuasively argues that this scene of shared narration also enables Quentin briefly to accept and enjoy his homoerotic desire; see "Coming Out," 345 and elsewhere.

78. Faulkner, *Absalom, Absalom!* 298. For an understanding of "working through" as a conscious and agential approach to one's own resistances, see Laplanche and Pontalis, *Language of Psycho-Analysis*, 488–89. On the pathos of this exchange's ending, see Kartiganer, *Fragile Thread*, 104–5.

79. For other critical models of thinking about cultural knowledge as "hidden in plain sight" through fetishization or the "unthought known," see, respectively, Matthews, "This Race Which Is Not One," 201–18; Yaeger, *Dirt and Desire*, 101–12.

80. Michaels, "*Absalom, Absalom!*" 137–39. Michaels argues that where Young is committed to a logic of cultural belonging and taste, Faulkner is committed to a logic of race (139–50). I am arguing that through pursuing questions of race, Faulkner elucidates a history of injustice that, as Michaels also notes, Young displaces (142).

81. Young, *So Red the Rose*, 17, 25, 34, 40.

82. Ibid., 103; Young, "Not in Memoriam," 329.
83. See, for instance, Godden, *Fictions of Labor*, 151–78.
84. Ibid., 178. See also Moreland, *Faulkner and Modernism*, 118.
85. T. Davis, *Games of Property*, 235–38.
86. Faulkner, *Go Down, Moses*, 369–383. See also T. Davis, *Games of Property*, 227–31; Matthews, "Touching Race," 22–26.
87. Faulkner, *Requiem for a Nun*, 80.
88. Moreland, *Faulkner and Modernism*, 216–18. Though there appears to be little chance that Temple's telling of her story to the governor will save Nancy Mannigoe, this is represented as Temple's primary motive for conceding to relate it (76).

Chapter 6. Provincial Cosmopolitanism

1. Lutz, *Cosmopolitan Vistas*, 14.
2. A. Anderson, "Cosmopolitanism, Universalism," 268.
3. Pollock et al., "Cosmopolitanisms," 586.
4. Soja, *Postmodern Geographies*, 163.
5. T. Mitchell, "Stage of Modernity," 1–16. For the significance of coevality and its denial, see Fabian, *Time and the Other*, 30–31.
6. Soja, *Postmodern Geographies*, 164.
7. Appadurai, *Modernity at Large*, 139–57.
8. Wallerstein, "What Can One Mean by Southern Culture?" 209–10.
9. Ransom, "Reconstructed but Unregenerate," 20, 22.
10. Dollard, *Caste and Class*, 364, 368.
11. C. Johnson, "Basis of Racial Antagonisms," 59. For his later analysis of dynamism in southern race relations, see C. Johnson, "Present Status of Race Relations."
12. C. Johnson, "Changing Attitude of the Negro," 534–42.
13. Hurston, *Mules and Men*, 2; see also Hurston, *Dust Tracks on a Road*, 127–28.
14. Cox, "Modern Caste School," 221, 220.
15. Cash, *Mind of the South*, 368, 384.
16. Ibid., 38, 39; Baker, *Turning South Again*, 20–21.
17. O'Brien, "W. J. Cash, Hegel, and the South," 385.
18. Cash, *Mind of the South*, 292–96, 428–29.
19. See Sitkoff, *Depression Decade*, 69–169; Klinkner, *Unsteady March*, 126–201.

20. Sullivan, *Days of Hope*, 88–118.
21. Singh, *Black Is a Country*, 103.
22. Ibid., 129.
23. President's Committee on Civil Rights, *To Secure These Rights*, 4, 151–73.
24. Brinkmeyer, "Faulkner and the Democratic Crisis."
25. Wright, *Lawd Today!* 33. Wright began submitting this novel for publication in 1935.
26. Stepto, *From behind the Veil*, 66–70.
27. Wright, *Black Boy*, 43. Werner Sollors notes that the early manuscripts of Wright's autobiography reveal his ambivalence about this passage and the degree to which his ultimately negative portrayal seems to stem from allegorical impulses. See Sollors, "Modernization as Adultery," 147.
28. Wright, *Black Boy*, 43.
29. Wright, "Blueprint for Negro Writing," 101.
30. Wright, introduction to *Black Metropolis*, xviii. On Chicago School nostalgia, see Maxwell, *New Negro, Old Left*, 160–61. On the "social pathology" thesis, see Bone, "Richard Wright and the Chicago Renaissance," 455–56.
31. Wright, "Blueprint for Negro Writing," 106, 99.
32. Kelley, *Hammer and Hoe*, 99–108.
33. Wright, *Black Boy*, 346–51, 378–407, 374.
34. Ibid., 394; Maxwell, *New Negro, Old Left*, 162–66.
35. Marx, "Eighteenth Brumaire," 608–11.
36. Wright, "How Bigger Was Born," 441. In "Invented by Horror," Smethurst argues that the "Eighteenth Brumaire" was particularly important to Depression-era U.S. communists (31). For an example of how "nonsynchronism" served to explain the rise of fascism, see Bloch, "Nonsynchronism."
37. Wright, *12 Million Black Voices*, xx, 17, 26.
38. F. Griffin, *"Who Set You Flowin'?"* 165; Wright, *12 Million Black Voices*, 144.
39. Wright, *Black Boy*, 40.
40. For a discussion of allochronic discourse, see Fabian, *Time and the Other*, 32–35.
41. Stepto, *From Behind the Veil*, 158, 136.
42. Whitted, "'Using My Grandmother's Life as a Model.'" For Wright's depiction of African American women as "the chains which bind black people to the premodern world" in *12 Million Black Voices*, see F. Griffin, *"Who Set You Flowin'?"* 81. For a concise analysis of how Wright's personal experiences may

have shaped his representations of African American women more generally, see DeCosta-Willis, "Avenging Angels and Mute Mothers."

43. Wright, "How Bigger Was Born," 441.

44. Couch, *Culture in the South*, x; Brearley, "Pattern of Violence," 686. Couch himself argued that, though "liberal southerners" regarded lynchings as "signs of general backwardness," they were in fact caused by "an economic system . . . that thrives on struggle between the poor and the less poor" (*Culture in the South*, 461).

45. Weatherford, "Negro Crime," 435; Myrdal, *American Dilemma*, 563. Myrdal also cites as causal factors the hormonally enhanced reactivity of teenage and menopausal white women.

46. Wright, *Uncle Tom's Children*, 48.

47. Wright, "How Bigger Was Born," 447, 443, 444, 441.

48. Ibid., 444–46.

49. Wright, *Uncle Tom's Children*, 25; Wright, *Black Boy*, 156.

50. Romine, *Narrative Forms of Southern Community*, 2.

51. Maxwell, *New Negro, Old Left*, 172.

52. Marx, "Eighteenth Brumaire," 611; Wright, *Native Son*, 392. For a broader reading of the gothicism in this novel, see Smethurst, "Invented by Horror."

53. *Plessy v. Ferguson*, 163 U.S. 537, 550 (1896).

54. Wright, *Long Black Song*, 135–38, 153–56. For similar readings of this story, see Sollors, "Modernization as Adultery," 122–23; and Maxwell, *New Negro, Old Left*, 169–70.

55. Hurston, "Stories of Conflict," 913.

56. Higashida, "Aunt Sue's Children," 410–18.

57. R. King, *Southern Renaissance*, 192.

58. Hale, *Making Whiteness*, 244. Though Smith later argued that her title does not refer to the blues song, the association is likely to have occurred to most of her readers (Boris, "'Arm and Arm,'" 6). For the significance of Holiday's song in national leftists' understanding of southern racism, see F. Griffin, "*Who Set You Flowin'?*" 15–16.

59. L. Smith, *Strange Fruit*, 118.

60. Fabian, "Of Dogs Alive," 199; Fabian, *Time and the Other*, 30. For a description of intersubjective time, see Luckmann, "Constitution of Human Life in Time," 156, 157–65.

61. Ellison, review of *American Dilemma*, 311.

62. Ibid., 311–12.

286   Notes to pages 198–205

63. For an overview of debates about migrants' agency, see F. Griffin, *"Who Set You Flowin'?"* 16–24. For an account of literary critics' attention to a "southern folk aesthetic," see Dubey, "Postmodern Geographies," 358–68.

64. Dubey, "Postmodern Geographies," 359, 362, 365. See Kelley, *Hammer and Hoe*; Woodruff, *American Congo*.

65. Williamson, *Crucible of Race*, 482.

66. Yaeger, *Dirt and Desire*, 104, 101; Bollas, *Shadow of the Object*, 281.

67. Appadurai, *Modernity at Large*, 180–81.

68. Agee and Evans, *Let Us Now Praise Famous Men*, 10.

69. Agee, *Let Us Now Praise Famous Men*, 178, 367. See Fabian, *Time and the Other*, 13–21, for the spatialization of evolutionary time; for its role in representations of southern tenant farmers, see my third chapter.

70. Staub, "As Close as You Can Get," 159; Stott, *Documentary Expression*, 299–302; T. Reed, "Unimagined Existence," 157–60; Lowe, *Creative Process of James Agee*, 87–126; Hilgart, "Valuable Damage," 87.

71. Hegeman, *Patterns for America*, 178.

72. T. Reed, "Unimagined Existence," 160.

73. Hilgart, "Valuable Damage," 111; Agee, *Let Us Now Praise Famous Men*, 9.

74. Hegeman, *Patterns for America*, 185.

75. Agee, *Let Us Now Praise Famous Men*, 52; Stott, *Documentary Expression and Thirties America*, 304.

76. For the suggestion of intimacy, see Wagner-Martin, "*Let Us Now Praise Famous Men*," 53; Folks, "James Agee's Quest for Forgiveness," 46–49; Stott, *Documentary Expression and Thirties America*, 300–302. Stott also notes the invasiveness of Agee's projections (302–4).

77. Schultz, "Off-Stage Voices," 81, 78, 101.

78. Agee, *Let Us Now Praise Famous Men*, 70, 18–19, 113, 52. It may be relevant here that traumatic anxiety about the mother's exhausted breast is associated, in the object relations school of psychoanalytic theory, with schizoid projection and narcissism: projecting both valued and despised elements of the self onto others, the subject is left empty and desperate for love but unable to perceive the distinctness of those around him, who appear as bearers of his discarded parts. See Fairbairn, "Schizoid Factors," 45–49; Klein, "Notes on Some Schizoid Mechanisms," 143–49.

79. Agee, *Let Us Now Praise Famous Men*, 365; Rubin, "Southern Literature," 101–2; Folks, "James Agee's Quest for Forgiveness."

80. McCullers, *Heart Is a Lonely Hunter*, 17.

81. For an overview of the critical focus on isolation in assessments of McCullers's work, see Logan, introduction to *Critical Essays*, 1–11.

82. Rubin, "Carson McCullers," 145.

83. McCullers, *Heart Is a Lonely Hunter*, 143, 193. For the prevalence of such stereotypes, see Cox, "Modern Caste School," 221.

84. McCullers, *Heart Is a Lonely Hunter*, 301, 302, 303. I cannot say whether McCullers had heard of interest in a march on Washington, which was reportedly proposed by a woman at a meeting of multiple activist groups in Chicago in early 1940, mere months after this novel was released (Sitkoff, *Depression Decade*, 314). The question is of interest in relation to Copeland's political transformation, as the March of Washington Movement, led by A. Philip Randolph, "explicitly excluded whites" (Singh, *Black Is a Country*, 99).

85. R. Adams, *Sideshow U.S.A.*, 89–111.

86. Karem, "'I Could Never Really Leave,'" 700–708.

Chapter 7. The Nation's Region Redux

1. Beard and Beard, *Industrial Era*, 6, 758.

2. Hartz, *Liberal Tradition in America*, 8, 199. For the lingering influence of Hartz's interpretation of U.S. political culture, see R. Smith, "Beyond Tocqueville, Myrdal, and Hartz," 555, 557.

3. Dudziak, "*Brown* as a Cold War Case," paragraphs 1–2.

4. *Brown v. Board (II)*, 349 U.S. 294, 300, 301 (1955); Klinkner, *Unsteady March*, 245–46.

5. *Plessy v. Ferguson*, 163 U.S. 537, 550 (1896).

6. Dudziak, *Cold War Civil Rights*, 149–50; Bell, "*Brown v. Board of Education*," 23.

7. Whitfield, *Culture of the Cold War*, 21–24.

8. Payne, "'Whole United States Is Southern!'" paragraph 16.

9. Ibid., paragraphs 4–6.

10. Singh, *Black Is a Country*, 151–56, 163–69; Sullivan, *Days of Hope*, 230–47.

11. Singh, *Black Is a Country*, 167.

12. President's Committee on Civil Rights, *To Secure These Rights*, 148.

13. Dudziak, *Cold War Civil Rights*, 13.

14. Dudziak, "*Brown* as a Cold War Case," paragraph 18.

15. See Latham, *Modernization as Ideology*, 33–59.

16. Singh, *Black Is a Country*, 144–49.

17. Myrdal, *American Dilemma*, 1015, 998–1018.

18. Ibid., 1003.
19. Frederickson, *Dixiecrat Revolt*, 6–7.
20. Rubin and Kilpatrick, preface to *Lasting South*, ix.
21. Ibid., ix–x.
22. A. Reed, "2004 Election in Perspective"; Fiorina, *Culture War?*
23. Faulkner, *Requiem for a Nun*, 205.
24. Leege et al., *Politics of Cultural Differences*, 6.
25. Ibid.
26. Ibid., 5.
27. A. Reed, "2004 Election in Perspective," 7; Mendelberg, *Race Card*, 1–15; Lamis, "Two-Party South," 3–8. In 2005 Ken Mehlman, chair of the Republican National Committee, acknowledged and decried that some members formerly had tried to "benefit politically from racial polarization." See M. Allen, "RNC Chief."
28. Rahv, "Myth and the Powerhouse," 140. For the Depression-era literary-critical prioritization of realism, see Irr, *Suburb of Dissent*, 32–33, 41–42.
29. Chase, "Fate of the Avant-Garde," 212.
30. For the convergence of conservative New Critics and more leftist New York intellectuals in building Faulkner's reputation during this period, see Schwartz, *Creating Faulkner's Reputation*, 73–98.
31. Aldridge, "Manners and Values," 350; Phillips, contribution to "Our Country and Our Culture," 587.
32. Howe, *William Faulkner: A Critical Study*, xii, 20–24, 53–56, 202; R. Lewis, *American Adam*, 198–99; Chase, "Fate of the Avant-Garde," 219; Cowley, introduction to *Portable Faulkner*, 22–23.
33. For one complaint about how "our greatest writer" had succumbed, in this novel, to *niaiserie* (inanity)—a failure leading the critic to diagnose "some lack of interior wisdom" in both regional and national culture—see Barrett, contribution to "Our Country and Our Culture," 422.
34. "The Jail," prologue to *Requiem for a Nun*'s third dramatic act, was published in *Partisan Review* 18, no. 4 (1951).
35. W. Brown, "Neo-Liberalism," paragraph 7.
36. See Ladd, " 'Philosophers and Other Gynecologists.' "
37. Pitavy, "William Faulkner and the American Dream," 76–77, 85.
38. Polk, *Faulkner's* Requiem for a Nun, 12; Parsons, "Imagination and the Rending of Time," 444.
39. Howe, *William Faulkner: A Critical Study*, 165.
40. W. Brown, *Politics out of History*, 6.

41. A. Reed, "2004 Election in Perspective," 12–13.
42. Ibid., 7.
43. On pop culture representations of the South and the midcentury emergence of a "southern identity," correlating with contemporary uses of the concept of "cultural identity," see Hoberek, "Flannery O'Connor."
44. Payne, " 'Whole United States Is Southern!' " paragraphs 10–11; Klinkner, *Unsteady March*, 236.
45. Faulkner, *Requiem for a Nun*, 103, 163; Ellison, "Twentieth-Century Fiction," 42.
46. Zender, "*Requiem for a Nun*," 282–84. Child sacrifice is, of course, a prominent trope in the Judeo-Christian tradition but seems particularly misguided here: though Nancy sought, as Temple argues, "to hold [Bucky's] normal and natural home together," that home is also characterized, again by Temple, as one that "couldn't possibly hold together . . even in decency, let alone happiness" (163).
47. Faulkner, *Requiem for a Nun*, 101. See also Towner, *Faulkner on the Color Line*, 68.
48. Kornblut, "Red or Blue?" Kornblut notes that these spatial differences are not reliable guides to political choices but asserts that they vitally shape cultural habits; in less playful accounts, as Fiorina argues, this way of thinking about such differences subsumes topics for political debate into discussions of cultural polarization.
49. McPherson, "Re-imagining the Red States."
50. K. Warren, *So Black and Blue*, 67.
51. For a popular account of contemporary political rhetoric that demonstrates the prominence of such oppositions without analyzing them in quite these terms, see T. Frank, *What's the Matter with Kansas?*
52. Fabian, "Of Dogs Alive," 189.
53. Bellow, "Man Underground," 28.
54. Ellison, "World and the Jug," 122; Ellison, "Remembering Richard Wright," 198.
55. Ellison, "Twentieth-Century Fiction," 42.
56. Ellison, "Art of Fiction," 182.
57. Ellison, "If the Twain Shall Meet," 91.
58. Ellison, *Invisible Man*, 7, 6.
59. Arac, "Toward a Critical Genealogy," 212.
60. Hegeman, *Patterns for America*, 5–6, 158–69.

61. For a thorough assessment of how these figures are associated with distinct yet related temporal forms, see M. Singer, " 'Slightly Different Sense of Time.' "

62. Nadel, *Invisible Criticism*, 112–14.

63. Singh, *Black Is a Country*, 175–76.

64. Ellison, "Harlem Is Nowhere," 296, 297.

65. Richardson, *Black Masculinity*.

66. Cohn, *History and Memory*, 106. See also Schaub, "Ellison's Masks."

67. Baker, "To Move without Moving."

68. Ellison, "Harlem Is Nowhere," 299, emphasis added. Although somewhat beyond my purview here, each of these novels associates determinate attachments to linear progressive time more directly with men; hence, in Faulkner's novel, women struggle with that temporality. See Ladd, "Dismantling the Monolith."

69. K. Warren, *So Black and Blue*, 67.

70. Cheng, *Melancholy of Race*, 155, 157, 155. This reading, though I find it very persuasive, is not typical of Ellison criticism.

71. Allen, *Talking to Strangers*, 112.

72. I take this project to offer some explanation of why *Invisible Man*, as Houston Baker rightly notes, offers no vision of southern African American "effective public-sphere activism" (*Critical Memory*, 34). The narrator's identification with white elites' ideas of progress serves precisely to blind him to people who are articulating alternate political messages.

73. Zinn, *Southern Mystique*, 218.

74. Ellison, "If the Twain Shall Meet," 90.

75. Zinn, *Southern Mystique*, 4. See Ellison, "If the Twain Shall Meet," 92–93.

76. Ellison, "If the Twain Shall Meet," 101. As Waligora-Davis argues, although Ellison never self-identified as a black nationalist, and was in fact severely criticized by many who did, his commitment to the importance of African Americans' cultural and political expressions was absolute. See Waligora-Davis, "Riotous Discontent," 388–89.

77. Zinn, *Southern Mystique*, 11; Ellison, "If the Twain Shall Meet," 95.

78. K. Warren, *So Black and Blue*, 58–64, 67.

79. Ransom, "Reconstructed but Unregenerate," 5, 13–14.

80. A. Reed, "2004 Election in Perspective," 9–13.

81. W. Brown, *Politics out of History*, 3–17.

82. This was Cason's assessment of the Agrarians' manifesto in "Is the South Advancing?" 510.

Works Cited

Abrahams, Roger. "Phantoms of Romantic Nationalism in Folkloristics." *Journal of American Folklore* 106 (1993): 3–37.

Adams, James Truslow. "The Crisis and the Constitution: III. Changes in the American People—Do We Need a Dictator?" *Scribner's* 99, no. 2 (February 1936): 65–69.

———. "The Crisis and the Constitution: V. The American Future—Unseen Consequences of Proposed Changes." *Scribner's* 99, no. 4 (April 1936): 210–15.

———. "Our Changing Characteristics." *Forum* 84, no. 6 (December 1930): 321–28.

Adams, Rachel. *Sideshow U.S.A.* Chicago: University of Chicago Press, 2001.

Agar, Herbert, and Allen Tate, eds. *Who Owns America? A New Declaration of Independence.* Boston: Houghton Mifflin, 1936.

Agee, James, and Walker Evans. *Let Us Now Praise Famous Men*. 1941. Boston: Mariner/Houghton Mifflin, 2001.

Aldridge, John W. "Manners and Values." *Partisan Review* 19, no. 3 (1952): 347–50. (Response to William Barrett, "American Fiction and American Values." *Partisan Review* 18, no. 6 [1951]: 681–90.)

Allen, Danielle. *Talking to Strangers: Anxieties of Citizenship since* Brown v. Board of Education. Chicago: University of Chicago Press, 2004.

Allen, Mike. "RNC Chief to Say It Was 'Wrong' to Exploit Racial Conflict for Votes." *Washington Post*, 14 July 2005: A04, accessed through Lexis-Nexis (6 Oct. 2005).

Alpers, Benjamin L. *Dictators, Democracy, and American Public Culture: Envisioning the Totalitarian Enemy, 1920s–1950s*. Chapel Hill: University of North Carolina Press, 2003.

Anderson, Amanda. "Cosmopolitanism, Universalism, and the Divided Legacies of Modernity." In Cheah and Robbins, *Cosmopolitics*, 265–89.

Anderson, Benedict. *Imagined Communities: Reflections on the Origin and Spread of Nationalism*. Rev. ed. London: Verso, 1991.

Anderson, Sherwood. *Puzzled America*. New York: Charles Scribner's Sons, 1935.

Appadurai, Arjun. "Disjuncture and Difference in the Global Cultural Economy." In *The Phantom Public Sphere*, ed. Bruce Robbins, 269–95. Minneapolis: University of Minnesota Press, 1993.

———. *Modernity at Large: Cultural Dimensions of Globalization*. Minneapolis: University of Minnesota Press, 1996.

Appiah, Kwame Anthony. "Cosmopolitan Patriots." In Cheah and Robbins, *Cosmopolitics*, 91–114.

Arac, Jonathan. "Toward a Critical Genealogy of the U.S. Discourse of Identity: *Invisible Man* after Fifty Years." *boundary 2* 30, no. 2 (2003): 195–216.

Armitage, Susan H. "From the Inside Out: Rewriting Regional History." *Frontiers* 22, no. 3 (2001): 32–47.

Aronovici, Carol. "Let the Cities Perish." *Survey Graphic* 68, no. 13 (1 Oct. 1932): 437–40.

Ayers, Edward L. "What We Talk about When We Talk about the South." In Ayers et al., *All over the Map*, 62–82.

Ayers, Edward L., Patricia Nelson Limerick, Stephen Nissenbaum, and Peter S. Onuf. *All over the Map*. Baltimore: Johns Hopkins University Press, 1996.

Baker, Houston A., Jr. *Critical Memory: Public Spheres, African American Writ-*

ing, and Black Fathers and Sons in America. Athens: University of Georgia Press, 2001.

———. "To Move without Moving: An Analysis of Creative and Commerce in Ralph Ellison's Trueblood Episode." *PMLA* 98, no. 5 (1983): 828–45.

———. *Turning South Again: Re-Thinking Modernism/Re-Reading Booker T.* Durham, N.C.: Duke University Press, 2001.

———. "Workings of the Spirit: Conjure and the Space of Black Women's Creativity." In Gates and Appiah, *Critical Perspectives*, 280–308.

Baker, Houston A., Jr., and Dana D. Nelson. "Preface: Violence, the Body and 'The South.'" *American Literature* 73, no. 2 (2001): 231–44.

Bakhtin, M. M. "Forms of Time and of the Chronotope in the Novel." In *The Dialogic Imagination: Four Essays,* ed. Michael Holquist and trans. Caryl Emerson and Michael Holquist, 84–258. Austin: University of Texas Press, 1981.

———. *Rabelais and His World,* trans. Helene Iswolsky. 1965. Bloomington: Indiana University Press, 1984.

Balibar, Etienne. "Racism and Nationalism." In *Race, Nation, Class: Ambiguous Identities* by Etienne Balibar and Immanuel Wallerstein, 37–67. New York: Verso, 1991.

Barbeito, Patricia Felisa. "'Making Generations' in Jacobs, Larsen, and Hurston: A Genealogy of Black Women's Writing." *American Literature* 70 (1998): 365–95.

Barkan, Elazar. *The Retreat of Scientific Racism: Changing Concepts of Race in Britain and the United States between the World Wars.* Cambridge: Cambridge University Press, 1992.

Barnard, Rita. *The Great Depression and the Culture of Abundance: Kenneth Fearing, Nathanael West, and Mass Culture in the 1930s.* Cambridge: Cambridge University Press, 1995.

———. "Of Riots and Rainbows: South Africa, the US, and the Pitfalls of Comparison." *American Literary History* 17, no. 2 (2005): 399–416.

Barr, Tina. "'Queen of the Niggerati' and the Nile: The Isis-Osiris Myth in Zora Neale Hurston's *Their Eyes Were Watching God.*" *Journal of Modern Literature* 25, no. 3 (2002): 101–13.

Barrett, William. Contribution to "Our Country and Our Culture" symposium. *Partisan Review* 19, no. 4 (1952): 420–23.

Bartov, Omer. "Defining Enemies, Making Victims: Germans, Jews, and the Holocaust." *American Historical Review* 103, no. 3 (June 1998): 771–816.

Bassett, John, ed. *William Faulkner: The Critical Heritage*. London: Routledge & Kegan Paul, 1975.

Beach, Joseph Warren. *American Fiction: 1920–1940*. New York: Macmillan, 1941.

Beard, Charles A., and Mary R. Beard. *The Industrial Era*. Vol. 2 of *The Rise of American Civilization*. New York: Macmillan, 1927.

Becker, Jane S. *Selling Tradition: Appalachia and the Construction of an American Folk, 1930–1940*. Chapel Hill: University of North Carolina Press, 1998.

Bell, Derrick A., Jr. "*Brown v. Board of Education* and the Interest Convergence Dilemma." In *Critical Race Theory: The Key Writings That Formed the Movement*, ed. Kimberlé Crenshaw et al., 20–28. New York: New Press, 1995.

Bellow, Saul. "Man Underground." 1952. In *Ralph Ellison: A Collection of Critical Essays*, ed. John Hersey, 27–30. Englewood Cliffs, N.J.: Prentice-Hall, 1974.

Bender, John, and David E. Wellbery, eds. *Chronotypes: The Construction of Time*. Stanford, Calif.: Stanford University Press, 1991.

Benjamin, Walter. *Illuminations*, ed. Hannah Arendt and trans. Harry Zohn. New York: Schocken, 1968.

Benton, Thomas Hart. *An Artist in America*. 4th rev. ed. 1937. Columbia: University of Missouri Press, 1983.

Bergson, Henri. *Time and Free Will: An Essay on the Immediate Data of Consciousness*, trans. F. L. Pogson. 1910. New York: Harper Torchbooks/Academy Library, 1960.

Berlant, Lauren. *The Anatomy of National Fantasy: Hawthorne, Utopia, and Everyday Life*. Chicago: University of Chicago Press, 1991.

———. *The Queen of America Goes to Washington City: Essays on Sex and Citizenship*. Durham, N.C.: Duke University Press, 1997.

Bhabha, Homi. *The Location of Culture*. London: Routledge, 1994.

Bishop, David W. "*Plessy v. Ferguson*: A Reinterpretation." *Journal of Negro History* 62, no. 2 (1977): 125–33.

Bleikasten, André. *The Ink of Melancholy: Faulkner's Novels from* The Sound and the Fury *to* Light in August. Bloomington: Indiana University Press, 1990.

Blight, David W. *Race and Reunion: The Civil War in American Memory*. Cambridge, Mass.: Belknap/Harvard University Press, 2001.

Bloch, Ernst. "Nonsynchronism and the Obligation to Its Dialectics." 1932. *New German Critique* 11 (1977): 22–37.

Blotner, Joseph. *Faulkner: A Biography,* Vol. 1. 2 vols. New York: Random House, 1974.
Boles, John B. *The South through Time: A History of an American Region,* Vol. II. 2nd ed. 2 vols. Upper Saddle River, N.J.: Prentice Hall, 1999.
Bollas, Christopher. *The Shadow of the Object: Psychoanalysis of the Unthought Known.* New York: Columbia University Press, 1987.
Bone, Robert. "Richard Wright and the Chicago Renaissance." *Callaloo* 28 (1986): 446–68.
Bontemps, Arna. "Saturday Night: Portrait of a Small Southern Town, 1933." *The Old South: "A Summer Tragedy" and Other Stories of the Thirties.* New York: Dodd, Mead, 1973.
Boris, Eileen. " 'Arm and Arm': Racialized Bodies and Colored Lines." *Journal of American Studies* 35, no. 1 (2001): 1–20.
Botkin, B. A. "Folk and Folklore." In Couch, *Culture in the South,* 570–93.
———. "Regionalism: Cult or Culture?" *English Journal* 25, no. 3 (1936): 181–85.
Bourdieu, Pierre. *Outline of a Theory of Practice,* trans. Richard Nice. New York: Cambridge University Press, 1977.
Boyd, Valerie. *Wrapped in Rainbows: The Life of Zora Neale Hurston.* New York: Scribner, 2003.
Bradford, Roark. *John Henry.* New York: Literary Guild, 1931.
Bramen, Carrie Tirado. *The Uses of Variety: Modern Americanism and the Quest for National Distinctiveness.* Cambridge, Mass.: Harvard University Press, 2000.
Brearley, H. C. "The Pattern of Violence." In Couch, *Culture in the South,* 678–92.
Brennan, Timothy. "The National Longing for Form." In *Nation and Narration,* ed. Homi K. Bhabha, 44–70. New York: Routledge, 1990.
Breuer, Josef, and Sigmund Freud. *Studies on Hysteria.* Vol. 2 of *The Standard Edition of the Complete Psychological Works of Sigmund Freud,* ed. and trans. James Strachey. 24 vols. 1893. London: Hogarth, 1955.
Brewer, William M. "Poor Whites and Negroes in the South since the Civil War." *Journal of Negro History* 15, no. 1 (1930): 26–37.
Brinkmeyer, Robert H., Jr. "Faulkner and the Democratic Crisis." In *Faulkner and Ideology: Faulkner and Yoknapatawpha, 1992,* ed. Donald M. Kartiganer and Ann J. Abadie, 70–93. Jackson: University Press of Mississippi, 1995.
———. "The Fourth Ghost: European Totalitarianism and the White Southern

Imagination, 1930–1950." Research supported by John Simon Guggenheim Memorial Foundation, 2004–5.

———. "Is That You in the Mirror, Jeeter? The Reader and *Tobacco Road*." In MacDonald, *Critical Essays*, 370–74. Essay first published in 1979.

Brodhead, Richard H. *Cultures of Letters: Scenes of Reading and Writing in Nineteenth-Century America*. Chicago: University of Chicago Press, 1993.

Brooks, Cleanth. *William Faulkner: The Yoknapatawpha Country*. New Haven, Conn.: Yale University Press, 1963.

Brooks, Peter. *Reading for the Plot: Design and Intention in Narrative*. New York: Alfred A. Knopf, 1989.

Brown, Bill. *The Material Unconscious: American Amusement, Stephen Crane, and the Economies of Play*. Cambridge, Mass.: Harvard University Press, 1996.

———. "Regional Artifacts (The Life of Things in the Work of Sarah Orne Jewett)." *American Literary History* 14, no. 2 (2002): 195–226.

Brown, E. Francis. "The American Road to Fascism." *Current History* 38 (July 1933): 392–98.

Brown, Sterling A. "More Odds." *Opportunity* 10 (1932): 188–89.

———. "Negro Character as Seen by White Authors." *Journal of Negro Education* 2, no. 2 (1933): 179–203.

———. *The Negro in American Fiction*. 1937. Port Washington, N.Y.: Kennikat, 1968.

———. "Unhistoric History." *Callaloo* 21, no. 4 (1998): 749–66. First published in 1930.

Brown, Wendy. "Neo-Liberalism and the End of Liberal Democracy." *Theory & Event* 7, no. 1 (2003), http//:muse.jhu.edu/journals/theory_and_event/ (14 Oct. 2005).

———. *Politics out of History*. Princeton, N.J.: Princeton University Press, 2001.

Brown v. Board of Education (II), 349 U.S. 294 (1955).

Bunche, Ralph J. "A Critique of New Deal Social Planning as It Affects Negroes." *Journal of Negro Education* 5, no. 1 (January 1936): 59–65.

Burke, Kenneth. "Caldwell: Maker of Grotesques." *The Philosophy of Literary Form: Studies in Symbolic Action*. 3rd ed., 350–60. Berkeley: University of California Press, 1973. Essay first published in 1935.

Burns, Robert E. *I Am a Fugitive from a Georgia Chain-Gang!* 1932. Savannah, Ga.: Beehive Press, 1994.

Burt, Struthers. "Democracy and the Broken South." *North American Review* 272, no. 4 (April 1929): 475–81.

"Bush and McCain Tiptoe around Battle Flag Issue." *Charleston Post and Courier*, 13 Jan. 2000: 6B, accessed through Lexis-Nexis (20 Jan. 2004).

Butler, Judith. "Subjection, Resistance, Resignification: Between Freud and Foucault." In *The Identity in Question*, ed. John Rajchman, 229–49. New York: Routledge, 1995.

Byrd, William, and Edmund A. Ruffin. *The Westover Manuscripts: The History of the Dividing Line betwixt Virginia and North Carolina*. 1841. Documenting the American South, http://docsouth.unc.edu (22 May 2004).

Caldwell, Erskine. "A Note about 'Tobacco Road,'" foreword for Kirkland, *Tobacco Road*.

———. *God's Little Acre*. 1933. Athens: Brown Thrasher/University of Georgia Press, 1995.

———. Letter to the editor. *New Republic* 79 (27 June 1934): 185.

———. *Tobacco Road*. 1932. New York: Signet/New American Library, 1982.

———. "Tobacco Roads in the South." *New Leader* 19 (1936). In MacDonald, *Critical Essays*, 50–53.

Caldwell, Erskine, and Margaret Bourke-White. *You Have Seen Their Faces*. New York: Duell, Sloan and Pierce, 1937.

Caldwell, Ira S. "The Bunglers: A Narrative Study in Five Parts." *Eugenics* 3 (1930): 209–10, 247–51, 293–99, 332–36, 377–83.

Calinescu, Matei. *Five Faces of Modernity: Modernism, Avant-Garde, Decadence, Kitsch, Postmodernism*. Durham, N.C.: Duke University Press, 1987.

Calverton, V. F. "The American Revolutionary Tradition." *Scribner's* 95, no. 5 (May 1934): 352–57.

———. "The Bankruptcy of Southern Culture." *Scribner's* 99, no. 5 (May 1936): 294–98.

Canby, Henry Seidel. "The Grain of Life." *Saturday Review of Literature* 9 (October 1932): 153.

Carby, Hazel. "Policing the Black Woman's Body in an Urban Context." *Critical Inquiry* 18, no. 4 (1992): 738–55.

———. "The Politics of Fiction, Anthropology, and the Folk: Zora Neale Hurston." *Cultures in Babylon: Black Britain and African America*, 168–85. London: Verso, 1999.

Cargill, Oscar. *Intellectual America*. New York: Macmillan, 1941.

Carpenter, C. T. "King Cotton's Slaves: The Fate of the Share-Cropper Becomes a National Issue." *Scribner's* 98, no. 4 (October 1935): 193–99.

Carr, Brain, and Tova Cooper. "Zora Neale Hurston and Modernism at the Critical Limit." *Modern Fiction Studies* 48, no. 2 (2002): 285–313.
Carson, Clayborne. "Two Cheers for *Brown v. Board of Education*." *Journal of American History* 91, no. 1 (2004), www.historycooperative.org (3 June 2004).
Carver, Thomas Nixon. "The Economic Test of Fitness." *Eugenics: A Journal of Race Betterment* 2, no. 7 (July 1929): 6–9.
Cash, Wilbur J. *The Mind of the South*. New York: Alfred A. Knopf, 1941.
Cason, Clarence. "Is the South Advancing?" *Yale Review* 20, no. 3 (March 1931): 502–14.
———. *90° in the Shade*. 1935. Tuscaloosa: University of Alabama Press, 1983.
Castoriadis, Cornelius. *The Imaginary Institution of Society*, trans. Kathleen Blamey. Cambridge, Mass.: MIT Press, 1987.
———. "Time and Creation." In Bender and Wellbery, *Chronotypes*, 38–64.
Cell, John W. *The Highest Stage of White Supremacy: The Origins of Segregation in South Africa and the American South*. Cambridge: Cambridge University Press, 1982.
Censer, Jane Turner. *The Reconstruction of White Southern Womanhood, 1865–1895*. Baton Rouge: Louisiana State University Press, 2003.
Chase, Richard. "The Fate of the Avant-Garde." In Phillips and Rahv, *Partisan Review Anthology*, 210–20. Essay first published in 1957.
Cheah, Pheng, and Bruce Robbins, eds. *Cosmopolitics: Thinking and Feeling beyond the Nation*. Minneapolis: University of Minnesota Press, 1998.
Cheng, Anne Anlin. *The Melancholy of Race*. New York: Oxford University Press, 2000.
Clark, Thomas D. Introduction to Dixon, *Clansman*, v–xviii.
Clifford, James. *The Predicament of Culture: Twentieth-Century Ethnography, Literature, and Art*. Cambridge, Mass.: Harvard University Press, 1988.
Cohen, Norman. "The Skillet Lickers: The Study of a Hillbilly String Band and Its Repertoire." *Journal of American Folklore* 78, no. 309 (1965): 229–44.
Cohn, Deborah N. "Faulkner and Spanish America: Then and Now." In Hamblin and Abadie, *Faulkner in the Twenty-First Century*, 50–67.
———. *History and Memory in the Two Souths: Recent Southern and Spanish American Fiction*. Nashville, Tenn.: Vanderbilt University Press, 1999.
Cole, Sarah. "Conradian Alienation and Imperial Intimacy." *Modern Fiction Studies* 44 (1998): 251–81.
Conforti, Joseph A. *Imagining New England: Explorations of Regional Identity*

from the Pilgrims to the Mid-Twentieth Century. Chapel Hill: University of North Carolina Press, 2001.

Conrad, Joseph. *Heart of Darkness*. 1899. New York: Penguin, 1995.

Conroy, Jack. "Passion and Pellagra." *New Masses* (1932). In MacDonald, *Critical Essays*, 17–18.

Cook, Sylvia Jenkins. *Erskine Caldwell and the Fiction of Poverty: The Flesh and the Spirit*. Baton Rouge: Louisiana State University Press, 1991.

Cooper, Anna Julia. *A Voice from the South*. 1892. New York: Oxford University Press, 1990.

Couch, W. T. "An Agrarian Programme for the South." *American Review* 3, no. 3 (June 1934): 313–26.

Couch, W. T., ed. *Culture in the South*. Chapel Hill: University of North Carolina Press, 1934.

Cowley, Malcolm. "Poe in Mississippi." *New Republic* (November 1936). In Bassett, *Critical Heritage*, 205–7.

Cowley, Malcolm, ed. *The Portable Faulkner*. 1946. New York: Viking, 1954.

Cox, Oliver C. "The Modern Caste School of Race Relations." *Social Forces* 21, no. 2 (1942): 218–26.

Crabités, Pierre. "A White South, or Black?" *North American Review* 272, no. 3 (March 1929): 277–81.

Cripps, Thomas R. "The Myth of the Southern Box Office: A Factor in Racial Stereotyping in American Movies, 1920–1940." In *The Black Experience in America: Selected Essays*, ed. James C. Curtis and Lewis L. Gould, 116–44. Austin: University of Texas Press, 1970.

———. "Winds of Change: *Gone with the Wind* and Racism as a National Issue." In Pyron, *Recasting*, 137–52.

Cullen, Jim. *The American Dream: A Short History of an Idea That Shaped a Nation*. New York: Oxford University Press, 2003.

Dabney, Thomas L. "Southern Negroes and Politics." *Opportunity* 8 (1934): 272–73.

Dabney, Virginius. "Dixie Rejects Lynching." *Nation* 145, no. 22 (27 Nov. 1937): 580.

Dahlberg, Edward. "Raw Leaf." *New Republic* (1932). In MacDonald, *Critical Essays*, 16–17.

Dainotto, Roberto Maria. *Place in Literature: Regions, Cultures, Communities*. Ithaca, N.Y.: Cornell University Press, 2000.

Dalgarno, Emily. " 'Words Walking without Masters': Ethnography and the Cre-

ative Process in *Their Eyes Were Watching God.*" *American Literature* 64 (1992): 521-41.
Davidson, Donald. "A Sociologist in Eden." *American Review* 8, no. 2 (December 1936): 177-204.
Davis, David Brion. "Free at Last: The Enduring Legacy of the South's Civil War Victory." *New York Times,* 26 Aug. 2001, late edition, sec. 4, p. 1, col. 5, accessed through Lexis-Nexis (23 March 2004).
Davis, Thadious. "Expanding the Limits: The Intersection of Race and Region." *Southern Literary Journal* 20, no. 2 (1988): 3-11.
———. *Games of Property: Law, Race, Gender, and Faulkner's* Go Down, Moses. Durham, N.C.: Duke University Press, 2003.
Dawahare, Anthony. *Nationalism, Marxism, and African American Literature between the Wars: A New Pandora's Box.* Jackson: University Press of Mississippi, 2003.
Dawson, Jan C. "The Puritan and the Cavalier: The South's Perception of Contrasting Traditions." *Journal of Southern History* 44, no. 4 (1978): 597-614.
DeCosta-Willis, Miriam. "Avenging Angels and Mute Mothers: Black Southern Women in Wright's Fictional World." *Callaloo* 28 (1986): 540-51.
DeLamotte, Eugenia C. *Perils of the Night: A Feminist Study of Nineteenth-Century Gothic.* New York: Oxford University Press, 1990.
Den Hollander, A. N. J. "The Tradition of 'Poor Whites.' " In Couch, *Culture in the South,* 403-31.
Denning, Michael. *The Cultural Front: The Laboring of American Culture in the Twentieth Century.* New York: Verso, 1997.
Derrida, Jacques. *Of Grammatology,* trans. Gayatri Chakravorty Spivak. Baltimore: Johns Hopkins University Press, 1976.
de Voto, Bernard. "Witchcraft in Mississippi." In *William Faulkner: The Contemporary Reviews,* ed. M. Thomas Inge, 144-49. New York: Cambridge University Press, 1995. Essay first published in 1936.
Dewey, John. "Americanism and Localism." *Dial* 68, no. 6 (June 1920): 684-88.
Dixon, Thomas. *The Clansman: An Historical Romance of the Ku Klux Klan.* 1905. Lexington: University of Kentucky Press, 1970.
Dollard, John. *Caste and Class in a Southern Town.* 3rd ed. 1937. New York: Doubleday/Anchor, 1957.
Donaldson, Susan V. "Making a Spectacle: Welty, Faulkner, and Southern Gothic." *Mississippi Quarterly* 50, no. 4 (1997): 567-83.
Dorman, Robert L. *The Revolt of the Provinces: The Regionalist Movement in America, 1920-1945.* Chapel Hill: University of North Carolina Press, 1993.

Doyle, Bertram Wilbur. *The Etiquette of Race Relations in the South: A Study in Social Control.* Chicago: University of Chicago Press, 1937.
Dubey, Madhu. "Narration and Migration: Jazz and Vernacular Theories of Black Women's Fiction." *American Literary History* 10 (1998): 291–316.
———. "Postmodern Geographies of the U.S. South." *Nepantla: Views from South* 3, no. 2 (Summer 2002): 351–71.
Du Bois, W. E. B. *Black Reconstruction: An Essay toward a History of the Part Which Black Folk Played in the Attempt to Reconstruct Democracy in America, 1860–1880.* New York: Harcourt, Brace, 1935.
———. *Darkwater: Voices from within the Veil.* 1920. In *The Oxford W. E. B. Du Bois Reader*, ed. Eric J. Sundquist, 483–623. New York: Oxford University Press, 1996.
———. "The Negro Mind Reaches Out." In Locke, *New Negro*, 385–414.
———. "Scottsboro." *Crisis* 41 (January 1934): 21.
———. "Segregation." *Crisis* 41 (January 1934): 20.
———. *The Souls of Black Folk.* 1903. New York: Bantam, 1989.
DuCille, Ann. "The Shirley Temple of My Familiar." *Transition* 73 (1997): 10–32.
Duck, Leigh Anne. " 'Rebirth of a Nation': Hurston in Haiti." *Journal of American Folklore* 117, no. 464 (2004): 127–46.
Dudziak, Mary L. "*Brown* as a Cold War Case." *Journal of American History* 91, no. 1 (June 2004), www.historycooperative.org (3 June 2004).
———. *Cold War Civil Rights: Race and the Image of American Democracy.* Princeton, N.J.: Princeton University Press, 2000.
Dwyer, Richard. "The Case of the Cool Reception." In Pyron, *Recasting*, 21–31.
Ekirch, Arthur A., Jr. *Ideologies and Utopias: The Impact of the New Deal on American Thought.* Chicago: Quadrangle, 1969.
Eliot, T. S. "Tradition and the Individual Talent." 1920. *Selected Essays*, 3–11. New York: Harcourt, Brace, 1950.
———. *The Waste Land.* 1922. New York: Faber & Faber, 1961.
Ellison, Ralph. "The Art of Fiction: An Interview." 1955. In *Shadow and Act*, 167–83.
———. "An Extravagance of Laughter." In *Going to the Territory*, 145–97.
———. *Going to the Territory.* 1986. New York: Vintage, 1995.
———. "Harlem Is Nowhere." 1948. In *Shadow and Act*, 294–302.
———. "If the Twain Shall Meet." 1964. In *Going to the Territory*, 88–103.
———. *Invisible Man.* 1952. New York: Vintage, 1980.

———. "Remembering Richard Wright." 1971. In *Going to the Territory*, 198–216.

———. Review of *An American Dilemma*. In *Shadow and Act*, 303–17.

———. *Shadow and Act*. 1953. New York: Vintage, 1972.

———. "Twentieth-Century Fiction and the Black Mask of Humanity." 1953. In *Shadow and Act*, 24–44.

———. "The World and the Jug." 1964. In *Shadow and Act*, 107–43.

Ely, James W., Jr. "The South, the Supreme Court, and Race Relations, 1890–1965." In *The South as an American Problem*, ed. Larry J. Griffin and Don H. Doyle, 126–44. Athens: University of Georgia Press, 1995.

Ermath, Elizabeth Deeds. "The Crisis of Realism in Postmodern Time." In *Realism and Representation: Essays on the Problem of Realism in Relation to Science, Literature, and Culture*, ed. George Levine, 214–24. Madison: University of Wisconsin Press, 1993.

Estabrook, Arthur H. "Country Slum." *Eugenics: A Journal of Race Betterment* 2, no. 7 (July 1929): 10–14.

Evans, Brad. "The Object-Life of Books: Regional Fiction's Access to the Ethnographic and the Fashionable." *Before Cultures: The Ethnographic Imagination in American Literature, 1865–1920*. Chicago: University of Chicago Press, 2005.

Everett, Anna. *Returning the Gaze: A Genealogy of Black Film Criticism, 1909–1949*. Durham, N.C.: Duke University Press, 2001.

Fabian, Johannes. "Of Dogs Alive, Birds Dead, and Time to Tell a Story." In Bender and Wellbery, *Chronotypes*, 185–204.

———. *Time and the Other: How Anthropology Makes Its Object*. New York: Columbia University Press, 1983.

Fairbairn, W. R. D. "Schizoid Factors in the Personality." First published in 1952, abridged in Scharff, *Object Relations Theory and Practice*, 43–49.

Fairclough, Adam. "The Costs of *Brown*: Black Teachers and School Integration." *Journal of American History* 91, no. 1 (2004), www.historycooperative.org (3 June 2004).

Faulkner, William. *Absalom, Absalom!* 1936. New York: Vintage, 1990.

———. *Flags in the Dust*. 1973. New York: Vintage/Random House, 1974.

———. *Go Down, Moses*. 1942. New York: Vintage, 1973.

———. *Light in August*. 1932. New York: Vintage, 1990.

———. *Requiem for a Nun*. 1951. New York: Vintage, 1975.

———. *The Sound and the Fury*. 1929. New York: Vintage, 1990.

Favor, J. Martin. *Authentic Blackness: The Folk in the New Negro Renaissance.* Durham, N.C.: Duke University Press, 1999.

Fearnow, Mark. *The American Stage and the Great Depression: A Cultural History of the Grotesque.* Cambridge: Cambridge University Press, 1997.

Feldstein, Ruth. *Motherhood in Black and White: Race and Sex in American Liberalism, 1930–1965.* Ithaca, N.Y.: Cornell University Press, 2000.

Fetterley, Judith. " 'Not in the Least American': Nineteenth-Century Literary Regionalism as un-American Literature." In *Rethinking American Literature,* ed. Lil Brannon and Brenda M. Greene, 33–49. Urbana: National Council of Teachers of English, 1997.

Fiedler, Leslie. *Love and Death in the American Novel.* Rev. ed. 1960. New York: Stein and Day, 1966.

Field, Louise Maunsell. "American Novelists vs. the Nation." *North American Review* 235 (June 1933): 556.

Fiorina, Morris P., with Samuel J. Abrams and Jeremy C. Pope. *Culture War? The Myth of a Polarized America.* New York: Pearson-Longman, 2005.

Fish, Stanley. *Is There a Text in This Class? The Authority of Interpretive Communities.* Cambridge, Mass.: Harvard University Press, 1980.

Fisher, Philip. *Still the New World: American Literature in a Culture of Creative Destruction.* Cambridge, Mass.: Harvard University Press, 1999.

Fletcher, Tom. Letter to the editor. *Scribner's* 98, no. 6 (December 1935): 384.

Foley, Barbara. *Radical Representations: Politics and Form in U.S. Proletarian Fiction, 1929–1941.* Durham, N.C.: Duke University Press, 1993.

Folks, Jeffrey J. "James Agee's Quest for Forgiveness in Let Us Now Praise Famous Men." *Southern Quarterly* 34, no. 4 (1996): 43–52.

Foucault, Michel. *Discipline and Punish: The Birth of the Prison,* trans. Alan Sheridan. 1977. New York: Vintage/Random House, 1995.

———. *An Introduction.* Vol. 1 of *The History of Sexuality,* trans. Robert Hurley. 3 vols. 1978. New York: Vintage/Random House, 1990.

Frank, Joseph. *The Idea of Spatial Form.* New Brunswick, N.J.: Rutgers University Press, 1991.

Frank, Thomas. *What's the Matter with Kansas? How Conservatives Won the Heart of America.* New York: Metropolitan Books, 2004.

Frank, Waldo. *Our America.* New York: Boni and Liveright, 1919.

Franklin, Wayne, and Michael Steiner. "Taking Place: Toward the Regrounding of American Studies." In *Mapping American Culture,* ed. Wayne Franklin and Michael Steiner, 3–23. Iowa City: University of Iowa Press, 1992.

Frazier, E. Franklin. "Durham: Capital of the Black Middle Class." In Locke, *New Negro*, 333–40.

Frederickson, Kari. *The Dixiecrat Revolt and the End of the Solid South*. Chapel Hill: University of North Carolina Press, 2001.

Freud, Sigmund. *Civilization and Its Discontents*, trans. James Strachey. 1930. New York: W. W. Norton, 1962.

———. *The Ego and the Id*. 1923. In Gay, *Freud Reader*, 628–58.

———. *Group Psychology and the Analysis of the Ego*, trans. James Strachey. 1921. New York: Boni and Liveright, 1922.

———. "Mourning and Melancholia." In Gay, *Freud Reader*, 584–89. Essay first published in 1917.

———. "On Narcissism: An Introduction." In Gay, *Freud Reader*, 628–58. Essay first published in 1914.

———. "Recollecting, Repeating, and Working Through (Further Recommendations on the Technique of Psycho-Analysis II)." In vol. 12 of *The Standard Edition of the Complete Psychological Works of Sigmund Freud*, trans. and ed. by James Strachey, 145–56. London: Hogarth, 1957. Essay first published in 1914.

———. "The Uncanny." In *Writings on Art and Literature*, trans. James Strachey, 193–233. Stanford, Calif.: Stanford University Press, 1997. Essay first published in 1925.

Gaines, Jane M. "Birthing Nations." In *Cinema and Nation*, ed. Mette Hjort and Scott MacKenzie, 298–316. New York: Routledge, 2000.

Gaines, Kevin. *Uplifting the Race: Black Leadership, Politics, and Culture in the Twentieth Century*. Chapel Hill: University of North Carolina Press, 1996.

Garland, Hamlin. *Crumbling Idols*. 1894. Cambridge, Mass.: Harvard University Press, 1960.

Gates, Henry Louis, Jr. "Zora Neale Hurston and the Speakerly Text." In Wall, *Zora Neale Hurston's* Their Eyes Were Watching God, 59–116. Essay first published in 1988.

Gates, Henry Louis, Jr., and K. A. Appiah, eds. *Zora Neale Hurston: Critical Perspectives Past and Present*. New York: Penguin-Amistad, 1993.

Gay, Peter, ed. *The Freud Reader*. New York: W. W. Norton, 1989.

Geismar, Maxwell. *Writers in Crisis: The American Novel between Two Wars*. Boston: Houghton Mifflin, 1942.

Gellman, David N., and David Quigley, eds. *Jim Crow New York: A Documen-*

tary History of Race and Citizenship, 1777–1877. New York: New York University Press, 2003.
Genette, Gérard. *Narrative Discourse: An Essay in Method,* trans. Jane E. Lewin. Ithaca, N.Y.: Cornell University Press, 1980.
Gerstle, Gary. *American Crucible: Race and Nation in the Twentieth Century.* Princeton, N.J.: Princeton University Press, 2001.
———. "The Protean Character of American Liberalism." *American Historical Review* 99, no. 4 (October 1994): 1043–73.
Gilroy, Paul. *The Black Atlantic: Modernity and Double Consciousness.* Cambridge, Mass.: Harvard University Press, 1993.
Glasgow, Ellen. "Heroes and Monsters." *Saturday Review of Literature* 12 (4 May 1935): 34–35.
Glover, David. "The 'Spectrality Effect' in Early Modernism." In Smith and Wallace, *Gothic Modernisms,* 29–43.
Godden, Richard. *Fictions of Labor: William Faulkner and the South's Long Revolution.* Cambridge: Cambridge University Press, 1997.
Goldberg, David Theo. *The Racial State.* Malden, Mass.: Blackwell, 2002.
Goldstein, Malcolm. *The Political Stage: American Drama and Theater of the Great Depression.* New York: Oxford University Press, 1974.
Grady, Henry. "The New South." Speech before the New England Society of New York, 22 Dec. 1886. In *The South in Perspective: An Anthology of Southern Literature,* ed. Edward Francisco, Robert Vaughan, and Linda Francisco, 528–34. Upper Saddle River, N.J.: Prentice Hall, 2001.
Graham, Allison. *Framing the South: Hollywood, Television, and Race during the Civil Rights Struggle.* Baltimore: Johns Hopkins University Press, 2003.
Grant, Susan-Mary. *North over South: Northern Nationalism and American Identity in the Antebellum Era.* Lawrence: University Press of Kansas, 2000.
Gray, James. Review of *Tobacco Road. St. Paul Dispatch* (1932). In MacDonald, *Critical Essays,* 13–15.
Gray, Richard. *The Literature of Memory: Modern Writers of the American South.* Baltimore: Johns Hopkins University Press, 1977.
———. *Southern Aberrations: Writers of the American South and the Problems of Regionalism.* Baton Rouge: Louisiana State University Press, 2000.
Greenfield, Liah. *Nationalism: Five Roads to Modernity.* Cambridge, Mass.: Harvard University Press, 1992.
Greeson, Jennifer Rae. "The Figure of the South and the Nationalizing Imper-

atives of Early United States Literature." *Yale Journal of Criticism* 12, no. 2 (1999): 209–48.

———. *Our South: Domestic Geography and Global Imagination from Independence to "Birth of a Nation."* Cambridge, Mass.: Harvard University Press, forthcoming.

Griffin, Farah Jasmine. *"Who Set You Flowin'?" The African-American Migration Narrative.* New York: Oxford University Press, 1995.

Griffin, Larry J. "Why Was the South a Problem to America?" In *The South as an American Problem,* ed. Larry J. Griffin and Don H. Doyle, 10–32. Athens: University of Georgia Press, 1995.

Grossman, James R. *Land of Hope: Chicago, Black Southerners, and the Great Migration.* Chicago: University of Chicago Press, 1989.

Grubbs, Donald. *Cry from the Cotton: The Southern Tenant Farmers' Union and the New Deal.* Chapel Hill: University of North Carolina Press, 1971.

Gruber, Ida. "All around the Town." *Golden Book* 20 (1934): 247.

Guérard, Albert. "Southern Memories: Sidelights on the Race Problem." *Scribner's* 77, no. 5 (May 1925): 492–98.

Hahn, Steven. *A Nation under Our Feet: Black Political Struggles in the Rural South from Slavery to the Great Migration.* Cambridge, Mass.: Belknap-Harvard University Press, 2003.

Hale, Grace Elizabeth. *Making Whiteness: The Culture of Segregation in the South, 1890–1940.* 1998. New York: Vintage, 1999.

Hall, Jacquelyn Dowd, et al. *Like a Family: The Making of a Southern Cotton Mill World.* Chapel Hill: University of North Carolina Press, 1987.

Hamblin, Robert W., and Ann J. Abadie, eds. *Faulkner in the Twenty-First Century: Faulkner and Yoknapatawpha, 2000.* Jackson: University Press of Mississippi, 2003.

Handley, George B. *Postslavery Literatures in the Americas: Family Portraits in Black and White.* Charlottesville: University Press of Virginia, 2000.

Harpham, Geoffrey Galt. "Doing the Impossible: Slavoj Žižek and the End of Knowledge." *Critical Inquiry* 29, no. 3 (Spring 2003): 453–85.

Harris, Joel Chandler. "William Henry at School." *Uncle Remus and His Friends: Old Plantation Stories, Songs, and Ballads with Sketches of Negro Character,* 330–38. Cambridge, Mass.: Riverside, 1892.

Hartz, Louis. *The Liberal Tradition in America.* New York: Harcourt, Brace, 1955.

Hathaway, Rosemary V. "The Unbearable Weight of Authenticity: Zora Neale

Hurston's *Their Eyes Were Watching God* and a Theory of 'Touristic Reading.' " *Journal of American Folklore* 117, no. 464 (2004): 168–90.

Hayworth, Donald. "A New Day in Oskaloosa." *Scribner's* 98, no. 4 (October 1935): 242–46.

Hechter, Michael, and Margaret Levi. "Ethno-Regional Movements in the West." In *Nationalism,* ed. John Hutchinson and Anthony D. Smith, 184–95. New York: Oxford University Press, 1994. Essay first published in 1979.

Hegeman, Susan. *Patterns for America: Modernism and the Concept of Culture.* Princeton, N.J.: Princeton University Press, 1999.

Hemenway, Robert. *Zora Neale Hurston: A Literary Biography.* Urbana: University of Illinois Press, 1977.

Hewitt, Andrew. *Fascist Modernism: Aesthetics, Politics, and the Avant-Garde.* Stanford, Calif.: Stanford University Press, 1993.

Hicks, Granville. *The Great Tradition.* New York: Macmillan, 1935.

Higashida, Cheryl. "Aunt Sue's Children: Re-viewing the Gender(ed) Politics of Richard Wright's Radicalism." *American Literature* 75, no. 2 (2003): 395–425.

Hilgart, John. "Valuable Damage: James Agee's Aesthetics of Use." *Arizona Quarterly* 52, no. 4 (1996): 85–114.

Hirsch, Jerrold. *Portrait of America: A Cultural History of the Federal Writers' Project.* Chapel Hill: University of North Carolina Press, 2003.

Hoberek, Andrew. "Flannery O'Connor and the Southern Origins of Identity Politics." *The Twilight of the Middle Class: Post–World War II American Fiction and White-Collar Work,* 95–112. Princeton, N.J.: Princeton University Press, 2005.

Hobsbawm, Eric. Introduction to *The Invention of Tradition,* ed. Eric Hobsbawm and Terence Ranger, 1–14. 1983. Cambridge: Cambridge University Press/Canto, 1992.

———. *Nations and Nationalism since 1780: Programme, Myth, Reality.* Cambridge: Cambridge University Press, 1990.

Hollinger, David A. "Authority, Solidarity, and the Political Economy of Identity: The Case of the United States." *Diacritics* 29, no. 4 (1999): 116–27.

———. *Postethnic America: Beyond Multiculturalism.* Rev. ed. New York: Basic Books, 2000.

Holt, Thomas C. *The Problem of Race in the Twenty-First Century.* Cambridge, Mass.: Harvard University Press, 2000.

Howard, June. *Form and History in American Literary Naturalism.* Chapel Hill: University of North Carolina Press, 1985.

———. "Unraveling Regions, Unsettling Periods: Sarah Orne Jewett and American Literary History." *American Literature* 68, no. 2 (1996): 365–84.

Howe, Irving. *William Faulkner: A Critical Study*. New York: Random House, 1951.

Howells, William Dean. *Criticism and Fiction*. New York: Harper, 1891.

Hughes, Langston. *The Big Sea*. 1940. New York: Hill and Wang, 1993.

———. "The Negro Artist and the Racial Mountain." In A. Mitchell, *Within the Circle*, 55–59. Essay first published in 1926.

Hunt, Frazier. "America Must Dream Again! Only in That Way Can She Get Back What She Has Lost." *Good Housekeeping* 96, no. 2 (February 1933): 16–17, 205–7.

Hurston, Zora Neale. "Characteristics of Negro Expression." In Wall, *Zora Neale Hurston*, 830–46. Essay first published in 1934.

———. "Court Order Can't Make Races Mix." In Wall, *Zora Neale Hurston*, 956–58. Essay first published in 1955.

———. "Crazy for This Democracy." 1945. In Wall, *Zora Neale Hurston*, 945–49. Essay first published in 1945.

———. *Dust Tracks on a Road*. 1942. New York: HarperPerennial, 1991.

———. "Hoodoo in America." *Journal of American Folklore* 44 (1931): 317–417.

———. *Mules and Men*. 1935. New York: HarperPerennial, 1990.

———. "The Sanctified Church." In Wall, *Zora Neale Hurston*, 901–5. Essay first published in 1938.

———. "Spirituals and Neo-Spirituals." In Wall, *Zora Neale Hurston*, 869–74. Essay first published in 1934.

———. "Stories of Conflict." In Wall, *Zora Neale Hurston*, 912–13. Essay first published in 1938.

———. *Tell My Horse: Voodoo and Life in Haiti and Jamaica*. 1938. New York: Harper & Row/Perennial, 1990.

———. *Their Eyes Were Watching God*. 1937. New York: HarperPerennial, 1998.

Huyssen, Andreas. "High/Low in an Expanded Field." *Modernism/Modernity* 9, no. 3 (2002): 363–74.

Irr, Caren. *The Suburb of Dissent: Cultural Politics in the United States and Canada during the 1930s*. Durham, N.C.: Duke University Press, 1998.

Irwin, John T. *Doubling and Incest/Repetition and Revenge: A Speculative Reading of Faulkner*. Baltimore: Johns Hopkins University Press, 1975.

Isaacs, Edith J. R. "News-Reel Theatre: Broadway in Review." *Theatre Arts Monthly* 18 (1934): 88–91.
Jameson, Fredric. "Beyond the Cave: Demystifying the Ideology of Modernism." *The Ideologies of Theory: Essays 1971–1986: The Syntax of History*, 115–32. Minneapolis: University of Minnesota Press, 1988.
Janet, Pierre. *Psychological Healing: A Historical and Clinical Study*, trans. Eden Paul and Cedar Paul. Vol. 1. New York: Macmillan, 1925.
Jarrell, Randall. Review of *Kneel to the Rising Sun*. In MacDonald, *Critical Essays*, 35–37. Review first published in 1935–36.
Johnson, Charles S. "The Basis of Racial Antagonisms." In Weatherford and Johnson, *Race Relations*, 50–64.
———. "The Changing Attitude of the Negro." In Weatherford and Johnson, *Race Relations*, 534–42.
———. "The New Frontage on American Life." In Locke, *New Negro*, 278–98.
———. *A Preface to Racial Understanding*. New York: Friendship Press, 1936.
———. "The Present Status of Race Relations, with Particular Reference to the Negro." *Journal of Negro Education* 8, no. 3 (1939): 323–35.
———. *The Shadow of the Plantation*. Chicago: University of Chicago Press, 1934.
Johnson, Charles S., Edwin R. Embree, and Will Alexander. *The Collapse of Cotton Tenancy: Summary of Field Studies and Statistical Surveys, 1933–35*. Chapel Hill: University of North Carolina Press, 1935.
Johnson, Gerald W. "The Ku-Kluxer." In *South-Watching: Selected Essays by Gerald W. Johnson*, ed. Fred Hobson, 15–21. Chapel Hill: University of North Carolina Press, 1983. Essay first published in 1924.
Johnson, James Weldon. "Harlem: The Culture Capital." In Locke, *New Negro*, 301–11.
———. *Negro Americans, What Now?* New York: Viking, 1935.
Jones, Anne Goodwyn. *Tomorrow Is Another Day: The Woman Writer in the South, 1859–1936*. Baton Rouge: Louisiana State University Press, 1981.
Jones, Gavin. "Poverty and the Limits of Literary Criticism." *American Literary History* 15, no. 4 (2003): 765–92.
Jones, Norman W. "Coming Out through History's Hidden Love Letters in *Absalom, Absalom!*" *American Literature* 76, no. 2 (2004): 339–66.
Jones, Suzanne W., and Sharon Monteith, eds. *South to a New Place: Region, Literature, Culture*. Baton Rouge: Louisiana State University Press, 2002.

Joyce, James. *A Portrait of the Artist as a Young Man.* 1916. New York: Viking Compass, 1970.

———. *Ulysses,* ed. Hans Walter Gabler. 1922. New York: Vintage, 1986.

Justus, James H. "Enduring Modernism: Stark Young and the Nashville Agrarians." *Southern Review* 39, no. 2 (Spring 2003): 418–36.

Kammen, Michael. "The Problem of American Exceptionalism: A Reconsideration." *American Quarterly* 45, no. 1 (1993): 1–43.

Kaplan, Amy. "Romancing the Empire: The Embodiment of American Masculinity in the Popular Historical Novel of the 1890s." In *Postcolonial Theory and the United States: Race, Ethnicity, and Literature,* ed. Amritjit Singh and Peter Schmidt, 220–43. Jackson: University Press of Mississippi, 2000.

Karem, Jeff. " 'I Could Never Really Leave the South': Regionalism and the Transformation of Richard Wright's *American Hunger.*" *American Literary History* 13, no. 4 (2001): 694–715.

Kartiganer, Donald M. *The Fragile Thread: The Meaning of Form in Faulkner's Novels.* Amherst: University of Massachusetts Press, 1979.

———. " 'So I, Who Had Never Had a War . . .': William Faulkner, War, and the Modern Imagination." *Modern Fiction Studies* 44 (1998): 627–44.

Kayser, Wolfgang. *The Grotesque in Art and Literature,* trans. Ulrich Weisstein. 1957. Bloomington: Indiana University Press, 1963.

Kazin, Alfred. "Faulkner: The Rhetoric and the Agony." *Virginia Quarterly Review* 18 (Summer 1942): 398–402.

Keely, Karen A. "Poverty, Sterilization and Eugenics in Erskine Caldwell's *Tobacco Road.*" *Journal of American Studies* 36, no. 1 (2002): 23–42.

Kelley, Robin D. G. *Hammer and Hoe: Alabama Communists during the Great Depression.* Chapel Hill: University of North Carolina Press, 1990.

Kennedy, Louise Venable. *The Negro Peasant Turns Cityward: Effects of Recent Migrations to Northern Centers.* 1930. New York: AMS Press, 1968.

Kern, Stephen. *The Culture of Time and Space, 1880–1918.* Cambridge, Mass.: Harvard University Press, 1983.

King, Desmond. *Making Americans: Immigration, Race, and the Origins of the Diverse Democracy.* Cambridge, Mass.: Harvard University Press, 2000.

King, Richard H. *A Southern Renaissance: The Cultural Awakening of the American South, 1930–55.* New York: Oxford University Press, 1980.

Kinney, Arthur F. *Faulkner's Narrative Poetics: Style as Vision.* Amherst: University of Massachusetts Press, 1978.

Kirby, Jack Temple. *Media-Made Dixie: The South in the American Imagination*. Baton Rouge: Louisiana University Press, 1978.
Kirkland, Jack. *Tobacco Road: A Three-Act Play*. New York: Viking, 1934.
Klarman, Michael J. *From Jim Crow to Civil Rights: The Supreme Court and the Struggle for Racial Equality*. New York: Oxford University Press, 2004.
Klein, Melanie. "Early Stages of the Oedipus Complex." *Contributions to Psycho-Analysis, 1921–1945*, 15–21. 1928. London: Hogarth, 1968.
———. "Notes on Some Schizoid Mechanisms." First published in 1946, abridged in Scharff, *Object Relations Theory and Practice*, 132–55.
Klinkner, Philip A., with Rogers M. Smith. *The Unsteady March: The Rise and Decline of Racial Equality in America*. Chicago: University of Chicago Press, 1999.
Kodat, Catherine Gunther. "Biting the Hand That Writes You: Southern African-American Folk Narrative and the Place of Women in *Their Eyes Were Watching God*." In *Haunted Bodies: Gender and Southern Texts*, ed. Anne Goodwyn Jones and Susan V. Donaldson, 319–42. Charlottesville: University Press of Virginia, 1997.
Kornblut, Anne E. "Red or Blue—Which Are You?" *Slate*, 14 July 2004, http://slate.msn.com (15 July 2004).
Kreyling, Michael. *Inventing Southern Literature*. Jackson: University Press of Mississippi, 1998.
Kristeva, Julia. *Powers of Horror: An Essay on Abjection*, trans. Leon S. Roudiez. New York: Columbia University Press, 1982.
Kroes, Rob. *Them and Us: Questions of Citizenship in a Globalizing World*. Urbana: University of Illinois Press, 2000.
Kronenberger, Louis. "Faulkner's Dismal Swamp." *Nation* 146 (1938): 212, 214.
Kruger, Loren. *The National Stage: Theatre and Cultural Legitimation in England, France, and America*. Chicago: University of Chicago Press, 1992.
Krutch, Joseph W. "Poor White." *Nation* 137 (12 Feb. 1933): 718.
Lacan, Jacques. *Écrits: A Selection*, trans. Bruce Fink. New York: W. W. Norton, 2002.
———. *The Seminar of Jacques Lacan, Book I: Freud's Papers on Technique, 1953–54*, ed. Jacques-Alain Miller and trans. John Forrester. 1988. New York: W. W. Norton, 1991.
———. *The Seminar of Jacques Lacan, Book VII: The Ethics of Psychoanalysis*,

1959–60, ed. Jacques-Alain Miller and trans. Dennis Porter. New York: W. W. Norton, 1992.

Ladd, Barbara. "Dismantling the Monolith: Southern Places—Past, Present, and Future." In Jones and Monteith, *South to a New Place,* 44–57.

———. *Nationalism and the Color Line in George W. Cable, Mark Twain, and William Faulkner.* Baton Rouge: Louisiana State University Press, 1996.

———. " 'Philosophers and Other Gynecologists': Women and the Polity in *Requiem for a Nun.*" *Mississippi Quarterly* 52, no. 3 (1999): 483–501.

Lamis, Alexander P. "The Two-Party South: From the 1960s to the 1990s." In *Southern Politics in the 1990s,* ed. Alexander P. Lamis, 1–49. Baton Rouge: Louisiana State University Press, 1999.

Lamont, Margaret Irish. Review of *Shadow of the Plantation. Opportunity* 12 (1934): 282–83.

Lamothe, Daphne. "Vodou Imagery, African American Tradition, and Cultural Transformation in Zora Neale Hurston's *Their Eyes Were Watching God.*" 1999. In Wall, *Zora Neale Hurston's* Their Eyes Were Watching God, 165–87.

Landsberg, Alison. "Prosthetic Memory: The Logics and Politics of Memory in Modern American Culture." Ph.D. diss., University of Chicago, 1996.

Laplanche, J., and J.-B. Pontalis. *The Language of Psycho-Analysis,* trans. Donald Nicholson-Smith. New York: W. W. Norton, 1973.

Larsen, Nella. *Quicksand.* 1928. In *An Intimation of Things Distant: The Collected Fiction of Nella Larsen,* ed. Charles R. Larson, 29–162. New York: Anchor, 1992.

Latham, Michael E. *Modernization as Ideology: American Social Science and "Nation Building" in the Kennedy Era.* Chapel Hill: University of North Carolina Press, 2000.

Lears, T. J. Jackson. *No Place of Grace: Antimodernism and the Transformation of American Culture, 1880–1920.* 2nd ed. Chicago: University of Chicago Press, 1994.

Leege, David C., et al. *The Politics of Cultural Differences: Social Change and Voter Mobilization Strategies in the Post–New Deal Period.* Princeton, N.J.: Princeton University Press, 2002.

Lehman, Peter, ed. *Close Viewings: An Anthology of New Film Criticism.* Tallahassee: Florida State University Press, 1990.

Leon, Juan Enrique. "A Literary History of Eugenic Terror in England and America." Ph.D. diss., Harvard University, 1989.

Leuchtenburg, William E. *The FDR Years: On Roosevelt and His Legacy.* New York: Columbia University Press, 1995.

Levine, Lawrence W. "Hollywood's Washington: Film Images of National Politics during the Great Depression." *Prospects* 10 (1985): 172–86.

Lévy, Maurice. *Le Roman "gothique" anglais, 1764–1824* [The English Gothic Novel]. Toulouse: Association des Publications de la Faculté des Lettres et Sciences Humaines de Toulouse, 1968.

Lewis, R. W. B. *The American Adam*. Chicago: University of Chicago Press, 1955.

Lewis, Sinclair. *Babbitt*. 1922. New York: Signet, 1980.

Leys, Ruth. "Traumatic Cures: Shell Shock, Janet, and the Question of Memory." *Critical Inquiry* 20 (Summer 1994): 623–62.

Liasson, Mara. "Impact of Gay Marriage and Civil Unions on the 2004 Political Scene." *National Public Radio Morning Edition,* 26 Dec. 2003, accessed through Lexis-Nexis (20 Jan. 2004).

Limerick, Patricia Nelson. "Region and Reason." In Ayers et al., *All over the Map*, 83–104.

Lipsitz, George. *The Possessive Investment in Whiteness: How White People Profit from Identity Politics*. Philadelphia: Temple University Press, 1998.

Lloyd, David. "Race under Representation." 1991. In *Culture/Contexture: Exploration in Anthropology and Literary Studies,* ed. E. Valentine Daniel and Jeffrey M. Peck, 249–72. Berkeley: University of California Press, 1996.

Locke, Alain. "Black Truth and Black Beauty: A Retrospective Review of the Literature of the Negro for 1932." *Opportunity* 11 (1933): 14–18.

———. "Deep River: Deeper Sea: Retrospective Review of the Literature of the Negro for 1935." *Opportunity* 14 (1936): 6–10, 42–43, 46.

———. "The Eleventh Hour of Nordicism: Retrospective Review of the Literature of the Negro for 1934." *Opportunity* 13 (1935): 8–13.

———. "Sterling Brown: The New Negro Folk Poet." In *Negro: Anthology Made by Nancy Cunard 1931–1933,* ed. Nancy Cunard, 312–14. London: Wishart, 1934.

———. "We Turn to Prose: A Retrospective Review of the Literature of the Negro for 1931." *Opportunity* 10 (1932): 40–44.

Locke, Alain, ed. *The New Negro*. 1925. New York: Atheneum, 1992.

Loewenberg, Peter. "The Construction of National Identity." In *Psychoanalysis and Culture at the Millennium,* ed. Nancy Ginsburg and Roy Ginsburg, 37–62. New Haven, Conn.: Yale University Press, 1999.

Logan, Lisa. Introduction to *Critical Essays on Carson McCullers,* ed. Beverly Lyon Clark and Melvin J. Friedman, 1–14. New York: G. K. Hall, 1996.

"A Long Road." *Nation* 141 (November 1935): 46.

Lord, Russell. "Back to the Farm?" *Forum and Century* 84, no. 2 (February 1933): 97–103.
Lott, Eric. "Love and Theft: The Racial Unconscious of Blackface Minstrelsy." *Representations* 39 (1992): 23–50.
Lowe, James. *The Creative Process of James Agee*. Baton Rouge: Louisiana State University Press, 1994.
Luckmann, Thomas. "The Constitution of Human Life in Time." In Bender and Wellbery, *Chronotypes*, 151–66.
Lükacs, Georg. "The Ideology of Modernism." *The Meaning of Contemporary Realism*, trans. John Mander and Necke Mander, 24–40. London: Merlin Press, 1962.
Lurie, Peter. "Some Trashy Myth of Reality's Escape: Romance, History, and Film Viewing in *Absalom, Absalom!*" *American Literature* 73, no. 3 (2001): 563–97.
Lutz, Tom. *Cosmopolitan Vistas: American Regionalism and Literary Value*. Ithaca, N.Y.: Cornell University Press, 2004.
Lynd, Robert S., and Helen Merrell Lynd. *Middletown: A Study in American Culture*. New York: Harcourt, Brace, 1929.
Lytle, Andrew Nelson. "The Hind Tit." In Twelve Southerners, *I'll Take My Stand*, 216–34. Essay first published in 1930.
MacDonald, Scott, ed. *Critical Essays on Erskine Caldwell*. Boston: G. K. Hall, 1981.
Magowan, Kim. "Coming between the 'Black Beast' and the White Virgin: The Pressures of Liminality in Thomas Dixon." *Studies in American Fiction* 27, no. 1 (Spring 1999): 77–102.
Mancini, JoAnne M. "'Messin' with the Furniture Man': Early Country Music, Regional Culture, and the Search for an Anthological Modernism." *American Literary History* 16, no. 2 (2004): 208–22.
Marlantes, Liz. "Make or Break? Primary Colors in South Carolina." *Christian Science Monitor*, 23 Dec. 2003, accessed through Lexis-Nexis (20 Jan. 2004).
Martín, Sara. "Meeting the Civilized Barbarian: Bram Stoker's *Dracula* and Joseph Conrad's *Heart of Darkness*." *Miscelánea: A Journal of English and American Studies* 22 (2000): 101–21.
Marx, Karl. "The Eighteenth Brumaire of Louis Bonaparte." 1852. In *The Marx-Engels Reader*, ed. Robert C. Tucker, 2nd ed., 594–617. New York: W. W. Norton, 1978.
Matthews, John T. "This Race Which Is Not One: The 'More Inextricable Com-

positeness' of William Faulkner's South." In Smith and Cohn, *Look Away!* 201–26.

———. "Touching Race in *Go Down, Moses*." In *New Essays on* Go Down, Moses, ed. Linda Wagner-Martin, 21–48. Cambridge: Cambridge University Press, 1996.

Maxwell, William J. *New Negro, Old Left: African-American Writing and Communism Between the Wars.* New York: Columbia University Press, 1999.

"McCain Flag Apology Extraordinary." Editorial. *St. Petersburg Times,* 21 April 2000: 20A, accessed through Lexis-Nexis (20 Jan. 2004).

McClintock, Anne. "The Angel of Progress: Pitfalls of the Term 'Postcolonialism.'" *Social Text* 31/32 (1992): 84–98.

McCullers, Carson. *The Heart Is a Lonely Hunter.* 1940. Boston: Mariner/Houghton Mifflin, 2000.

McGowan, Todd. "Liberation and Domination: *Their Eyes Were Watching God* and the Evolution of Capitalism." *MELUS* 24, no. 1 (1999): 109–28.

McIlwaine, Shields. *The Southern Poor-White: From Lubberland to Tobacco Road.* Norman: University of Oklahoma Press, 1939.

McPherson, Tara. *Reconstructing Dixie: Race, Gender, and Nostalgia in the Imagined South.* Durham, N.C.: Duke University Press, 2003.

———. "Re-imagining the Red States: New Directions for Southern Studies." *Southern Spaces,* Emory University, 14 Dec. 2004, http://southernspaces.org (7 June 2005).

McWilliams, Carey. *The New Regionalism in American Literature.* 1930. N.p.: Folcroft, 1971.

Mencken, H. L. "The Sahara of the Bozart." In *Prejudices: A Selection,* ed. James T. Farrell, 69–82. New York: Vintage, 1958. Essay as published in 1920.

Mendelberg, Tali. *The Race Card: Campaign Strategy, Implicit Messages, and the Norm of Equality.* Princeton, N.J.: Princeton University Press, 2001.

Merriam, C. E. "Government and Society." *Survey Graphic* 22, no. 1 (January 1933): 33–36.

Merritt, Dixon. "Democracy and the South." *Outlook and Independent* 151 (27 Feb. 1929): 341–43, 354–55.

Merritt, Russell. "D. W. Griffith's *The Birth of a Nation*: Going after Little Sister." In Lehman, *Close Viewings,* 215–37.

Michaels, Walter Benn. "*Absalom, Absalom!* The Difference between White Men and White Men." In Hamblin and Abadie, *Faulkner in the Twenty-First Century,* 137–53.

———. "Local Colors," *MLN* 113, no. 4 (1998): 734–56.

———. *Our America: Nativism, Modernism, and Pluralism.* Durham, N.C.: Duke University Press, 1995.

Miller, Dan. *Erskine Caldwell: The Journey from Tobacco Road.* New York: Alfred A. Knopf, 1995.

Miller, Guy A. Letter to the editor. *Nation* 141 (25 Dec. 1935): 741.

Miller, Kelly. "Howard: The National Negro University." In Locke, *New Negro,* 312–22.

Mitchell, Angelyn, ed. *Within the Circle: An Anthology of African American Literary Criticism from the Harlem Renaissance to the Present.* Durham, N.C.: Duke University Press, 1994.

Mitchell, Lee Clark. *Determined Fictions: American Literary Naturalism.* New York: Columbia University Press, 1989.

Mitchell, Margaret. *Gone with the Wind.* New York: Macmillan, 1936.

Mitchell, Timothy. "The Stage of Modernity." In *Questions of Modernity,* ed. Timothy Mitchell, 1–34. Minneapolis: University of Minnesota Press, 2000.

Mixon, Wayne. *The People's Writer: Erskine Caldwell and the South.* Charlottesville: University Press of Virginia, 1996.

Moran, Jeffrey P. "Reading Race into the Scopes Trial: African American Elites, Science, and Fundamentalism." *Journal of American History* 90, no. 3 (2003): 891–911.

Moran, Kathleen, and Michael Rogin. "'What's the Matter with Capra?' *Sullivan's Travels* and the Popular Front." *Representations* 71 (Summer 2000): 106–34.

Moreland, Richard. *Faulkner and Modernism: Rereading and Rewriting.* Madison: University of Wisconsin Press, 1990.

Moton, Robert Russa. *What the Negro Thinks.* New York: Doubleday, Doran, 1929.

Müller, Harro. "Identity, Paradox, Difference: Conceptions of Time in the Literature of Modernity" (trans. Jan Mieszkowski). *MLN* 111, no. 3 (1996): 523–32.

Muscio, Giuliana. "Roosevelt, Arnold, and Capra, (or) the Federalist-Populist Paradox." In *Frank Capra: Authorship and the Studio System,* ed. Robert Sklar and Vito Zagarrio, 164–89. Philadelphia: Temple University Press, 1998.

Mustafa, Jamil. "Mapping the Late-Victorian Subject: Psychology, Cartography, and the Gothic Novel." Ph.D. diss., University of Chicago, 1999.

Myrdal, Gunnar. *An American Dilemma: The Negro Problem and Modern Democracy.* New York: Harper & Brothers, 1944.

Nadel, Alan. *Invisible Criticism: Ralph Ellison and the American Canon.* Iowa City: University of Iowa Press, 1988.
National Emergency Council. *Report on the Economic Conditions of the South.* Washington, D.C.: Government Printing Office, 1938.
National Resources Committee. *Regional Factors in National Planning and Development.* Washington, D.C.: Government Printing Office, 1935.
Nicholls, David Greene. "Migrant Labor, Folklore, and Resistance in Hurston's Polk County: Reframing *Mules and Men.*" *African American Review* 33, no. 3 (1999): 467–79.
Nissenbaum, Stephen. "Inventing New England." In *The New Regionalism,* ed. Charles Reagan Wilson, 105–26. Jackson: University Press of Mississippi, 1998.
North, Michael. *Reading 1922: A Return to the Scene of the Modern.* New York: Oxford University Press, 1999.
Norton, Anne. *Reflections on Political Identity.* Baltimore: Johns Hopkins University Press, 1988.
O'Brien, Michael. *The Idea of the American South, 1920–1941.* Baltimore: Johns Hopkins University Press, 1979.
———. "W. J. Cash, Hegel, and the South." *Journal of Southern History* 44, no. 3 (1978): 379–98.
O'Donnell, George Marion. "Looking Down the Cotton Row." In Agar and Tate, *Who Owns America?* 161–78.
Odum, Howard. *Race and Rumors of Race: Challenge to American Crisis.* Chapel Hill: University of North Carolina Press, 1943.
———. *Southern Regions of the United States.* Chapel Hill: University of North Carolina Press, 1936.
Odum, Howard W., and Harry Estill Moore. *American Regionalism: A Cultural-Historical Approach to National Integration.* 1938. Gloucester, Mass.: Peter Smith, 1966.
Ong, Aihwa. "Cultural Citizenship as Subject Making: Immigrants Negotiate Racial and Cultural Boundaries in the United States." In *Race, Identity, and Citizenship: A Reader,* ed. Rodolfo D. Torres, Louis F. Mirón, and Jonathan Xavier Inda, 262–93. Malden, Mass.: Blackwell, 1999.
Onuf, Peter S. "Federalism, Republicanism, and the Origins of American Sectionalism." In Ayers et al., *All over the Map,* 11–37.
Osborne, Peter. "Modernity Is a Qualitative, Not a Chronological Category." *New Left Review* 192 (1992): 65–84.

Page, Thomas Nelson. *Red Rock*. New York: C. Scribner's Sons, 1899.

Parsons, Marnie. "Imagination and the Rending of Time: The Reader and the Recreated Pasts of *Requiem for a Nun*." *Mississippi Quarterly* 41, no. 3 (Summer 1988): 433–46.

Pate, James E. "Federal-State Relations in Planning." *Social Forces* 15, no. 2 (1936): 187–95.

Pavlic, Edward. "Papa Legba, Ouvrier Barriere Pour Moi Passer: Esu in *Their Eyes* and Zora Neale Hurston's Diasporic Modernism." *African American Review* 38, no. 1 (2004): 61–86.

Payne, Charles M. " 'The Whole United States Is Southern!' *Brown v. Board* and the Mystification of Race." *Journal of American History* 91, no. 1 (June 2004), www.historycooperative.org (3 June 2004).

Pease, Donald E. "Ralph Ellison and Kenneth Burke: The Nonsymbolizable (Trans)Action." *boundary 2* 30, no. 2 (2003): 65–96.

Perrow, E. C. "Songs and Rhymes from the South." *Journal of American Folklore* 26, no. 100 (1913): 123–73.

Phillips, William. Contribution to "Our Country and Our Culture" symposium. *Partisan Review* 19, no. 5 (1952): 587–89.

Phillips, William, and Philip Rahv, eds. *The Partisan Review Anthology*. New York: Holt, Rinehart, and Winston, 1962.

Pickens, William. "Re-Visiting the South." *Crisis* 37 (1930): 127–28.

Pinckney, Josephine. "Bulwarks against Change." In Couch, *Culture in the South*, 40–51.

Pitavy, François L. "The Gothicism of *Absalom, Absalom!* Rosa Coldfield Revisited." In *"A Cosmos of My Own": Faulkner and Yoknapatawpha, 1980*, ed. Doreen Fowler and Ann J. Abadie, 199–226. Jackson: University Press of Mississippi, 1981.

———. "William Faulkner and the American Dream: A Furious Affirmation." In *Faulkner: After the Nobel Prize*, ed. Michel Gresset and Kenzaburo Ohashi, 74–87. Kyoto: Yamaguchi Publishing, 1987.

Plessy v. Ferguson, 163 U.S. 537 (1896).

Poague, Leland. *Another Frank Capra*. Cambridge: Cambridge University Press, 1994.

Polk, Noel. *Faulkner's* Requiem for a Nun: *A Critical Study*. Bloomington: Indiana University Press, 1981.

Pollock, Sheldon, et al. "Cosmopolitanisms." *Public Culture* 12, no. 3 (2000): 577–89.

Polman, Dick. "If Democrats Look away from Dixie, Winning White House May Be Tough." *Philadelphia Inquirer*, 27 Nov. 2003, accessed through Lexis-Nexis (20 Jan. 2004).

Pondrom, Cyrena N. "The Role of Myth in Hurston's *Their Eyes Were Watching God*." *American Literature* 58, no. 2 (1986): 181–202.

Pound, Ezra. "The Wisdom of Poetry." *Selected Prose 1909–1965*, ed. William Cookson, 359–62. New York: New Directions, 1973. Poem first published in 1912.

Prahlad, Sw. Anand. "Guess Who's Coming to Dinner: Folklore, Folkloristics, and African American Literary Criticism." *African American Review* 33 (1999): 565–75.

Preece, Harold. "The Negro Folk Cult." 1936. In *Mother Wit from the Laughing Barrel: Readings in the Interpretation of Afro-American Folklore*, ed. Alan Dundes, 34–38. New York: Garland, 1981.

President's Committee on Civil Rights. *To Secure These Rights: The Report of the President's Committee on Civil Rights*. Washington, D.C.: Government Printing Office, 1947.

President's Research Committee on Social Trends. *Recent Social Trends in the United States: Report of the President's Research Committee on Social Trends*. New York: McGraw-Hill, 1933.

Pryse, Marjorie. "Writing out of the Gap: Regionalism, Resistance, and Relational Reading." *Textual Studies in Canada* 9 (1997): 19–34.

Punter, David. "Hungry Ghosts and Foreign Bodies." In Smith and Wallace, *Gothic Modernisms*, 11–28.

———. *The Literature of Terror: A History of Gothic Fictions from 1765 to the Present Day*. London: Longman, 1980.

Pyron, Darden Asbury, ed. *Recasting: Gone with the Wind in American Culture*. Miami: University Presses of Florida, 1983.

Quinones, Ricardo J. *Mapping Literary Modernism: Time and Development*. Princeton, N.J.: Princeton University Press, 1985.

Rable, George C. "The South and the Politics of Anti-Lynching Legislation, 1920–1940." *Journal of Southern History* 51, no. 2 (1985): 201–20.

Radway, Jan. "What's in a Name?" In *The Futures of American Studies*, ed. Donald E. Pease and Robyn Wiegman, 45–75. Durham, N.C.: Duke University Press, 2002.

Rafter, Nichole Hahn. Introduction to *White Trash: The Eugenic Family Studies, 1877–1919*, ed. Nicole Hahn Rafter, 1–31. Boston: Northeastern University Press, 1988.

Rahv, Philip. "The Myth and the Powerhouse." 1953. In Phillips and Rahv, *Partisan Review Anthology*, 135–44.

———. Review of *Absalom, Absalom!* In Bassett, *Critical Heritage*, 208–10. Review first published in 1936.

Railton, Ben. " 'What Else Could a Southern Gentleman Do?': Quentin Compson, Rhett Butler, and Miscegenation." *Southern Literary Journal* 35, no. 2 (2003): 41–63.

Ransom, John Crowe. "Reconstructed but Unregenerate." In Twelve Southerners, *I'll Take My Stand*, 1–27.

———. "The South Is a Bulwark." *Scribner's* 99, no. 5 (May 1936): 299–303.

"Recovery in the South." *Opportunity* 12 (1934): 72.

Reed, Adolph, Jr. "The 2004 Election in Perspective: The Myth of 'Cultural Divide' and the Triumph of Neoliberal Ideology." *American Quarterly* 57, no. 1 (2005): 1–15.

Reed, T. V. "Unimagined Existence and the Fiction of the Real: Postmodernist Realism in *Let Us Now Praise Famous Men*." *Representations* 24 (1988): 156–76.

Renda, Mary A. *Taking Haiti: Military Occupation and the Culture of U.S. Imperialism, 1915–1940*. Chapel Hill: University of North Carolina Press, 2001.

Richardson, Riché. *Black Masculinity and the U.S. South: From Uncle Tom to Gangsta*. Athens: University of Georgia Press, forthcoming.

Ring, Natalie. "The Problem South: Region, Race, and 'Southern Readjustment,' 1880–1930." Ph.D. diss., University of California, San Diego, 2003.

Riquelme, John Paul. "Toward a History of Gothic and Modernism: Dark Modernity from Bram Stoker to Samuel Beckett." *Modern Fiction Studies* 46, no. 3 (2000): 585–605.

Riskind, Jonathan. "Gore Calls Bush, McCain 'Morally Blind.' " *Columbus Dispatch*, 21 Feb. 2000: 3A, accessed through Lexis-Nexis (20 Jan. 2004).

Rogin, Michael. " 'The Sword Became a Flashing Vision': D. W. Griffith's *The Birth of a Nation*." *Representations* 9 (1985): 150–95.

———. "The Two Declarations of American Independence." *Representations* 55 (1996): 13–30.

Rolfe, Edwin. Review of *God's Little Acre*. In MacDonald, *Critical Essays*, 23–25. Review first published in 1933.

Roller, Bert. "No More Swords and Roses." *Outlook and Independent* 153 (25 Sept. 1929): 136–37, 158–59.

Romine, Scott. *The Narrative Forms of Southern Community*. Baton Rouge: Louisiana State University Press, 1999.

———. "Things Falling Apart: The Postcolonial Condition of *Red Rock* and *The Leopard's Spots*." In Smith and Cohn, *Look Away*, 175–200.

Roosevelt, Franklin D. Democratic primary campaign speech (Barnesville, Georgia, 11 Aug. 1938). In *The Roosevelt Reader: Selected Speeches, Messages, Press Conferences, and Letters of Franklin D. Roosevelt*, ed. Basil Rauch, 197–203. New York: Rinehart, 1957.

Rorty, Richard. *Achieving Our Country: Leftist Thought in Twentieth-Century America*. Cambridge, Mass.: Harvard University Press, 1998.

Rose, Jacqueline. *States of Fantasy*. Oxford: Clarendon, 1996.

Rourke, Constance. *American Humor: A Study of the National Character*. New York: Harcourt, Brace, 1931.

Rozario, Kevin. " 'Delicious Horrors': Mass Culture, the Red Cross, and the Appeal of Modern American Humanitarianism." *American Quarterly* 55, no. 3 (2003): 417–55.

Rubin, Louis D., Jr. "Carson McCullers: The Aesthetic of Pain." *A Gallery of Southerners*, 135–51. Baton Rouge: Louisiana State University Press, 1982. Essay first published in 1977.

———. "Southern Literature and the Great Depression." In *Literature at the Barricade*, ed. Ralph F. Bogardus and Fred C. Hobson, 96–113. Tuscaloosa: University of Alabama Press, 1982.

Rubin, Louis D., Jr., and James Jackson Kilpatrick, eds. *The Lasting South: Fourteen Southerners Look at Their Home*. Chicago: Henry Regnery, 1957.

Said, Edward W. *Culture and Imperialism*. 1993. New York: Vintage, 1994.

———. *Orientalism*. New York: Pantheon, 1978.

Sánchez-Eppler, Benigno. "Telling Anthropology: Zora Neale Hurston and Gilberto Freyre Disciplined in Their Field-Home-Work." *American Literary History* 4 (1992): 464–88.

Sartre, Jean-Paul. Introduction to *The Colonizer and the Colonized* by Albert Memmi, trans. Lawrence Hoey. 1957. New York: Orion, 1965.

Scharff, David E. *Object Relations Theory and Practice: An Introduction*. Northvale, N.J.: Jason Aronson, 1996.

Schaub, Thomas. "Ellison's Masks and the Novel of Reality." In *New Essays on Invisible Man*, ed. Robert O'Meally, 123–56. New York: Cambridge University Press, 1988.

Schmidt, Hans. *The United States Occupation of Haiti, 1914–1934*. New Brunswick, N.J.: Rutgers University Press, 1971.
Schultz, William Todd. "Off-Stage Voices in James Agee's *Let Us Now Praise Famous Men*: Reportage as Covert Autobiography." *American Imago* 56, no. 1 (1999): 75–104.
Schuyler, George S. "The Negro-Art Hokum." 1926. In A. Mitchell, *Within the Circle*, 51–54.
Schwartz, Lawrence H. *Creating Faulkner's Reputation: The Politics of Modern Literary Criticism*. Knoxville: University of Tennessee Press, 1988.
Scott, Joan W. "Fantasy Echo: History and the Construction of Identity." *Critical Inquiry* 27 (Winter 2001): 284–304.
"Scottsboro." *Opportunity* 11 (1933): 134.
Sedgwick, Eve Kosofsky. *The Coherence of Gothic Conventions*. New York: Arno Press/New York Times, 1980.
Segrest, Mab. *My Mama's Dead Squirrel: Lesbian Essays on Southern Culture*. Ithaca, N.Y.: Firebrand, 1985.
Seltzer, Mark. *Bodies and Machines*. New York: Routledge, 1992.
Shaw, Roger. "Fascism and the New Deal." *North American Review* 238, no. 6 (December 1934): 559–64.
Shimakawa, Karen. *National Abjection: The Asian American Body Onstage*. Durham, N.C.: Duke University Press, 2002.
"Shoes for Southerners? Never!" *Literary Digest* 115 (17 June 1933): 116.
Singal, Daniel Joseph. *The War Within: From Victorian to Modernist Thought in the South, 1919–1945*. Chapel Hill: University of North Carolina Press, 1982.
Singer, Brian C. J. "Cultural versus Contractual Nations: Rethinking Their Opposition." *History and Theory* 35, no. 3 (1996): 309–37.
Singer, Marc. "'A Slightly Different Sense of Time': Palimpsestic Time in *Invisible Man*." *Twentieth Century Literature* 49, no. 3 (Fall 2003): 388–419.
Singh, Nikhil Pal. *Black Is a Country: Race and the Unfinished Struggle for Democracy*. Cambridge, Mass.: Harvard University Press, 2004.
———. "Culture/Wars: Recoding Empire in an Age of Democracy." *American Quarterly* 50, no. 3 (1998): 471–522.
Sitkoff, Harvard. *The Depression Decade*. Vol. 1 of *A New Deal for Blacks: The Emergence of Civil Rights as a National Issue*. New York: Oxford University Press, 1978.
Smethurst, James. "Invented by Horror: The Gothic and African American Literary Ideology in *Native Son*." *African American Review* 35, no. 1 (2002): 29–40.

Smith, Andrew, and Jeff Wallace, eds. *Gothic Modernisms*. New York: Palgrave, 2001.

Smith, Anthony D. "The Origins of Nations." In *Becoming National: A Reader*, ed. Geoff Eley and Ronald Grigor Suny, 106–31. New York: Oxford University Press, 1996. Essay first published in 1989.

Smith, Jonathan R. "Southern Culture on the Skids: Punk, Retro, Narcissism, and the Burden of Southern History." In Jones and Monteith, *South to a New Place*, 76–95.

Smith, Jonathan R., and Deborah Cohn, eds. *Look Away: Comparatist Approaches to U.S. Southern Cultures*. Durham, N.C.: Duke University Press, 2004.

Smith, Lillian. *Strange Fruit*. 1944. New York: Harvest-HBJ, 1992.

Smith, Rogers M. "Beyond Tocqueville, Myrdal, and Hartz: The Multiple Traditions in America." *American Political Science Review* 87, no. 3 (September 1993): 549–66.

———. *Civic Ideals: Conflicting Visions of Citizenship in U.S. History*. New Haven, Conn.: Yale University Press, 1997.

———. *Stories of Peoplehood: The Politics and Morals of Political Membership*. Cambridge: Cambridge University Press, 2003.

Smoodin, Eric. "'Compulsory' Viewing for Every Citizen: *Mr. Smith* and the Rhetoric of Reception." *Cinema Journal* 35, no. 2 (Winter 1996): 3–23.

Soderbergh, Peter A. "Hollywood and the South, 1930–1960." *Mississippi Quarterly* 19, no. 1 (Winter 1966): 1–19.

Soja, Edward. *Postmodern Geographies: The Reassertion of Space in Critical Social Theory*. New York: Verso, 1989.

Sollors, Werner. "Modernization as Adultery: Richard Wright, Zora Neale Hurston, and American Culture of the 1930s and 1940s." *Hebrew University Studies in Literature and the Arts* 18 (1990): 109–48.

Sommer, Doris. "Irresistible Romance: The Foundational Fictions of Latin America." In *Nation and Narration*, ed. Homi K. Bhabha, 71–98. New York: Routledge, 1990.

Southwick, Ron. "Humanities Centers Face a Shaky Future." *Chronicle of Higher Education*, 22 March 2002: 22, accessed through Lexis-Nexis (27 Oct. 2003).

Southworth, Caleb. "Aid to Sharecroppers: How Agrarian Class Structure and Tenant-Farmer Politics Influenced Federal Relief in the South, 1933–1935." *Social Science History* 26, no. 1 (2002): 33–70.

Spillers, Hortense J. "'All the Things You Could Be Right Now, If Sigmund

Freud's Wife Was Your Mother': Psychoanalysis and Race." *boundary 2* 23, no. 3 (1996): 75–141.

Stallybrass, Peter, and Allon White. *The Politics and Poetics of Transgression*. London: Methuen, 1986.

Staub, Michael. "As Close as You Can Get: Torment, Speech, and Listening in *Let Us Now Praise Famous Men*." *Mississippi Quarterly* 61, no. 2 (1988): 147–60.

Steiner, Michael. "Regionalism in the Great Depression." *Geographical Review* 73, no. 4 (October 1983): 430–46.

Stepto, Robert. *From behind the Veil: A Study of Afro-American Narrative*. Urbana: University of Illinois Press, 1979.

Stoker, Bram. *Dracula*. 1897. New York: Barnes & Noble, 1992.

Stone, Albert E., Jr. "Seward Collins and the *American Review*: Experiment in Pro-Fascism." *American Quarterly* 12, no. 1 (1960): 3–19.

Stone, Geoffrey. Review of *Light in August*. *Bookman* 75 (November 1932): 736–38.

Stott, William. *Documentary Expression and Thirties America*. New York: Oxford University Press, 1973.

Styron, Arthur. "A Southern View of Northern Reformers." *North American Review* 238, no. 1 (July 1934): 149–57.

Sullivan, Patricia. *Days of Hope: Race and Democracy in the New Deal Era*. Chapel Hill: University of North Carolina Press, 1996.

Sumida, Stephen H. "East of California: Points of Origin in Asian American Studies." *Journal of Asian American Studies* 1, no. 1 (1998): 83–100.

Sumner, William Graham. *Folkways: A Study of the Sociological Importance of Usages, Manners, Customs, Mores, and Morals*. Boston: Ginn, 1906.

Sundquist, Eric. *Faulkner: The House Divided*. Baltimore: Johns Hopkins University Press, 1983.

Susman, Warren I. *Culture as History: The Transformation of American Society in the Twentieth Century*. New York: Pantheon, 1984.

Swint, Henry L. "Northern Interest in the Shoeless Southerner." *Journal of Southern History* 16, no. 4 (November 1950): 457–71.

Sykes, Gerald. "The Poetry of Unfeeling." *Nation* 133 (1931). In MacDonald, *Critical Essays*, 7.

Szalay, Michael. *New Deal Modernism: American Literature and the Invention of the Welfare State*. Durham, N.C.: Duke University Press, 2000.

Tabachnick, Steve. "The Gothic Modernism of T. S. Eliot's *Waste Land* and What Martin Rowson's Graphic Novel Tells Us about It and Other Matters." *Readerly/Writerly Texts* 8, no. 1 (2001): 79–92.

Tate, Allen. "The Man of Letters in the Modern World." *Essays of Four Decades*, 3–16. Chicago: Swallow Press, 1968.

———. "Notes on Liberty and Property." In Agar and Tate, *Who Owns America?* 80–93.

———. *Poems 1922–1947*. New York: Charles Scribner's Sons, 1948.

———. "Remarks on the Southern Religion." In Twelve Southerners, *I'll Take My Stand*, 155–75.

Tate, Claudia. *Psychoanalysis and Black Novels: Desire and the Protocols of Race*. New York: Oxford University Press, 1998.

Thompson, Charles H. "Editorial Note: The Availability of Education in the Negro Separate School." *Journal of Negro Education* 16, no. 3 (1947): 257–71.

Thurman, Wallace. *Infants of the Spring*. 1932. Freeport, N.Y.: Books for Libraries Press, 1972.

Tindall, George B. "The Benighted South: Origins of a Modern Image." *Virginia Quarterly Review* 40, no. 2 (1964): 281–94.

———. "The 'Colonial Economy' and the Growth Psychology: The South in the 1930's." *South Atlantic Quarterly* 64, no. 4 (Autumn 1965): 465–77.

"'Tobacco Road' Runs on and on, a Saga of Cussing and Turnips." *Newsweek*, 27 Nov. 1939: 32–33.

Tolson, Melvin B. *Caviar and Cabbage: Selected Columns by Melvin B. Tolson from the* Washington Tribune, *1937–1944*, ed. Robert M. Farnsworth. Columbia: University of Missouri Press, 1982.

Tompkins, Lucille. Review of *Their Eyes Were Watching God* by Zora Neale Hurston. In Gates and Appiah, *Critical Perspectives*, 18–19. Review first published in 1937.

Toomer, Jean. *Cane*, ed. Darwin Turner. Norton Critical Edition. 1923. New York: W. W. Norton, 1988.

Towner, Theresa. *Faulkner on the Color Line: The Later Novels*. Jackson: University Press of Mississippi, 2000.

Trachtenberg, Alan. *The Incorporation of America: Culture and Society in the Gilded Age*. New York: Hill and Wang, 1982.

Trilling, Lionel. "Mr. Faulkner's World." *Nation* 133 (1931): 491–92.

Turner, Frederick Jackson. "Sections and Nation." *The Significance of Sections in American History*, 315–39. 1932. Gloucester, Mass.: Peter Smith, 1959. Essay first published in 1922.

Turner, Victor. *From Ritual to Theatre: The Human Seriousness of Play*. New York: Performing Arts Journal Publications, 1982.

Twelve Southerners. *I'll Take My Stand: The South and the Agrarian Tradition.* 1930. Baton Rouge: Louisiana State University Press, 1977.

Vance, Rupert B. *Human Geography of the South: A Study in Regional Resources and Human Adequacy.* Chapel Hill: University of North Carolina Press, 1932.

van der Kolk, Bessel A., and Otto van der Hart. "The Intrusive Past: The Flexibility of Memory and the Engraving of Trauma." In *Trauma: Explorations in Memory,* ed. Cathy Caruth, 158–82. Baltimore: Johns Hopkins University Press, 1995.

Vaughan, Malcolm. "Exit Mammy." *Scribner's* 80, no. 4 (October 1926): 405–14.

Volkan, Vamik D. "The Narcissism of Minor Differences in the Psychological Gap between Opposing Nations." *Psychoanalytic Inquiry* 2, no. 6 (1986): 175–91.

———. "Psychoanalysis and Diplomacy: Part I. Individual and Large Group Identity." *Journal of Applied Psychoanalytic Studies* 1, no. 1 (1999): 29–55.

Wagner-Martin, Linda. "*Let Us Now Praise Famous Men* and Women: Agee's Absorption in the Sexual." In *James Agee: Reconsiderations,* ed. Michael A. Lofaro, 44–58. Knoxville: University of Tennessee Press, 1992.

Wainwright, Mary Katherine. "The Aesthetics of Community: The Insular Black Community as Theme and Focus in Hurston's *Their Eyes Were Watching God.*" In *The Harlem Renaissance: Revaluations,* ed. Amritjit Singh, Williams S. Shiver, and Stanley Brodwin, 233–43. New York: Garland, 1989.

Waligora-Davis, Nicole. "Riotous Discontent: Ralph Ellison's 'Birth of a Nation.'" *Modern Fiction Studies* 50, no. 2 (2004): 385–410.

Wall, Cheryl A. "*Mules and Men* and Women: Zora Neale Hurston's Strategies of Narration and Visions of Female Empowerment." *Black American Literature Forum* 23 (1989): 661–80.

———, ed. *Zora Neale Hurston: Folklore, Memoirs, and Other Writings.* New York: Literary Classics, 1995.

———, ed. *Zora Neale Hurston's* Their Eyes Were Watching God: *A Casebook.* New York: Oxford University Press, 2000.

Wallace, Henry A. "The Search for an American Way." *Scribner's* 100, no. 1 (July 1936): 22–27.

Wallace, Michelle Faith. "The Good Lynching and *The Birth of a Nation*: Discourses and Aesthetics of Jim Crow." *Cinema Journal* 43 (2003): 85–104.

Wallerstein, Immanuel. "What Can One Mean by Southern Culture?" *Geopolitics and Geoculture: Essays on the Changing World-System,* 200–214. Cambridge: Cambridge University Press, 1991. Essay first published in 1988.

Warren, Kenneth W. "Appeals for (Mis)Recognition: Theorizing the Diaspora." In *Cultures of United States Imperialism*, ed. Donald Pease and Amy Kaplan, 392–406. Durham, N.C.: Duke University Press, 1994.

———. *So Black and Blue: Ralph Ellison and the Occasion of Criticism*. Chicago: University of Chicago Press, 2003.

Warren, Robert Penn. "The Briar Patch." In Twelve Southerners, *I'll Take My Stand*, 246–64.

Watson, Jay. "The Rhetoric of Exhaustion and the Exhaustion of Rhetoric: Erskine Caldwell in the Thirties." *Mississippi Quarterly* 46, no. 2 (1993): 215–29.

Weatherford, Willis D. "Negro Crime and the Treatment of Criminals." In Weatherford and Johnson, *Race Relations*, 424–41.

Weatherford, Willis D., and Charles S. Johnson. *Race Relations: Adjustment of Whites and Negroes in the United States*. 1934. New York: Negro Universities Press, 1969.

"The Week." *New Republic* 84 (November 1935): 348.

Weinstein, Philip. *Faulkner's Subject: A Cosmos No One Owns*. New York: Cambridge University Press, 1992.

Weiss, Richard. "Ethnicity and Reform: Minorities and the Ambience of the Depression Years." *Journal of American History* 66, no. 3 (December 1979): 566–85.

Westen, Drew. "Beyond the Binary Opposition in Psychological Anthropology: Integrating Contemporary Psychoanalysis and Cognitive Science." In *The Psychology of Cultural Experience*, ed. Carmella C. Moore and Holly F. Matthews, 21–47. Cambridge: Cambridge University Press, 2001.

White, Kenneth. Review of *Tobacco Road*. *Nation* 135 (1932). In MacDonald, *Critical Essays*, 18–19.

Whitfield, Stephen A. *The Culture of the Cold War*. 1991. Baltimore: Johns Hopkins University Press, 1996.

Whitted, Qiana. " 'Using My Grandmother's Life as a Model': Richard Wright and the Gendered Politics of Religious Representation." *Southern Literary Journal* 36, no. 2 (2004): 13–30.

Williams, Linda. *Playing the Race Card: Melodramas of Black and White from Uncle Tom to O. J. Simpson*. Princeton, N.J.: Princeton University Press, 2001.

Williams, Raymond. *Marxism and Literature*. Oxford: Oxford University Press, 1977.

———. "Metropolitan Perceptions and the Emergence of Modernism." In *The Politics of Modernism: Against the New Conformists*, ed. Tony Pinckney, 37–48. New York: Verso, 1989.

Williams, Walter L. "United States Indian Policy and the Debate over Philippine Annexation: Implications for the Origins of American Imperialism." *Journal of American History* 66, no. 4 (1980): 810–31.

Williamson, Joel. *The Crucible of Race: Black-White Relations in the American South since Emancipation.* New York: Oxford University Press, 1984.

Wilson, Charles Reagan. "Religion of the Lost Cause: Ritual and Organization of the Southern Civil Religion, 1865–1920." *Journal of Southern History* 46, no. 2 (1980): 213–38.

Winnicott, D. W. "Primitive Emotional Development." Essay first published in 1945, abridged in Scharff, *Object Relations,* 179–86.

Wolfe, Charles. "*Mr. Smith Goes to Washington*: Democratic Forums and Representational Forms." In Lehman, *Close Viewings,* 300–332.

Wolfe, W. Béran. "Psycho-analyzing the Depression." *Forum and Century* 87, no. 4 (April 1932): 209–14.

Woodruff, Nan Elizabeth. *American Congo: The African American Freedom Struggle in the Delta.* Cambridge, Mass.: Harvard University Press, 2003.

Woodward, C. Vann. *The Strange Career of Jim Crow.* 3rd ed. New York: Oxford University Press, 1974.

Wright, Richard. *Black Boy (American Hunger): A Record of Childhood and Youth.* 1945. New York: HarperPerennial, 1993.

———. "Blueprint for Negro Writing." In A. Mitchell, *Within the Circle,* 97–106.

———. "How Bigger Was Born." In *Native Son,* 431–63. Story first published in 1940.

———. Introduction to *Black Metropolis: A Study of Negro Life in a Northern City* by St. Clair Drake and Horace R. Cayton, xvii–xxxiv. New York: Harcourt, Brace, 1945.

———. *Lawd Today!* 1963. Boston: Northeastern University Press, 1993.

———. *Native Son.* 1940. New York: HarperPerennial, 1998.

———. Review of *Their Eyes Were Watching God.* In Gates and Appiah, *Critical Perspectives,* 16–17. Review first published in 1937.

———. *12 Million Black Voices.* 1941. New York: Thunder's Mouth, 2002.

———. *Uncle Tom's Children.* 1940. New York: HarperPerennial, 1993.

Wrobel, David M. *The End of American Exceptionalism: Frontier Anxiety from the Old West to the New Deal.* Lawrence: University of Kansas Press, 1993.

Wyatt, Euphemia Van Rensselaer. Review of Masque Theatre production of *Tobacco Road. Catholic World* 138 (1933–34): 603–4.

Yaeger, Patricia. *Dirt and Desire: Reconstructing Southern Women's Writing, 1930–1990.* Chicago: University of Chicago Press, 2000.

Young, Stark. "Not in Memoriam, but in Defense." In Twelve Southerners, *I'll Take My Stand,* 328–59.

———. Review of Masque Theatre production of *Tobacco Road. New Republic* 74, no. 994 (4 Dec. 1933): 168–69.

———. *So Red the Rose.* New York: Charles Scribner's Sons, 1934.

Zagarell, Sandra A. "Troubling Regionalism: Rural Life and the Cosmopolitan Eye in Sarah Orne Jewett's *Deephaven.*" *American Literary History* 10, no. 4 (1998): 639–63.

Zender, Karl. "*Requiem for a Nun* and the Uses of Imagination." In *Faulkner and Race: Faulkner and Yoknapatawpha, 1986,* ed. Doreen Fowler and Ann J. Abadie, 272–96. Jackson: University Press of Mississippi, 1987.

Zinn, Howard. *The Southern Mystique.* New York: Alfred A. Knopf, 1964.

Žižek, Slavoj. *Looking Awry: An Introduction to Jacques Lacan through Popular Culture.* Cambridge, Mass.: MIT Press, 1991.

———. *Tarrying with the Negative: Kant, Hegel, and the Critique of Ideology.* Durham, N.C.: Duke University Press, 1993.

Index

abjection, 93–95, 108–14, 169, 236–39
Abrahams, Roger, 124–25
Absalom, Absalom! (Faulkner), 149, 157–58, 161, 166, 168–73
activism, 79, 178; anticolonial, 145; antiracist, 38, 48; antisegregation, 144, 173, 182–85, 214; importance of coevality in, 118, 123, 125, 130; labor, 35, 78–79, 97, 106–8; mentioned, 7, 13, 17
Adams, James Truslow, 56
aesthetic narrative, distinctness of, 7–8, 246
African American press, 38, 67–68
Agee, James, 13, 178, 200–204
Agrarians, 22, 73, 77–78, 180, 220, 245. *See also* Ransom, John Crowe; Tate, Allen; Warren, Robert Penn; Young, Stark
agriculture, southern, 18; sharecropping and tenant farming in, 74, 77–78, 99, 106–8, 123–25, 127
Alabama Sharecroppers Union, 107

332 Index

Aldridge, John, 220
alienation, modernity and, 6, 89–90, 121, 223
Allen, Danielle, 241
American Dilemma, An (Myrdal), 23, 73, 189, 215
Americanization, 38, 53–55, 97
Anderson, Benedict, 5, 52–53, 272n5
Anderson, Sherwood, 74–75, 77, 81
antiracism, 38, 48
antisegregationism, 144, 173, 182–85
apartheid, use of term, 4, 250n9
Appadurai, Arjun, 179, 199
Appalachia, representations of, 98
Arac, Jonathan, 233
As I Lay Dying (Faulkner), 165
avant-garde, literary, 85, 178, 184, 200. *See also* proletarian fiction

Babbitt (Lewis), 54, 72
backwardness, southern, 23–24, 178–79, 185–89, 199–200, 215, 245; domestication of, 216, 218, 226; as problem for nation, 2, 7, 21–22, 52, 74–80; as rationale for segregation, 22–27, 104–6, 158–59, 179–82, 246; as strategy for nationalist disavowal, 2–6, 18–20, 38
Baker, Houston A., Jr., 35, 181–82, 192, 238–39
Bakhtin, Mikhail, 91–92, 95
Balibar, Etienne, 25
Beard, Charles and Mary, 212–13
Bell, Derrick, 213
Bellow, Saul, 232
Benton, Thomas Hart, 76
Berlant, Lauren, 65–66, 109, 254n45
Bhabha, Homi, 30, 45
Bilbo, Theodore, 79
Birth of a Nation, The (Griffith), 11, 37–39, 44–48, 63, 68
Black Boy (American Hunger) (Wright), 187–88, 190, 210–11
"Blueprint for Negro Writing" (Wright), 186
blues, 23, 126
Bollas, Christopher, 199
Botkin, B. A., 61–62, 76
Bourdieu, Pierre, 165
Bourke-White, Margaret, 86
Bradford, Roark, 125–26
Brinkmeyer, Robert, 184
Brodhead, Richard, 30–31
Brown, Bill, 31
Brown, Sterling, 68, 123, 125–26
Brown, Wendy, 221, 225
Brown v. Board of Education, 213
Bunche, Ralph, 56, 77–78
Burke, Kenneth, 86–88, 91, 113
Bush, George H. W., 227

Cable, George Washington, 36
Caldwell, Erskine, 12, 86–87, 113; goals of, 88–89, 92, 104; *God's Little Acre*, 85, 88–90, 103, 105–7; journalism of, 92; reception of, 92–96, 103; *Tobacco Road*, 85, 88–90, 99–101, 105, 107; *You Have Seen Their Faces*, 86
Caldwell, Ira, 101–3
Calverton, V. F., 56, 61, 76
Cane (Toomer), 121–22
Capra, Frank, 8, 11, 51, 62–67

Carby, Hazel, 121, 128, 131–32, 134, 140, 144
Caribbean cultures, 10, 130–31, 138–39
"Casey Jones," 126
Cash, W. J., 181–83
censorship, 86, 92–94
chain-gang labor, 21–22
Chase, Richard, 220
Cheng, Anne Anlin, 240
Chesnutt, Charles, 36
chronotope, literary: defined, 133; gothic novels and, 148–55, 158; marginalization and, 99–101, 200–204; modernization and, 127–32, 185–95, 204–10; southern modernism and, 12–13, 81–82, 86–87, 184–85, 199–200; unconscious and, 203, 238–39
chronotypes, 5–10
Civil War, representation of, 39, 45. *See also* Confederate memorialization
Clansman, The (Dixon), 11, 39–42, 264n77
Cohn, Deborah, 238
Communism: as form of political organization, 55, 214, 235; as social movement, 63, 78, 190, 194–95; as theory, 186–87, 208–9, 233
Confederate memorialization, 20, 112, 158–63, 224–26; contemporary, 36; national, 20, 26–27. *See also* plantation romance
Connelly, Marc, 125
Conrad, Joseph, 153–57
consumer culture, 54, 59–60, 72, 104

Cooper, Anna Julia, 27, 36
cosmopolitanism, 31, 38, 177–78, 200
Couch, W. T., 189
country music, 24, 126
Country of the Pointed Firs, The (Jewett), 31, 34
Cowley, Malcolm, 149
Cox, Oliver, 181, 287n83

Dabney, Virginius, 79
Darkwater (Du Bois), 25
Davidson, Donald, 73
Davis, David Brion, 20
Democratic Party, 24, 35–36, 79, 227, 246
Denning, Michael, 55, 91
Dewey, John, 52–53, 57
disavowal: grotesque and, 91–93; in identity construction, 26, 239; national, 4–6, 18–20, 23, 32–35, 247; southern, 170–72, 199
Dixiecrats (States' Rights Democratic Party), 24, 216
Dixon, Thomas, 11, 37, 39–42, 49, 68–69, 144, 264n77
documentary, 57, 74–75
Dollard, John, 180
Dracula (Stoker), 153–57
Dubey, Madhu, 199
Du Bois, W. E. B., 25–26, 37, 68, 117–19
Dudziak, Mary, 213–14

ego ideal, 109, 163, 229, 254n45
Eisenhower, Dwight, 227
Eliot, T. S., 146, 150

Ellison, Ralph, 198, 229, 245; "An Extravagance of Laughter," 9, 36, 91–92, 110–14; "If the Twain Shall Meet," 3, 242–44; *Invisible Man*, 13, 217–19, 232–42
eugenics, 97–99, 101–3
Evans, Walker, 200, 202

Fabian, Johannes, 152, 196, 232
Fair Employment Practices Commission, 214
fantasy: affiliative, 42–47, 64–71, 167–72, 181–82, 204–6; identity, 26, 166, 197, 240–41, 257n97, 258–59n120; nationalist, 18–19, 26, 32–35, 41–42, 87; projective, 2–3, 26, 202–3. *See also* abjection
fascism, 7, 55, 187, 190, 205–6, 208; compared to southern white supremacy, 74, 77–79
Faulkner, William, 8, 12, 87, 146–47, 153, 232–33; reception of, 148–49, 157, 161, 219–20, 224
Faulkner, William, works of: *Absalom, Absalom!*, 149, 157–58, 161–66, 168–73; *As I Lay Dying*, 165; *Flags in the Dust*, 162–65; *Go Down, Moses*, 172–73; *Light in August*, 149, 165, 167–70, 185; *Requiem for a Nun*, 13, 174–75, 217–30, 233; *Sanctuary*, 150, 165, 228; *The Sound and the Fury*, 149, 165, 168, 171–72
Favor, J. Martin, 120
Flags in the Dust (Faulkner), 162–65
folk culture, southern African American, 114, 236; modernization and, 124, 129–32, 143, 194–95; pathology thesis and, 120–21, 185–86; temporal debates concerning, 115–24, 187–91. *See also* Hurston, Zora Neale
folklore: as apolitical, 12; debates concerning representation of, 124–27; Depression-era interest in, 61, 76; hegemony and, 137–39; motility of, 126–28. *See also* Hurston, Zora Neale
Frank, Waldo, 54
Freud, Sigmund, 203; on affiliation, 10–11, 42–43, 251n34; on identity development, 108–9, 254n45, 257n97; on mourning, 135; on "slips," 217; on trauma, 155, 165

Garland, Hamlin, 30
Glasgow, Ellen, 148, 150
Godden, Richard, 172
Go Down, Moses (Faulkner), 172–73
God's Little Acre (E. Caldwell), 85, 88–90, 103, 105–7; reception of, 92–93, 95–96
Gold, Mike, 89
Gone with the Wind (Fleming/Selznick), 11–12, 52, 67–68, 70–73, 74, 226
Gone with the Wind (Mitchell), 11–12, 52, 67–70, 71–73
Good Housekeeping, 56
gothic, 192; chronotopes of, 148–55, 158; South as, 18, 80, 147; southern, 12, 148, 159–61. *See also* Faulkner, William

Grady, Henry, 6
Great Depression, 48; U.S. nationalism and, 50, 55–56, 80, 86–87
Great Migration, 24, 55, 121, 128–29, 133, 198–99
Green Pastures (Connelly), 125
Griffin, Farah Jasmine, 187
Griffin, Larry, 2
Griffith, Andy, 226
Griffith, D. W., 11, 37–39, 44–49, 68
grotesque, 12, 90–93. See also Caldwell, Erskine

Hale, Grace Elizabeth, 27, 195
Harris, Joel Chandler, 27
Hartz, Louis, 213
Heart Is a Lonely Hunter, The (McCullers), 204–10
Heart of Darkness (Conrad), 153–57
Hegeman, Susan, 86, 201–2
Hewitt, Andrew, 152
Hitler, Adolf, 43, 79
Hoberek, Andrew, 226
Holt, Thomas, 5
Hoover, Herbert, 24, 55
"How Bigger Was Born" (Wright), 188, 190, 192
Howe, Irving, 220–24
Howells, William Dean, 81
Hughes, Langston, 55, 78
Hurston, Zora Neale, 12, 87, 114–15, 194; "Hoodoo in America," 129–30; *Mules and Men*, 116, 124–31, 133, 181; political views of, 124, 132, 144–45; *Tell My Horse*, 130–31; *Their Eyes Were Watching God*, 116, 130–44, 185
Huyssen, Andreas, 116

I Am a Fugitive from a Chain Gang (LeRoy/Wallis), 80
identity, performative, 110–11
I'll Take My Stand (Twelve Southerners), 104, 160, 245. See also Agrarians
immigration, 31, 35, 38, 97
imperialism, 250n20; narrative and, 152–57; U.S., 6, 35, 48, 222–23
industry, southern, 106–8, 127–28
Infants of the Spring (Thurman), 273n26
International Labor Defense, 78
interpretive communities, 9, 87, 161
Invisible Man (Ellison), 13, 217–19, 232–42

Jameson, Fredric, 152
Janet, Pierre, 155
Jewett, Sarah Orne, 31, 34
Jezebel (Wyler), 68–69
John Henry (Bradford), 125
Johnson, Charles S., 117, 120, 123; *Race Relations* (with Weatherford), 180–81, 189; *Shadow of the Plantation*, 74, 127–28
Johnson, James Weldon, 17–18
Joyce, James, 146, 156–57, 161

Kaplan, Amy, 35
Kayser, Wolfgang, 91–92
Kelley, Robin D. G., 186–87, 198
Kennedy, Louise Venable, 121

Kilpatrick, James Jackson, 216
Kirkland, Jack: *Tobacco Road*, 85, 88–92, 100–101; —, responses of critics to, 92–96, 110
Kreyling, Michael, 158
Kristeva, Julia, 93, 108
Kruger, Loren, 100
Ku Klux Klan (KKK), 38, 41, 45, 78–79, 131

labor activism, 35, 78–79, 97, 106–8
Lacan, Jacques, 47, 108, 254n45
Ladd, Barbara, 222
Lamarckianism, 97–98
Lamothe, Daphne, 132, 141
Larsen, Nella, 122–23
Lasting South, The (ed. Rubin and Kilpatrick), 216
Latin American literature, 34, 147
Let Us Now Praise Famous Men (Agee and Evans), 200–204
Lewis, Sinclair, 54
liberalism: assessments of, 14; during cold war, 213, 244–45; in 1930s, 17, 23, 57; regionalism and, 11, 14, 31, 56–62; as state ideology, 20, 25, 256n80; temporality of, 5–6, 225, 233; U.S. nationalism and, 1–6, 53
Liberal Tradition in America, The (Hartz), 213
Light in August (Faulkner), 149, 165, 167–70, 185
Lipsitz, George, 4
local color fiction, 30–34, 59
Locke, Alain, 68, 116–18, 123–24, 126, 131

Long, Huey, 78
lynching, 41, 47, 111–12, 188–90, 241; efforts to combat, 25, 78–79
Lynd, Robert S. and Helen Merrell, 54

mammy figure, 70–74, 123, 250–51n20
Marx, Karl, 187, 192
Maxwell, Bill, 187, 191
McCullers, Carson, 178, 204–10
McPherson, Tara, 70, 231
McWilliams, Carey, 58
media, 23, 59–61, 190, 200, 205
memory: collective, 147, 167–68; nationalism and, 31, 242–43; screen, 38, 168. *See also* Confederate memorialization
Mencken, H. L., 20, 96
Michaels, Walter Benn, 35, 38, 42, 58, 143–44, 170
Middletown (Lynd and Lynd), 54
Midwest, 29, 54, 94
Mind of the South (Cash), 181–82
minstrelsy, 33–34, 39; stereotypes from, 121, 124
Mitchell, Margaret, 49; *Gone with the Wind*, 11–12, 52, 67–75, 226
modernism, 7–8, 85–86, 116, 146–47; critiques of, 151–52; folklore and, 132–35, 140–42; gothic, 150–57, 161, 172; sexuality and, 86, 88–90, 92; southern, scope of, 12–13; temporal multiplicity in, 8, 12, 149–52, 156, 161, 172
modernization: ideology of, 179, 213–16, 221–23, 232, 234–37, 242; southern, 8–9, 23–25

Moton, Robert R., 74
mourning, 135–41, 163
Mr. Smith Goes to Washington (Capra), 8, 11, 51, 62–67
Mules and Men (Hurston), 116, 124–31, 133, 181
Myrdal, Gunnar, 23, 73, 189, 215

Nadel, Alan, 235
National Association for the Advancement of Colored People (NAACP), 78, 183
nationalism, U.S.: abjection and, 87, 93–96, 108–13; capitalism and, 29–32, 37; civic (liberal) vs. particularist, 1–6, 21, 27–28, 53, 63, 252n12; compared with regionalism, 28–35, 52–53; disavowal and, 2–6, 18–20, 23, 32–35, 247; fantasy and, 11–12, 26; Great Depression and, 50, 55–56, 80, 86–87; materialism and, 54–55; multiple traditions of, 2–9, 13, 48, 183–84, 193, 213, 234–36; narrative and, 27, 52–53; temporality and, 5–6, 13, 30–34; triumphalist, 50, 98–99, 145, 174, 210–11, 214; white supremacy and, 39–48
Native Americans, representations of, 6, 33–34, 221–22
Native Son (Wright), 190–93
nativism, 23, 48
New Critics, 220
New Deal, 7, 55–58, 75–77, 79, 104, 106–7
New England, 29, 30, 220

New Negro, The (ed. Locke), 116–18
New South ideology, 6, 72, 158, 160
Nixon, Richard, 231

Odum, Howard, 17, 21, 60
Osborne, Peter, 5

Page, Thomas Nelson, 27
Payne, Charles, 6, 214
Pepper, Claude, 183
Perkins, Frances, 77
plantation romance, 11, 35, 51–52; examples of, 37–42, 44–49, 68–74; influence of, 124, 164–71; popularity of, 26–27, 67–68, 148
Plessy v. Ferguson, 5, 19, 22, 47, 193, 213–14
Poague, Leland, 63–64
politics, U.S.: contemporary, 35–36, 219, 230–32, 245–46; identity and, 216–17, 225–26, 230–31; postcolonial nations and, 234–36; race-baiting in, 24; temporality and, 218–19, 227–33
Politics of Cultural Differences, The (Leege et al.), 217
Polk, Noel, 223
Pound, Ezra, 156
poverty, southern, 7, 21, 205, 207; as alterity, 13, 86–88, 92; racialization of, 96–99, 101–2
President's Committee on Civil Rights, 184, 214–15
President's Committee on Social Trends, 55
proletarian fiction, 89–91

Protestantism, southern, 18, 107, 186, 188, 194–95
psychoanalysis, 10–11, 44, 198, 243–44
Puzzled America (S. Anderson), 74–75, 77, 81

Quicksand (Larsen), 122–23

race, representation and, 31–34, 115–16, 250n9
Race Relations (Weatherford and Johnson), 180–81, 189
race relations, southern, 24, 73–74
racism, 33, 256n81; sexual hysteria and, 38, 46. *See also* white supremacy
Rahv, Philip, 148, 219–20
Ransom, John Crowe, 61, 67, 180, 245
Raper, Arthur, 73
realism, literary, 81, 88, 92–93, 100, 151
Reconstruction, 21, 37, 112, 243
Reed, Adolph, Jr., 225–26
regionalism, 51, 179; liberal models of, 11, 14, 31, 57–67; as restrictive model of affiliation, 3–6, 11–14, 21, 28–35, 252n38. *See also* Agrarians; nationalism, U.S.; sectionalism
Republican Party, 35–36, 218, 226–27, 245–46
Requiem for a Nun (Faulkner), 13, 174–75, 217–30, 233
Richardson, Riché, 236–37
Riquelme, John Paul, 152–53

Rise of American Civilization, The (Beard and Beard), 212–13
Robinson, Bill, 67–68
Rogin, Michael, 34, 45–46
Roosevelt, Eleanor, 79
Roosevelt, Franklin D., 23–24, 56–57, 77, 79, 144
Rourke, Constance, 58
Rubin, Louis D., Jr., 216

Said, Edward, 2
Sanctuary (Faulkner), 150, 165, 228
Schuyler, George, 119
Scopes ("monkey") trial, 23, 96
Scottsboro trial, 78, 140, 191–92
sectionalism: conflict and, 29–30; reconciliation and, 35
segregation, racial, 17–18, 143–44; activism against, 144, 173, 182–85, 214; federal approaches to, 4, 21–22, 25, 79, 182, 213, 227; as particularist model of collectivity, 4, 19–20; propagandists for, 6, 25, 27, 38, 144, 213; rationales for, 22–27, 104–6, 158–59, 179–82, 246. See also *Plessy v. Ferguson*
Selznick, David O., 11, 67–75
sexuality: identity and, 166; modernism and, 86, 88–90, 92; nationalist fantasy and, 41–42; politics and, 36
Shadow of the Plantation (Johnson), 74, 127–28
shame, 166, 205–6, 240
sharecropping. *See under* agriculture, southern

Shimakawa, Karen, 108–9
Singh, Nikhil Pal, 114, 183, 256n81
Smith, Jon, 158
Smith, Lillian, 178, 195–99
Smith, Rogers, 2, 32
sociology, concerning the South, 22, 25, 97–98, 123–24, 186
sociopsychology, 22, 180, 189
Soja, Edward, 179
So Red the Rose (Young), 68, 71, 170–71
Souls of Black Folk, The (Du Bois), 25
Sound and the Fury, The (Faulkner), 149, 165, 168, 171–72
South, images of: as anticommunist, 4, 144, 213, 226; as icon of conservatism, 35–36; as ideological victor of Civil War, 20, 49. *See also* backwardness, southern
Southern Conference for Human Welfare, 79, 183
Southern Mystique, The (Zinn), 242–45
southern studies, 9–10, 247
Southern Tenant Farmers Union, 107–8
space: narrative and, 99–100, 132–34, 149, 151–57, 158; nationalism and, 29, 98–101, 103, 113–14
Stalin, Josef, 187
Stepto, Robert, 188
Stoker, Bram, 153–57
Strange Fruit (L. Smith), 195–98
Sumner, William Graham, 22
supplementation, 32–35
Susman, Warren, 54

Tate, Allen, 68, 160–61
Tate, Claudia, 10, 134–35
Tell My Horse (Hurston), 130–31
Temple, Shirley, 67
temporality: capitalist modernity of, 5, 8, 117–18; changing views of, 59, 218–20; distancing and, 200–204, 208–10, 236–38, 242; intersubjective, 196, 200, 204; mapping of, 13, 173, 184–98; multiplicity within, 174, 199, 210, 224, 242, 246; narrative and, 81–82, 86–87, 99–100, 128–30, 239–41; nationalism and, 5–6, 30–34, 51, 60–62, 213–16, 233–35; politics and, 218–19, 227–33
tenant farming. *See under* agriculture, southern
Their Eyes Were Watching God (Hurston), 116, 130–44
Thurman, Wallace, 273n26
Thurmond, Strom, 216
Tobacco Road (E. Caldwell), 85, 88–90, 99–101, 105, 107; responses to, 92–93, 95–96, 103
Tobacco Road: A Three Act Play (Kirkland), 85, 88–92, 100–101; responses to, 92–96, 110. *See also* censorship
Tolson, Melvin, 49, 71, 79
Toomer, Jean, 121–22
Tourgée, Albion, 36, 47
trauma, narrative and, 154–60, 162–69, 229
Trujillo, Rafael, 138
Turner, Frederick Jackson, 28–29

Turner, Victor, 139, 141
12 Million Black Voices (Wright), 187

Ulysses (Joyce), 146, 156–57, 161
uncanniness, 18, 116, 121, 130, 133, 169
Uncle Remus, 27, 69
Uncle Tom's Children (Wright), 188–91, 193–94
unconscious, 238–39, 242–44
uneven development, 59, 60, 86, 152, 179, 211

Vance, Rupert, 96–97
Vincent, Sténio, 138

Wallace, Henry, 56
Wallace, Michelle, 37, 48
Warren, Kenneth, 36, 118, 231, 240, 256
Warren, Robert Penn, 68, 97, 104
Waste Land, The (Eliot), 150
Weatherford, Willis D., 189
Weinstein, Philip, 165
West, 28, 31, 33–34
white supremacy, 183, 214, 218; nationalist fantasy and, 11, 19–20, 34, 110–13; southern, 182, 190, 192, 215–16, 224–26, 246, 250–51n20; temporality and, 18, 122. *See also* lynching; plantation romance; segregation, racial
Whitted, Quiana, 188
Williams, Linda, 69, 71
Williamson, Joel, 199, 260n131
Winnicott, D. W., 71
Wolfe, W. Béran, 50–51
Woodruff, Nan Elizabeth, 199
Woodward, C. Vann, 226
working through, 169, 199, 239–41
World War I, 48, 43, 163–64, 195
World War II, 182–83
Wright, Richard, 133–34, 178, 185, 198–99; *Black Boy (American Hunger)*, 187–88, 190, 210–11; "Blueprint for Negro Writing," 186; "How Bigger Was Born," 188, 190, 192; *Native Son*, 190–93; *12 Million Black Voices*, 187; *Uncle Tom's Children*, 188–91, 193–94
Wyler, William, 68–69

Yaeger, Patricia, 199
You Have Seen Their Faces (E. Caldwell), 86
Young, Stark, 67–68, 71, 96, 170–71

Zender, Karl, 229
Zinn, Howard, 242–45
Žižek, Slavoj, 33, 43–44, 47–48, 256n80

THE NEW SOUTHERN STUDIES

The Nation's Region: Southern Modernism, Segregation, and U.S. Nationalism
by Leigh Anne Duck

Black Masculinity and the U.S. South: From Uncle Tom to Gangsta
by Riché Richardson

Grounded Globalism: How the U.S. South Embraces the World
by James L. Peacock

Disturbing Calculations: The Economics of Identity in Postcolonial Southern Literature, 1912–2002
by Melanie R. Benson

www.ingramcontent.com/pod-product-compliance
Lightning Source LLC
Chambersburg PA
CBHW030127240426
43672CB00005B/50